MW00674404

DEVELOPMENTAL CONFLICTS AND DIAGNOSTIC EVALUATION
IN ADOLESCENT PSYCHOTHERAPY

OTHER BOOKS BY RICHARD A. GARDNER

The Boys and Girls Book About Divorce

Therapeutic Communication with Children:
The Mutual Storytelling Technique

Dr. Gardner's Stories About the Real World,
Volume I

Dr. Gardner's Stories About the Real World,
Volume II

Dr. Gardner's Fairy Tales for Today's
Children

Understanding Children: A Parents Guide to
Child Rearing

MBD: The Family Book About Minimal Brain
Dysfunction

Psychotherapeutic Approaches to the
Resistant Child

Psychotherapy with Children of Divorce

Dr. Gardner's Modern Fairy Tales

The Parents Book About Divorce

The Boys and Girls Book About One-Parent
Families

The Objective Diagnosis of Minimal Brain
Dysfunction

Dorothy and the Lizard of Oz

Dr. Gardner's Fables for Our Times

The Boys and Girls Book About Stepfamilies

Family Evaluation in Child Custody
Litigation

Separation Anxiety Disorder:
Psychodynamics and Psychotherapy

Child Custody Litigation: A Guide for
Parents and Mental Health Professionals

The Psychotherapeutic Techniques of Richard
A. Gardner

Hyperactivity, the So-Called Attention-Deficit
Disorder, and the Group of MBD Syndromes

The Parental Alienation Syndrome and the
Differentiation Between Fabricated and
Genuine Child Sex Abuse

Psychotherapy with Adolescents

Family Evaluation in Child Custody
Mediation, Arbitration, and Litigation

The Girls and Boys Book About Good and
Bad Behavior

Sex Abuse Hysteria: Salem Witch Trials
Revisited

The Parents Book About Divorce–Second
Edition

The Parental Alienation Syndrome: A Guide
for Mental Health and Legal Professionals

The Psychotherapeutic Techniques of Richard
A. Gardner–Revised

Self-Esteem Problems of Children:
Psychodynamics and Psychotherapy

True and False Accusations of Child Sex
Abuse

Protocols for the Sex-Abuse Evaluation

Testifying in Court

Conduct Disorders of Childhood:
Psychodynamics and Psychotherapy

Psychogenic Learning Disabilities:
Psychodynamics and Psychotherapy

Psychotherapy with Sex-Abuse Victims: True,
False, and Hysterical Dream Analysis in
Psychotherapy

The Parental-Alienation Syndrome: A Guide
for Mental Health and Legal Professionals–
Second Edition

The Utilization of the Gardner Children's
Projective Battery

DEVELOPMENTAL CONFLICTS AND DIAGNOSTIC EVALUATION IN ADOLESCENT PSYCHOTHERAPY

RICHARD A. GARDNER, M.D.

JASON ARONSON INC.
Northvale, New Jersey
London

This book was printed and bound by Book-mart Press, Inc. of North Bergen, NJ.

Copyright © 1999 by Richard A. Gardner
The hardcover edition was entitled *Psychotherapy with Adolescents*

10 9 8 7 6 5 4 3 2 1

All rights reserved. No part of this book may be used or reproduced in any manner whatsoever without written permission from Jason Aronson Inc. except in the case of brief quotations in reviews for inclusion in a magazine, newspaper, or broadcast.

Library of Congress Cataloging-in-Publication Data

Gardner, Richard A.
    Developmental conflicts and diagnostic evaluation in adolescent psychotherapy / Richard A. Gardner.
        p.   cm.
    Originally published as part of: Psychotherapy with adolescents. Cresskill, N.J. : Creative Therapeutics, 1988?
    Includes bibliographical references and index.
    ISBN 0–7657–0206–1 (softcover : alk. paper)
    1. Adolescent psychotherapy.   2. Behavior disorders in children—Treatment.   I. Gardner, Richard A.   Psychotherapy with adolescents.
    [DNLM: 1. Mental Disorders—in adolescence.   2. Mental Disorders—diagnosis.   3. Psychotherapy—in adolescence.   WS 463 G223d 1999]
    RJ503.G376   1999
    616.89'14'0835—dc21
    DNLM/DLC
    for Library of Congress   98–54479

Printed in the United States of America on acid-free paper. For information and catalog write to Jason Aronson Inc., 230 Livingston Street, Northvale, NJ 07647-1726, or visit our website: www.aronson.com

I dedicate this book to

> My teachers at The Bronx High School of Science and Columbia College.
>
> Their formidable influence on me during my own adolescence — as teachers, models, and mentors — has served me well throughout the course of my life.
>
> This book represents only one small derivative of their influence.

PSYCHOTHERAPY WITH ADOLESCENTS

A Series of Books by
Richard A. Gardner

VOLUME I:
**Developmental Conflicts
and Diagnostic Evaluation
in Adolescent Psychotherapy**

VOLUME II:
**Individual and Group Therapy
and Work with Parents
in Adolescent Psychotherapy**

VOLUME III:
**Psychotherapy
of Antisocial Behavior
and Depression in Adolescence**

Contents

ACKNOWLEDGMENTS

I wish to express my gratitude to my secretaries, Linda Gould, Carol Gibbon, and Donna La Tourette for their dedication to the typing of the manuscript of this book in its various renditions. I am indeed fortunate to have such committed assistants. I am grateful, as well, to Robert Mulholland for his astute editing of the manuscript. He did more than edit; he gave good reasons for his changes and taught me some useful grammatical principles in the course of our work together. I appreciate the contributions of Jo-Nell Long and Elizabeth Quackenbush for their careful reading of the page proofs.

My greatest debt, however, is to my adolescent patients who have taught me much over the years about the kinds of problems they can have. From their parents, as well, I have learned much that is included here. Although their names and other identifying data have been disguised, their experiences have been recorded herein. My hope is that what I have learned from them will be put to good use through this series and will contribute to the prevention and alleviation of grief and stress in others.

INTRODUCTION

This series represents the cumulative experience of over 40 years of working intensively with adolescent patients. It includes references to the works of others who have influenced my thinking as well as my own ideas regarding how to conduct psychotherapy with adolescents. But even those theories and techniques that I consider my own were probably thought of by others in the past. New and unique ideas are very rare; it is only that others have not published the innovative theories and approaches described herein or I have not come across them in my researches. But this should be of little concern to the reader. What is important is that this is the amalgam of the ideas and techniques I have found most useful in work with adolescents. The reader does well to select from that which is presented here those elements that seem reasonable and those that show promise for effective utilization.

My next point was said better previously by D.J. Holmes (1964) in the preface to his book *The Adolescent in Psychotherapy*:

> In our teaching we frequently go the way of the arrogant house mouse who advised the shivering grasshopper that he

would survive the winter better if he were to change into a mouse. Heartened by the suggestion, the grasshopper inquired how he might proceed with this, and the mouse replied: "I can only give you the general idea — you will have to work out the details for yourself."

During the course of my training, all too often my supervisors only gave me general principles. Most of the details I had to work out myself. Holmes' book provides many useful details. And this book, published almost 35 years later, provides additional details. Like Holmes' it is not intended to be a comprehensive statement of all forms of treatment for all adolescent disorders. Rather, the series focuses on the areas with which I have had the most experience and presents those therapeutic techniques that I have found most reliable in the course of my work.

Of the three age groups — childhood, adolescence, and adulthood — adolescence is generally viewed as the most difficult to work with psychotherapeutically. The youngsters' arrogance, rebellion, and general unreceptivity to adult authority results in their often being viewed as extremely poor candidates for psychotherapy. There are even therapists who will work with children and adults but who steer clear of adolescents. Working with each of these three groups has its advantages and disadvantages. Each group has its areas of receptivity and areas of unreceptivity. All things considered, however, I believe the adolescents are the easiest group in which to bring about psychotherapeutic change — and this is especially the case for youngsters from the mid- to late-adolescent period.

The rambunctiousness and distractibility of younger children make them difficult candidates for treatment and one must utilize a wide variety of seductive techniques (such as psychotherapeutic games) in order to engage them. In contrast, the adult patient generally exhibits none of these childlike characteristics, but comes to treatment with deeply entrenched problems that may have been years in the making. Also, an adult's opportunity for flexibility in such areas as job and marriage may be seriously compromised, thereby reducing the chance that one may alter environmental factors operative in the development and perpetuation of the psychopathology. The adolescent is halfway between these two groups. Adolescents (especially the older ones) will often sit and talk — the rebellious and sneering facade notwithstanding. Their narcissism is so enormous that they can spend hours talking about the minutiae of themselves, their appearance, their clothing, and so forth. And this is just the kind of thing we want people to do in treatment. Also, their life situation is one that still allows for significant flexibility because they are not locked, like most adults, into fixed vocational and personal arrangements. And, because of their youth, their problems are not generally as deeply entrenched as those of the adult (but certainly more so than those of the young child).

Of the three age groups, adolescents may very well be the most introspective. They may preoccupy themselves with fundamental questions of the world, the universe, God, and the meaning of life. These same deliberations make them good candidates for introspection into the causes of their underlying psychological processes. Although they may be rebellious, they are still at a stage in life in which they are quite dependent on adults, especially their parents and teachers. Although they need to rebel against their parents, in order to achieve a reasonable degree of independence and autonomy, they may not have to rebel against their teachers and teacher surrogates (and a therapist is a teacher surrogate). Their receptivity to the therapist, then, may be greater than that enjoyed with adults and younger children (especially the latter).

Another factor that may contribute to adolescents' being good candidates for treatment relates to educational and career choices. Previously, adult life was viewed as being an infinite number of years away. Most children do not feel any compulsion to concern themselves with such remote future eventualities. In adolescence (particularly late adolescence) the future is almost here. The youngster stands at the doorstep of adult life and may suffer many anxieties about education and career. These fears will enhance his or her motivation to enlist the aid of a therapist to help sort out the options and work through the problems interfering with one's choice. In short, the immediacy of the situation can enhance the adolescent's motivation for therapy. Accordingly, when one considers all these factors, I find myself significantly attracted to many of my adolescent patients and have more optimism regarding their therapeutic prognosis than I have for patients in the other two age groups.

The book begins in Chapter One with the description of certain developmental conflicts of adolescence, the understanding of which I consider important if one is to deal effectively with adolescent psychopathology. Some of these developmental theories are derived from the work of others and some of the ideas are considered to be my own (at least I have never read them elsewhere). Because so much of adolescent psychopathology is an outgrowth of these conflicts, it is important that the reader review these from the start. I consider particularly important the theory proposed of the five stages in the development of what I refer to as the *internal guilt-evoking mechanisms*. I consider this theory of particular value in understanding and treating antisocial youngsters. However, extensions of it are applicable to our understanding of the increasing psychopathy of Western society (a phenomenon that I mention on a number of occasions throughout the course of the series). In the first chapter I also introduce the term *delusions of invulnerability*. Although just about everyone who works with adolescents is aware of this phenomenon, and although others may very well have utilized the term, I have not seen it nor heard it used. I consider it a useful concept for understanding many of the psychological phenomena that we are dealing with when we treat adolescent patients.

In Chapter Two I discuss certain environmental situations (especially family) that are conducive to the development of psychopathological reactions in adolescence. I place particular focus on factors that result in the deprivation of parental affection — a common central element in bringing about psychopathology. It may be of interest to the reader to appreciate that prior to the 1940s, therapists did not generally see a link between childhood psychopathology and deprivation of parental affection. This is a relationship that we routinely investigate in our evaluations of youngsters who come for treatment. Nowhere in Freud's description of Little Hans is there any mention of this potential relationship. It is reasonable to conclude that Freud may not have even considered this linkage. In fact, he tells us that he considered Hans' parents to be healthy people who had not in any way exposed their child to psychopathological processes within themselves nor were they utilizing what he considered to be improper child-rearing tactics. Freud presents as support of this conclusion the statement that the mother had been in psychoanalytic treatment with him and the father was a friend. Clearly, we can only assume then that Freud considered himself to have "cured" the mother and that any person who would be a friend of his could not possibly suffer with psychopathology.

Chapter Three is devoted to a detailed description of the two-hour initial evaluation that I conduct with the youngster and both parents. I do not follow the traditional approach of interviewing the parents alone first and then evaluating the child. I prefer to see at the outset the flesh and blood human being who is likely to become my patient. In that two-hour meeting I can interview the youngster and parents in any possible combination. This gives me the opportunity to learn about intrapsychic as well as interpersonal processes. Chapter Four is devoted to a detailed description of the intensive evaluation I conduct for patients who are going into treatment. This is an exhaustive data-collection process, which includes individual interviews with the patient and each of the parents. It also includes joint interviews with the parents together as well as a family interview. The information so obtained not only serves as a foundation for treatment but the relationships that I form with the patient and parents during this comprehensive evaluation serve as a foundation for that which will ensue.

ONE

SELECTED DEVELOPMENTAL CONSIDERATIONS RELEVANT TO ADOLESCENT TREATMENT

Of the three age brackets: childhood, adolescence, and adulthood, the adolescent period is the one in which the differentiation between normality and pathology is most difficult. The main reason for this is that the adolescent period is normally so tumultuous that it is common for youngsters to exhibit behavior so bizarre that it could be considered psychotic—especially if exhibited at other age levels. Accordingly, it may be extremely difficult to ascertain the line at which the normal "craziness" of adolescence ends and pathological manifestations begin.

The problem is further compounded because many therapists may be easily misled into believing that the adolescent is more mature than he or she really is. The examiner may equate physical maturity with psychological maturity and thereby believe that the adolescent is capable of acting much more judiciously than is actually possible for youngsters in that phase of life. A good guideline for the therapist when assessing and treating adolescents is to view them as having the bodies of adults, but the minds of children. Although physiologically capable of procreation they are

1

generally psychologically incapable of taking care of themselves, let alone progeny. Furthermore, the therapist should not be deceived by the adolescent who scores at the 99th percentile on the SATs. Although that youngster's brain may very well be hypertrophied in certain cognitive areas, the rest of the brain substance may be functioning at infantile levels. I often say that the therapist does well to consider the adolescent as one whose pneumoencephalogram would reveal the head to be largely filled with air, with the cortical substance reduced to pea-sized material lying at the base of the skull just above the brain stem.

These principles apply especially to the traditional poor judgment of the adolescent. Considering the short stay that the adolescent has had thus far on earth, and considering the paucity of experiences that he or she has had, it could not but be otherwise. Good judgment derives from and must be based on experience, and the adolescent has not been around long enough to have enough experiences to enable him or her to have reliable judgment in many areas of living. The cigarette companies know this well. They can rely on the adolescent's being gullible enough to believe that smoking a cigarette makes one more mature and/or attractive to the opposite sex. They can rely upon adolescents' delusions of invulnerability (about which I will have much to say throughout the course of this book) enabling them to deny that cigarette smoking will increase the risk that someday they will get cancer of the lung and/or one or more of the other diseases caused by cigarette smoking. A few years later, when the young adult finally realizes how he or she has been duped, it is too late—so deep-seated may be the tobacco addiction.

Politicians and military leaders also know well how poor is the judgment of adolescents. Visiting any military cemetery, especially those wherein are buried battle casualties of wars fought prior to the 20th century, one cannot but note how young were the boys who fell in battle. Traditionally, wars have been fought by teenagers, or even youngsters no more than 10 to 12 years of age. It is only in the 20th century that we have required our soldiers to be 17 or 18 years of age. Leaders know well that adolescents are physically strong enough to fight wars, but mentally weak and gullible enough to believe propaganda, stirring war cries, and exhortations that evoke murderous rage. They know also that adolescents, because of their delusions of invulnerability, can charge into battle believing that all those around them may fall, but that they somehow will survive. Recently I learned that the motto of the 82nd Airborne Division of the U.S. Army is *Death Before Dishonor*. I personally would much prefer *dishonor before death*. If my choice is only (and it is unlikely that it will be) between death and humiliation, I'll choose *humiliation* anytime. Call me any name you want: "coward," "yellow," "chicken-shit," etc. I'll still choose disgrace. Somehow adolescents do not seem to appreciate this obvious wisdom.

It is also important for the therapist to appreciate that many of the adolescent behavioral manifestations we refer to as symptoms are outgrowths of normal adolescent developmental conflicts and stages. Accordingly, in this first chapter I focus on what I consider to be some of the most important of these. I am not claiming to present an all-encompassing theory of development. In fact, I do not believe that anyone has thus far been able to do so. All of the proposed developmental theories I know of, whether they be those of Freud, Erikson, or Piaget (to mention three of the most well known) are still selective. They focus only on relatively narrow aspects of the developmental process. I present here developmental considerations that I have found to be most important in understanding adolescent psychopathology, which is often best viewed as an outgrowth of these normal developmental stages. Without the understanding of what is normal, therapists are compromised in their ability to understand and treat what is abnormal in their adolescent patients.

One last introductory comment. The reader may be familiar with Francois Villon's "But where are the snows of yesteryear?" One can similarly ask the question "But where are the adolescents of yesteryear?" Where are the crazy kids, juvenile delinquents, and other adolescent maniacs who have caused their parents so much grief? The answer is that most of them have blended into the mainstream of adult life. They are no longer walking the streets in their weird costumes, an eyesore to behold. They are no longer keeping the neighbors up all hours of the night with their earsplitting music and raucous drinking. Most of the delinquents are no longer committing their crimes. Most end up as solid citizens. It is important for the therapist to appreciate this because it provides some optimism when one is considering the prognosis of the adolescent patient. It also provides therapists with the reassurance that time is on their side and that even if the therapy is unsuccessful there is a high degree of probability that the adolescent will end up a sober and solid citizen anyway.

A THEORY OF THE DEVELOPMENT
OF THE CAPACITY TO
EXPERIENCE GUILT

I use the word *guilt* to refer to the feeling of low self-worth individuals experience when they have entertained thoughts, experienced feelings, or performed deeds that they have been taught are wrong or bad by significant figures in childhood (especially parents). Each society, culture, and family has its own collection of such phenomena that are considered unacceptable. Not only has the individual been *taught* that these thoughts, feelings, and acts are wrong but he or she has come to *believe* that they are so. Furthermore, although the earliest significant figures are generally the parents and/or their surrogates, others such as teachers and clergymen also play a role in teaching children what is good, bad, right, and wrong.

   The word *guilt* that I am referring to here is very different from the word *guilt* that is used by the judge who asks the accused whether he or she pleads guilty or innocent: "Do you admit that you committed the crime or do you deny it?" The judge uses the word guilt to refer to a purely *external* phenomenon, i.e., whether or not a particular act was indeed performed. In contrast, I am referring to an *internal* psychological phenomenon that may result from the performance of such an act. A criminal may admit guilt (perpetration) but not feel guilt (reactive self-loathing). These two utilizations of the word guilt are so different that they should probably be represented by two entirely different words. Nor am I referring here to a *third* use of the word guilt: the delusion a person has that an event was his or her fault. There are children, for example, who believe that their parents' divorce was their fault—that the divorce was the result of their transgressions. Such children may then develop the delusion that their parents will reconcile if they were never again to so transgress. The feelings of self-blame here are basically related to the need to gain control over an uncontrollable situation (R.A. Gardner, 1969, 1970). Unless specifically mentioned otherwise, I will be using the term guilt to refer only to the first category: the feeling of low self-worth that is associated with thoughts, feelings, and deeds that one has been taught are bad or wrong.

I have specifically avoided using the word *superego* in this discussion because its use sometimes introduces confusion. In S. Freud's original concept the superego was considered to be a composite of the conscience (the agency via which guilt is evoked) and the ego-ideal (the collection of images of the standards by which one wishes to live, especially those derived from early childhood models). The word superego, however, is often used as if it were just synonymous with conscience, or the guilt-evoking mechanisms. In order to avoid such confusion, I will rarely use the term superego, but rather use the term guilt—to refer only to the first of the three aforementioned types.

The ability of people to experience guilt is crucial for the survival of civilized societies. Without it individuals prey upon one another in a predatory world in which no one can feel safe. Under such circumstances leaders must be constantly policing their followers to insure compliance with standards and rules. Guilt internalizes the standards of the society so that leaders can relax somewhat their vigil. The members of the society can then be relied upon to some extent to police themselves and deter themselves from engaging in unacceptable behavior. Many forms of psychopathology involve either weakness or exaggerated utilization of the guilt-evoking mechanisms. Various forms of antisocial behavior are often the result of weakness of the guilt-evoking mechanisms; and some forms of neurotic disturbance are caused by an exaggerated utilization of these processes.

I present here a theory of the development of the guilt-evoking mechanisms. My theory is derived from information gathered over the years, both from my patients and the works of others. It is basically a synthesis of ideas, many of which have been described previously. Though I have not seen this particular synthesis elsewhere, I suspect others have viewed the development of the guilt-evoking mechanisms in a similar way. It is a multi-step process and I will proceed developmentally from the earliest to the latest steps.

The Genetic-Neurological Substrate

It is obvious that guilt, like all other mental processes, must have a neurological substrate. To have a thought one must have nerve cells. It is reasonable also to state that lower animals do not have the capacity to develop guilt. They do not have an internalized inhibitory mechanism that results in a lowering of their self-esteem when they perform an act which is considered reprehensible by others in their environment. Although some may claim that lower animals do have such capacity (especially beloved domesticated pets), most would agree that the capacity for such guilt is far less than that which the human being is capable of developing. Many who work intensively with higher apes also claim for them the capacity for what appears to be guilt. I do not believe, however, that higher apes have the capacity to develop the *degree* of sophisticated guilt-evoking mechanisms of which humans are capable. It is reasonable, therefore, to speculate that the intermediary forms between the higher apes and homo sapiens developed progressively more complex neurological structures that serve as a substrate for environmentally-induced, guilt-evoking mechanisms.

At any given point along this evolutionary continuum it is reasonable to consider there to have been a range with regard to the guilt-evoking capacity, a range that might very well have represented itself on a bell-shaped curve. Also, over time, the mean of this curve shifted progressively to the right as the average individual exhibited ever more sophisticated capacity to develop guilt. It is also reasonable to speculate that one factor operative in this shift was an environmental selective process in which there was preferential survival of those who had the capacity to deter themselves from antisocial behavior by these internal inhibitory mechanisms. In contrast, those who were poorly endowed with such a neurological substrate were less likely to develop the internalized guilt-evoking mechanisms, more likely therefore to exhibit antisocial behavior, and more likely therefore to get punished, incarcerated, and even killed for their transgressions—thereby selectively removing from the genetic pool those individuals with weak consciences. Unfortunately, we still appear to have a long way to go in this regard. (I am not suggesting any particular method for such removal; I am only stating that their representation is still very much with us.)

If this theory is correct, then it is reasonable to view children today as also falling somewhere along the continuum of the bell-shaped curve, from a low genetically determined neurologically based guilt-potential substrate to a very powerful capacity for the development of such mechanisms. It is important to appreciate that this theory does not preclude the environmental input into any individual's final functioning in this area. An individual with a very sophisticated, complex, and highly developed capacity for guilt evocation needs very little environmental input to manifest what might be considered a normal or even a high degree of guilt. In contrast, individuals who are poorly endowed with these neurological structures may require formidable environmental guilt-engendering exposures to develop guilty feelings. And many may not be able to do so, even with optimum exposure to such influences.

I recognize that this concept is somewhat reminiscent of the 19th-century theory of the "constitutional psychopath." At that time there was a prevailing view that some individuals were born to be psychopaths because of a constitutional weakness in the capacity to develop guilt mechanisms. One 20th century derivative of this notion was the so-called "bad seed" child who was destined from birth to be "bad." Primarily as an outgrowth of the psychoanalytic movement in the 20th century, the concept of the constitutional psychopath is generally considered to be somewhat outdated. My theory here may be viewed as an attempt to disinter this now presumably defunct concept. I have no problem doing this as long as the reader appreciates that I still view psychopathy to be multidetermined and that only a small segment of those who are psychopathic are so because of a genetically determined weak neurological substrate for the implantation of environmental guilt-evoking mechanisms. Whereas the 19th century concept was all inclusive and served as an explanation for all psychopathy, my view is that a *small* percentage of psychopaths are best viewed as manifesting psychopathy because of a constitutional or genetically based neurological weakness.

One confirmation I have for this theory is my observation on numerous occasions of families in which one child showed evidences of an extremely weak capacity to develop guilt, whereas other siblings and the parents manifested normal guilt capacity. After detailed evaluation and prolonged therapy, I was unable to delineate the family factors that caused the child's impairment and reluctantly came to agree with the parents that the patient might have been "born that way." Of course, one could always argue that the environment of each child in a family is different from every other sibling, and that each child enters into and grows up in a different family constellation. Although this is certainly the case, it does not explain satisfactorily the isolated child (one of three, or four, or five, regardless of sequence of birth) who exhibits impairment in this area. I am not claiming that these anecdotal and incidental observations are "proof" of my theory; only that they lend some confirmation to it.

The genetic-neurological factor is the substrate upon which all subsequent factors (to be described) are supported. When it is weak all subsequent factors rest on an unstable foundation and the internalized guilt-evoking mechanisms are likely to be compromised. Each factor presented below must occur in the proper sequence if the whole structure is to be stable. I do not believe that one can "skip" any particular step and still end up with an adult who has the capacity for a strong sense of guilt.

Imprinting

Imprinting in Lower Animals   In recent years ethologists have described the phenomenon of *imprinting*. This term refers to a response pattern that develops in the earliest hours of life, arises under very specific circumstances, and cannot be extinguished by subsequent experiences. This response pattern occurs during what is referred to as the *critical period* because it will not develop if the same circumstances are operative significantly before or significantly after this particular segment of time.

Some of the seminal work in this area was done by K. Lorenz (1937, 1950) who introduced the term *imprinting* to refer to this phenomenon. Lorenz worked primarily with Greylag geese, but the principles of the imprinting process have been verified in many other species by a variety of workers. The basic principle is well demonstrated by studies on ducklings, for example, those conducted by E.H. Hess (1966). The fertilized egg of a duck is removed from the nest of the biological mother and placed in the nest of a surrogate duck. Once hatched, the duckling is allowed to remain with the surrogate mother during the first two to three days of life, during which time the duckling will demonstrate various manifestations of an attachment bond with the surrogate. One of these is the tendency to follow her wherever she goes. If, after the first few days, the duckling is returned to the nest of its biological mother, it will show few if any manifestations of attachment, especially the "following" response. And no amount of effort on the biological mother's part to involve the duckling will be successful.

If one studies this phenomenon further, one finds that there is a critical period during which this attachment response develops, and that involvement with the surrogate before and after this critical period is less likely to result in the formation of an attachment bond. For Mallard ducklings the critical period is from 13 to 16 hours. The imprinting response cannot be viewed as an example of a learned reflex in that it cannot be "taught" before or after the critical period, and it cannot be extinguished by traditional negative reinforcement. Furthermore, it is somewhat indiscriminate in that if the surrogate is a mechanical toy the bond will develop in association with it and the duckling will follow the mechanical toy throughout its life—no matter how many attempts are made to get it to follow the biological mother. Attempts to suppress the response by such techniques as shocking the duckling each time it touches the mechanical toy will often serve instead to strengthen the response. This further demonstrates the point that this phenomenon is not to be considered an example of a learned or conditioned response. Last, if the egg is hatched in a situation in which the newborn duckling is deprived of all contact with any kind of moving figure, animate or inanimate, for a length of time that extends beyond the critical period, then no following response at all will be evoked. Under these circumstances the duckling will not be capable of attaching itself to any caretaking figure, whether it be the biological mother, a surrogate mother, or a human being. The implications of this last phenomenon will be discussed in detail subsequently. It is reasonable to assume that the capacity to form the imprinted response is genetically programmed in that each species has its own critical period for the elicitation of it. Accordingly, I consider it reasonable to refer to it as *instinctual*.

The Question of Imprinting in Human Beings   I believe that human infants exhibit a similar phenomenon during the earliest months of life. I do not believe, however, that it is so specific that one can measure accurately an exact critical period—as one can in lower animals. One of the ways in which human beings differ from lower animals is the flexibility of the instinctual response and its capacity to be modified to varying degrees by the individuals themselves and the social environment. Certain birds, for example, are compelled to perform specific ritualistic mating dances during the mating season. They have no choice but to do so. The capacity for the particular response is programmed into their genes and is elicited by certain environmental stimuli that occur at specific times of the year. Although we human beings have procreative urges that produce the desire to mate, we are not compelled to act out on these instinctual responses in a reflex manner. We have a certain amount of conscious control over them and our social environment can play a significant role in modifying these instinctive responses.

Like the duckling, the human infant forms an attachment bond with its mother or her surrogate. If the human infant is not provided tender loving care during infancy, the child may literally waste away and die. In less extreme situations—in which the caretaker simply does not provide significant affection, tenderness, cuddling, protection, etc.—the infant is not likely to form this bond and, I believe, may never form it. Like the duckling who does not develop a following response if it has been deprived of contact with moving figures for a time that extends beyond the critical period, humans who have been significantly deprived during their critical periods for imprinting will similarly be unable to form an attachment bond— regardless of how benevolent, devoted, dedicated, and loving the caretaking individual. Although I cannot specify a particular segment of time—such as one can with a duckling and other lower species—I believe that this critical period exists in humans within the first few months of life. I cannot be more specific. To do so would be not only presumptuous, but would imply a specificity that probably does not exist in humans. And, as is true of lower species, if a human infant does not form this bond during the critical period *it can never be formed*. I believe that one of the results of the failure to develop this bond is that the individual will never develop significantly strong internalized guilt-evoking mechanisms. Just as the aforementioned genetic-neurological factor serves as a substrate for the imprinted factor, the imprinted factor serves as a substrate for the subsequent contributions (to be described below) to the development of the internalized guilt-evoking mechanisms. Without such imprinting there will be no guilt, because without it the next steps will not be successfully accomplished.

The Pleasure-Pain Stage

At the earliest levels of life, young infants deter themselves from behavior that may be detrimental to themselves and/or society by following the pleasure-pain principle. In the healthy family situation the pleasure the child experiences from being "good" or doing the "right" things results from the love and affection the child receives when it manifests such behavior. And the healthiest form of discipline is the threatened loss of such affection. The mother of a three-year-old may say, "Mary, I'm very proud of you. You've been a wonderful girl *all* day. You've been very good to your little brother and helped Mommy feed him. You're very useful to have around the house. I'm so happy with you that I want to give you a big hug and a kiss (mother hugs child affectionately and kisses her on both cheeks). I'm so happy with you today that I want to tell Daddy all about how good you were as soon as he comes home." Such a child is not only likely to respond with enhanced feelings of self-worth and a glow of loving tenderness toward mother, but is also likely to remember well what those behavioral patterns were that evoked such wonderful responses from mother. These patterns then are likely to be repeated in future situations in order to elicit similar positive reinforcement from mother.

On another day, however, the same mother may say, "Mary, I've had it with you today. I'm so upset with you, I'm ready to climb the walls. I don't know what's got into you today. You've been a mess from the minute you got up. You spilled your milk, threw your muffin on the floor and stepped on it and, worst of all, you poked your little baby brother in the eye. Thank God nothing happened to him. Just go to your room and stay away from me. I'm ready to explode. I can't wait until your father comes home so he can take care of you." I do not believe that these comments reflect any deficiency on this mother's part. Her statements are natural and humane, and they get across the message to the child that the unacceptable behavior is going to result in temporary loss of affection from her mother. I consider such comments to reflect healthy and humane forms of punishment in the upbringing of children. It is an extremely effective way of "helping the child remember" to be good.

But more direct examples of punishment are also important in healthy and humane upbringing. A two-year-old who runs into the street will not be deterred from doing so by being lectured on the dangers of automobiles. The child has little capacity to project him- or herself into the future and appreciate the ultimate consequences of such irresponsible behavior. A slap on the backside or strong castigation is much more likely to be effective. The child learns restraint with the internal message: "If I run into the street, my mother or father will hit me—I'd better not." Living for the moment, the child at that age cannot be expected to say, "I'd better not run into the street because some day I might get hit by a car." As long as the slap on the backside does not produce physical trauma—but is more psychologically than physically painful—I would consider it to be a healthy form of punishment in the learning process.

Crucial to the child's successfully passing through this stage in a healthy fashion is the presence of a loving parent or parental surrogate. In the earlier stage of imprinting, the primary goal was to establish an attachment bond with an affectionate parenting figure. There was little in the way of formal cognitive processes operating. In this phase, the affectionate parenting figure must be present to provide linguistic input in the service of teaching the child what is good, bad, right, and wrong. Linguistic and cognitive factors are operative here, but the learning is based on simple pleasure-pain principles. If such significant figures are absent then the child is not going to accomplish this phase successfully. And the learning occurs because of the affection the child will predictably receive when "good" and the threat of its withdrawal when "bad."

Once again, the hierarchal nature of the sequence in the development of the internalized guilt-evoking mechanisms requires that the previous stages be present if the next stage is to be accomplished. Accordingly, a child with a genetic-neurological factor with high guilt-evoking potential, who may have had good imprinting and the development of a strong attachment bond, will not successfully accomplish this third phase if the parenting figure is removed, not sufficiently present, or significantly unpredictable in providing positive reinforcement. Also, it is difficult to ascertain the exact time span when this phase is operative. Roughly, I believe it begins at the time when the child starts to appreciate formal language, during the end of the first year of life. There is no particular time of life when this phase comes to an end; however, the earlier in life the conditioning is provided by loving figures, the stronger will be its effects and the more important it will be in the child's development.

The Shame Stage

In the fourth stage, the shame stage, the child's primary deterrent to performing a prohibited act is the fear that he or she will be discovered by significant environmental figures who will then reject him or her. Of importance here is the child's fear of being *seen* performing the transgression by parents or surrogates, and thereby rejected. It is as if the child is standing in the middle of a circle of parenting figures all of whom are pointing at him or her and simultaneously shouting "shame on you!" This stage coincides with E.H. Erikson's (1950) second stage in which the primary conflict to be resolved is that of "Autonomy vs. Shame." Erikson makes reference to the ashamed person's words to the observers: "God damn your eyes." At this stage, the deterrent forces are still externalized; one blushes in front of someone, not alone. In Eastern cultures, such as the Japanese, shame as a deterrent to undesirable behavior is ubiquitous. When a man commits a crime his whole family suffers disgrace and it is not simply the individual who need be ashamed. (This is probably one of the reasons for the low crime rate in countries like Japan.) In this phase, as well, there must be caring figures who still provide praise and affection when the child is "good" and who care enough to threaten loss of affection (at this stage "publicly") when the child exhibits undesirable behavior. There is a definite similarity between the pleasure-pain and the shame stage in that in both an external factor operates to discourage unacceptable behavior. They differ, however, in that in the pleasure-pain stage the deterrent can be any of a variety of external noxious stimuli—both physical and psychological. In the shame stage a very specific external threat is employed, namely, the overt disapproval of one or more significant figures in a public (as opposed to private) setting.

The Guilt Stage

In the fifth and final stage, the self-blame or guilt stage, the child has internalized the parental values. Here, the inner rather than the outer voice deters (G. Piers and M.B. Singer, 1953). This corresponds to Erikson's (1950) third stage, "Guilt versus Initiative." Alone and unobserved, the child suffers the admonition of the voices of the internalized authorities. Once this phase has been reached, the parents can relax their vigil. The child can be trusted to behave because this mechanism is powerful—so powerful that it not only functions with exaggerated severity, but lends itself well to the formation of many psychopathological mechanisms.

S. Freud considered the ages of three to five to be important ones in superego development. He related this to the resolution of the Oedipus complex. According to Freud, boys develop incestuous designs on their mothers during this phase and anticipate that their fathers will castrate them in punishment for these illicit cravings, which violate the incest taboo. In order to protect themselves from this consequence, they incorporate their fathers' superego dictates against incest. In this process, they also carry down from their fathers' superegos other dictates that are designed to inhibit a wide variety of unacceptable behaviors via the formation of guilt. I am in agreement with Freud that there is indeed rapid development of the child's capacity to experience guilt during this phase. However, I am not in agreement with him that it has anything to do with the resolution of the Oedipus complex. (I have discussed in detail elsewhere 1973a, 1986a my views on the Oedipus complex.) Rather, I believe that this is the period in children's lives when they are beginning to spend significant amounts of time outside the parental home. They start attending nursery school and begin visiting the homes of other children, unaccompanied by their parents. In these new situations they have to learn the "rules" of the new authorities who take command over their lives. In order to adjust properly in these new environments they must learn quickly the new rules or else suffer rejection. I believe that children's rapid superego development during this phase is much more reasonably explained by these developments in the child's life than by anything related to sexual attraction toward the parent of the opposite sex.

In this phase, as well, there must be present in the child's environment loving and affectionate individuals with whom the child will identify and whom the child will emulate. Without such identification and emulation there will be no incorporation and internalization of the parental standards. Such incorporation is central to the development of the guilt-evoking mechanisms. The child then has his or her own guidelines for behavior and will secretly feel a sense of low self-worth if these rules are broken. Guilt, therefore, differs from shame. One is ashamed only when others learn of the reprehensible behavior; when there is guilt, only the perpetrator need know. Shame is public; guilt is private.

I have defined guilt as the feeling of low self-worth that an individual experiences after having thoughts, experiencing feelings, or performing deeds which one has learned in early childhood are unacceptable to significant figures. I believe that this mechanism is central to what we refer to as guilt, but there are other operative factors. One of these is the capacity to put oneself in another person's position. This is another cognitive capacity which, although separate from guilt, is also an element within it. Let us take, for example: "It is bad and wrong to hurt other people." One could simply say that an individual might feel guilty if he or she were to break this rule, because such transgression had been associated with criticism and/or loss of parental affection in early childhood. However, it is reasonable also to say that this rule will be strengthened if the individual appreciates that the person whom one has harmed will suffer. Such appreciation is likely to strengthen the internalized guilt-evoking mechanisms. Another cognitive factor that is operative in the guilt mechanism is the ability to project oneself into the future, especially the appreciation of the future consequences of one's unacceptable behavior. The anticipation of pain or pleasure, as mentioned, is operative in the development of guilt. In order to utilize this contributing factor, however, the individual must have the cognitive capacity to project him- or herself into the future.

Accordingly, there are two kinds of projective mechanisms operative in guilt: 1) The capacity to project oneself into the position of those who might suffer from one's transgressions and 2) the ability to project oneself into the future in order to appreciate the possible consequences (both positive and negative) of one's behavior. These mechanisms also have their own evolutionary development and it is reasonable to speculate that the aforementioned bell-shaped curves are applicable to these mechanisms as well. Consequently, it is probable that individuals vary with regard to the genetic endowment that determines the strength of these functions. Accordingly, children with weak superegos may very well have these genetic impairments contributing to their difficulties.

I believe that there are gender differences in the strength of the internal guilt-evoking mechanisms. Specifically, I believe that women are more likely to feel guilt on a genetic basis than men and are more likely, as well, to be able to put themselves in the position of other people, i.e., exhibit sympathy and empathy. I believe that this difference not only exists but also that it cannot be explained simply as due to environmental influences. Up until the 20th century men were primarily the hunters and fighters (protectors and warriors) and women were primarily the child rearers. I am not placing any particular value judgments on these role differences; I am only stating that this is what the situation was. Men who were genetically strong in hunting/fighting capacities were more likely to survive than those who were weak in these areas. The weaker ones were more likely to fall in battle and less likely to protect their families from enemies. They were also less likely to compete successfully for food for themselves and their families. Accordingly, they were less likely to pass their genes down to subsequent generations. Women who were stronger in the child-rearing realm were more likely viewed as desirable mates and their genes, therefore, were more likely to be passed down to their progeny.

Now to go more specifically to the guilt-evoking mechanisms. Men with high development of the capacity for guilt were generally less effective warriors than those who were more psychopathically inclined. To be a good soldier one must not think too long about the fact that one is murdering another individual—depriving that person thereby of the one life he or she has on this earth. Guilt-ridden neurotics make the poorest soldiers; criminal psychopaths probably make the best soldiers. Wars give them the opportunity to murder and plunder with social sanction. In contrast, there was no particular survival advantage for women with low genetic programming for the guilt-evoking mechanisms. In fact, having strong guilt mechanisms may have been of preferential value to them in that it lessened the likelihood that they would abandon their children or treat them badly. This difference in the sexes, justifies, I believe, my view that men today are less likely to feel guilt than women. I believe that this is *one* of the reasons why there are many more male than female criminals.

Women also are generally more sympathetic and empathetic than men. I believe that this difference relates also to the aforementioned evolutionary selective processes. Putting oneself in the position of one's enemy lessens the likelihood of killing that individual. Weakness in this capacity is an asset on the battlefield. Strength in such capacity is an asset in child rearing. Babies cannot verbalize their needs. The mother's sympathy and empathy, the ability to project herself into the child's position and understand its needs, was crucial for the survival of the human species. This speculation, therefore, explains this gender difference.

The ability to project oneself into the future may also have genetically determined gender differences. The opposite of this capacity is generally referred to as impulsivity. Although the warrior must utilize such thinking to some degree, there must be a certain weakness in this area when one goes into battle. There must be the capacity to deny that one may get killed. Such denial requires some blindness to future consequences and more attention to immediate action. As men are recruited to march off to war, they have to deny that they might not march back. The effective soldier must often shoot first and ask questions later. Impulsivity, then, over the course of history, may have contributed to the survival of men. Women, in contrast, had to be thinking more about the future if their babies were to survive. Quietly thinking about the future was probably conducive to the survival of women. I am not claiming that conducting warfare does not involve any consideration of the future; I am only claiming that conducting successful warfare, at the foot-soldier level, involves more impulsivity than quiet deliberation. The generals, behind the lines, can indulge themselves in future planning and strategies. Consistent with this theory is my belief that there would probably be less war in this world if women were the leaders of nations. Unfortunately, at this time, it is more often the case that women who are able to reach such levels of power and influence are generally those who have taken on male qualities of combativeness, competition, and ruthlessness. Perhaps that was the only way they could have reached their high positions in today's world. Later in this chapter, in my discussion of differences in mating patterns, I will make reference to these speculations again.

Clinical Implications of the Theory

I believe this theory has important implications for therapy. If I am correct, then many patients who present with deficiencies in their capacity to feel guilt have a poor therapeutic prognosis. One cannot change the genes and so those whose impairments in this area relate to weak genetic-neurological programming are not likely to be helped by a psychotherapeutic approach. Furthermore, those who (in addition or separately) have suffered deprivations of affection during the critical imprinting period of infancy are also not likely to be helped by treatment because of their deep-seated impairment in forming meaningful relationships. Although these are certainly pessimistic implications regarding the treatability of patients who have these defects, this should not be a reason for denying their reality. If this is the way the world is then we have to recognize and accept these realities and not delude ourselves into believing that we can help people whose disorders are not reversible by our psychotherapeutic techniques. One way of enhancing the efficiency of psychotherapy is to be more selective with regard to our patients and not attempt to treat those who are untreatable. Such differentiations also open up new avenues of research for *appropriate* therapeutic measures for those who are not candidates for our psychotherapeutic programs. A behavior modification approach, for example, probably offers more hope than psychotherapy for changing a psychopathic person who has not had a healthy imprinting experience with an affectionate parenting figure during early infancy. (I will discuss this further below.)

At this point I would like to present a clinical vignette that will serve as a basis for my subsequent discussion of the implications of this theory. A number of years ago I saw a 15-year-old boy named

Bob, who presented with moderately severe psychopathic behavior. He had become involved with a group of delinquent youngsters and had been picked up by the police on a number of occasions for recklessly driving stolen cars, stealing from department stores, and burglarizing homes. He had practically no motivation to learn in school, and had no hesitation cheating on tests. He would usually lie about his grades and often "lose" his report cards. He was disruptive in the classroom in a kind of playful and mocking way. He frequently propositioned his female cousins and on two occasions was found fondling the genitalia of little girls who were relatives.

The patient's mother was unmarried when she became pregnant at the age of 18. She was a seriously disturbed woman, who did not inform her family that she was pregnant. Rather, she found some excuse to remove herself entirely from her family and moved to a distant part of the city in which they lived. Over the course of the pregnancy there was good reason to believe that she deteriorated significantly, to the point that she was psychotic at the time of Bob's birth. She took the newborn infant home to an apartment, where she lived alone, and would often leave the child alone for hours and even days. During these periods the child would not be fed and would lie crying in his own wastes. After numerous interventions by neighbors, the child's neglect was brought to the attention of the police and subsequently of the mother's family. By that time the child was about five months of age. It took another six months, however, before the mother was finally declared unfit and the child was turned over to the mother's sister, who was married and five years the mother's senior. It was the maternal aunt who raised the patient and brought him to me.

In the initial session she said: "Doctor, since the day he came into my home, when he was about one year old, I've been turning myself inside out trying to be a mother to this child. But nothing's worked. In spite of all my efforts, he still treats me like a piece of furniture. I think that if I died today, he wouldn't even cry. He has absolutely no feelings for people. He never feels guilty about anything he's done and punishments don't seem to work. I've tried them all. He couldn't care less whether I send him to his room, ground him, take away television, take away his allowance, or anything else. Nothing works! He's never ashamed of anything he's done. He often says he's sorry and then he apologizes, but he just does that to get people off his back. I know him well enough to know that he really doesn't mean it. Sometimes he can convince people that he's really sorry about what he's done, but he just goes on and does what he wants anyway—no matter how terrible. He lives for the moment and doesn't seem to concern himself with the future consequences of what he does.... He has no concern for other people's feelings. I've never seen him cry about anything terrible that has happened to another person, even death. He's been to a couple of funerals now. One was the funeral of my mother two years ago and he showed absolutely no emotion at all.... My other two children are just fine. In fact, I've done less for them, even though they're my own biological offsprings, than I've done for him. Sometimes they resent how much I go out of my way for him because I feel I have to keep trying.... He has never known his mother. She's been in the hospital all these years. A few years ago I took Bob to visit her and he couldn't care less one way or the other. So we never went again. I just didn't see the point.... He's also a con man. He can put on a sweet smile and con people into doing things for him. I started taking him to psychiatrists when he was about seven. You're the fifth one. The others all said the same thing. They said they couldn't help him and that maybe when he's older he might be helped. You've come very highly recommended and I hope you can help him."

In my interview with Bob he was calm and "smooth." At no point did he exhibit any manifestations of guilt over his various forms of antisocial behavior. When I pointed out to him that his reckless driving was dangerous and might result in people being killed, he shrugged his shoulders and said, "No one lives forever." When I reminded him that he himself might be killed, he replied, "I don't drive that fast." When I asked him about his fondling the genitalia of little girls he replied, "It was fun. I told them I was only tickling them. I don't know why everybody's getting so upset." Bob showed absolutely no interest in coming for treatment, but stated that he would come if his mother insisted because it made her happy. He didn't think that he had any problems and so thought treatment would be a waste of time and money.

I informed Bob's mother (I will call her *mother* because psychologically she was, even though biologically she was his aunt) that I regretted that I could not be of help to him. I explained to her my belief that he had not formed a psychological tie with an affectionate adult during a critical period for such bonding during the first year of his life and that there was no possibility that he would be able to do this subsequently. I discussed with her the phenomenon of imprinting and compared Bob to the duckling who had been deprived completely of meaningful caretaking input during the critical period of his infancy. I explained to her, as well, that for psychotherapy to be meaningful, the patient must have a good relationship with the therapist. Because Bob was not capable of forming a meaningful affectionate relationship, he did not satisfy a primary and fundamental criterion for successful treatment. I explained to her that if he had shown any evidence, no matter how small, of having formed a meaningful relationship with another human being throughout the course of his life, I would consider revising my conclusion. However, I pointed out to her that there was no evidence that he had done so, and that even his relationship with her was one that could not satisfy the criterion of being a genuinely human one. She had described Bob as treating her "like a piece of furniture," and I agreed that this was basically the way he viewed all other human beings.

The mother pleadingly asked me if I would still try to treat him. I told her that without conviction for the possibility of a positive therapeutic outcome, I would be exploiting her. Again, she repeated that I had come highly recommended and that I was her last hope. Again, I tried to impress upon her the futility of a psychotherapeutic program, but finally agreed to try for a few sessions with the full understanding that the likelihood of my helping Bob was practically zero. And the prediction came true. We discontinued after a few months of treatment, when I felt that I was getting absolutely nowhere. One could argue that my initial pessimism resulted in my fulfilling my prophecy that therapy would be doomed. In response, I believe that the failure of therapy had nothing to do with my initial prophecy, but was related to the child's being untreatable because of the aforementioned reasons. And I believe, further, that even the most optimistic therapist (whose optimism would have to be based on delusion) would still have come forth with the same result. During the four or five years following the cessation of Bob's treatment I intermittently received letters from other therapists and clinics asking for reports. Obviously, the mother did not give up and I doubt seriously whether the subsequent therapists were successful.

Bob's case demonstrates in an extreme way the principles outlined in the theory presented above. But he is not the typical patient who presents with antisocial behavior. The more typical youngster has generally suffered less serious compromises at the levels of imprinting and the subsequent pleasure/pain, shame, and guilt levels. These children are more readily treatable because they have had at least some experience with a meaningful relationship during the imprinting phase and so have the potential for forming a relationship with the therapist.

The therapist does well to view antisocial behavior on a continuum. At one end is the extreme psychopath who may have a high genetic loading for psychopathy (because of a weak genetically based substrate to serve as the foundation for guilt-evoking mechanisms), and/or who has suffered formidable deprivations of affection during the imprinting period, and/or who has experienced antisocial inducing influences during the three phases in which parental disciplinary measures influence the development of the conscience. At the other end of the continuum is the normal, healthy child who has not suffered any significant deficiencies in the five levels of development of the internalized guilt-evoking mechanisms. The closer the child is to the healthy end of the continuum the greater the likelihood a therapeutic relationship will be possible and potentially useful.

A scenario sometimes seen in television sitcoms is that of a severely antisocial boy of seven or eight who has spent practically all his life being shuttled from one foster home to another. He is then adopted by Mr. and Mrs. *Goody Two Shoes* who take him under their benevolent wings and provide him with love, understanding, and sympathy. Whereas at the beginning of the program, the school principal is tearing his hair out with frustration over the boy's delinquent antics, by the end of the program he is a class leader, star student, and the loveliest little fellow you could imagine. All this is Hollywood pap and is just another one of the fairy tales that sell a product. Unfortunately, gullible listeners believe this stuff and will use it as a guideline when adopting children who have had formidable deprivations in the early years of their lives. Promulgating this myth is a disservice to all concerned. Elsewhere in this book, I will be making reference to this theory when it provides a useful explanation for the clinical phenomena being discussed.

REBELLION

Adolescent rebellion can be divided into three types: 1) healthy and constructive rebellion, 2) neutral and/or innocuous rebellion, and 3) destructive rebellion. It is extremely important for the examiner to make these differentiations, especially because of their therapeutic importance. Healthy or constructive rebellion should be encouraged; neutral or innocuous rebellion might very well be left alone; destructive rebellion must be discouraged.

Accordingly, rebellion may not be all that bad. Constructive rebellion may very well be considered the stuff of which progress is made. In fact, if not for constructive rebellion we might still be living in caves. There are societies in which centuries pass and there is absolutely no difference in lifestyle from one generation to the next. The family may remain living in the same home for hundreds of years. There is no rebellion; and there is no progress. One could argue that my criticism of this lifestyle is a reflection of a prejudiced value judgment, and that my preference for societies that progress over those in which one generation is no different from the next reflects an inappropriate bias. I cannot deny that people in the nonprogressive category might very well lead fulfilling and enriched lives. In such societies, however, we do not observe the impetus to make new discoveries, expand human knowledge, and solve ever-present problems. If one has appendicitis, it's nice to know there are surgeons around who can perform the life-saving appendectomy. When giving birth and the baby is "stuck," it's nice to know there are obstetricians around who can perform a caesarean delivery that may very well save the life of both the mother and child. These are just two of countless examples of the benefits of progress—benefits which, I believe, far outweigh what appear to me to be the disadvantages (I would say stagnation) of a nonprogressive society.

Rebellion is an important element in human progress. The rebellious person is basically saying: "I do not agree with that which those before me have accepted as fact. I will reject it, or I will expand upon it, or improve it." The people whom we refer to as geniuses are often individuals who are able to look upon a generally accepted fact—something believed by the vast majority of their predecessors—question it, and not only consider the possibility that it is wrong, but prove it to be so. Albert Einstein is just one such example. Prior to his time, the consensus among scientists was that light is weightless. Einstein believed that light has weight—not very heavy, but weight nevertheless. In his famous eclipse experiment he demonstrated that light waves bend as they pass celestial bodies and that only an entity with some weight would exhibit such changes in its path. Einstein also questioned the general notion that time passes at a fixed rate. He demonstrated that the rate at which time passes is related to the speed of the platform on which one measures time's rate of passage. Although these differences are significant only when one approaches the speed of light, he still proved that the rates of time passage do indeed change at these extremely high speeds. Although this may not appear to be of much practical interest to the everyday person, it has profound implications for our understanding of the nature of the universe. It was healthy rebellion on Einstein's part that was a central factor in these important discoveries.

Another more practical and mundane example: Up until the last 10 to 15 years, Rh+ babies who were born to Rh- mothers might develop erythroblastosis fetalis, a disease that might be fatal or crippling. The people who developed RhoGAM, a drug that can prevent the development of this disorder in such babies, had to reject some basic immunological principles before they could proceed with their work. They had to disbelieve what was being said by most professors and most textbooks, namely, that the baby's Rh+ cells cross the placenta during the intrauterine period and stimulate the mother to produce antibodies to Rh+ cells during the course of the pregnancy. Once this notion was tested and rejected, and it was found that the baby's Rh+ cells only entered the mother's circulation at the time of delivery, the investigators were able to go on with their important work. Again, healthy rebellion was a central element in this important discovery from which mankind has benefited immensely.

As mentioned, the various developmental issues focused on in this chapter are not completely separate from one another; there is much overlap. Rebellion is no exception to this principle. I discuss rebellion first because it infuses many of the other conflicts and problems with which adolescents must deal, especially their dependency problems, their attempts at forming a separate identity, and the maneuvers that they utilize to enhance their self-esteem. Rebellion can serve to compensate for feelings of inadequacy. Rebellion, especially when it is associated with great anger, may provide the youngster with a feeling of strength and power that he or she does not actually possess. And this is especially the case when the rebellion takes place in the context of a group, which generally provides the youngster with a sense of power far greater than he or she possesses. It is truly an example of the principle of the whole being greater than the sum of its parts. Rebellion can very well be viewed as the energizer of the adolescent's solutions to these basic developmental problems. It adds a vitality to the problem-solving processes and to the solutions themselves and thereby enhances the likelihood that they will be effective.

The examiner should try to ascertain in which of the three aforementioned categories the rebellion lies—healthy, neutral, or destructive—and should attempt to determine the point at which normal and expected adolescent rebellion ends and the pathological begins. These differentiations may sometimes be very difficult. For example, in recent years some adolescents have become deeply identified with the "punk rock" movement. These youngsters pride themselves on bizarre and outlandish dress that is not only gaudy but designed to frighten. Infused in all of this is a strong sadistic element; their songs often center on themes of violence and murder. Is this necessarily pathological? Although I do not claim vast experience with this group, from what I know of them I would consider their preoccupation with these sadistic themes to be pathological— especially if the youngster engages in antisocial behavior as an outgrowth of participation in such a group. Accordingly, I would say that such membership is at best a prepathological manifestation and certainly a warning sign that the youngster may very well move into the pathological realm.

Another example: A number of years ago a mother brought a 13-year-old girl to me for treatment. While cleaning her daughter's room one morning she found a note on her desk that she had written to a friend. It had not yet been folded or put into an envelope for mailing. The segment that was particularly upsetting to the mother read: "Dear Mary, I had a great time at your house this weekend. Thanks for inviting me. That was a real great time we had with the boys you invited over. I really liked that big guy, the 18-year-old. I really liked sucking his big cock." Not surprisingly, the mother was shocked by the "discovery" of this letter, considered it a definite sign of severe psychopathology, and requested the earliest possible appointment with me. On the basis of my evaluation I concluded that there had been no such encounter and that the note was left as a prank. Examiners do well to work on the assumption that unsealed letters left in "public" places are placed there so that they will be read by those who are likely to notice them. People who genuinely do not wish their letters read do not make such "mistakes."

Was this a pathological act? The question cannot be answered without considering the broader context in which the letter was written. In this girl's case, it was an isolated example of a "prank" and she was basically functioning well in all areas: school, the neighborhood, and at home. Had she not been functioning well in these areas, and had this been one of a series of such pranks, then I would have considered her to have had problems warranting treatment. In this case, I advised the mother that I saw no reason for treatment at that point and that I was taking the girl's statement at face value. It was an age-appropriate prank (although probably a little more creative than that devised by most 13-year-old girls). I also advised the mother to call me if there was a repetition of such antics and asked her to call in a few months, even if there were no such recurrences, in order to inform me of the outcome. The mother did indeed call me a few months later and told me that there had been no repetition of pranks of this kind. My final conclusion, then, was that this prank was an example of normal adolescent rebellion in the somewhat creative and provocative category.

Another example: An 18-year-old girl, while sitting at the dinner table with her family, nonchalantly says, "You know, I've missed my period this month. I wonder if I'm pregnant?" Is dropping such a *bomb* necessarily pathological? Again, one cannot come to a conclusion unless one considers the total context of the setting in which the comment was made. If the girl, for example, engages in indiscriminate sex in order to compensate for feelings of low self-worth, then that is her primary problem. If she is feigning nonchalance as a way of covering up underlying fears of pregnancy, then one must still look into other aspects of the situation before deciding whether psychopathology is present. If she is frequently dropping provocations of this kind, totally unrelated to real events, then the problem is not one of pregnancy, but provocation. And persistent provocation is pathological. My hope here is that the reader will be impressed with the fact that placement of adolescent rebellion into one of the three aforementioned categories may not be easy. In many situations, therefore, one must explore a variety of factors in the attempt to make such a determination.

It is important also for the therapist to appreciate that adolescent rebellion does not exist separate from the reactions of the individuals against whom the youngster is rebelling. An important determinant as to whether or not the rebellion will have served its purposes is whether parents and other adult authorities are shocked, disgusted, nauseated, or react in other ways that reveal their revulsion from the rebellious act. If the parents do not provide these reactions, the youngster is deprived of one of the important gratifications of the rebellious act. Failure of parents to respond in these ways may result in the youngster's feeling the need to utilize more dramatic methods of rebellion. In such cases this may result in a shift from innocuous to pathological modes of rebellion.

A good example of this phenomenon is the long-hair style that became common in the early to mid-1960s, primarily as a result of the popularity of The Beatles. Of all the forms of adolescent rebellion one could imagine, I believe long hair is one of the most innocuous, and therein lies the ingenuity of the person who first devised this mode of adolescent rebellion. I do not know who he or she was, but I believe that the individual may have contributed more to the lessening of violence on earth than many who have won Nobel Peace Prizes. After all, what more innocuous way could there be to rebel than to grow one's hair long? However, the success of this maneuver relies upon parental revulsion. Otherwise, the rug is pulled out from under it and the youngster may have to resort to more dramatic methods of rebellion.

During the time when the long-hair mode of rebellion was in vogue, I would generally recommend that parents provide the youngster with reasonable degrees of revulsion in order to insure the perpetuation of this innocuous rebellious maneuver. This interchange typifies the kind of conversation I recommended at that time. It takes place between 16-year-old Tom, whose hair is down below his shoulders, and his father.

Father: Tom, I would like to have a chat with you, son.

Tom (as if granting a favor): Yeah, Pop. What is it you want?

Father (apologetically): Well, Tom, it's just that I would like to have a father-son talk with you, boy.

Tom (impatiently): Yeah what is it, Dad?

Father: Well, Tom, the first thing I want you to know is that your mother and I *love you deeply*.

Tom: Yeah, Dad, I know that. What do you have in mind?

Father (hesitantly): Well, son, I'm going to make a criticism of you, but I want you to know that it doesn't mean that I don't love you very much.

Tom (now even more impatient): I know, Dad. Will you please get to the point. What's the bottom line?

Father: Well, Tom, to tell you the truth, it's that hair of yours. To tell you the truth, it really upsets your mother and me to see you that way, especially because from the back we can't tell whether you're a boy or a girl.

Tom (angrily): This is a *free* country and I'll wear my hair any way I want!

Father: Listen, Tom, I recognize that. I know you're free to wear your hair any way you want. However, I have the freedom to tell you how upset I am over it.

Tom: Well, is that all?

Father: No. There's more. You see this Saturday night your mother and I are having some dinner guests, some people from the office. Some of them are senior people in my firm and it's important that we make a good impression.

Tom: So what's that got to do with me?

Father: Well, son, you see it's that hair. It's not that we don't love you, but it'll be a little embarrassing for us if the guests see you. Therefore, your mother and I would both appreciate if you would leave the house about 7:00 or 7:30 on

Saturday night. They'll be coming at about 8:00 and, to be honest with you, it'll be a little embarrassing for us if they see you this way. Also, your mother and I have decided that you can extend your curfew Saturday and can come home around 1:00 a.m. We expect the guests to leave around midnight.

Tom (even more angrily): No one's going to tell me when I leave this house and when I come back. This is a free country and this is *my* house also. What is this a jail or a penitentiary or something? If you're ashamed of me that's your problem, not mine. There's nothing wrong with the way I wear my hair. That's the way *I* like it. And if those asshole friends of yours don't like my hair, that's their problem.

Father (somewhat timidly): Please don't get angry, Tom. It's just that we want you to know how we feel about it. We just hoped you'd take our feelings into consideration and not embarrass us Saturday night. We don't want you to feel that this house isn't yours; it's just that we want you to take our feelings into consideration here.

Tom (getting up): Well you're not taking my feelings into consideration and I'll come and go when I please. (Exit Tom.)

That Saturday evening Tom will stay in his room until approximately 8:30, to insure that even the latest guest will have by then arrived. Then, wearing his heaviest boots, he will stomp down the stairs (to insure that everyone can hear him approaching) and make a grand entrance into the dining room, hair waving in the breeze. He'll make the rounds of all the guests, politely inquiring about their welfare and that of their children. A more sensitive and well-mannered boy would be hard to imagine. Each greeting of each guest will be accompanied by enough head-nodding to insure once again that his mane is fully displayed. And one can be sure, as well, that he will prance into the house at 11:30 p.m., before any of the guests have left, in order to once again insure that his grand entrance will be noticed by the guests—who will politely hide their revulsion. Of course, Tom will be acutely sensitive to the suppressed disgust of the guests and the embarrassment he has caused his parents. This is the scenario I recommended during the 60s and 70s. Those parents who were wise enough to follow this advice and who carried out their role helped prevent their children's having to resort to more dramatic and serious forms of rebellion.

One of the purposes of adolescent rebellion is to help mobilize the youngster to leave the home and assuage the anxieties attendant to such separation. The facts are that the vast majority of parents will be far more loving and affectionate of the adolescent than any other human being on earth. Except for the most rejecting and abusive parents, most are willing to make more sacrifices and to provide more guidance, support, affection, and money than any other person on earth. Furthermore, they will take more "shit" from the adolescent than any other human being. I suspect that on some level (probably *very* deep in the unconscious) the adolescent is appreciative of this and thereby fears the separation. By viewing the parents as village idiots, as anachronisms from the Middle Ages, as people who are not up with the latest trends, the adolescent can justify rebellion and refusal to comply with parental standards. Rebellion, then, may serve to lessen separation anxieties. Such rebellion also has the fringe benefit of helping the parents deal with their own "empty nest syndrome." On the one hand, the parents anticipate that the home will be somewhat lonely when the adolescent is gone. On the other hand, the *Sturm und Drang* of adolescent rebellion is often such a nuisance and a source of ongoing provocation for the parents that there is also a sense of relief when the youngster is finally out of the house.

DEPENDENCY CONFLICTS

Twentieth-century teenagers are growing up in a somewhat unique environment in that their childhoods are being artificially prolonged by the demands of our modern technological society. Prior to this century, children generally were considered adults as early as the age of six or seven, but no later than puberty, and were expected to go out into the adult world and assume adult responsibilities. Such expectations are no longer realistic in modern technological societies. The many years of training required to achieve competence in most occupations is so great that one cannot reasonably expect youngsters to complete their education and training until the late teens and beyond.

Accordingly, the realities are that most teenagers *are* dependent upon their parents for food, clothing, shelter, and the other necessities of life. With physical dependency comes psychological dependency—the adolescent's attempts to deny it notwithstanding. The adolescent would like to believe that he or she is truly independent of the parents and tries to deny frequently the humiliating realization that just the opposite is most often the case. The adolescent is perpetually proclaiming independence in a situation where there is significant dependence. Accordingly, the sense of independence is specious. In earlier centuries the transition from childhood to adulthood was short. Youngsters had little time to gratify dependency needs because they were so swept up in the fight for survival. They were too preoccupied with the acquisition of the bare necessities of life to indulge themselves in the kind of frivolous dependency conflicts that are so widespread today. In short, many of the adolescent phenomena we are discussing in this book are manifestations of 20th-century indulgences, especially in affluent families and societies.

Dependence on Parents vs. Rejection of Parents

A common way in which adolescents deal with the transition from dependence to independence is to scorn and denigrate their parents. I recall my daughter Nancy, when she was three-years-old, sitting between her mother and me saying, "Mommy, you're the best mommy in the whole wide world and I'm the luckiest little girl in the whole world to have a mommy as wonderful as you. And Daddy, you're the best daddy in the whole world, and I'm the luckiest little girl in the whole world to have a daddy like you. I don't ever want to leave this house in my whole life. I want to stay living here with the two of you forever and ever." Her mother and I welled up with joy and pride after such a wonderful and loving comment. However, if a child is making the same statement at the age of 18, the parents have problems! Somewhere along the line the child has to give up the notion of living with the parents for the rest of his or her life, or else the youngster will be crippled with regard to entering into adult society as a self-sufficient individual.

One way in which the separation becomes easier and the dependency longings are squelched is to transform the parents from loving, kind, and giving individuals into morons, loathsome odd-balls, and people who have not been keeping up with the latest developments in mankind's progress and who know nothing about "where it's all at." Once the parents are transformed into such despicable imbeciles, it is much easier for the adolescent to have the courage to go forth into the cold cruel world. The reality is that no one will ever treat the adolescent as well as the parents do. Even the most ardent lover is not as likely to make the sacrifices and tolerate the privations that a parent will. By denigrating the parents the adolescent can deny this obvious reality and provide him- or herself with an excuse to "get out of that shit-house once and for all." It would be nice if this could solve the dependency problem. Such deprecation of the parents is rarely successful in resolving the dependency problem, however, because the reality · is that the youngster is still very much dependent on the parents – denigration and rejection of them notwithstanding. Scorning them is easy; it does not provide, however, the wherewithal for genuinely independent living. Now that the parents have been transformed into stupid ogres, however, it is more difficult to believe that they can be reliable sources of gratification of the youngster's still ever-pressing dependency needs.

Many adolescents take the position that parents should provide their services from hidden places. This concept of the ideal parent derives from the belief that only children and babies do things with their parents, but mature individuals no longer have such infantile needs. Accordingly, it may be a source of mortification for an adolescent to be seen in public with a parent. This phenomenon was demonstrated well a number of years ago when I was shopping one Saturday afternoon with my youngest daughter, Julie, then 14 years old. We were strolling through a mall, nonchalantly window shopping. Suddenly, the following interchange took place:

> *Julie* (speaking very firmly and slowly): Dad, don't turn around. Don't look sideways. Don't look back. Just look straight ahead and follow me.

I suspected that Julie had seen some friends and the prospect of their seeing her with her father (ugh!) was mortifying to her.

Accordingly, she wanted to get out of that mall as fast as possible, without being seen. I did not consider it useful to confront Julie with my speculation. Rather, I decided that it would be judicious to go along with the plan.

> *Gardner* (feigning curiosity): Why do you want me to do that, Julie?
> *Julie* (firmly): Don't ask questions. Just do what I say. Let's get out of here as soon as we can.
> *Gardner*: Okay.

I then began following Julie. Her steps were deliberate, stiff, and mechanical and so were mine. Neither of us even turned sideways (and certainly not backwards) as we hastily left the store. I suspected, however, that if a store detective were to have seen us at that point, he probably would have stopped us as two "suspicious characters" in that we certainly appeared as if we had something to hide and might very well have been sneaking out with stolen goods. I complied here with Julie's request because of my appreciation that she needed to be seen as a separate entity from her father, and that her humiliation at the prospect of being seen with me in public was a normal adolescent manifestation of her need to break away from me and be seen by herself and others as a separate person.

On another occasion, while sitting in the living room, Julie initiated the following conversation:

> *Julie*: You know, Dad, you turn me off!
> *Gardner*: Why do you say that, Julie?
> *Julie*: I don't know, just everything about you turns me off.
> *Gardner*: Well, Julie, you know that I'm always receptive to try to rectify any deficiencies I may have, especially deficiencies that may be interfering with the relationship I have with my children. So if you'll be just a little more specific, perhaps we can do something about this problem of my "turning you off."
> *Julie*: I don't know, it's just your whole lifestyle!
> *Gardner*: Well, Julie, it's very difficult for me to respond to that. If you could pinpoint some particular aspects of my lifestyle that are particularly alienating to you, then I would be in a better position to address myself to them. Perhaps I would

be in agreement with you that these qualities are indeed deficiencies, that their removal would improve our relationship, and would make you less critical of my lifestyle. However, it may be that I might not be in agreement with you, and then I would do nothing about them. However, I'm in no position to make such a decision until you can be more specific about what these possible deficiencies are.

Julie: I can't think of them right now.

Gardner: Well, why don't you give it some thought and when you can be more specific about what these characteristics are, then I'll be happy to address myself to them. Then I can promise you great receptivity to trying to change them, if I'm in agreement with you that they are indeed defects.

Julie never brought up the subject again. A classical Freudian analyst might say that her statement that I "turned her off" was a manifestation of the suppression of sexual feelings toward me. Although I cannot deny this possibility, I am dubious. I believe that the comment stemmed more from her need to totally reject my "lifestyle" in order to provide a sense of independence for herself. Some adolescent youngsters will manifest such rejection of their parents' lifestyle by embracing a religious creed that is totally antithetical to theirs. Others embrace political philosophies that are exactly the opposite of their parents' deep-seated convictions. Children of highly academically oriented parents may decide that they want to think seriously about a menial career that does not require formal education. A healthy youngster entertains these alternatives in constructive ways; the unhealthy youngster may do so in a self-destructive manner.

Transfer of Dependency from Parents to Peers

Adolescents cannot allow themselves the humiliation of overt expression of their still-present dependency desires and must gratify these symbolically, surreptitiously, or by structuring a situation in such a way that they are seemingly coerced into such gratification. One of the ways in which the adolescent satisfies the now suppressed and repressed dependency needs is to transfer dependency gratification from parents to peers. Via this maneuver adolescents convince themselves that they are no longer dependent because the parents have been rejected. However, one does not have to look too deeply into the nature of their relationships with peers to see how dependent they basically are. Under the guise of considering themselves independent thinkers, adolescents are extremely dependent on peer pressure and peer opinion. They feel compelled to embrace the ideology in vogue with their peers, regardless of how absurd. They are slavishly dependent on the adolescent clothing styles that are "in" at that moment and fear diverting from them, even in the smallest way. This reflex dependency on their peers may get them into trouble, e.g., when they fear being the only one in a group who does not engage in a particular form of antisocial behavior. Many become addicted to smoking because they cannot tolerate the prospect of being the only one in their group who doesn't smoke.

In mid-1987, there was a movie in which an adolescent boy did a handstand on the front of an automobile driven by a friend. This act of bravado was copied many times over by youngsters all across the United States—with the result that at least a few were killed while involved in this stunt. Such dependency on peers contributes to the seemingly inexplicable waves of bizarre behavior that periodically break out. For example, it is well known that the widespread reporting of two or more adolescent suicides in the same community is likely to result in an "epidemic" of further adolescent suicides. Some newspapers make it a policy not to report such events because of their awareness of this phenomenon. Such is the power of adolescents' dependency on peers and the forces within them that drive them to mimic behavior that is in vogue among teenagers.

This dependence is demonstrated well by an experience I once had with my son Andrew, then 14 years old. He was preparing to go to summer camp, in this instance a tennis camp. As his mother and I were helping him with his final packing, he became increasingly agitated. This is the conversation that ensued:

> *Gardner*: What's the trouble, Andy?
> *Andrew*: I don't know whether to put my stuff in a duffel bag or a suitcase. I'm afraid if I use a duffel bag, that most of the kids will have suitcases and I'll be embarrassed. Also, I'm

scared that if I choose the suitcase, most of the kids will have duffel bags and then I'll look different and funny.

Gardner: Andy, I've got an idea. First, let me ask you a question. Which do you think is more likely, duffel bags or suitcases?

Andrew: I would say duffel bags in favor of suitcases by a ratio of 51 to 49. (Andy was always mathematically inclined.)

Gardner: Well, I have a suggestion. Why don't we put your stuff in a duffel bag, and we'll take an empty suitcase and put it in the trunk of the car. Then we'll drive past the bus stop, as if we're strangers, and we'll look the situation over to see whether there are more duffel bags or more suitcases. If there are more duffel bags, then out you'll go and everything will be all right. However, if there are more suitcases, then we'll just drive on, as if we don't even belong there, and find an empty lot or alley a few blocks away. Then, when no one is looking, we'll switch things and then we'll drive you back to the bus stop.

Andrew: Gee Dad, every once in a while you say things that make me realize you aren't so stupid after all!

The vignette demonstrates, of course, the need of the adolescent to denigrate his father. The main point here, however, is the obvious one that this bright boy was still slavishly dependent on his peers, so much so that he would experience terrible mortification if he packed his clothing in the less common carrier. It is important for the reader to appreciate, however, that this dependency on the group should not be just viewed merely as a kind of pathological substitute of peers for parents. Rather, it is a step outside the home and is best viewed as a necessary part of the adolescent's transition to independence.

I recall a personal experience when in junior high school that demonstrates quite well the strength of the adolescent's dependency on peers. There were two classmates of mine who were well known for their antisocial antics. One day, as we were leaving an English class, to move on to mathematics, the two boys decided to make what was then called a "stink bomb." This was prepared by mixing photographic negatives with paper and then igniting the "bomb." The smoke was particularly noxious and calculated to produce revulsion in even the most phlegmatic. Because of the obvious fire danger, stink bombs were generally utilized outdoors.

In this case, however, the boys thought it would be a great idea to throw a stink bomb into a desk as we left the English class to go on to mathematics. They chose English because the teacher was one who had great difficulty controlling the class and was easy prey for tormentors. She had just left the room at the time the boys ignited the bomb. As I filed out of the room with my classmates I saw the smoke pouring out of the desk. My immediate impulse was to go over to the desk, pull out its contents, and stomp out the flames. What stopped me was the anticipation that my classmates would call me "chickenshit" and accuse me of a variety of other forms of cowardice. About five minutes later, soon after we were seated in mathematics, we heard the inevitable sound of a fire alarm. Approximately 2,000 students quickly left the building as the fire department engines surrounded it. Fortunately, no one was injured and the amount of damage done to the classroom was minimal.

In those days there were repercussions for such behavior in the New York City Public Schools. (Unfortunately, such incidents are probably commonplace today with few consequences, except for the most egregious offenders.) The boys were expelled. The class they were expelled from was an honors' class, then referred to as a "rapid advance" class. Most of us in that track went on to highly competitive academic high school programs. These boys did not. I know nothing of what ultimately happened to them. Perhaps their expulsion and failure to go on to a specialized academic high school did not affect their lives one iota. Perhaps their failure to have gone on to a more demanding high school played a role in their not having achieved as much in life as they might otherwise have. I can only wonder whether if I had had the courage at that time to stomp out the flames the boys might have led very different lives. Although I do not know whether my having acted more assertively would have protected them from the dire consequences of what ultimately occurred, I do know that my failure to do so was a reflection of typical adolescent passivity and fear of doing that which might engender the rejection and/or disapproval of peers.

Another way in which the adolescent can satisfy dependency cravings in a socially acceptable manner is to "fall in love." I will discuss in detail my views on romantic love in a later section of this chapter. Here I focus on its value for socially acceptable dependency gratifications. As part of the obsessive involvement with the loved partner the individual is ever craving to be in the presence of the loved one and feels lost when that party is not available. The dependency may often be parasitic, and one of the ways in which the relationship may become compromised is the feeling on the part of at least one of the parties that he or she is being drained and constrained by the other. Their physical caressing of one another is certainly reminiscent of the pattern of the parent and the infant. If the reader concludes from this that I am suggesting that all lovemaking is pathological, that would be a serious error. We all need some dependency gratifications. In a mature loving relationship between a man and a woman these play a definite but relatively small role. In adolescent romantic love (regardless of the age of the person) the dependency gratifications reach pathological levels, as manifested by the obsessiveness with which the individuals crave them. The common term "puppy love" is applicable here — implying as it does that the relationship is much more like two little puppies snuggling up against one another than more mature loving partners whose relationship is a far richer one with less time spent in infantile gratifications.

The adolescent's dependence on peers can be utilized in a healthy way in group therapy. I will discuss group therapy in detail in Vol. II (1999a). Here, I mention it only in the context of its value in utilizing the adolescent's dependency on peers for therapeutic purposes. The therapist is viewed as close enough to the parents to be distrusted. As mentioned, he or she is not considered to be up with the latest trends, whereas one's peers are. Because the adolescent views peers as omniscient, he or she considers them far more judicious choices when seeking those to depend on for guidance. Therapists who do not make use of these all-knowing individuals in their therapeutic groups are depriving themselves of valuable assistants in the treatment process.

Dependency on Heroes and Mentors

Another way in which adolescents gratify their dependency needs and, at the same time, transfer dependency gratifications away from parents is to involve themselves with heroes. Movie stars and athletes probably are the most well-known examples of this phenomenon. Adolescents not only emulate and identify with film stars, but try to conform to their lifestyles. Another and more blatant manifestation of such hero worship is the phenomenon of the religious cult in which the followers become slavishly dependent on their leader—who may be viewed as God appointed, God derived, or even God incarnate. Healthier adolescents may become involved with a revered teacher or mentor. This person may become a respected confidant and there may be many healthy elements in this relationship, especially if the teacher exhibits qualities that would serve the youngster well to emulate. Also, if the dependency gratifications are kept within healthy boundaries then the relationship may be even more salutary. Many accomplished people consider themselves to have lifelong debts to their mentors, because of the formidable positive influences they have had on their lives.

The ''Winter Camp'' College

College is an institution that provides many adolescents with gratification of pathological dependency needs. I believe that most colleges in the United States are not serving primarily as educational institutions; rather, they are serving as what I call "winter camps" for immature youngsters. Most youngsters attending colleges are not really looking for an education, but for another four years of prolongation of their dependent state. We have a unique disease in the United States which I call *the college disease*. Millions of parents believe that it is crucial that their children attend college and really believe that the schools to which they are sending their children are actually serving educational purposes. When there is a demand for something there will always be individuals who will be pleased to provide a supply of the item, especially when there is good money to be made in the business. Most college institutions in the United States are basically businesses. Yes, they have their academic hierarchy, their assistant professors, associate professors, and full professors. They have their college-style buildings (especially red brick and ivy), their alumni associations, their football teams, and their fund-raising campaigns. But the vast majority of students are not there to learn; rather they are there primarily to have a "good time"—which often includes significant indulgence in alcohol, drugs, and sex. When the "students" are not engaged in these activities, they go through the motion of attending classes, but little is learned. Grade-inflation insures that even those with borderline intelligence will get high grades. It is rare for someone to flunk out. And why should they fail? Does one kick a good customer out of the store? If a customer's parents are willing to continue to pay for the services provided, it would be self-destructive of the college in this highly competitive market to cut off a predictable supply of money because of the student's failure to consume the product being offered.

It is important for the reader to appreciate my use of the word *most*. I did not say that the aforementioned criticisms apply to *all* collegiate institutions and *all* students. If I had to give a percentage of those academic institutions in the U.S. that fit the above description, I would say that it is in the 75 to 80 percent range. My main purpose in mentioning this here relates to the use of these colleges for the gratification of pathological dependency needs. Such colleges also serve as a mechanism for transferring dependency from parents to those who administer these institutions. And thwarting college authorities (especially by antisocial behavior and refusal to study) is often a mere transfer of rebellion from parents to school authorities—a rebellion in which the dependency denial element is often operative.

The Role of Coercion in Providing Adolescents with Dependency Gratification

Adolescents may often structure situations in such a way that they get themselves coerced into satisfying their dependency needs. Therapists do well to appreciate this phenomenon. Psychotherapy is basically a dependent situation. In fact, it may be one of the most dependent. Many adolescents, however, cannot openly state that they need treatment, but may inwardly recognize their need for it. Such youngsters may require coercion to provide them with the excuse to attend the sessions. An adolescent will often state that the only reason he or she comes to treatment is because "my mother makes me." I have had adolescent boys, over six feet tall, weighing over 200 pounds, telling me that their 95-pound scrawny mothers, "make them come to treatment." The therapist who responds to this with incredulity and tries to help such a youngster appreciate that his mother cannot possibly force him into therapy is making an error. And, if the therapist goes further and tries to impress upon such a youngster that therapy is only for people who can consciously appreciate that they have problems, and who are motivated to change them, then that therapist is making an even worse technical error. Such confrontations will only deprive the adolescent of the excuse needed for attending the sessions and may result in the youngster leaving treatment. My usual response to such a comment is to say something along these lines: "Yeah, I understand, parents have a way of forcing kids into doing a lot of things they don't want to. But as long as you're here, and your parents are paying for it anyway, why don't we use the time? So what's on your mind? What would you like to talk about?" One boy, in this situation, stood up following the aforementioned comment, reached deeply into his pocket, pulled out a crumbled slip of paper, and said, "Well, I have this dream here...." When entering group adolescent therapy, most newcomers are asked by other members why they have come to the group. A common response includes parental coercion and denial of any psychological difficulties at all. I find it interesting that most often other group members do not pin the youngster down on this point. Rather, "they understand" and then go on directly to discuss "problems."

Hospitals and prisons may also provide an adolescent with dependency gratifications, without the youngster's having to appreciate that this is one of the functions they are serving. In both of these situations the adolescent can profess that he or she was forced into the institution and the purpose of residence therein has nothing to do with dependency gratification, but treatment and rehabilitation. One need not look hard, however, to see how these institutions provide a formidable amount of dependency gratification. The youngster's life is structured 24 hours a day by powerful authorities upon whom the youngster is dependent. However, the youngster need not openly admit that these institutions provide dependency gratifications. In prison, especially, these are well hidden because everybody knows that prisoners are tough characters who resent authority, never cry, and have nothing but hatred for those who have incarcerated them. They have nothing but scorn for those who predictably provide them with three meals a day, a bed, clothing, and other basic necessities of life.

IDENTITY CONFUSION

Adolescents are often confused about their identities. This is not surprising considering that they are part child and part adult. For most youngsters, however, the transition is quite rapid—some seeming to have been transformed in a matter of months. One girl goes to summer camp flat-chested and comes back buxom at the end of the summer. Another youngster "shoots up like a string bean" in a matter of a few months. I recall when I was about 16 years old, standing in front of my apartment house in the Bronx, in New York City where I grew up. I must have grown about five or six inches in the previous year. I looked like one could "slide me under the door." As I was standing there, a little boy of about five years of age was walking past me. He stopped, looked up at me and said, "Are you a boy or a man?" I hesitated, thought a minute about his question, and then responded, "You know, I really don't know." And I really didn't know. Like most adolescents I felt I was some of both and neither of both—at the same time.

Adolescents need to have a separate identity from their parents if they are to break away in a healthy fashion. They often don't know what identity to take, only that it must be one that is different from that of their parents. Accordingly, it is common during this period for adolescents to suddenly decide to change their religion from that of their parents. Children from religious families abruptly become agnostics or atheists, much to the chagrin of their parents. Sometimes such religious conversions follow fads as in 1960s and 1970s when Zen Buddhism was very much in vogue. Similarly, a youngster who previously couldn't care less about politics suddenly becomes obsessed with a particular political philosophy. Politically conservative parents find themselves (much to their embarrassment) with a super-liberal adolescent in their midst. Less common are the liberal parents who suddenly find themselves with an ultra-conservative. Adolescent clothing styles, as well, are often adopted in the service of establishing a separate identity. However, one will generally find the adolescent slavishly dependent on peers for information about the particular styles that are in vogue at the time, the style that is designed to be just the opposite of what is preferred by the adult generation.

In the mid-1970s a 14-year-old girl once came to a session quite upset. When I asked her what was wrong she replied, "I'm having a lot of trouble with my father lately. Up until a couple of months ago he was just like any other father. He wore standard suits and went to the office each day with his attaché case. However, in the last few months, he's become totally different. He suddenly started wearing these bell-bottom jeans that all the kids are wearing now. He wears these open collars in order to show the hair on his chest. He's also wearing these beads around his neck. They sure look stupid. He walks around the house with this little radio with an ear plug in his ear listening to rock music. Up until now all he wanted to hear was classical stuff. Now he's starting to grow this Afro haircut. I don't know what he's doing with an Afro haircut. We're Jewish and it looks stupid on him. When my friends come to the house he wants to sit around, Yoga-style, and have rap sessions with us. It's all very embarrassing and I'm ashamed to bring my friends to the house anymore. I know what's wrong with him. He's having an *identity crisis*. He's 49 years old and can't stand the fact that he's soon going to be 50. I think he's trying to recapture his youth."

One could argue that such a father might be perfect for an adolescent in that "being one of the guys" would be just what a youngster would want, i.e., a parent, who is "on the same wavelength" and can relate to the youngster at his or her own level. Such a position does not take into consideration the importance of the adolescent's having a separate identity. A youngster with a father like that may be driven back into conservative clothing in order to establish a separate identity. I am in full agreement with the girl's analysis of her father's behavior, namely, that he was truly having an "identity crisis" and was trying to recapture his youth because of his inability to accept gracefully the aging process.

Typically, adolescents are quite receptive to detailed information about how they appear to others. Girls, especially, will spend long hours discussing with one another the details of their appearence: their eyes, ears, noses, breasts, figures, etc. Generally, they are painfully dissatisfied with the most minute deviation from what they consider to be some idealized norm. And such differences may cause them significant grief. It is common for an adolescent to stand in front of the mirror for many hours in order to master the exact pose, complexion, coiffure, etc. that they consider necessary to acquire. This cannot be considered simple narcissism; rather, it relates more to the desire to get information about one's identity and to provide oneself with an identity that would be acceptable to one's peers. The same behavior in adult life would justifiably be labeled narcissism, the ubiquity of such behavior notwithstanding. During lovemaking, as well, the two youngsters may spend long hours describing in detail their opinions on the loved one's various body parts. They seem never to tire of what to the adult might appear to be an endless discussion on picayune topics.

The parents of a 14-year-old girl once described a problem they had with their daughter during a vacation trip to the Caribbean. The family was preparing to go out to the beach, but the girl adamantly refused to join them. She claimed there was a disfiguring pimple on her face, which she was quite certain would be apparent to all on the beach. No one in the family had noticed any particular disfiguration and when she was asked where it was, she pointed to a small, almost microscopic, pimple on her chin. Reassurances that this "pimple" could hardly be seen, even from six inches, were to no avail. She insisted that her appearance on the beach would subject her to terrible mortification. Finally, she was prevailed upon to join the family, but only did so after she had covered her head almost completely with a towel. As she walked on the beach, she parted the towel in front—just enough to see her way to the beach chair. She walked quickly through the crowd to lessen the likelihood that her "defect" would be noticed and thereby become the subject of conversation of all the vacationers. Then, when she finally reached her beach chair, she was sure to place the towel in such a position that it covered her "scar." This youngster was exhibiting typical adolescent fear of appearing atypical; yet, at the same time, she professed to be an independent thinker, unconcerned with the opinions of others—especially her parents and other adults.

Therapists do well to utilize this propensity of adolescents to dwell on the minutiae of their appearance. Often the adolescent who was unreceptive to therapeutic involvement may be willing to involve him or herself in long discussions on this subject. Providing this service can entrench the relationship between the youngster and the therapist and may pave the way to other discussions that might not have been possible previously.

In the process of forming a separate identity adolescents are likely to model themselves after others, especially older teenagers and certain adults (but not consciously the parents). Sometimes these models are very specific, such as a movie star or teacher. At other times these identifications are nonspecific, such as the "macho man" or the "sexy woman." The cigarette companies are well aware of this phenomenon and capitalize on it to a significant degree. They have been successful in getting adolescents to believe that smoking a cigarette makes one appear adult and to consider the cigarette to be the ticket of admission into adult society. They can rely, as well, on the adolescent's aforementioned delusion of invulnerability to deny the health consequences of cigarette addiction. Companies that peddle alcohol are also appreciative of this phenomenon. They too have convinced adolescents to equate drinking with adulthood and they also know that the adolescent is simple-minded enough to deny the possibility of addiction in him- or herself.

During this period, as well, there may be experimentation with a number of different identities. It is almost like the changing hobbies of the latency-aged child: one month the child is into one hobby and the next month into another. These transitional identifications are best viewed as steps toward finding one's own identity, after trying out that of others.

For many (if not most) adolescents group identity plays an important role in this transitional process. For many the group almost becomes a substitute family. It is as if the adolescent is saying: "I am no longer a member of my family; I am now a member of this group." Senior members of the group may be reacted to as if they were substitute parents, even though the adolescent may be the last one to admit this. Many adolescents are likely to gravitate toward healthy groups that have salutary goals. These include sports, social contribution, recreation, etc. Some adolescents gain identity as good students; others are good in sports; and others may select music, theater, or art to gain a sense of a special identity. Some may pride themselves on being the kind of a person who is quite social and has many friends. And many can claim competence in two or more of these areas, which produces a more enhanced sense of personal identity.

If a youngster reaches puberty and has not developed a strong sense of identity in one or more of these areas, then the individual is likely to utilize pathological mechanisms for gaining a sense of identity. One such method is to gravitate toward pathological groups, especially those involved with substance abuse and/or antisocial behavior. Often they are attracted to these fringe groups because they have not developed the skills and personality patterns that would enable them to join meaningfully with youngsters who are members of the healthier groups. However, for such adolescents the choice may be between a fringe group and no group at all. In such a situation, most choose the fringe group. The adolescent generally works on the theory that it is better to be a member of an antisocial gang than not to be recognized as a human being in any way at all. Better to be a drug addict than someone who isn't even noticed. Rather have the reputation of a "slut" than be someone whom no one ever talks about at all. Often, there is little or no conscious realization that they are making such a choice. Rather, they rationalize with other group members that they are superior to their traditional peers in that they know "where it's all at" while the others do not. Their scorn of normal youngsters merely serves to compensate for and deny the feelings of rejection and isolation that they harbor within.

E. Erikson (1968) considers the adolescent's identity confusion to be a central element in psychological development at that age level. He refers to this stage as "Identity vs. Role Confusion." He states that during this phase adolescents "... are now primarily concerned with what they appear to be in the eyes of others as compared to what they feel they are and with the question of how to connect the roles and skills cultivated earlier for the occupational prototypes of the day... and they are ever ready to install lasting idols and ideals as guardians of a final identity." Erickson also addresses himself to the traditional intolerance that adolescents have toward others who do not live up entirely to the specific codes of the group. He states that "... such intolerance is a defense against a sense of identity confusion. For adolescents not only help one another temporarily through much discomfort by forming cliques and by stereotyping themselves, their ideals, their enemies, they also perversely test each other's capacity to pledge fidelity. The readiness for such testing also explains the appeal which simple and cruel totalitarian doctrines have on the minds of the youth of such countries and classes as have lost or are losing their group identities...."

One of the important purposes of all this, obviously, is the ultimate acquisition of an adult identity. The process involves proceeding along a course that leads to a career or role in the adult society of their parents. In association with these identity and career role considerations adolescents may spend significant time wondering about the world, the universe, and where they fit in. They have grave concerns about the future course of their lives and wonder about exactly what roles they will play. As children, the future seemed like a million years away; now it is at their very doorsteps. Definite choices have to be made soon, *by them*; they can no longer be made *for them*. They have to try to envision themselves in various careers and social positions and take appropriate steps toward the attainment of these goals. All this can be very anxiety provoking; the decisions are awesome; they affect the youngster's whole life, and he or she may regret forever the decisions now being made. At its best and healthiest, this identity search can be a rewarding and creative period of self-discovery—these anxieties notwithstanding. Even when the confusion becomes so great that the term "identity crisis" seems appropriate, it might not be a deleterious experience.

There are those who can handle this crisis only by taking "time out" to "find themselves." They have to remove themselves from their main activities, to take stock, to think, to try new things, and to try to see things from another vantage point. Most accomplish this on evenings and weekends while remaining in school (at least until graduation from high school). Others, however, may have to leave school (whether it be high school or beyond) in order to do this. When this occurs it may be very difficult to ascertain whether the step is a healthy one. One way of determining this is to observe what the youngsters are doing while they are trying to "find themselves." If they are actively out in the world—involved, committed, trying to make it on their own—then it may very well be a salutary experience. However, if they withdraw into themselves and find solutions through philosophizing about them—without having reality experiences against which to test their ideas—they may be labeling the withdrawal an "identity crisis" in order to cover up its pathological significance to both themselves and those around them. If the pursuit of the "true self" requires parasitic dependence on parents and involves no meaningful efforts toward self-sufficiency, then it is probably sick. If "doing their own thing" means a life of hedonistic self-indulgence at the parents' expense (or at the expense of anyone else who is misguided enough to support this way of life), then there is more of a "crisis" going on than just that of "identity." In addition, the longer it takes for the youngster to accomplish this task, the greater the likelihood it is pathological.

Never before in the history of the world have so many youngsters been so indulged. Never before has Western society been more affluent. Never before has there been such a long gap between the time one is born and the time one is capable of self-sufficiency. Never before has there been so much psychologizing to parents about what their children are doing, how to "understand" them, and how to bring them up to be psychologically healthier. There is probably no better example of a sick fusion of all these phenomena than a disturbed adolescent's being supported (financially and psychologically) in a neurotic (and even psychotic) flight from reality with the rationalization (borrowed from psychology) that the youngster is only having an "identity crisis."

COMPENSATING FOR FEELINGS
OF INADEQUACY

Alfred Adler took issue with Freud regarding his emphasis on sexuality as the central element in the development of psychopathological processes. He considered feelings of inadequacy and the various methods people utilize to compensate for them to be more important factors. I am in agreement with Adler on this point. Although I believe that Adler took his theory too far—thereby repeating Freud's mistake of exaggerated emphasis on one point— he has nevertheless provided us with valuable insights into the factors that contribute to the development of psychopathology. In fact, there may not be a single psychopathological symptom that does not relate, at least in part, to the problem of feelings of inadequacy and the attempts to deal with it. H.L. Mencken said that "self-confidence is the delusion that others don't know how inadequate you feel about yourself." There is great wisdom in this statement. When a therapist says that a patient is suffering with low self-esteem, I believe that what is really being said is that the therapist believes that the patient's feelings of self-worth are lower than his or her own. (And this may or may not be the case.) More specifically, I believe that most symptoms contain, in part, an element that serves to enhance self-worth or to avoid situations that may lower it.

Examples are not difficult to find. In fact, one could randomly select any symptom and not have too much difficulty finding confirmation for this principle. Consider the common student symptom of cheating on tests. Youngsters who cheat on tests do not believe they have the capacity to get a good grade honestly (they may or may not have such ability) and fear the feelings of low self-worth that they will suffer if they do poorly. Children who bribe others for friendships do not believe they have the personality qualities that will predictably attract companions and have to delude themselves into believing that those who are "bought off" are genuinely friends. In this way they protect themselves from ego-debasing feelings of loneliness. Those who brag are generally individuals who feel inadequate; those who have the "real stuff" generally do not need to brag. Delusional grandiosity is the extreme example of this mechanism. Paranoid projections often include an element of attributing to others the self-denigratory feelings that one harbors within oneself. Considering others to be falsely criticizing is less ego-debasing than recognizing that the criticisms are self-derived and genuinely valid. Of course, there are many symptoms in which the self-esteem element plays only a small role; however, I do not know of a symptom in which it plays no role at all.

Adolescents have much to feel inadequate about. In our modern technological society they generally cannot acquire the skills necessary for them to function independently, yet they would like to believe that they can. The disparity between their actual situation and that which they fantasize can contribute to feelings of inadequacy. A common way with which adolescents deal with the feelings of inadequacy that derive from this obvious disparity is by scorning their elders and viewing them as "idiots." This mechanism of compensation is especially seen among the intellectual types who will use their newfound knowledge to lord their superiority over their elders. They may try to flaunt their knowledge to their parents and thereby show them up as imbeciles. They commonly do this with teachers and relish the opportunity to point out the inevitable errors that any teacher will occasionally make. They generally fail to appreciate how limited is their knowledge and that by virtue of their youth they cannot possibly have accumulated the depth and breadth of information that serves as a solid foundation for the expertise of their elders. I am not claiming that their elders are *necessarily* more knowledgeable and wiser, only that there is a greater likelihood that this will be the case.

Mention has already been made of the adolescents' delusions of invulnerability. I consider this an important adolescent manifestation which, in part, serves to compensate for feelings of low self-worth. Military leaders are well aware of the phenomenon. Adolescents make wonderful soldiers. They are old enough to have the physical stamina and strength to fight, yet simple-minded enough to believe that they are not likely to be killed. They can thereby be encouraged to walk into the cannon's mouth and believe that those around them may fall, but they, somehow, will be spared. Visit any military graveyard; look at the ages of those who are buried there; the average in 20th-century cemeteries is the late teens. In earlier centuries it was the early to mid-teens. In short, wars have been fought primarily by children. Adults are smart enough to stay far behind the lines and spare themselves.

Mechanisms to compensate for feelings of inadequacy pervade the adolescent's life. Adolescent girls will spend many hours a day attempting to improve their appearance. The multi-billion dollar cosmetic industry is not simply for adult women, but for adolescents as well. The industry knows that the best time to get women "hooked" on these products is during the adolescent years, when people are most vulnerable to believing the advertising and most likely to be obsessed with their appearance. These preoccupations are not simply for the purpose of attracting the opposite sex; they also serve to enhance feelings of self-worth. (The two go together.) Concern with the details of one's appearance also serves to insure admission to the peer group—admission often being dependent on scrupulous imitation of the prevailing style. Acceptance into the group also serves to compensate for feelings of low self-worth, because such acceptance essentially communicates the message that the youngster is indeed a worthwhile individual if he or she can gain admission into a particular "exclusive" club.

The half-naked muscle men that we so frequently see in public may be spending hours each day subjecting themselves to the most grueling exercises in order to enjoy the fantasy that others are impressed with their power, strength, enormous muscles, etc. Competition over who can consume the most alcohol can also serve to compensate for feelings of low self-worth. The youngster may actually hate beer, but will guzzle down as many cans as possible in order to impress his peers and thereby enhance his feelings of self-worth. Or, he may brag about how fast he has driven his car, or how flashy or expensive it is. Advertising companies, of course, are very happy to capitalize on this inanity of thinking, which, of course, extends into adult years for many (if not most) people. Of significance here is that the attribute selected for self-aggrandizement is *easily* acquired. What many adolescents fail to appreciate is that easily acquired attributes do not enhance self-worth as well as those that require long hours of dedicated labor. It is no particular feat to drink formidable amounts of beer; it is a feat to play the violin well, to be a champion chess player, to be an extremely competent basketball player, or to get very high grades on one's college entrance examinations. Youngsters who do not believe they can achieve healthy self-confidence in the latter areas are likely to resort to the former.

There is an anecdote that demonstrates this point quite well. Actually, it is best told by first asking the listener if he or she can figure out the moral or the lesson of this story:

> One day a mouse was walking through the jungle and suddenly heard the deep voice of another animal crying out, "Help, help, help! I'm sinking in the quicksand. Please help me. Help, help, help!!" The mouse quickly ran to the source of the pleas and there saw a huge elephant sinking rapidly into the quicksand.
>
> The mouse ran over to the edge of the quicksand and yelled to the elephant, "Don't worry. I'll save you. I have a Cadillac and I'll use it to pull you out of the quicksand." At this

point, the mouse went over to his Cadillac and backed it up so that the rear bumper was at the edge of the pool of quicksand. He then yelled to the elephant, "Put your trunk around my rear bumper and I'll pull you out. Hurry, Hurry!" And so the elephant wrapped his trunk around the rear bumper of the Cadillac and the mouse after great effort, with grinding of his Cadillac's motors, was finally successful in pulling the elephant out of the quicksand.

After wiping himself off the elephant said to the mouse, "I want you to know that I will never forget what you've done for me here today. As you know, we elephants have wonderful memories and never forget anything. I want you to know, then, that if you're ever in trouble, just send word through the jungle and I'll do everything in my power to help you, even at the risk of my own life."

About a year later, the same elephant was walking through the jungle and he suddenly heard a little squeaky voice yelling, "Help, help, help! I'm sinking in the quicksand. Please come and help me. Please! Please!"

The elephant ran toward the source of the noise and there he saw this little mouse sinking in the quicksand. He then said, "Why you're the very same mouse who saved my life last year. As I told you then, I'll never forget the good deed you did for me. And so now I'm going to return the favor and I'm going to save your life." The elephant then went over to the edge of the quicksand and, while lowering his huge penis into it, said to the mouse, "Hurry, grab on to the end of my penis and I'll pull you out of the quicksand." And so the mouse reached up, grabbed on to the end of the elephant's penis, and the elephant pulling his penis in, hand over hand, finally pulled the mouse out of the quicksand! The end.

The listener is then asked for the moral or lesson of this story. (For those who haven't figured it out): "If you've got a big penis, you don't need a Cadillac!"

Sexual activities, as well, may serve to compensate for feelings of inadequacy. Adolescents are typically concerned with whether or not they are sexually attractive to members of the opposite sex. The best way to prove such attractiveness, of course, is to actually have sexual experiences. Normally, an adolescent boy will not feel that he is "a man" until he has had sexual relations. I do not consider this belief necessarily to be pathological, as long as it is put in proper perspective and the boy does not become obsessed with losing his virginity or walk around feeling worthless if he has not yet achieved the exalted status of nonvirgin. It is even within the normal range to relate the details of his sexual experiences to his peers, even with some exaggeration. Although there is some insensitivity here to the "reputation" of the girl involved, I consider such sharing and even boasting to be so common that I cannot necessarily label it pathological. It is really asking too much of a teenage boy to tell absolutely no one about his first sexual experience.

In recent years, however, there has been less stigma for the girls who have been used more for the purposes of the boys' self-aggrandizement than for sexual gratification. The boy who is obsessively preoccupied with the number of his "conquests" and who is frequently bragging about them is likely to have psychiatric difficulties, especially in the realm of low self-esteem. The more secure boy does not generally need to brag so extensively. And girls who feel inadequate may use sexual receptivity to attract boys and thereby prove to themselves that they are worthwhile. An element in girls' sexual promiscuity is the need to compensate for feelings of low self-worth. They are even willing to suffer the reputation of being a "slut" or a "whore" for the benefits they believe they are deriving in the realm of enhancing their self-worth.

E. Becker (1973, 1975) has proposed that a central element in the development of psychopathological symptoms is the denial of the painful feelings associated with our realization that someday we will die. One of the ways in which human beings differ significantly from lower animals is our ability to appreciate that we are mortal. It may be the greatest price we pay for our superior intelligence. Many psychological phenomena, both normal and abnormal, include the element of denial of our fallibility and mortality. We involve ourselves in activities in which we flirt with death in order to prove to ourselves that we, in contrast to other humans, need not be grasped by death's claws. We place ourselves in extremely precarious positions and then pride ourselves on our ability to come out unscathed. Sky-divers, tightrope walkers, mountain climbers, speed racers, and bullfighters are just a few examples of people with a strong need to prove to themselves that they, unlike others, are invulnerable to death. The general populace admires those who demonstrate such fearlessness and will make them heroes. However, the admirers need to maintain the delusion that their heroes are invulnerable. If events destroy the delusion, then the hero no longer serves his or her purpose and is dispensed with. Once Achilles is wounded in his heel, he is no longer revered. But it is a two-way arrangement. Achilles needs to feel invulnerable to compensate for the feelings of vulnerability he feels over his appreciation of his mortality. And his worshipers need to maintain the image that Achilles is invulnerable in order to give them hope that they are so as well.

This phenomenon is related to the aforementioned adolescent's delusion of invulnerability. The adolescent smokes and believes that he is immune to lung cancer and the other diseases caused by smoking. He drives at high speeds, while inebriated, and believes that he will neither be injured nor killed. He even plays "chicken" on the open road. For those not familiar with this "game," two cars—driving head on in the same lane—approach each other at high speeds. The first one who veers off the collision path is viewed as "chicken" and the "loser" of the game. It is not just simple-mindedness that is required for willingness to involve oneself in this idiocy. Also involved is the need to compensate for feelings of inadequacy by attempting to prove that one is indeed courageous. Another element, however, is its value in dealing with death fears. Once the youngsters have survived, they can flaunt their invulnerability to death.

I introduce my next point anecdotally. A number of years ago I visited my son Andrew's junior high school in association with a parent-teacher's meeting. The parents made the rounds of the various classrooms that their children were attending and met with their teachers. I was quite pleased with Andy's teachers, but the one that impressed me most was the shop teacher. This was basically the message he gave to the group of parents:

> I want to tell you, first, that I don't know very much about theories of teaching. In fact, to be absolutely honest, when I go to teachers' conferences I really don't understand what they're talking about when they speak about educational psychology

and philosophy. But I can tell you this: when a kid makes something here in the shop—something that he can be proud of—it really makes him feel good. (These were the days when there were no *hers* in shop class.) For example, if a kid makes a tree sign with the family name on it, and nails it up on a tree outside his house, he really feels good every time he walks into that house and sees *his* sign there. It really makes him proud. If a kid makes a little lamp—I have one here—it looks like a water pump and everytime you pull down the handle, a chain that is attached to it turns on the light, he really feels good about himself when he sees that lamp sitting there in the house and when he sees people using it, it really makes him feel good about himself....

And let's say I have a kid who is shy and timid. What I do is make that kid a *monitor* for the whole row. It's his job to be sure that no boy leaves his row without cleaning up completely. His job is to inspect that row before anyone can leave, and he inspects every kid's work bench to be sure that it's completely spic and span before that boy has permission to leave the room. And the monitor works under my authority. When I give a shy kid this kind of a job it really makes him stand taller. It makes him feel better about himself....

I want you to know that I run a tight ship here. In order to pass my course you've got to produce. Also, I've got to run a tight ship here because we have a lot of equipment that could be dangerous. We have electrical saws and drills here that could literally kill someone. So safety is *number one* here; I can't be lax in this room. The safety monitors, too, know that I mean business and there will be absolutely *no* horsing around in this shop. There is absolutely no running here. If a kid runs I boot him out for the day. And there's no wise-guy back talk. These kids have got to know that I'm boss around here and that I won't put up with any wise-ass characters....

Although some of this shop teacher's colleagues had Ph.D.s, I believe that he knew more about educational philosophy than most of them. This man was one of the most admired teachers in the school. He was the one, more than others, whom graduates would return to visit. This man knew about self-esteem and healthy ways to help youngters deal with the inevitable feelings of low self-worth with which adolescents (like all people) suffer. He knew that competence and hard work are very valuable antidotes to feelings of low self-worth and provide healthy self-esteem. He knew that vigorous self-discipline—when humane and reasonable—is also ego-enhancing. This man was "building character"—something we don't hear much about these days. I am convinced that this man probably did more good for his junior-high-school students than most of the other teachers in that school. Years later, most of the graduates, I am convinced, remembered little of what they had learned in their academic subjects; but I believe that the living experiences that this man provided his students probably contributed to lifelong personality changes of far greater educational value.

In recent years competition has been viewed by many educators and psychologists as a detrimental influence in personality development. Particular emphasis is given to the fact that those who lose in a competitive activity will suffer with low feelings of self-worth. I believe that this is a misguided view. I believe that proper discrimination has to be made between healthy and unhealthy competition. Success in competition can enhance self-esteem. We should not deprive the more successful ones from the ego-enhancement that comes from that success, even though those who lose may experience lowered feelings of self-worth. Furthermore, healthy individuals do not suffer psychologically traumatic feelings of low self-worth when they lose; nor do healthy individuals turn into egomaniacs when they win. In healthy competition there is respect for one's competitor and the appreciation that it's "not the end of the world" if one loses.

In healthy competition one puts the competition into proper perspective and recognizes that it is of secondary importance to the primary *activity* (sports, art, writing, debate, etc.) into which the competitive element has been introduced. In unhealthy competition the primary aim is to degrade, humiliate, and even slaughter one's opponent. Denigrating and even destroying the opponent is "the name of the game." Certainly, we could very well dispense with unhealthy competition; but we should preserve healthy competition and make every attempt to derive what benefits we can from it. If not for healthy competition we might still be living in caves; if not for unhealthy competition many people would not have suffered severe physical and psychological trauma, and even premature death.

Many schools in recent years have tried to remove competition entirely. There are "noncompetitive camps." I believe such attempts are naive and predictably will fail. When students in these situations still demonstrate competitive strivings, in spite of the allegedly noncompetitive atmosphere, the administrators claim that these children have been so imbued by society to be competitive that their own attempts to provide a healthier atmosphere have proven futile. I disagree. I believe that competitive strivings are locked into the genetic structure of the human animal. All other forms of life are in active competition for survival. Darwin said it well: "Survival of the fittest" is the basic law of evolution. Although we humans need not utilize our competitive strivings in the service of murdering one another, we certainly have residua of them which can be put into healthy channels.

One patient of mine attended a Quaker school which prided itself on being noncompetitive. Even the coaches were warned that the youngsters should be encouraged to play games for the fun of it and not to concern themselves with winning or losing. Unfortunately, this created problems when the Quaker school was playing against other schools in various sports. In these schools just the opposite was occurring, namely, the youngsters were being imbued with a "fighting spirit" and were being encouraged by their coaches to "get in there and win." An adolescent patient of mine was on the school's basketball team and described this pep talk given by the coach:

> Now listen you guys. What I'm telling you now is just between us. I don't want you to breath a word of this to the people upstairs in the classrooms. When you get out there in the field, I want you to wipe up the floor with those guys. I want you to burn their asses off. I want you to beat them into the ground.

Although one might take issue with this coach's use of language, and although one might say that he is going a little too far, I believe that his is basically the healthier approach to competitive sports. It is not that only fiercely competitive sports can be healthy. I certainly believe that one can engage in sports "just for the fun of it," without concerning oneself with who wins or loses. I also believe, however, that fiercely competitive sports too can be psychologically healthy – if put in proper perspective. Encouraging these boys to play their best in their basketball games is not encouraging them to be fiercely competitive in any other aspect of their lives, nor does it necessarily teach them to be insensitive to all human beings whom they may encounter.

An excellent example of many of the principles presented in this section on self-esteem is to be found in D. Holmes' book on adolescent psychotherapy (1964). Dr. Holmes has graciously given me permission to quote the following material from his book.

> At the outset I had very few doubts about how the recreational therapy program should work. Miss B, who was then in charge of girls' "RT," proposed that they all be required to attend a weekly swimming class, and I confidently advised her that this would be unwise. "All people," I explained, "have an inherent phylogenetic dread of water," and we could logically expect this to be pathologically exaggerated in mentally ill persons. (The reader will understand that the recollection of this incident worked upon me a distinctly emetic effect.) Swimming was declared an optional activity and failed after several weeks of trial because none of the girls attended.
>
> A similar plan for instructing the boys in the fundamentals of various physical skills was proposed by Mr. K, director of "RT" for the boys. I pointed out to him the need for emphasizing the recreational aspects of this activity, and further urged that competition and score-keeping be omitted in order not to intensify the low estimation in which our patients already held themselves.
>
> The "RT" staff strove conscientiously to carry out the program as it had been precisely and asininely defined, but in spite of their best efforts the patients refused to cooperate. They were scornful, rebellious, and utterly perverse in their refusal to have fun while discharging their pent up aggressive energy. It was all very disappointing, and once again I reminded myself that one could hardly expect more from sick, delinquent youngsters. They were told they needed the exer-

cise, and we tried to convince them of the therapeutic value of having a good time. Although they were rather casually required to attend the regularly scheduled daytime "RT" sessions, individual patients who were unusually "threatened" by fear of physical injury or competition were frequently excused.

A few months after the opening of the service, I began to hear disturbing reports from several of the boys about how things were being changed in "RT." Jerry, a 15-year-old delinquent boy, explained in persuasive detail his reasons for refusing to attend the activity any longer. He explained that it wasn't fun any more. For the past three weeks, five days per week, they had done nothing but figure eight basketball drill, shooting practice, and running laps. Mr. K, Jerry observed, was a "mean bastard" who gave them neither praise nor respite. He was routinely requiring each boy to run an additional lap for each deliberate "mistake" made during drill and was holding them overtime, making them late for dinner whenever the entire group lagged in completing the day's exercises.

Calisthenics, deep knee bends, and push-ups were required for warming up at the beginning of each hour. And to make matters even worse, Mr. K had started coming up on the ward before each period for the purpose of applying firm, personal, though unobtrusive pressure on each of the boys to attend.

It was a grim picture indeed, and in light of Jerry's proved capacity for revising reality to suit his convenience, there was little reason to believe that it could possibly be true. I spoke with Mr. K about it, and he modestly confirmed every detail of Jerry's account. It seemed to me that no great harm had been done, so I advised him to "ease up on the patterning approach and get back to recreation."

But, as it developed, there are some things too great for the human soul to endure—cruelty to children being one of them. Mr. K stood firm and courageously defended his approach without benefit of theoretical rationale. He simply insisted that "it's better for them."

We called in the head nurse, and she confirmed my suspicions that for the past several weeks the number of complaints from the boys about the "RT" sessions had increased markedly. However, she also noted that attempts to refuse the activity had fallen almost to zero. I decided to see for myself, and it was immediately apparent that Jerry had understated his complaints. After they had finished their grueling workout, I finally saw what I had long since despaired of ever seeing. The boys left the gymnasium perspiring, panting, and bone-weary. They complained lavishly and in chorus. They were bright-eyed, square-shouldered, and flushed with pride in the aftermath of battle. The evidence was incontestable.

From this moment on, "cruel regimentation" became the official guiding policy, and "recreation," in this area at least, gave way to physical education.

Explaining the psychological rationale for this paradoxical reaction was a simple matter, after the fact. Mr. K was advised to proceed according to his own judgment, with the added assurance we would be happy to provide the theoretical explanations for his successes after he had accomplished them.

Since then problems centering around the "RT" program have been isolated and infrequent occurrences. The physical education program, like the school, functions without a respectable rationale which can dignify it as therapy. The boys follow a year-round schedule of coaching in tackle football with full equipment, basketball, boxing, baseball, and track. Each of these endeavors requires *many consecutive weeks of monotonous drill, all without a prospect of immediate reward.* When they have acquired sufficient skill and strength to qualify for competition the boys are forthwith subjected to the "threat" of winning or losing. The approach has provided them with an *earned and well-deserved* sense of masculine accomplishment.

The physical education program for the girls also emphasized the teaching of physical skills, although it is not nearly as demanding as for the boys. Basketball, swimming, volleyball, modern dance, and choral music are stressed. Periodic courses in some of the fundamental do's and don't's of hairstyling, cosmetics, clothing, bearing, and posture are also included.

Despite their symphonic complaints the patients are as a group more dedicated to these activities than are the staff. They understand and readily accept the idea that intercurrent psychological symptoms are insufficient cause for their failing to fulfill this obligation to themselves.

SEXUAL DEVELOPMENT

Gender Differences in Mating Patterns

Adolescents' reactions to their sexual development are extremely important to understand if one is is to place in proper perspective the psychopathological reactions that may emerge from this developmental phenomenon and its attendant conflicts. The fact that I have placed it last in this section in no way means that it is the least important. The central conflict for many adolescents is that of gratifying or not gratifying their sexual urges. For the girl, the conflict is generally one between how much she should allow boys to gratify themselves with her and how much restraint she must show. If she avoids or rejects opportunities for sexual gratification she will suffer frustration; indulging herself such gratifications often results in fears that she will be viewed as promiscuous and thereby compromise her reputation. Furthermore, she may feel strongly that she wants the sexual experience to be associated with tenderness and emotional involvement and may find that boys are much less concerned with these aspects of the sexual experience – their professions of commitment to these values notwithstanding. For boys, especially after the mid-teens, the conflict is less internal than external. They generally want as much sex as they can get, and most often feel little guilt over their sexual experiences. The confict, more often, is between them and the girls who resist them, rather than between one intrapsychic compartment and another.

I do not believe that the aforementioned differences between boys and girls are entirely socially induced. Rather, I believe that genetic programming plays a role in these differences. I recognize that this is an unpopular thing to say at a time when male/female egalitarianism is very much in vogue. However, I believe that I have good arguments to support my position here. No one can deny that up until the 20th century men were primarily the hunters and fighters (protectors and warriors). Women, in contrast, were primarily the child rearers. I am making no statement regarding whether this was good or bad or right or wrong, only that it was the reality of the world up until the 20th century for the vast majority of societies on earth. Of course, there were and still are occasional societies in which this principle did not hold, but these exceptions do not in any way detract from the validity of my generalization. (There is always an island in the South Pacific that will demonstrate any point—in support or in refutation.)

It is reasonable to state that those men who were genetically strong in the hunting/fighting functions were more likely to survive than those who were not. Accordingly, those who were weaker in these functions were less likely to have food for survival or to protect themselves from their enemies. Consequently, their genes were not as likely to be passed down to subsequent generations. Also, those who were weak in these areas were less likely to attract women, in that women would tend to consider as desirable mates men who exhibited high capacity for food gathering for themselves and their children and high capability for protecting the potential family from enemies. This was another reason why genes of men who were weaker in these areas were less likely to survive in the genetic pool. Similarly, women who were stronger in the child-rearing realm were more likely to be viewed by men as desirable mates and their genes, as well, were more likely to be passed down to their progeny. And the greater aggressiveness of the male was not, I believe, simply confined to hunting and warring; it was also utilized in the service of mating. Specifically, more aggressive men were more likely to be successful in acquiring mates. And so we have another factor favoring the selective survival of more aggressive men.

Youngsters today of both sexes carry within them these genetic programs. Although we human beings are less beholden to our instinctual drives than are lower animals, we are still affected by them. A bird, for example, during the mating season, may have no choice other than to go through the mating ritual of its species. We humans have procreative urges, but we are not compelled to mate in any particular season nor are we compelled to follow rigid mating patterns of behavior. However, this does not preclude our being programmed for such mating patterns with the resultant pressure for their expression. In short, then, I believe that adolescent boys are more likely to be assertive and aggressive during this phase and adolescent girls more likely to be passive – present-day social pressures for egalitarianism notwithstanding.

There is another factor operative in what I believe to be gender differences in mating patterns during adolescence. This relates more directly to reproductive capacity. It is a principle of Darwin's theory of natural selection and survival of the fittest that each species generally produces far more offspring than can possibly survive. Those particular forms that are most adaptable to the environment in which they have been born are more likely to survive and perpetuate the species. Those that are less adaptable to the particular environment will generally die off. This is the central element in the Darwinian theory. If one examines this further, one finds that there are two factors operative here: *quantity* and *quality*. With regard to *quantity*, the number of offspring produced is far greater than can possibly survive in a particular environment.

With regard to *quality*, the quality or type of offspring that is most adaptable to the specific environment is more likely to survive. Accordingly, one must consider both quantity control and quality control. Furthermore, with regard to quantity, the general thrust is for an organism to produce as many offspring as possible, i.e., the greatest quantity possible – most often far more than will survive. With regard to quality, the general thrust is to select, narrow down, and restrict survival to those forms that will best adapt to and survive in a particular environment. The two processes of control, then, are antagonistic. The quantity control factors work toward the survival of the greatest number of offspring. The quality control factors operate to reduce and/or limit the number of offspring that will survive. Those forms that ultimately survive represent a balance of these two antagonistic forces.

In many forms of life one of the sexes is specifically designated to provide quantity and the other quality. Often, it is not difficult to determine which sex is primarily involved in which function. This is certainly the case for the human being. Men are clearly the ones involved in producing the greatest quantity of offspring and women are the quality controllers. If one were to simply view human beings as baby factories, whose main purpose is to perpetuate the species (a not absurd view), and if one were to ask the question which sex is more likely to produce a high quantity of offspring, it is clearly the male. If a man were to devote his whole life to the procreative process, it is reasonable that he could father one to two babies a day providing, of course, he was provided with women who were in the fertile stages of their menstrual cycles. Accordingly, the male is reasonably capable of fathering 500 babies a year. We know that we could start using males for this purpose at about the age of 13 or 14, but we do not know the upper age at which such utilization would no longer be possible. There are men in their 90s who have viable sperm. But let us, more practically, end the male's fecund period at 75, because most men do not live beyond that age and older men are less likely to father 500 babies a year. Accordingly, it is reasonable to say that the average male has a fecund period of 60 years. Fathering 500 babies a year for 60 years would enable a man to father 30,000 babies. (I am not addressing myself here to practicality; only to the issue of maximum possible reproductive capacity if one were to make use of men and women for this purpose.) In contrast, if a woman were to devote her fecund life to being a baby factory, she could reasonably reproduce one a year from age 13 to about 54 (the oldest "proven" age at which a woman has been demonstrated to give birth). This will give her approximately 40 babies. Accordingly, it is reasonable to conclude that the male is very much the one capable of producing the greatest quantity of offspring.

What I have said thus far relates purely to biological capacity. The next question relates to the actual behavior of each of the sexes regarding the procreative process. The *potential* for being a repro-ductive factory is there, but in practice individuals generally have other things to do with their lives besides fornicating and propagat-ing. And probably the most important of these other functions is child rearing. If no concern is given to the protection of the young then the young will not survive and there would be no point to devoting one's life solely to manufacturing babies. This brings us to quality control, the second step necessary for species survival. It is here that women have played the more formidable role. In order to carry out this function, it behooved women to be more circumspect with regard to mate selection. Those who were so were more likely to be chosen as mates and more likely to pass their stronger child-rearing genes down to their offspring. Men, I believe, have been programmed to be promiscuous, i.e., to impregnate as many women as possible. From the roving bands of men in perpetual heat, a woman must select the man who is most likely to remain around after impregnation and serve the role of food gatherer and protector. In order to serve ideally in this capacity women do best to be less impulsive with regard to gratifying indiscriminately their sexual urges – in order that they assess more objectively a potential father of their children. Women who were slower in sexual arousal were more likely to be judicious in mate selection and, therefore, more likely to survive. They were more likely to select men who would provide food, clothing, shelter, and protection. Accordingly, I believe that the *average* (I did not say all) present-day woman is slower in sexual arousal than the average man. Once aroused, however, a woman is more likely to attempt to maintain an ongoing relationship with her mate.

The old saying is applicable here: "Men are looking for girls, and girls are looking for husbands." Men are on the prowl. They are not only out hunting for prey to kill and eat, but hunting for female prey to serve as sexual companions. From the roving bands of men in heat the woman must reject the large majority or else she will find herself impregnated by a man who has already gone on to the next cave or condo. She is much more concerned with relationships. I believe that this is one of the factors involved in women having greater orgastic capacity than men. Although the woman is more likely to need caressing and tender overtures to be aroused, once aroused she is more likely to remain aroused longer. The male reaches his orgasm and immediately goes into a refractory period ("zonks out," falls asleep). The vast majority of women have the potential for multiple orgasms. This serves, I believe, the purpose of enhancing procreative capacity. Her multiple orgastic capacity enables her to "hang in there longer" and insure that the male who is slow to ejaculation is likely to be sustained in his interest and involvement.

Last, I believe that what I have said here is one explanation for the fact that men are generally more likely to be sexually excited by visual stimuli, whereas women are more likely to respond to tactile stimuli. The roving bands of men spot their prey at a distance and can get excited merely at the sight of a woman. Women, however, need caressing, tenderness, and reassurance that the man will remain around for supplying food and protection for herself and her children. This is one of the reasons why men are more likely to be sexually aroused by visual pornographic material than women.

In today's world, boys' greater self-assertion in the "dating game" is generally not as blunt and crass as described above. More subtle techniques are utilized, techniques to impress the girl. One of the factors that enables "jocks" to endure the grueling periods of practice in their sports is the fantasy that they will win the affection of some pretty young girl in the stands. Academically/intellectually oriented youngsters are similarly trying to impress, but they are often interested in winning girls who are more "turned on" by their intellectual feats. And those boys who devote themselves to the arts have, somewhere not so far in the back of their minds, the fantasy that some girl will be turned on by *their* particular talents or skills.

Boys in our society are programmed to be the entertainers. They are encouraged to "show the girl a good time." And the girls are programmed to be entertained. The boys tell the jokes and the girls laugh at them. This is one of the reasons, I believe, why men have much greater memories for jokes than women. When men get together they are much more likely than women to spend their time swapping jokes, especially the ones that are making the rounds at that particular time. These joke-telling encounters serve many purposes. They provide men with the opportunity to compete with their peers for the reputation of having the greatest collection and/or telling them best. This is a male competitive endeavor. In addition, in the course of such competition, they enhance their repertoires of jokes for use in attracting women. The fact that women generally have less facility to recall jokes has nothing to do with any brain inferiority on their part. Men need to remember them if they are to be effective entertainers of women; women, as the traditional "entertainees," are less motivated to remember them. However, women do well to be receptive to laughing at them. If they are unreceptive to serving in this function, they may find themselves at a disadvantage when competing with other women for the attraction of men. This phenomenon, I believe, explains why there are so many more professional comedians who are male than female. The reader should know that I am not placing any value judgments in my comments regarding these different gender roles; I am only describing what I consider to be the reality of the world today.

This theory also serves as an explanation for the fact that most studies of marital infidelity conclude that married men are more likely to be sexually unfaithful than their wives. Although the gap has narrowed somewhat in recent years, with women's new liberation, men are still more likely to involve themselves with extramarital lovers than are their wives. Therapists who work with men toward the goal of reducing significantly their urges for sexual variety have a formidable task ahead of them because they are working against their patients' genetic programming. The more reasonable goal for most men, I believe, is to bring them to the point where their relationships with their wives are so good that the urge for infidelity will be reduced to the point of toleration. Such suppression can also be enhanced by guilt (both anticipatory and "after the fact"), by the desire to avoid the hassles and ego-debasement of surreptitiousness, and the belief that there is more to lose than gain if the affair becomes known to the wife, i.e., irreparable compromise, if not destruction, of the marital relationship.

In conclusion, then, I believe that females are likely to be more passive and desirous of exclusivity in their sexual/romantic involvement with men and that these differences are not simply culturally induced. As mentioned, I recognize that this is an unpopular thing to say in this age of sexual egalitarianism, but I believe that the aforementioned arguments provide compelling support for my position. Again, this is not to say that these patterns cannot be modified somewhat by environmental influences. I am only saying that therapists who counsel youngsters must be aware of these genetic factors and not deny their reality or make attempts to impose an unnatural egalitarianism on their patients, whether adolescent or adult.

Dealing with Sexual Urges

The Therapist's Values   It is impossible to discuss adolescents' sexual urges without taking into consideration the therapist's values. For example, if the therapist believes that all sexual activity of any kind, heterosexual, auto-erotic, or homosexual is bad and sinful then that therapist is going to react very differently from the one who views such behavior as part of normal adolescent development. As I will discuss in detail in Vol. II (1999a), I believe that all therapeutic interchange involves some attempt on the therapist's part to impose his or her own values on the patient. It is hoped that the values so imposed will be in the patient's best interests. Accordingly, I have no hesitation stating that the views on adolescent sexuality I presented here are reflective of my own values. I do not claim any right or wrong answers on this subject, only that these opinions on sexual behavior reflect my own values.

Take, for example, the issue of pre-marital sex. Perhaps it is the case that all pre-marital sex is indeed a sin and that those who engage in it will be punished by God, in this life and/or after death. Perhaps it is not a sin and there are no repercussions from higher powers for engaging in this activity. Therapists like myself, then, who sanction such behavior (in accordance with the limits described below) may very well be punished for having contributed to the corruption of youth. Accordingly, the therapist's work is "risky business" and therapists should appreciate this before entering the field.

Parents are certainly entitled to the therapist's views on these subjects. Of course, when presenting such opinions, the therapist does well to explore with the parents other aspects of the issue, especially their thoughts and feelings that might reflect psychopathology. The parents may not be receptive to such exploration, but they are still entitled to the therapist's position. If they are uncomfortable with the answers they receive, then the therapist does well to discuss the possibility of their seeing another therapist – someone who might have different values on these particular sexual issues. Under these circumstances I would generally not refer a specific person, but leave it to the parents to find someone whose values are the same as theirs. To make a specific referral only complicates matters. The new person may also not have values consistent with what the parents want and they may become critical and further irritated with both the original therapist as well as the one to whom they were referred. In addition, it is generally a bad policy to refer to a colleague whose therapeutic orientation is one for which the referrer does not have conviction.

For example, as will be discussed in Vol. III (1999b), I believe that behavior modification programs are contraindicated for many (but not all) children with antisocial, acting-out behavior. If I see a youngster in consultation for whom I consider a behavior modification program to be contraindicated, and the parents request a behavior modification program rather than the psychotherapeutically oriented program that I am recommending, I will not accede to their request that I refer them to someone who would provide behavior modification. The therapist who makes such a referral is similar to the surgeon who recommends appendectomy and, when the patient asks to have it treated with an ice bag and penicillin, refers them to a person who would be willing to provide such treatment. Although one could argue that different values on the subject of sex are not the same as different therapeutic persuasions, I am not in agreement. I would not refer to a therapist who believes that pre-marital sex is a sin, because I believe that such a therapist is going to induce inordinate guilt in the youngster—guilt that is psychopathological. Accordingly, I advise parents who have different values from mine to find for themselves another therapist, a therapist who will tell them what they want to hear.

Masturbation   Adolescents do well to masturbate. It is one of the best ways to deal with sexual urges in a situation in which heterosexual activities cannot be readily satisfied. They should be helped to appreciate that there is absolutely no excuse why anyone in the world should walk around "horny." I am not recommending masturbation as being preferable to heterosexual experiences throughout life, only that in the early adolescent period it may be a superior form of sexual activity. In years past parents tended to induce great guilt in their children over masturbatory behavior; this is far less true today, but we are still not free from it. I believe that such guilt, in part, is directly related to parents' reacting negatively and even punitively to the occasional masturbatory activity of small children. I use the term *masturbatory activity* here to refer to the occasional touching of the genitalia that all children engage in. I am not referring to masturbation to orgasm, which generally is less frequently seen in pre-pubertal children (but can be present when there has been artificial stimulation, physical or psychological).

Some parents induce masturbatory guilt by carrying down to yet another generation what they have been taught about the practice. Others may be threatened by the child's masturbation because it may imply to them that the child is turning to him- or herself for gratification because the parent is inadequate in the capacity to provide it. Some parents are threatened by the activity because it presages (to them) heavier sex, with all its implications of promiscuity, pregnancy, and sexually transmitted diseases. They believe that squelching sexual expression early is likely to forestall and even prevent these dangers. Whatever its psychodynamics, the therapist does well to make every attempt to reduce such guilt if present. However, the alleviation of such guilt may not be necessary for the vast majority of adolescents today. I recall recently seeing in consultation a girl of 14 who sought my opinion because she was not yet masturbating and feared that she might be different from her friends who were doing so. She wondered whether she had a psychological problem. I certainly would not have been consulted for this purpose 15 to 20 years ago.

When discussing masturbation with adolescents I generally do not try to convey the notion that this practice is simply confined to people during this period. Rather, I inform them that it is a widespread practice at all ages and that it would generally be considered normal even when there is heterosexual opportunity. I inform them that the general opinion among mental health practitioners today is that it becomes pathological when a person routinely engages in it in preference to heterosexual activities or involves oneself in it to an obsessive degree. I tell them, as well, that when other opportunities for sexual gratification are not available, then it is perfectly healthy for masturbation to be the only outlet at that time. If the person routinely prefers the masturbatory outlet over seeking heterosexual experiences then there may be a problem. In the context of such a discussion I may tell the youngster the maxim: "If God didn't want people to masturbate, he wouldn't have made people's arms long enough to reach down there." Or I might quote the limerick:

> There once was a woman named Croft
> Who played with herself in a loft.
> Having reasoned that candles
> Rarely cause scandals,
> Besides which they never go soft.

For a girl who may have difficulty reaching orgasm I may recommend a vibrator or suggest that the youngster try other methods

that may prove successful, such as a high-speed shower head. I try
to assuage any guilt a youngster might have about being turned on
by sexually explicit magazines. In fact, I have often said that an
excellent confirmation present for a 13-year-old boy would be a
five-year subscription to one of these magazines. For the 13-year-old
girl, an analogous present would be a five-year subscription to a
romantic love magazine and a vibrator.

In the last few years there have been additional reasons for my
encouraging masturbation, specifically the risk of herpes and more
recently AIDS. Any therapist who does not warn adolescent patients about the risk of these diseases is negligent. Because of the
adolescent's capacity for delusions of invulnerability (the reader
hasn't heard the last of this one), they are likely to consider
themselves immune to these disorders. Therapists do well to instill
a reasonable (not paralytic) amount of fear in adolescents when
discussing these and other sexually transmitted diseases in order to
counterbalance some of this delusion. Last, I wish to impress upon
the reader that I do not routinely encourage the initiation of
masturbation when working with adolescents. Rather, I encourage
it among youngsters who have strong sexual urges, but do not have
a reasonable outlet for them, and may find themselves getting into
various kinds of difficulties because they do not give the masturbation option proper respect. Such difficulties would include promiscuity, frequenting prostitutes, seeking inappropriate partners, and
suffering unnecessary sexual frustration.

Sexual Relationships　I believe it is normal and healthy for
youngsters to begin having mild heterosexual experiences ("pet-
ting" and caressing) in the early to mid-adolescent period and to
begin having sexual relations in mid- to late adolescence. Whether
or not I think this is healthy is almost irrelevant, in that the vast
majority of youngsters have had sexual relations by the late adolescent period anyway—regardless of what I or anyone else thinks
about it. The therapist does well, however, to help the youngster
differentiate sharply between sexual activity in which the sole
purpose is some release and sexual activity in the context of a
relationship. The youngster should be helped to appreciate that the
latter is generally the more gratifying and rewarding experience.
Some experience with the former, however, may still be useful in

that one still learns better about this contrast from actual experience than from some statement made by the therapist.

As mentioned, it is crucial that the therapist impress upon youngsters the risks of sexually transmitted diseases, especially herpes and AIDS. The therapist should attempt to differentiate between sexual behavior that is normal and that which is abnormal. Abnormal sexual behavior generally involves compulsivity. In boys it can often serve to compensate for feelings of inadequacy. For such youngsters the therapist has to attempt to differentiate the normal boy's need to flaunt sexual "conquests" from the pathological degree of such boasting. This may be quite difficult because the normal boy is likely to brag significantly anyway. For girls, one of the most common reasons for promiscuity is feelings of low self-worth and the belief that the only way she can get a boy's attention is to provide sex. One must deal here with the underlying factors that have contributed to the feelings of low self-worth.

When discussing the sexual activities of adolescents, the subject of confidentiality often comes up. In Vol. II (1999a), I will discuss in detail my views on confidentiality in treatment. As will be elaborated there, I do not consider sexual intercourse to be a "reportable" event to the parents of the adolescent in therapy. I will, however, *consider* reporting an adolescent's sexual behavior to parents if there are definite risks associated with it. Let us take, for example, the situation in which a girl is clearly trying to get pregnant. If, after discussion of the problem in individual and group therapy, she is still trying to do so, I believe that some communication with the parents is warranted. Or if promiscuity is exposing the youngster to sexually transmitted diseases, I would consider this also to be a reportable issue. It is not that the parents can do much about such a girl's sexual activities, but they may be able to take some precautions that may lessen the likelihood of the youngster's being exposed to these dangers. For example, they may be more circumspect with regard to leaving the girl at home alone when they go off at night and on weekends. And they might check more on where their daughter "actually" is when visiting the homes of friends.

A number of years ago I had an experience during one of my presentations that elucidates an important point with regard to confidentiality and a youngster's sexual activities. I was speaking to a group of pastoral counselors in Tennessee. They were mainly ministers, deeply committed to their religious beliefs. Following a presentation of mine on the treatment of adolescents I invited questions from the floor. One minister raised his hand and the following interchange took place:

Minister: I'm having a problem in the treatment of a 16-year-old girl and I want your opinion on it.

Gardner: Yes, what's the problem?

Minister (somewhat dramatically): *She's having sexual intercourse!*

Gardner: Yes. (This was said with intonation implying that I was waiting for more information.)

Minister: That's it. She's *having sexual intercourse!*

Gardner (in a somewhat incredulous tone): I heard that. But what I want to know is *what* is the problem?

Minister (somewhat angrily): That's the problem! She's having sex!

Gardner: Why is that a problem?

Minister: It's a problem because it's a *sin*, and I have an obligation to do everything possible to stop her from sinning.

Gardner: How do you plan to do that?

Minister: Well, the first thing I'm going to do is to tell her parents.

Gardner: Let me say this to you. I suspect that what I am going to say now may never have been considered before by many of you. I suspect that many of you have never considered the possibility that sex before marriage may *not* be a sin. Now I do not claim to know *with certainty* whether or not it is. I know that some of you here believe deeply, with 100 percent certainty, that pre-marital sex is a sin. And you may be right. I just don't know. My guess is that it is not.

All therapy involves the imposition of one's own values on one's patients. Clearly, the values of most of the people here in this room are different from many of mine. You (now turning to the questioner) may be correct that you must do everything to protect her from what you consider to be the consequences of her sins, both in this life and in the hereafter. I do not know whether you are or are not correct on this issue. However, there is one thing I can say to you with 100 percent certainty. And that is this: If you do tell her parents against her will, you will no longer have a patient. The disclosure may very well protect her from eternal damnation, but it will have destroyed the therapy. This is a choice you must make.

Needless to say, I was never invited to return to speak again at that facility. In fact, I would suspect that they probably tried to find out who the person was who had so many screws loose in his head that he invited me to speak there in the first place. The vignette is presented because it demonstrates well my point regarding the importance of therapists' appreciating that they cannot avoid imposing their values on their patients; the sexual situation is only one example of this phenomenon. To try to follow the dictum that one should never impose one's values on one's patients is impossible. Therapists must appreciate that they are continually doing so; one has to accept the consequences of so doing, whether these consequences be here on earth or potentially in the hereafter.

Homosexuality   Here I discuss what I consider to be normal homosexual desires in adolescence. In Chapter Two I will discuss what I consider to be pathological manifestations of homosexuality. At the outset, I wish to state quite directly that I am not in agreement with those colleagues of mine who hold that obligatory homosexuality is a normal variant. By obligatory I refer to the person who is compelled to have homosexual experiences only, and has never had any desire for heterosexual experiences at any time in his or her life. I would also include in the pathological group those whose homosexual orientation is so strong that they have rarely, if ever, engaged in or had the desire for heterosexual activities, especially when opportunities for such behavior were readily available. Rather, they have sought and engaged in homosexual behavior only. I believe that for some people there may very well be a genetic predisposition to the development of homosexual behavior, but this does not negate the argument that such an orientation can be pathological. Most diseases, both organic and psychogenic, probably have genetic contributing determinants. Their presence does not warrant our concluding that they are therefore not disorders. I believe, however, that genetic predisposition notwithstanding, environmental factors play an important role in determining whether such predisposed individuals will develop into obligatory homosexuals. In Chapter Two I will elaborate in detail on my views on homosexuality. Here, I will focus on adolescent homosexual manifestations that are so common that I consider them to be within the normal range of behavior.

Even though we have experienced in recent years what has been referred to as the "sexual revolution," youngsters in early adolescence still do not generally have as much heterosexual opportunity as they would like. Under these circumstances, a certain amount of homosexual activity may be seen. The principle is similar to the one found among adults who are placed in situations in which heterosexual opportunity is either severely restricted or not possible at all. People in prison would be an excellent example of this. In past centuries sailors on long ocean voyages would serve as another example. Under these circumstances homosexuality is quite common and might very well be considered "normal."

I believe that in recent years there has been a shift among adolescent boys with regard to homosexual behavior. Prior to the last 10 to 15 years, many adolescent boys found outlets through mutual masturbation. This practice generally discontinued by the mid-teens when the boys began dating and having heterosexual experiences. Since the late 1960s and early 1970s boys have had more heterosexual opportunities and so this practice appears to be less widespread. When I have seen it, in the last 10 to 15 years, it generally occurs among those boys who are more homosexually oriented and are likely to take the homosexual route. Accordingly, it has different diagnostic significance in the 1980s than it had in the 1950s and early 1960s. What was then "normal" may now very well be a sign that the youngster is heading in a pathological direction.

A less overt form of homosexual gratification engaged in by early adolescent boys involves comparing penis size, especially in locker rooms and when lining up at urinals. There may be "horseplay" in which they grab one another's genitalia. Whereas in early childhood this was an inevitable part of wrestling matches in which one "grabbed for the soft spots," it takes on a new function in the early adolescent period. Specifically, it enables the youngster to get an idea of how "well hung" his peers are (in comparison to himself) and also provides for some mild and transient homosexual gratification.

With regard to girls, I have not seen any changes in recent years in their early adolescent "homosexual" patterns. Rather, their "homosexuality" in the early teen period does not generally manifest itself in overt sexual activity, such as mutual masturbation. Rather, they often develop "crushes" on other girls and become intimate confidantes of their friends. Mutual sexual involvement was and still is far less common. If anything, if there is some "normal" homosexuality occurring in girls in the 1980s it is to be found at the college level. There, girls who have not previously been introduced into homosexuality may become so, especially at all-girls institutions. These girls have, I believe, been swept up in what I consider to be a pathological environment, an environment in which homosexuality is viewed as a normal alternative and healthy lifestyle with no implications of psychopathology. (This will be discussed in greater detail in Chapter Two.) Some of these girls will, I believe, switch back onto the heterosexual track, the one they were destined to proceed on anyway. Others, however, especially those with a homosexual predisposition, may very well become more entrenched in the homosexual track—perhaps irretrievably.

I fully appreciate that many readers will take exception to what I have said here with regard to homosexuality. However, I believe that all readers will agree (those who agree with me about the etiology of homosexuality and those who do not) that it is important that I state clearly my position on this subject, both with regard to what I consider normal and what I consider to be pathological. I do not claim to have any final answers here. I do believe, however, that those who claim complete certainty on the issue of the etiology of homosexuality are somewhat premature considering our present state of knowledge (or, more accurately, ignorance) in this area.

Romantic Love

Romantic love is very much an adolescent phenomenon. It generally is not seen before the adolescent period and thrives best during adolescence. Although adults may find themselves indulging in it, they are less likely to be swept up by its delusions because of the improvement in judgment that comes as we mature.

Common Concepts of Romantic Love   In the United States (and throughout most of the Western world) the socially acceptable reason for getting married is *love,* and more specifically *romantic love.* Individuals who marry for other reasons, or who fail to include love in their list of reasons for marrying, are likely to be considered injudicious, misguided, or possibly suffering with a psychopathological disturbance. When "in love" the individuals find that they experience certain ecstatic feelings when thinking about or being in the presence of a specific person of the opposite sex. In its full-blown form the blissful state appears to be all-pervasive. It enhances the pleasure that the individual may derive from even the simplest everyday activities and makes many of life's inevitable pains more tolerable. The person in love comes to the conclusion that the particular party who is the object of his or her affection is the only one in the whole world capable of inducing this special state of elation. Lovers soon develop the deep conviction that these blissful feelings will last throughout their lives, even though they have never personally observed anyone—except on the movie or television screen—who has sustained this state beyond a few years. Yet, this does not deter people in love from making vows about how they will feel and behave toward one another many years hence (even the rest of their lives). Here again, the fact that the vast majority of people have not proven themselves capable of or inclined to keep these vows does not deter lovers from making them.

A type of romantic love that is particularly attractive to adolescents is the kind that I refer to as the *Some-Enchanted-Evening-Across-a-Crowded-Room* type of romantic love. In this variety, two complete strangers, merely on viewing one another (from across a crowded room is desirable but not crucial to the phenomenon), are suddenly struck, as if by a lightning bolt, from out of the blue, with intensive feelings of affection and sexual attraction for one another. I also refer to this type of romantic love as the *bifurcated lightning bolt* kind of love. Here, God in heaven decides that it is now the time for these two particular individuals to fall in love. He therefore thrusts a lightning bolt down toward earth which, just before it reaches the ground, splits into two parts, each one of which invests the lovers. So magnetized, they make a beeline for one another, stomping over people in between, and "read life's meaning in one another's eyes." I also refer to this as the *acute infectious disease* type of romantic love. Here the individuals are suddenly afflicted with cravings for one another, as if stricken with an illness. This is one of the reasons why individuals with this kind of love may refer to themselves in popular song as having been "bitten by the lovebug." In medicine we have a term: *pathognomonic sign*, which refers to that sign that clinches the diagnosis of a disease. The lovebug disease has a pathognomonic sign—a sign that differentiates it quickly from all other diseases known to medicine. Patients who are suffering with any other disease known to medicine would be quite upset if a doctor, when admitting them to the hospital, would inform them that they will have to share a bed with another patient suffering with that disorder. People with the "lovebug disease" have no such objections; in fact, they welcome being in the same bed together. This is the one pathognomonic sign that differentiates it from all other diseases known to medicine.

In all these cases the individuals view their attraction to come from mysterious, almost magical, forces that instantaneously and irresistibly draw them together. Although some view the cause of the overwhelming attraction to be external (as planned for by God, for example), others attribute it to internal factors (such as "body chemistry"). I, personally, suspect that internal psychological and biological factors are the most important elements in producing this phenomenon. The individuals enter the room predisposed to the experience, and even hoping for it, because of a lack of meaningful involvement with anyone else at the time. And loneliness may intensify the craving for such an involvement. The need for an esteem-enhancing experience as an antidote to one's pains and frustrations may also be present. Perhaps the object of the intense attraction bears some physical resemblance to an earlier love object, such as an opposite-sexed parent or a former lover. Sexual frustration is in all probability present as well. All of these cravings may be particularly great at the time—explaining thereby the suddenness with which the individuals are drawn to one another. All these factors together result in a copious outpouring of hormones into the bloodstream that enhances formidably the desire of the two individuals to spend as much time as possible with one another, both physically and psychologically. In fact, they may give such high priority to being with one another that they may ignore obligations vital to their well-being. And when the two people become more involved with one another the attraction becomes solidified by a dovetailing of both healthy and neurotic needs. (Both of these factors will be elaborated upon below.)

The risks that one takes by falling in love with a stranger are no different from those one takes when one, for example, buys a used car from a stranger or lends money to a stranger. One does better to get a little more information before entering into such transactions, and yet it is both amazing and pathetic how individuals who would never be injudicious enough to buy cars from or lend money to strangers will be willing to sign a contract in which they take an oath to live together for the rest of their lives with a "stranger from across a crowded room."

The Psychodynamics of Romantic Love   Before discussing what I consider to be the important psychodynamic factors operative in bringing about the state of romantic euphoria, I wish to emphasize that I do not necessarily equate psychodynamics with psychopathology. Most, if not all, forms of psychological behavior have psychodynamic elements, but not all psychologically determined behavior should necessarily be considered psychopathological. Each of the psychodynamic factors I describe here runs the gamut from the normal to the pathological. Each person who is "in love" utilizes one or more of these mechanisms. And each person may utilize them in either normal or pathological degrees and in any combination in between these extremes.

One factor operative in the romantic love phenomenon is compliance with social convention. In our society we consider "love" to be the most important reason for marrying another person. Of course, in other societies other criteria have been used. In some, money and power were unashamedly utilized as criteria for matchmaking. The ancient Pharaohs routinely married brothers and sisters in order to keep power and wealth within the family. Unfortunately for the Pharaohs, genes for intellectual retardation were quite common in their families—resulting in an unusually high

percentage of retarded monarchs. Marrying cousins and near relatives was a routine practice among European royalty, even up to this
century. Unfortunately for the European aristocracy, genes for
hemophilia were quite prevalent. The presence of these defective
genes, however, did not seem to deter marriages between close
relatives because of the great desire to keep wealth and power in the
family. And even among commoners, marriages planned by parents
is an ancient tradition, the parents considering themselves to be
more judicious than their children for making such an important
decision. Here again, considerations other than romantic love were
generally operative in the parents' decision-making process. Although I would not recommend that we resume the practice of
parents deciding whom their children shall marry, I cannot say that
the practice is not without its merits.

Social convention, then, deems it normal for people, especially
when young, to have the experience of falling in love. In fact, people
who claim that they have never had the experience are often viewed
as being somewhat deficient and even unfortunate. We are much
more like sheep than we would like to admit and there are many for
whom the social-compliance factor is an important one. When one's
friends start falling in love, then one starts falling in love as well. It
is similar to the phenomenon by which anorexia/bulimia and even
adolescent suicide have come into vogue in recent years. When it
becomes "the thing to do" in the adolescent set, many adolescents
are likely to go along with the crowd, even if it means acquiring
some dreaded disease and even if it means killing oneself.

I believe that an important contributing factor to the development of feelings of romantic love is the need to provide oneself with
a narcotic. Like the narcotic, it quickly produces intense pleasurable
sensations and thereby provides enjoyment—practically on demand. One need not apply oneself diligently over time to gain
pleasure; one merely need spontaneously induce the state within
oneself and revel. (One need not even have encouragement or
reciprocity from the object of one's affection; "unrequited love" can
produce the same euphoric state.) In addition, like the narcotic, it
makes one insensitive to pain. There are many painful feelings
associated with the prospect of marriage—if one is to allow oneself
to think about them. One is committing oneself to a lifelong
arrangement—a decision that cannot but be extremely anxiety

provoking. The prospect of living — for the rest of one's life — with the same person cannot but make an intelligent and sensitive human being shudder. And the awesome responsibility of rearing children is certain to produce further anxieties. Romantic love is an extremely potent tranquilizer for the treatment of such anxieties. Narcotics also dull one's senses and make one less discriminating about what is happening in the world around. And romantic love assists the lover in denying deficiencies in the partner, deficiencies that may be obvious to almost everyone else, deficiencies that might cause most judicious individuals to pause before making such an important commitment. As with the narcotic, the ecstatic feelings are experienced only early in its use. As time passes the drug becomes less and less capable of producing the blissful state. Alas, such is also the case with romantic love.

One of the important attractions of the romantic love experience is that it is an esteem enhancer. We generally admire most those who have the good sense to like us (and conversely, we are quickest to dislike intensely those who are stupid or blind enough to hold us in low regard). We cannot but find attractive a person who has selected us — from all the billions of other people on earth — to respect, confide in, and communicate sexual attraction to as well. Typically, the individuals bestow praises on one another to a degree not generally seen in any other situation. All stops are pulled out in the service of this goal. Even one's own mother does not hold one in as high regard as one's lover. The process may start, for example, with A bestowing on B some complimentary comment. B, thereby flattered, returns the favor. A then considers B to be quite judicious for having such high regard for him or her and thinks then even more highly of B. B, receiving even greater positive feedback, esteems A even more highly and communicates this. A mutual admiration society thereby develops with an upward spiraling of the compliments. The society is founded on the agreement that "if you'll admire, praise, respect, and find me sexually attractive, I'll do the same for you." This is indeed one of the important attractions of the phenomenon.

Unfortunately, there are only about 400,000 words in most unabridged dictionaries of the English language, only a small fraction of which are useful in the service of complimenting one's beloved. It is even more unfortunate that the majority of individuals have only a few of these in their repertoire. As a result, the praises tend to become somewhat repetitious and they thereby lose some of their efficacy. In addition, the individuals may believe that it behooves them to maintain the high frequency of compliments and this can be somewhat taxing and draining. Healthy people can allow the romantic love experience to simmer down somewhat and have ongoing experiences that enable them to supply fresh compliments. Those who do not may then become frustrated with this aspect of the romantic love experience. Last, individuals with profound feelings of low self-worth are more likely to gravitate toward this aspect of the romantic love phenomenon because the praises provide compensation for low self-esteem.

There is yet another element in this phenomenon that enhances even further the feelings of self-worth of the individuals involved. If the object of one's affections is perfect, and if one is in turn loved by that perfect person, then one must indeed be a most admirable person indeed. It is as if the young man in love were saying: "She is perfect. Among her perfections is wisdom. She loves me. If she is wise enough to love me, I must be unique, adorable, lovable, wise, and maybe even perfect like her. Why, she even tells me that 'we're a perfect match.'"

Another factor operative in the romantic love experience is reaction formation to underlying anger. All human relationships are ambivalent, and those who are in love are no exception to this principle. However, there are individuals who believe that it behooves them to have a relationship in which there is no anger expressed—lest the relationship be viewed by themselves and others as not "the real thing." In most (if not all) human relationships angry feelings are inevitably going to arise at some point, often very early. We cannot satisfy one another's desires all the time; the frustrations that ultimately result in all close human encounters must produce resentments at times. In healthy relationships, the individuals express these at the earliest possible times, in a civilized manner, in the hope that the problems may be resolved. If a problem cannot be resolved, and if there are many such problems, then the individuals usually part ways. If, however, they are successful in resolving the inevitable conflicts that arise, they may then be in a position to maintain a relationship that may ultimately mature. Individuals who are too guilty to express their resentments or who need to feel that there are none, are likely to use the romantic, loving feelings in the service of reaction formation. Obsessive love may then be used to suppress deep-seated hatred. Accordingly, romantic love not only provides a cover-up of angry feelings—for those who believe that they should not be present in good relationships—but lessens the likelihood that the individuals will work out the problems that are producing the anger in the first place. In this way it contributes to the perpetuation of difficulties in the relationship and even to its deterioration.

Romantic love can also be used to satisfy pathological dependency cravings. It is much more socially acceptable to gratify pathological dependency with a spouse than with a parent. This would be an extension of the previously described shift in which the adolescent transfers dependency on parents to dependency on peers. In romantic love, the dependency gratifications may be even greater and a marriage based on such cravings is not likely to be stable, because in any parasitic relationship the host as well as the parasite ultimately get to hate one another. The host resents the parasite because his or her blood is being sucked; and the parasite resents the host because of his or her vulnerability. At any point the host may flick off the parasite, leaving him or her with no sustenance. And such resentments may, over time, develop into hatred when the two individuals become "locked in" with one another.

Another factor that may be operative in the romantic love phenomenon is the desire to outdo one's friends and even evoke their jealousy. One can boast to friends that one is loved, adored, admired, and even worshipped by another party. When one's friends are not at that time having that fortunate experience, then it places the beloved in a superior position in the competition for success in the dating/mate-acquisition arena. One can then boast of the "good catch" and flaunt the beloved to one's friends. Again, individuals with low feelings of self-worth are more likely to utilize this maneuver.

I wish to emphasize again my point that psychodynamics should not necessarily be equated with psychopathology. Each of the above contributing factors, when present in mild degree, may very well be considered normal. To the degree that romantic love becomes obsessive and prolonged, to the degree that it becomes delusional, to the degree that it interferes with important functions (school, work, etc.), to that degree should it be considered psycho-pathological. The healthiest situation for the adolescent, I believe, is to have a few such experiences, but not to make any commitments under the influence of the romantic-love feeling. Adolescents are generally too young to marry and have children and the romantic experience may result in their taking these steps. My final advice, whether it be to the adolescent or to the adult who is "in love," is this: Romantic love is a wonderful experience. Enjoy it while it lasts, but don't make important decisions under its influence—like marriage, for example!

It would be unfortunate if the reader concluded from this somewhat cynical description that I am totally condemning the phenomenon. I believe that in moderation it can be an enriching, uplifting experience that makes life more meaningful. It has served to inspire some of the world's greatest artistic and scientific creations. The person who has not tasted its sweet fruits has missed out on one of life's most rewarding experiences, but when it is indulged in to excess, when people are so blinded by it that they enter into self-destructive involvements, I consider it a type of psychological disturbance. One can compare romantic love to the occasional alcoholic beverage. Used in moderation it can ennoble our spirits; when we are addicted to it, it can destroy us. I think that it is possible that in recent years there may have been some decrease in the tendency of people to become addicted. The "tell it like it is" philosophy that has become so popular in recent years may very well lessen the tendency of people to enter into this self-induced delusional state to such an extreme degree.

Factors Operative in a Mature Heterosexual Relationship   I believe that a more judicious concept of love between adults is to view it as a composite of many factors, each of which is on its own continuum—from a very low to a very high level. One factor, of course, would be the romantic love element. This is generally strongest when one has very little information about the other party. A number of years ago there was a movie entitled *Lovers and Other Strangers*. This title itself is a clear statement of one important aspect of the romantic love phenomenon. We can love most ardently those about whom we know least. Romantic loving feelings tend to decrease in situations in which there is ongoing close contact – such as when the two people live together. The feelings do not survive well under the competition of hair in the sink, bathroom smells, snoring, etc. Accordingly, a relationship that is based purely on this factor, and has little else, is not likely to survive long. As mentioned, romantic loving feelings may include formidable psychopathological elements, and this is a further reason for distrusting them. I am not claiming that romantic feelings have no place at all in a mature relationship, only that they be considered to be one part. Ideally residua of the initial feelings survive over time, to re-express themselves in periods of relaxation, tenderness, and sexual intimacy.

Another factor to be considered is sexual attraction. Here too sexual feelings can range from very strong to very weak, and even to the point of nonexistence. Generally, these are strongest in the earliest phases of the relationship when there is much novelty and even a "forbidden fruit" element. In the healthiest relationship, however, the sexual feelings may still remain strong over many years, even after these initial factors are no longer operative. But here too fluctuations may be present and still be considered within the normal range.

Another factor, one that is quite important, is that of genuine respect. Here, too, there is the continuum from very low to very high. In a good relationship there is a high regard for the other person's opinions in important areas – so much so that the partners are willing to take action on the basis of their respect for one another's opinions. And respect also includes respect for the other person's rights, space, freedom, aspirations, and a wide variety of other needs. Related to respect is admiration. Here there is high respect to the point of real esteem. When there is admiration the loving relationship is likely to be even stronger. However, it is important for the reader to appreciate that respect and admiration must be based on realistic qualities, not fantasized ones. They must be qualities that are genuinely considered worthy of respect, not easily attained attributes.

Another important element in a good loving relationship is the desire to share with one another. Here again there is the same continuum from very little desire to share to very strong desire. Probably the most common area for sharing is child rearing. However, there are some couples who may not enjoy this kind of sharing, but other kinds of mutual endeavors. Of course, the more areas in which the couple enjoys mutual sharing, the stronger will be the relationship. I would not consider the ideal, however, to be one of complete togetherness on practically every area of functioning. Marriage should not be a "three-legged race." I make reference here to the traditional children's game in which the children race in pairs, each tied together as if they had three instead of four legs. In such a marriage, as in such a race, the individuals are likely to fall flat on their faces. There must be opportunities for decompression and for each to have his or her own living space. They must each have the opportunity to enjoy the benefits of other relationships as well, but not to the point where the loving relationship takes second place.

Another factor that is important in a good loving relationship between adults is the willingness to make *reasonable* sacrifices for the other party. I emphasize the word reasonable because I consider an inordinate desire to sacrifice (or to be sacrificed for) to be unhealthy. Accordingly, sacrifices that are motivated by masochistic and martyristic tendencies are not what I am referring to here. Rather, I am talking about the willingness to deprive oneself and do things for the other party under circumstances of personal inconvenience and sacrifice, but not to the point of seeking or creating situations in which one can provide oneself with morbid extensions of the willingness for self-abnegation in the service of the loved one.

The reader may be wondering why I have included here such an extensive discussion of those factors that are operative in the mature adult heterosexual relationship. My reason is that adolescents are extremely unlikely to exhibit such elements. Accordingly, their loving relationships rarely satisfy these criteria and so are likely to be transient. There are rare occasions, however, when the adolescent relationship may indeed serve as the basis for the development of these more stable and mature qualities. It behooves a therapist to be appreciative of these differentiations and to recognize that it is only over time that one can tell whether the relationship will mature in the aforementioned directions.

In addition, there are the psychopathological processes that are operative in even the healthiest relationships. She claims she wants a husband and he claims he wants a wife. What she really wants is a child and what he really wants is a mother; and so the relationship takes on all the hallmarks of a parent/child relationship. He is a very quiet, uptight kind of person who is ill at ease in social situations and has little to say. She is very voluble, extremely gregarious, and enjoys speaking with others. Accordingly, he can rely upon her to "fill up the vacuum" in social situations. So we have a man with verbal constipation who falls in love with a woman with verbal diarrhea—and the match is made. She says she wants a husband and he says he wants a wife. Basically, she wants a sadist and he wants a masochist, and they "fall in love." I am not referring here to the full-blown type of sado-masochistic relationship in which the partners reach orgasm via beating and torturing one another. Rather, I am referring to the more common and less dramatic form in which there is cruelty, maltreatment, and denigration. The alcoholic man is likely to fall in love with a woman who has some kind of a savior complex, in which she believes that she is going to cure him of his drinking. Another woman is going to cure her betrothed of homosexuality by giving him a good heterosexual sex life. Schizoid or severely suppressed people may gravitate toward one another because each would feel uncomfortable with a partner who is freer to express emotion.

L. Kubie (1956) considers the need to "settle old scores" and "right old wrongs" to be an important psychopathological factor in many heterosexual relationships. A woman, for example, who was rejected by her father may involve herself with a man who is similarly rejecting in order to extract love from her husband, who is viewed as a surrogate father. What she didn't get from her own father she now hopes to get from his substitute. Finding a loving man in the first place might seem simpler and more judicious, yet it would deprive her of the opportunity of going through the process of converting the unloving to a loving man and thereby accomplishing the transformation. Another example: A man might want to make his bad mother (now equals wife) good or use her as a target for the present expression of past resentments originally felt toward his mother. For individuals to do this they must marry people who have the very same alienating qualities that they claim they never want to have in a spouse. These qualities exist as internal bad objects in the individuals themselves, and these are then projected out onto the spouse, even when they don't exist. The spouse is then viewed as a "bad internal object representation." The distorted view of the spouse, then, results from two processes: 1) a transference onto the spouse of feelings originally felt toward one's own parent in childhood and 2) a projection of one's own internal bad object parental representations that have been incorporated. The real personality of the family member then hardly exists because the individual is seen primarily, if not exclusively, as a bad object representation and/or as someone who is distorted by one's own transferences.

According to Kubie these two processes contribute significantly to the individual's desire to use the spouse to settle old scores and/or to right old wrongs. The list of such psychopathological interactions goes on and I am sure the reader can provide his or her own examples. The examiner must appreciate that one or more of these pathological types of interaction are likely to be present along with the more normal factors delineated above. Although adults will often manifest these pathological types of interaction in full-blown form, one observes them *in statu nascendi* in adolescents. Therapists do well to detect these developing pathological manifestations and do what they can to interrupt the process in its earliest stages.

Clearly, by the definition I have just presented, adolescents are not likely to qualify as good candidates to have strong mature loving relationships. And they generally don't. The romantic euphoric element is often predominant and they do not have the experiences to entrench in depth the other elements. The relationships are often transient and this lessens even further the likelihood for such entrenchment. Unfortunately, they often have the foundations for the kinds of pathological interactions that may contribute to disturbed adult heterosexual relationships. It behooves the therapist to be aware of these and to do everything possible to alleviate them in order to reduce the likelihood that these will contribute significantly to the youngster's ultimate heterosexual difficulties.

Parental Reactions to the
Adolescent's Sexual Development

Generally the greatest fear of the parents of adolescent girls is that their daughters will become pregnant. To a lesser degree, parents of adolescent boys fear that their sons will prematurely become fathers. Healthy parents take proper precautions, provide reasonable sexual education, and, at the appropriate times, provide information about contraception if they have no religious or ethical proscriptions against the utilization of such safeguards. They also inform their youngsters, at the proper time, that if a pregnancy were to occur the youngster should feel comfortable telling the parents at the very outset. Disturbed parents instill formidable fears of sex in their children, the result of which may be a pregnancy that is not disclosed to them, or disclosed when it is too late to handle it in the most expeditious fashion (again, depending upon the parents' religious values).

It is normal for parents to have a certain amount of jealousy of their adolescents' sexual freedom. Healthy parents, however, put this in proper perspective and the jealousy does not play an important role in the way they deal with their youngsters. Parents who cannot tolerate their adolescents' emerging sexuality may become punitively restrictive with regard to the youngsters' sexual opportunities. A father, for example, may be obsessively concerned with his daughter's clothing, especially with regard to how revealing it is. He may refuse to let her leave the home with low-cut blouses and be extremely punitive when she uses even occasional cosmetics and perfume. Some fathers who exhibit such concerns are actually fighting their own sexual urges toward their daughters and may be unconsciously taking the position: "If I can't have her, then I'm not going to let anyone else have her either." And the daughters, too, are not immune from having sexual feelings toward their fathers. Many would describe the feelings of such a child as "oedipal." As I have discussed elsewhere (R.A. Gardner, 1968, 1973a, 1986a), I believe that only a small percentage of the patients I see have what I would consider justifiably to be called "oedipal problems." When such problems are present, there are usually special situations in the family that are conducive to the development of these difficulties. These will be discussed in Chapter Two.

I mention here what I consider to be a normal way for an adolescent girl to deal with occasional sexual feelings toward her father by excessive criticism, disgust, and even frequent fighting, in order to disguise (to both her father and herself) her sexual attraction. And a father may respond in kind, with regard to his own sexual feelings, by frequently bickering with his daughter. A similar phenomenon may exist between mothers and sons. I consider such fighting to be within the normal range when it is occasional and does not interfere with functioning in major areas. When, however, it becomes a deep-seated pattern, then I would view it to be pathological.

CONCLUDING COMMENTS

I have presented in this chapter what I consider to be normal developmental conficts of the adolescent. Rather than confining myself to any particular developmental theory, I have focused on those developmental conflicts that I have seen over the years to be the most important for youngsters during this stage. Nor do I claim to have covered all developmental problems. I do believe, however, that I have dealt with those that are most likely to serve as a foundation for psychopathology. Because psychopathology so often emerges from these normal conflicts, the understanding of these will place the reader in a better position to understand the psychopathological processes that I will be describing in this series.

TWO

COMMON SITUATIONS CONDUCIVE TO THE DEVELOPMENT OF PSYCHOPATHOLOGY IN ADOLESCENTS

In this chapter I will discuss those situations I have found to be most conducive to the development of psychopathology in adolescents. This chapter, therefore, should not be viewed as a comprehensive statement of the wide variety of situations that can produce psychopathology in adolescence. Rather, it describes those situations that, in my own personal experience, are most commonly conducive to the development of such difficulties in these youngsters. I recognize that others, with different patient populations, would describe different situations—some similar to mine and some not. The developmental conflicts described in Chapter One are at the foundation of the psychopathology of most of these youngsters. The particular situations described in this chapter combine with these underlying developmental conflicts to bring about the psychopathological reactions. The conflicts described in Chapter One may very well be normal; the situations described in this chapter are generally pathological and play an important role in determining whether the normal developmental conflicts will serve as the foundation for psychopathology or merely become resolved through the process of maturation.

The reader will perhaps note what may initially appear to be be an emphasis on situations that produce antisocial behavior in these youngsters. This over-representation is not related, I believe, to any particular bias on my part. Rather, it reflects my experience that antisocial behavior is the most common category of difficulty in the adolescent patients referred to me. As I have mentioned frequently in other publications of mine, when I collect data for a book, I invariably find that anger problems are the ones I am most commonly asked to treat and so the sections in my various books related to anger problems are usually the most extensive (R.A. Gardner, 1971, 1973a, 1976, 1977, 1979a and 1986a).

SOCIAL, CULTURAL, AND EDUCATIONAL FACTORS

Day-care Centers

In recent years we have witnessed a burgeoning of day-care centers. This growth has paralleled the shift of women from the home into the work place. Obviously, when women are no longer at home taking care of the children someone has to take over this role. As far back as the late 19th century, at the time of the establishment of the kibutzim in Israel, this problem had to be faced. The young pioneers who first established these settlements designated certain women, called *metapelets*, to involve themselves primarily in child rearing — thereby freeing up mothers to work in the fields, factories, etc. The day-care center is the American equivalent of this phenomenon. The success or failure of the day-care principle rests on the quality of the care given the children and the hope that it will be as good as that provided by the biological mother. On the basis of my experiences with children who have spent many years in such centers, I believe that many of these facilities are significantly deficient in providing such quality care. Of course, when the biological mother herself is somewhat impaired in maternal capacity then the day-care center may very well be a boon for her child — its deficiencies notwithstanding. But when one compares the care given in the average center with that given by the average mother, I believe that the mothers come out significantly ahead (and the children in day care, therefore, significantly behind).

In the last few years the problem of sex abuse of children in day-care centers has received widespread attention, but I believe that physical and emotional abuse are also common. It is unreasonable to expect that people who would be depraved enough to sexually abuse children are completely free from tendencies to abuse children in other ways—ways not directly related to sex abuse. Of course, it is impossible to get accurate statistics regarding the prevalence of such practices. This is especially the case for emotional abuse, for which objective criteria cannot be utilized. I believe, however, that the lower the cost of the facility, the less the regulation by the community, and the greater the number of children per care provider, the greater the likelihood that one or more of the three forms of abuse is likely to take place—especially emotional abuse. And I consider neglect to be a form of emotional abuse. It is difficult to learn exactly what is going on in these facilities because the children, most often under the ages of three and four, are ill equipped to describe exactly what has happened behind their parents' backs. It is important to appreciate that people who choose careers in these centers are not always motivated by the noble desire to provide children with loving care; many are motivated by money and some by the opportunity to find helpless scapegoats for their sadistic impulses and objects for the pedophilic gratification.

I believe that many of the children "dumped" into these facilities suffer with deprivation of affection and that such deprivation may contribute to a wide variety of psychiatric disturbances. In fact, it is reasonable to say that the vast majority of psychogenic disturbances include deprivation of affection in childhood as an important contributing etiological element. Elsewhere (1973a) I have described in greater detail the specific relationship between such privation and the development of various forms of psychogenic disturbance in childhood.

A particular form of such disturbance, which I focus on here because of its increasing ubiquity, is that of *psychopathic behavior*. I use the word *psychopath* to refer to an individual who has an impairment in the development of internal conscience mechanisms. The individual feels little if any guilt over the infliction of pain and suffering on others. There is little capacity to put oneself in another individual's position, especially an individual who is the object of one's persecution, exploitation, etc. For the psychopath the primary deterrent to such behavior is the immediate threat of external punishment. I believe that western society has become increasingly psychopathic in the last 20–25 years. I see the trend to have started in the early to mid-1960s and to be continuing. There is far more exploitation of individuals, far less honesty, far less dignity, and far less concern for the feelings of others. We are living in a much more exploitive world than we did 20–25 years ago.

I am not claiming, for one moment, that the history of mankind prior to that time was characteristically free from psychopathy. There were certainly times when psychopathy was probably even more widespread than it is now. For example, following the period of the Black Plague in the mid-14th century, when Europe was depleted of about 25 to 30 percent of its population, society became almost entirely predatory with a nearly complete deterioration of moral standards in church, government, and even family life. And there have certainly been other periods in mankind's history when similar situations prevailed. Unfortunately, we are moving with increasing frequency into such an era. In day-care centers young children are not being provided with good models for the development of conscience because their caretakers themselves have grown up in a psychopathic society and have taken on its values. In addition, a child is most likely to learn to be "good" when he or she is rewarded for goodness by loving caretakers. In Chapter One I described in greater detail how the absence of caring parental figures at the imprinting, pleasure-pain, shame, and guilt stages produces failure in the development of the internal guilt-evoking mechanisms.

It would be an error for the reader to conclude that I am condemning entirely the whole day-care concept. It would also be an error for the reader to conclude that I am condemning all day-care centers and all their personnel. Rather, I am sharply critical of many with which I have had personal experience. Furthermore, I do not believe, even under the most ideal circumstances, that day-care center personnel can provide the same kind of love and affection that the natural average, healthy parent is capable of giving. There is something about the biological tie that increases the likelihood that the child will develop a strong psychological tie. Day-care personnel do not have this foundation for the development of this important psychological bond. And the inevitable turnover of both children and caretakers makes it even more unlikely that such bonds will develop.

As women enter increasingly into the work force they are spending less time with their children. The growth of day-care centers helped fill the need for a place for mothers to leave their children during the workday. Obviously, a mother cannot be in two places at the same time; she cannot be at work and at home taking care of the children. Although these new trends certainly serve well the needs of women, especially those who consider a full-time job as child rearer to be boring and unsatisfying, they do not serve well the needs of their children. Most mothers in this situation find themselves on the horns of a dilemma. To the degree they satisfy their work interests, they neglect their children; and to the degree they satisfy their children's needs, they neglect their careers. We are witnessing an ever burgeoning growth of "latchkey children," i.e., children who carry their house keys with them to school in order to be able to enter their empty home at the end of the school day and then wait for their parents to return from work.

What is the solution then? Should mothers return to their traditional roles as homemakers? I do not think so. But even if I did think so, there would be no turning back. The answer, interestingly, I believe to be a very simple one. There are few simple answers to the problems of the world, yet I believe we have one here—as difficult as it may be to accomplish. The answer lies in restructuring society so that mothers and fathers can divide child-rearing obligations. All we need do is have each parent work outside the home half the days of the week. The mother, for example, might work outside the home on Monday, Wednesday, and half of Friday; and the father could then work outside on Tuesday, Thursday and the other half of Friday. Such an arrangement is entirely feasible. Everyone has had the experience of calling an office in order to speak with Mr. Jones. One is informed that Jones is not available that day and that he will be in the following day. However, if one wants to speak with Mr. Smith, who is equally capable of handling the situation, then he is available. All of us are expendable. There is no one whose job is so vital and/or unique that there aren't other individuals who can take over. Life goes on even when the most vital people become incapacitated, retired, or die.

Many feminists are clamoring for more money for day care. I think this is an error. Some of the more vociferous of these women are individuals who abhor child rearing and denigrate homemaking. These women would do far better to use their influence in bringing about the aforementioned changes in the work place: changes that would accommodate a 50/50 split by parents in child rearing and work obligations. This arrangement would be the optimum one for younger children, during the first four to five years of life. After the youngest child enters school, the parents would then be freer to involve themselves more extensively in the work force. I consider this arrangement to be entirely viable at the present time. The vast majority of organizations could implement it for most of their employees without formidable difficulty. Its implementation would remove one important contributory factor to the psychopathology of children and, by extension, adolescents.

Unfortunately, the seemingly utopian plan of each parent working half time and spending the remaining time at home with the children is not close to being realized. What can we do then at this point? In presenting my recommendation, I will use the mother as the example of the primary caretaking person because, at the present time, she is more likely to be the one who is providing such care. In part I believe this is a "good" thing because mothers are more likely than fathers to have a stronger psychological tie with the infant at the time of birth. However, it is also a "bad" thing because it is a statement of society's failure to provide adequate opportunities for men to participate fully in the child-rearing process. The optimum program, I believe, is one in which the younger the child the greater the amount of time the mother has with it. Certainly in the first six months or so the mother should be spending most of the time at home. I am not stating that there be no respite. She too needs some decompression and alleviation of child-rearing involvements. And most mothers probably need this daily or at least a few times a week. Such respites should be taken while the child is sleeping and/or while the child is cared for by persons such as the father, grandparents, and close relatives and friends. These people are much more likely than the strangers at the day-care center (no matter how sophisticated and devoted) to provide the child with optimum care. It is important for the reader to appreciate that the six-month figure given above may vary and that is why I stated, "six months or so."

During the second half of the first year (I know that I am being particularly vague here) I would suspect (I am not certain) that children can tolerate maternal absence for longer periods. I suspect, as well, that if a mother returned to work for one to two days a week at that time *and* the child was cared for by one of the aforementioned individuals (as opposed to someone in a day-care center) the child would probably be all right. By extension, the older the child the greater will be its tolerance for separations while mother is working. By 2-1/2 to 3 years of age children are certainly more capable of tolerating longer times away from their mothers and are more likely to profit from the group and peer experiences that are so important for healthy development. *If* the care provided is warm, humane, and tender and *if* the ratio of caretakers to children is adequate, then the day-care experience at this age is likely to be salutary. But there are very big *ifs* here because, as mentioned, I am dubious about the quality of the care provided in most centers.

Like many other things in life the rich have a much greater chance of getting quality day care than the poor. In the early grade-school period children still do better if, on returning from school, they find mother or some other well-known figure who will provide love, affection, and attention. I recognize that my position on this point would be considered "sexist" by many feminists. Many women's desire to enter the workplace is so strong that they have to blind themselves to the psychologically detrimental effects of turning their children over to the care of strangers. They have to deny the fact that no one loves our children more than biological parents and close relatives (and on occasion close friends). If one were to interpret my comments here to indicate that I want to drive women back into the home, that would be a serious distortion of my intent. Rather, I want to bring mothers *as well as fathers* back into the home. However, I want mothers to be in the home more than fathers during the infancy period. And then, by age two to three, both parents should be involved equally in the child-rearing process.

Socioeconomic Deprivation

Children who grow up in homes and neighborhoods in which they suffer socioeconomic deprivation are likely to be angry; and such anger is likely to contribute to the development of a variety of psychopathological manifestations, especially in adolescence. In childhood the youngster is generally not capable of acting out on such hostile impulses or expressing fully the symptoms derived from such deprivation. In adolescence, however, the youngster may very well exhibit psychopathology, especially in the realm of drug abuse and antisocial behavior. The drugs serve in part to provide some pleasure in a situation which is generally viewed as pleasure-less. And the antisocial acting out serves as a vehicle for the expression of the rage engendered by the deprivation. The sense of deprivation is enhanced further by the inevitable exposure to situations that provide opportunities for comparison between what the youngster has in reality and what the child might very well have had under more favorable circumstances. Movies, television, news-papers, magazines, and other aspects of the mass media perenially bombard the youngster with the "good life" out there—a life which the child is continually being rejected from and which he or she may consider an impossible goal toward which to aspire.

The economic deprivation is generally apparent in the home, the neighborhood, and the schools. Such youngsters are brought up in an atmosphere in which they consider themselves to be among the "have-nots" and there is continual comparison with the "haves." Accordingly, the child grows up in an environment of ongoing deprivation, frustration, and anger. Unfortunately, the youngsters with whom the child associates during the formative years are exposed to similar privations, and they too exhibit the same kinds of psychopathology that derive from the deprivation. As a result there are few if any peer models with whom the child might make healthier identifications.

I believe that one of the most important determinants as to whether a child in this situation will develop psychopathology is the presence of a father in the home. In those homes in which a father is present, there is less likelihood that the youngster will develop antisocial behavior, abuse drugs, or manifest other symptoms derived from deprivation—the economic privation notwithstanding. Even when the neighborhood is one in which drugs and crime pre-vail, if there is stability within the home, especially a stable marriage between the parents, then the likelihood that the child will become involved in such activities is reduced significantly. Although there might be present healthy adult models such as ministers, recreation directors, teachers, etc. for more salutary emulation, these figures generally have far less influence on such youngsters than fathers.

The rectification of this situation obviously goes far beyond what therapists can do in their offices. It is only via changes in those factors that have contributed to the socioeconomic deprivation in the first place that one can hope to reduce significantly the frequency of the kinds of adolescent disturbances derived from such privation. The therapist does well to appreciate the formidable forces operative in producing such psychopathology and must recognize, thereby, how impotent he or she is to change such children—especially when they do not reach the therapist's office until the adolescent period.

Schools

Whereas the home plays the most important role in the child's psychological development during the first three or four years, the schools play an increasingly important role during the next decade or so (at least for most children). Those who are unfortunate enough to be provided with inadequate educational programs are likely to develop psychopathology, both in childhood and in adolescence. I believe there to have been a progressive deterioration of our educational systems (both public and private) in the last 15 to 20 years. A number of factors have contributed to this deterioration. One relates to teachers' salaries. It is unreasonable to expect that schools can attract high quality, well-educated individuals when other careers provide much greater pay. In most municipalities garbage men make as much as, if not more than, elementary school teachers. The public sector can generally afford to provide higher salaries than private and parochial schools; yet the public schools seem to be getting the poorest quality teachers. The more dedicated ones are willing to take positions for lower salaries in order to work in the more academically stimulating atmosphere of the private and/or parochial schools.

I believe there has been a general diminution in the commitment of teachers to the educational process. I am not claiming that this is true of all teachers, only that the percentage of teachers who are deeply committed to their profession has been sharply reduced in the last 15 to 20 years. One manifestation of this trend is the decreased frequency with which children are required to do homework. Giving children homework most often involves homework for the teacher. And less dedicated teachers are not willing to take on this extra responsibility. In previous years there were many more teachers generally viewed to be somewhat hard nosed and dictatorial, yet their despotism was benevolent and years later their students have looked back with gratitude on what they were "forced" to do. These days "respect" for the child often involves a degree of permissiveness and indulgence that does not serve children well in the course of their education. A good educational experience helps the child learn that there are times when one has to do things that may be unpleasant in order to derive future benefits. "Respecting" the child's wish not to suffer such discomforts is basically not in the child's best interests. True respect for children involves the *requirement* that they do what is best for them, not the indulgence of their avoidance of reasonable responsibilities. The net result of these unfortunate trends is that children learn less during their primary and secondary school years—with the subsequent result that SAT scores have dropped significantly during the last 15 to 20 years and many studies have demonstrated that the majority of children are abysmally ignorant of basic facts about history, literature, english, and mathematics.

Another factor operative in the deterioration of the educational system has been the growth of a generation of teachers who themselves have not learned very much during their own educational processes. Often, these are teachers who went to college during the 1960s when students' self-indulgence may have reached an all-time high. Grammar, punctuation, spelling, and foreign languages were dismissed as "irrelevant." Many other subjects that required self-abnegation, self-discipline, and hard work were also often viewed as irrelevant. These are the people who are now teaching our youngsters. Not only do many of these teachers serve as poor models for their students, because of their impaired commitment to the educational process, but they are compromised as well in what they can teach. I routinely ask parents to bring in my child patients' report cards. Often I see egregious errors in grammar, punctuation, and spelling. I have had secretaries whom I have had to let go after a week or two because of their ignorance of basic

English. They were not people who I felt needed time to adjust to a new job; rather, it might have taken years to get them to reach the point where they could function adequately in a standard secretarial position. They often did not even appreciate how ignorant they were. They didn't even recognize that a misspelled word looked misspelled and so had no motivation to consult a dictionary for the correct spelling.

In their book *What Do Our 17-Year-Olds Know?*, D. Ravitch and C. E. Finn (1987) report a study conducted with approximately 18,000 17-year-olds who were selected to reflect the makeup of the population as a whole regarding region, sex, race, type of school, and type of community. Some of their findings: Thirty percent of the students did not know that Christopher Columbus reached the New World before 1750. More than 35 percent were not aware that the Watergate scandal took place after 1950. More than 30 percent believed that one consequence of the Spanish-American War was the defeat of the Spanish Armada. Approximately half of the students believed that *Nineteen Eighty-Four* dealt with the destruction of the human race in a nuclear war. Over one-third did not know that Aesop wrote fables. Over 42 percent did not know that Senator Joseph R. McCarthy conducted anti-Communist investigations. Seventy percent were unable to identify the Magna Carta. And the book goes on and on with many more examples of the abysmal ignorance of the average American teenager. But these findings should not be surprising, considering the kinds of educational programs these youngsters are being provided.

This deterioration of the educational process has extended up into the college and university levels as well. When I went to college we generally went from nine a.m. to five p.m. Monday through Friday and a half-day on Saturday. Most courses met four or five times a week and laboratory courses two to three afternoons a week. It was expected that one would do four or five hours of homework a night. School began the day following Labor Day and continued right through early June. There was a one-week Christmas vacation, possibly a one-week Easter vacation, and of course national holidays. Otherwise we went to school. This is no longer the case. Even in the so-called "best" colleges and universities the formal academic program is far less rigorous. Most students average two or three hours a day of classes while professors may only have to come in five to ten hours a week and are otherwise unseen. These days, the academic year, although it may start around Labor Day, generally ends in early May. Some institutions use the Christmas and/or Easter season as an excuse for an extended holiday (two to four weeks). Others have long vacations (lasting two to four weeks) between semesters. Many need no other excuse for a long break than the season (spring or winter vacation). These students are being short-changed. "Educations" of this kind may cost $15,000 a year or more.

Recently, a mother of a patient, who teaches at one of the public universities in New York City, related to me an incident that demonstrates well the deterioration of our educational systems, even at the highest level. The woman is a highly intelligent, well-trained, scholarly individual with a Ph.D. in a very demanding field. One day her chairman called her into his office and told her that he was having a problem with her, namely, that too many of her students were failing. He informed her that a 40 percent failure rate was unacceptable. She informed him that she was actually being quite generous, and that if she had marked in a less generous way about 60 percent of her students would fail. He told her that he had sat in on a couple of her classes, knew exactly what the problem was, and considered it easily rectifiable. He then went on to explain to her that she was not giving tests in the "correct" manner. What she was doing was to tell students on Friday, for example, that there would be a test on Monday covering the material in certain chapters of the textbook. This he considered "unfair" to the students. Rather, the "correct" way to give a test was to tell the students on Friday exactly what questions would be asked on Monday. Under the new system the failure rate dropped from 40 to 20 percent, but even then she found herself being quite generous. Such procedures are a manifestation of a bastardization of the educational system. They make a farce of education and, worse, are a terrible disservice to students. The next step, of course, is merely to tell what questions will be asked and give the answers that will be expected. If one extends this further one might as well give out (or sell) the diplomas in advance and save everybody a lot of trouble.

Things are even worse at some of the lower level colleges. Many of these merely go through the motions of providing an education and are basically a sham. Students are given textbooks that are seemingly rigorous and demanding, yet in actuality the students are only required to learn a small fraction of what is presented therein. Those in charge recognize the travesty but are party to it, even at the highest levels. The net result of all this is that students are not getting a bona fide education and are thereby entering into the workplace ill equipped to handle jobs for which they are ostensibly being trained. Also they are being deprived of the feelings of accomplishment and high self-worth enjoyed by those who have acquired skills and talents through hard labor and dedication over years. The situation, thereby, contributes to psychopathology, because feelings of low self-worth are an important contributing factor in the development of psychogenic symptoms. In addition, it contributes to psychopathic trends (I am not saying gross psychopathy) because of the sanctions the youngsters are given for "cutting corners," taking short-cuts, and otherwise doing shabby work.

Accordingly, I consider most colleges in the United States to be little more than "winter camps." Most (but certainly not all) colleges are nothing more than businesses that cater to a gullible population of parents who consider it crucial that their children go to college. Four years are spent in which the "students" indulge themselves in alcohol, sex, and drugs—with little serious attention to academics. And no one flunks out because colleges need the parents' money. (No sane businessman throws a paying customer out of the store.) Grade inflation gives students the specious feeling that they are learning something. As long as there are parents who believe it is *crucial* that their children (no matter how simple and/or unmotivated) have a college education (no matter how specious and inferior), there will be people happy to supply the "product." These educational depravities become progressively worse, because for each successive generation there is greater distance from traditional models in which healthy values were practiced and preached. Elsewhere (1973a), I have described in greater detail other deficiencies in our educational system that contribute to psychopathology.

Television and Movies

There is little question that television and movies contribute to the development of various forms of psychopathology. I wish to emphasize, at the outset, that I believe that the detrimental influences of these media can be offset to a significant degree by a healthy, stable home situation. However, even in the most healthy and stable homes, parents are still working against the nefarious influences of these media on their children's psychological development.

Prior to the early 20th century, people were required to derive their own sources of home entertainment. It was an active experience and necessitated a certain amount of ingenuity and creativity. Watching television and movies is an easy and passive experience, which deprives the individual of the gratifications to be derived from the more traditional home entertainment activities. And this passivity extends itself into other areas of life in which individuals have become accustomed to being served and catered to. This contributes to both physical and mental laziness—the latter type being much more psychologically detrimental than the former.

Although still denied by some (especially those who produce television programs), there is compelling evidence that television violence contributes to violent behavior among viewers. One of the earliest studies in this area was that of A. Bandura et al. (1963) who found that physical and verbal aggressiveness increased in nursery school children after brief exposure to violence. Over the years, many (but not all) studies have lent strong confirmation to Bandura's original conclusions. The notion that the observation of violence in movies and television has cathartic value and thereby reduces pent-up anger is now generally discredited. Whatever cathartic benefits individuals may derive are far less important than the factor of inciting the viewer to further violence. L. Berkowitz and E. Rawlings (1963) were among the earliest to discredit the cathartic value of such observations. More recently G. Comstock and his associates (1978, 1983, 1986) have demonstrated a positive association—especially for boys—between exposure to television violence and antisocial behavior. Comstock et al. consider the evidence strongest for "interpersonal aggression," that is for fighting, minor theft, and name-calling. The relationship is less obvious for the more extreme and harmful types of antisocial behavior, such as criminal activity. I consider the difference in the two types of violence to be related to the home environment, especially with regard to its degree of psychopathy and sanction for the more severe forms of antisocial behavior. N.M. Malamuth and E. Donnerstein (1982) have also found there to be an increase in sexual violence after exposure to sexually explicit movies in which women are assaulted.

Many studies have found that there are specific factors in television and movies that are likely to evoke violent reactions. One factor is the implication, either overt or covert, that the aggressive behavior is rewarded or not punished. Another is that the particular action is normal, usual, and a reasonable adaptation to real-life circumstances. Another factor is related to whether or not the violent behavior is so portrayed that it arouses distaste or disgust. If the viewer is not shown the victim's pain or suffering, the sorrow of friends, or remorse on the part of the perpetrator, it is more likely that it will stimulate antisocial behavior. If the situation is similar to one that the viewer is involved in, it will serve to increase the likelihood of violent acting out on the part of the viewer. When sexual aggression is the theme, it is more likely to be reproduced by the viewer if the woman eventually relishes the assault. If prior to exposure the viewer is already angry, the likelihood is increased that antisocial behavior will subsequently be exhibited.

Some might argue at this point that the implications of this research are that we should strictly avoid exposing our children to any kind of violent material in movies, television, etc. Some might even ask about the judiciousness of exposures to Shakespearean tragedies (*Hamlet* and *Macbeth*, for example), such classics as the *Iliad*, and even biblical passages in which violence is portrayed. Are not these works equally capable of inciting violent reactions? There is most often (but not always) a difference between the violence portrayed in these great works of literature and the kinds of violence one sees in most movies and television. The main difference is that in the great works of literature violent acts are not simply reflex responses, but are embedded in a context of deliberation. One of Hamlet's problems is that he deliberates too long; he cannot make up his mind. We are told that he is a man who "thinks too much." In the process of his deliberations, however, the viewer is treated to many "lofty thoughts" and valuable wisdoms about the world. In contrast, in most television programs the violence is impulsive and is used as the *first* method of dealing with a difficult situation. In addition, in the great works of literature there are many other redeeming elements in the story that enhance the reader; this is most often not the case in the typical movie and television story in which the violence predominates.

The ancient Roman emperors knew that the best way to gain popularity among the general populace was to give them "bread and circuses." By circuses, they were not referring to clowns and acrobats. Rather, they were referring to gladiatorial conflicts in which the combatants fought to the death or spectacles in which prisoners, political dissidents, and individuals of religious persuasions unacceptable to the emperor were fed to lions. We have our equivalents today in such sports as boxing, wrestling, bull fights, and cock fights. To the degree that we can replace the more primitive forms of hostile entertainment with the more sophisticated and humane types, to that degree will we contribute to the prevention of psychopathology derived from such exposures and, by extension, will move toward the enhancement of ourselves as civilized human beings. The Nobel laureate Konrad Lorenz once said: "I have found the missing link between the higher apes and civilized man. It is we."

The Legal System and Penal Institutions

One factor contributing to the development of psychopathology in adolescents, especially antisocial behavior, is the present structure of the legal system and penal institutions. I do not claim to be an expert in these matters and I fully appreciate that they are exceedingly complex. I also appreciate that the solutions to the problems presented herein are also complex and some of them may not have any solutions. Yet, I will make some recommendations which, if implemented, could reasonably contribute to the prevention of certain forms of adolescent psychopathology.

Our legal system is much too lenient in the way it deals with adolescent offenders. It has been said, (and I don't know who said it): "A criminal is a very old man who has committed a series of violent crimes." This statement, of course, reflects the penal system's leniency toward juvenile offenders. First offenders are rarely punished and those who have the wherewithal to hire clever attorneys are even less likely to suffer repercussions for breaking the law. Such leniency only serves to sanction antisocial behavior. Compensation to victims is rarely considered and this only lessens the likelihood that discomforting and painful repercussions will deter offenders. Many policemen do not even bother arresting many offenders, because they recognize that nothing is likely to happen to them. Even when a youngster is found guilty of a crime, the records may be destroyed after a period of good behavior. One could argue that such leniency is humane, and that a youngster should not have his or her record marred for life because of an indiscretion committed in adolescence. Whatever the merits of this argument, there is no question that leniency increases the likelihood that a youngster will commit a crime because of the knowledge that one's record may still remain clean. I sincerely believe that fewer crimes would be committed if reasonable and humane punishment were more predictable and criminal records could not be destroyed or the information expunged—no matter how young the convicted offender.

Another problem relates to the apprehension of criminals. In order to protect the rights of those who might be falsely apprehended and convicted, legislators have passed many laws in recent years that serve to protect individuals from such miscarriages of justice. Whatever benefits society may derive from such laws, there is no question that they have been so manipulated by attorneys that perpetrators have succeeded in avoiding prosecution and punishment for their offenses. Attorneys are taught in law school to protect the rights of their clients, even though they may not have conviction for their causes. Lawyers are taught that their personal convictions regarding the nature of the criminal's behavior (no matter how heinous) should not deter them from fighting for their client's cause. Although I recognize the right of a person to have legal representation, I still believe that a better system would be one in which lawyers were taught that they should not represent a person for whose position they have no conviction. Under such a system criminals would have a more difficult time getting legal protection and this, I believe, would contribute to a reduction in crime. Furthermore, clients whose lawyers do not have conviction for their positions are not being given as effective representation as those whose attorneys have such conviction. The notion that the attorney can serve equally well under both circumstances is misguided, psychologically naive, and a disservice to clients. Elsewhere (1982, 1986b, 1987a, 1987c) I have commented on this and other criticisms I have of the adversary system.

Judges, with justification, are loathe to send youngsters to penal institutions where they will be mixed in with hardened criminals and thereby made worse rather than better. This problem could be obviated by the creation of institutions designed for younger offenders. Although such facilities exist there are far too few of them, certainly not enough to accommodate more than a small fraction of youngsters whose placement there might "help them remember" not to commit crimes. Another problem relates to the overcrowding of jails. There have been times when courts have ordered jails to release criminals before their sentences have been completed, because of overcrowded conditions. Although attempts have been made to release the less dangerous criminals, the process has on occassion resulted in violent crimes and even murders being committed by such released individuals. Clearly, under such a program, prisons are going to free individuals who are considered "safer" — for example, younger criminals who have committed fewer crimes.

DEPRIVATION OF
PARENTAL AFFECTION

Examiners today generally make the assumption that there will often be found a relationship between deprivation of parental affection and the development of psychogenic pathology in their child patient. Although a wide variety of parental deficiencies may be considered, most if not all of them have in common a basic impairment in the parent's capacity to provide the child with the love, guidance, affection, nurture, and protection that is so vital to its well being. Most examiners do not appreciate that this relationship, which is viewed as being so obvious today, was not always appreciated. For example, at no point in Freud's discussion of the analysis of Little Hans does he mention the possibility that there might be some relationship between Hans' symptoms and parental deprivation of affection (S. Freud, 1909). Although Hans' phobia was termed a "psychoneurosis," Freud considered the symptoms to be basically developmental in etiology (a derivative of the "normal" oedipal phase) and even went further to point out that he considered the parents to be normal and healthy, without any evidence of impairment in their parenting capacity.

It was not until the 1930s that we first saw articles suggesting the possibility that there might be some relationship between a child's psychopathology and parental impairment in providing affection. D.M. Levy (1937) introduced the term "affect hunger" to describe this phenomenon. Using the model of the nutritional deficiencies that result from deprivation of vitamins, he considered various childhood psychogenic symptoms to be the result of such deprivation. In 1944 J. Bowlby published the results of a study in which he tried to determine whether there was any relationship between juvenile delinquency and parental deprivation of affection. His finding that a significant percentage of juvenile delinquents came from homes that were disturbed seems unsurprising to us today; however, in Bowlby's time the article was considered to be a landmark contribution. It ultimately resulted in the *World Health Organization* asking Bowlby in the late 1940s to review the world's literature and try to ascertain if there was indeed a relationship between parental deprivation in childhood and the development of psychopathology. In his monograph *Maternal Care and Mental Health* (1952) he concluded that there was indeed such a relationship. Again, his publication was considered a landmark in the history of the field of child psychiatry.

In subsequent years numerous studies have lent confirmation to this theory. The consensus has been that a wide variety of disorders can result from parental absence and/or impaired parenting capacity. The absence of the father (or deficiencies in his ability to serve well in this capacity) has been particularly linked with impaired superego development and the appearance of antisocial behavior. One of the most well known of these studies was done by A. Bandura and R.H. Walters (1958). In their study of antisocial youngsters and their families, they found a high frequency of disruption of the relationship between delinquents and their fathers. They concluded that these impaired relationships interfered with the youngsters' identification with their fathers and internalization of their values. A. Kardiner and L. Ovesey (1951), in their studies of black families, found a correlation between delinquency and the absence of a suitable male model for identification. In addition, when these absentee fathers did have contact with their youngsters they often encouraged, either overtly or covertly, the antisocial behavior of their sons. R.J. Marshall (1983) has written an excellent summary of important contributions in this area.

Another way in which parental deprivation of affection contributes to the development of psychopathology in youngsters relates to the anger engendered in children by parental deficiencies. When there is little guilt over the expression of such anger, then antisocial behavior is likely to develop. (In contrast, when the child has been taught to feel shame and/or guilt over the expression of his or her resentment then the symptoms of anger inhibition may develop.) Rage over the parental privation is another important factor contributing to antisocial behavior, a factor separate from the aforementioned superego deficiencies that are likely to be found, especially in situations where the father is absent or psychologically impaired.

There are some deficient parents who basically do not want to have children. In extreme cases they will murder their children. Body parts of infants may be flushed down the toilet, or the dead infant may be buried, or simply placed in the garbage. In less extreme situations children are brutally beaten as they serve easily as scapegoats for the venting of parental hostility. Such brutalized children are inevitably going to develop psychopathology. There are parents who want their children removed from the home, but cannot permit themselves to overtly abandon the youngster. They thereby create situations so intolerable to the youngster that he or she runs away. These children are prime candidates for becoming prostitutes (either male or female) and every large city has its collection of them. As well-meaning workers with such children know, when the families are called and told that their youngster has been found, not uncommon responses include: "Who asked you to butt in?" "If you like her so much, why don't you take her?" and "I don't know what you want. You must have the wrong number. We never heard of her." These, of course, are the most extreme examples of parental deprivation.

Separating and divorced parents are also likely to create a situation in which the youngster suffers with feelings of deprivation of affection. This is not simply related to the absence of one of the parents (usually the father) from the home. Prior to the separation the child may have been exposed to and embroiled in the parental hostilities. Most often the child is used as a weapon or a tool in the parental warfare, and this is especially likely to be the case around the time of the divorce. Often, the parents are so swept up in their hostilities that they pay little attention to their children. Elsewhere (1976, 1977, 1979a) I have described in detail the variety of psychiatric disturbances likely to arise in the divorce situation. And, if the parents are sick and/or foolish enough to involve themselves in protracted litigation (especially custody litigation) then more severe forms of psychopathology are likely to develop. Elsewhere (1986b, 1987c) I have described these disorders in detail.

IDENTIFICATION WITH PATHOLOGICAL PARENTAL TRAITS

Although I believe there to be certain genetically determined components to personality structure, and even the propensity for the development of certain forms of psychopathology, there is no question that identification with pathological parental traits plays an important role in the development of childrens' and adolescents' psychiatric disturbances. The modelling process is far more extensive than most parents (and many therapists) appreciate. Linguistic development is an excellent example of this phenomenon. Most three-year-olds are reasonably fluent in the language of their parents and will utilize with uncanny accuracy the parental intonations, pronunciations, and associated linguistic gestures. When one considers how formidable a task it may be for an adult to learn a new language, one can appreciate how much time and energy children put into this process. Yet, it is done in what is seemingly an effortless way. I believe that the impulse to mimic a caretaking figure is genetically determined, and that over the course of human evolution those individuals who were weak in this area were less likely to survive—because they did not acquire those parental traits necessary for optimum functioning.

The first-born child emulates and identifies with the parents. The second born has three models for identification: the two parents and the older sibling. I often have said that the three-year-old is the parrot of the five-year-old, especially if the two children are of the same sex. Five-year-old Billy says he wants a cracker. His three-year-old brother, Jimmy, will in all likelihood reflexly decide that he too wants a cracker. Parents may jestingly say, "I wonder where Jimmy got the idea?" The traditional game of "house" is a good example of the process by which children entrench their identification models into their psychic structure via the process of reiteration. Children most often start such a game with the assignment of roles and there may be some arguments as to who should be the father, the mother, the baby, etc. (And it may take a long time to settle the arguments over which role each child shall assume.) Once the game gets rolling, one sees an exact repetition of what goes on in the household. Typical household scenes are reenacted: serving breakfast, sending the children off to school, eating lunch, meeting the children upon their return from school, giving them milk and cookies, instructing them in their afternoon activities, feeding them supper, involving them in after-supper play, getting them to bed, and lulling them to sleep. Disciplining the children is also a common preoccupation and the "parents" are traditionally far more punitive than the real parents. I believe that this phenomenon relates to the fact that children's superegos are generally weak and a certain amount of "overkill" is necessary if they are to develop a normal level of conscience.

The list of parental traits that children identify with is long, in fact as long as the list of parental traits that exist. Parents who are committed to the educational process, who continue to learn long after their formal education has ended, are likely to have children who will similarly become committed to school. On a number of occasions I have seen youngsters with little if any commitment to the educational process who are brought by parents who similarly lack conviction for academics. Both may have been high school drop-outs and rarely show any interest in reading, expanding their intellectual horizons, and even watching programs on television that are above the level of pap. Generally the school refers the child and the parents reluctantly come, hoping that the therapist will disagree with the school authorities and conclude that the child has no problems. On occasion I have had parents in this category who have literally fallen asleep during the consultation. The chances of a therapist helping such a child develop more academic enthusiasm is extremely small.

Another common situation in which the identification process contributes significantly to the development of adolescent psychopathology is the one in which the parents are involved in vicious divorce litigation. Such youngsters live in an atmosphere of ongoing animosity between the parents. They are likely to identify with one or both parents and then exhibit antisocial behavior themselves. The antisocial behavior is not simply related to the acting out of anger the youngster feels over the privations associated with the parents' preoccupation with their marital difficulties. It is also related to the identification process wherein the child's repertoire of behavioral patterns becomes increasingly restricted as he or she is exposed continually to the parental battles. These patients are frequently brought to therapists who are asked to help them without direct work with the parents. Therapists who take on such cases are at the same time grandiose and simple-minded. The likelihood of helping such youngsters without reducing the parental animosity is almost at the zero level.

Another common situation that contributes to the development of psychopathology in children is the child's emulation of and identification with parents who themselves exhibit psychopathic tendencies. As mentioned, I believe that we have experienced over the last 15 or 20 years a definite increase in psychopathic traits in our society. The increasing crime rate is the most blatant confirmation of this phenomenon. But there are many other examples: hijacking of airplanes; terrorist attacks against innocent women and children; killing policemen (armed and unarmed); defaulting of debts to the government by students; scientists who falsify their data; and crimes committed by policemen, lawyers, and judges. There has been a deterioration of values that extends to almost every area of functioning. Doctors can no longer trust their patients to pay a bill at the end of the month; most require payment at the time services are rendered if they are to survive in practice. Most homes are not considered to be complete without burglar alarm systems. Clergymen are no longer considered unlikely candidates to commit child sex abuse. The standards for getting a job as a teacher become progressively lower, to the point where many teachers write report cards with gross errors in grammar, spelling, and punctuation. It is no surprise that SAT scores are getting lower.

Another identification phenomenon contributing to the development of psychopathology in children and adolescents is that of "identification with the aggressor." The youngster who observes a parent treating others in a cruel fashion may fear that he or she will similarly become a target of the parental hostility. One way of protecting oneself from this eventuality is to join the hostile parent as an ally. This decision follows the principle: "If you can't fight 'em, join 'em." An extreme example of this phenomenon occurred in concentration camps where Jews became Nazi sympathizers and even attempted to join the ranks of their persecuters. The records from the period of the Spanish Inquisition reveal the execution of thousands of monks and nuns, many of whom were Jews who had taken on such guise in order to protect themselves from being killed.

PARENTAL SANCTION OF
PATHOLOGICAL BEHAVIOR

The acquisition by a youngster of parental pathological patterns via the aforementioned process of identification is a relatively passive process with regard to the parent. The parent just serves as a model for the child's pathological patterns. In this section I discuss a more active type of transmission of parental pathological patterns. Here the parent consciously or unconsciously attempts to bring about the pathological manifestations in the child and receives definite gratifications from the child's behavior. Certainly these two processes can coexist; in fact, one generally finds a combination with one or the other form predominating.

Antisocial Behavior

It is in the realm of antisocial behavior that parental sanction is quite common. Although juvenile delinquency is seen in all economic strata, it is generally more prevalent in the socioeconomically deprived. Many factors contribute to this, but an important one relates to the resentment of the "have nots" toward the "haves." Adults who are chronically enraged over the disparity between their own situation and that of those who are more fortunate and/or enterprising are generally judicious enough to appreciate that direct expression of their resentment may result in serious repercussions—such as going to jail. Youngsters, however, because of their cognitive immaturity, are less likely to appreciate the long-range consequences of their acts. Furthermore, adolescents' delusions of invulnerability make them excellent candidates for acting out parental anger.

A storekeeper complains to a father that his son stole some goods. The father responds, "My Bill would never do such a thing." The parent may suspect that the storekeeper's complaint is justifiable, but may rationalize his failure to discipline or punish with the belief that only a disloyal and defective parent takes a stranger's side against one's own child. Another parent in the same situation responds, "Don't bother me. All kids do that. It's normal. I used to do the same thing when I was a kid. Get out of here. Don't bother me!" Another parent responds, "Jimmy, tell the man you're sorry." Jimmy then perfunctorily says that he's sorry. The stranger, quite frustrated, responds, "But aren't you going to do anything?" To which the father replies, "He told you he's sorry. What more do you want? Now get out of here and don't bother me!" In this situation Jimmy knows well that there will be no repercussions for his antisocial behavior, and he can rely on his father to protect him from those who might want to punish him or make him suffer other consequences for his delinquency.

I once saw a 12-year-old boy who was brought by his parents because of fire setting. When I asked the parents how they were dealing with the problem the mother replied, "Well, Doctor, what I do is this. When he comes home from school I tell him he can go into the backyard and set fires in a garbage can. I tell him he can do that as much as he wants as long as the fires are confined to the garbage can. In this way I want him to get it out of his system."

In response I said to the mother, "You told me that you also have a 14-year-old daughter. I would expect that, if you're like most mothers, you're becoming somewhat concerned about how she'll handle her sexual urges which, at this point, are probably getting stronger. If you're like most mothers you're probably wondering about whether she might become promiscuous, get pregnant, or acquire some sexually transmitted disease. Am I correct?" The mother responded affirmatively. I then continued, "Now suppose I suggested that you put up notices in local supermarkets, your church, and other prominent places in your community announcing that during a certain week all young boys in your neighborhood should come to your house and will have the opportunity to have sexual intercourse with your daughter. The purpose here would be for her to get the sexual urges 'out of her system.' What would you think of that suggestion?"

The mother replied, "Why that's insane. I would never do such a crazy thing."

To which I responded, "Well, I don't see much difference between the way you're handling the fire-setting problem and the plan I proposed for your dealing with your daughter's sexual urges. Both plans are based on the assumption that there exists a finite amount of urge that needs to be expressed, and once this amount is 'out of the system' nothing is left and the problem is then resolved." The mother was not too happy with my analogy, but did discontinue the practice of allowing the boy to build fires in the garbage cans.

There are parents who provide their children with money in order that they may buy drugs. When asked why they do this, some common replies are: "If I don't give him the money, Doctor, he'll go out and steal it and then he may have to go to jail." or "I've got to give her the money, Doctor. If I don't, she'll probably have to go into the streets and become a prostitute. How else can a girl of 15 earn $100 a day?" I have seen a number of parents who routinely cover their adolescents' forged checks. They usually justify this practice with the rationalization that they are protecting the youngster from the police and the courts. They seem not to appreciate that they are perpetuating the pathological behavior that they ostensibly want to discourage.

A common maneuver utilized by middle- and upper-class parents is to find a lawyer who will "get the kid off." They look for the shrewdest and most cunning attorney they can find, one who is well known for his or her ability to manipulate the judicial process in order to protect the client from suffering consequences for illegal behavior. Such parents may try to use political influence, contact people who can influence the judges, "pull strings," and otherwise manipulate the judicial process in order to protect their youngsters from suffering any consequences for their antisocial behavior. A far better position for such parents to take is that of asking the judge to implement the usual punishment for youngsters of that age, who have committed that specific crime, that particular number of times. They should neither ask for leniency nor request Draconian punishment, only the usual and reasonable punishment for that crime. This is the best way to help such youngsters "remember" not to repeat their offenses.

I present here an example that demonstrates well the phenomenon of parental sanction of pathological behavior. Henry, a 14-year-old boy, was referred for treatment because of delinquent behavior. His defiance of authority was ubiquitous. He was not only continually thwarting his parents but his teachers and school authorities as well. He refused to do homework, was often truant, and was failing most of his courses. He joined with friends in petty thievery and occasional mugging. He was also starting to experiment with drugs and alcohol. His father was an extremely rigid and punitive person who made Henry feel quite impotent. From ages ten to twelve he had worked with another therapist without too much success. Unfortunately, this therapist had died a year previously.

When he entered his first session he smugly looked around and said, "You shrinks are all the same...same stupid couch...same stupid diplomas on the walls...same damn pictures of your family on the desk." I understood Henry to be trying to lessen his anxiety in this new situation. By finding similarities between my office and that of his previous therapist he was reducing his feelings of strangeness. In addition, he was trying to identify me with his former therapist in order that I could better serve as his replacement. The hostile veneer was also anxiety alleviating; acting like a tough guy is a typical teenage defense against fear. Although anger displaced from his father onto me was also contributing to Henry's hostility, I considered the anxiety-alleviating factor to be the most important at that time. To have delved into the hostility at that point would have missed the aforementioned important issues and would have robbed the patient of his defenses at a time when he was very much in need of them. Appreciating his need for reassurance that his therapist and I did indeed have many similarities, I replied, "Yes, we psychiatrists often have much in common." This comment made Henry less tense and less hostile.

In spite of a promising beginning, I cannot say that Henry and

I had a very good relationship during the subsequent months. This was primarily due to my failure to identify with him when he engaged in antisocial behavior—especially when it took on dangerous proportions. I was, however, making some headway when the father angrily stated in a joint session that he was fed up with Henry's long hair and that he wanted him to cut it shorter. (This occurred in the mid-1960s when the long hair vogue its antisocial value had reached a peak.) I tried to dissuade the father from putting pressure on Henry and explained to him that it was one of the most innocuous forms of rebellion ever invented and he should be happy that Henry was resorting more to it and less to the more destructive and violent forms. The father was deaf to my advice. Following the session he took Henry to a barber shop. There he and a barber held Henry down while another barber gave him a very short haircut. Following this, Henry completely refused to attend school. (During the course of the therapy he had gotten to the point of attending most of the time.) There was also an intensification of his antisocial behavior, to the point where I was convinced that he would soon be in trouble with the police. In subsequent sessions it became apparent that Henry considered himself to have been castrated by his father. His rage was enormous.

About two weeks after this incident in the barber shop Henry came to my office with a teenage friend and asked if the latter could wait for him in the waiting room. The meeting was not particularly eventful. During my session with the patient who followed, she thought she smelled smoke. I didn't smell anything and neither of us thought it was necessary to investigate. At the end of the session, when we walked out of my consultation room, I was horrified to see that attempts had been made to set my waiting room on fire. Fortunately, the curtains were made of fire-resistant material and so did not ignite completely. The bathroom toilet tissue and paper hand towels had all burned, but the flames did not spread to the walls. Had the waiting room caught fire, my only exit would have been out the 13th story window.

I summoned Henry and his family back for a session at the end of my day. When I asked Henry about the incident, he admitted that he and his friend were responsible. When I asked him if he appreciated that I might have been killed, he smugly replied, "Doc, you gotta die sometime." I concluded that this was not a time for analytic inquiry. Since I was discharging Henry from treatment, such inquiry would have served little, if any, purpose. Besides, I was not particularly interested in spending time helping Henry to gain insight into such things as his act being a reflection of rage felt toward his father displaced onto me. At this point, "I didn't care two shits about the transference." I was just interested in getting rid of him as quickly and efficiently as possible. I called his parents in, told them about the fire incident, explained that I could not effectively treat anyone who had tried to kill me, and I was therefore discharging him from treatment. Without any particular sense of concern for what almost happened to me, they requested that I refer them to someone else. This I refused, explaining that I had too much concern for my respected colleagues to refer someone such as Henry to them. Although I recognized that this rejection might help Henry appreciate that there could be untoward repercussions to his dangerous behavior, this was not my motivation in discharging him. Nor was it my intent to provide him with any kind of therapeutic "corrective emotional experience"; rather, I just wanted to get rid of him.

Before they left I suggested the parents give me the name of Henry's friend, so I could call his parents and inform them about what their son had done. I called the boy's father, a lawyer, and told him that his son and my patient had tried to set fire to my office and, if they had been successful, my only exit would have been out the 13th story window. His immediate response was, "Can you prove it?" I replied, "You and your son deserve one another," and I hung up. A more blatant example of a parent's sanctioning a son's antisocial behavior (so often the case) would be hard to find.

Pathological Sexual Behavior

Two mechanisms are most often operative, either alone or in combination, in parents' sanctioning abnormal sexual behavior in adolescents. The first is vicarious gratification. Via this mechanism the adolescent is utilized to gratify unfulfilled parental sexual yearnings. The parent, by virtue of age and possibly marital restrictions, is generally not as free to engage in as wide a variety of sexual activities as the adolescent. The adolescent, therefore, lends him- or herself well to satisfying vicariously parental sexual cravings. It is as if each time the youngster engages in a sexual activity the parent enjoys similar satisfaction. However, in order to enjoy such gratification the parent must have information, details, and even on occasion observation of the sexual activity. Vicarious gratification may be conscious and/or unconscious.

The other mechanism is reaction formation. Here the parent is not consciously aware of the underlying desires that the adolescent involve him- or herself in the sexual activity. Rather, it is expressed as its opposite, that is, the prohibition and denial of the adolescent's sexual activities. There is an obsessive preoccupation with the adolescent's sexual life in the form of obsessive denunciation and excessive restriction. Such a parent, however, does not realize that each time the condemnation is verbalized a mental image of the adolescent engaging in the sexual activity appears in the parent's mind. Accordingly, the wish is gratified via the visual imagery that the preoccupation provides, and the guilt is alleviated via the denunciation process. It is as if the parent is saying: "It is not that I want my adolescent to have sex. No, it's just the opposite: I *don't* want my adolescent to have sex. In fact, I hate the thought and will do everything possible to prevent such a terrible thing from happening."

For example, a mother gives her daughter long lectures about the evils of sex and warns her before each date about the terrible things that can happen if a girl engages in such activities. Following each date she cross-examines the youngster—especially with regard to every single detail of any possible sexual encounters. When the youngster denies such involvement, the mother is incredulous and accuses her of lying. When, inevitably, she describes some activities the mother's facial expression changes completely. Although her words are words of condemnation, her facial expression is one of agitated excitation. She craves more and more facts and unconsciously relishes every detail. This situation is reminiscent of the name of a song that was popular when I was a teenager: "Your lips tell me no-no, but there's yes-yes in your eyes." At some level the youngster recognizes what is going on and complies with the mother's wishes, gratifying vicariously thereby the mother's desires and protecting the mother from guilt via the utilization by the mother of the mechanism of reaction formation.

While I was in residency training, during the late 1950s, I saw a 14-year-old girl, Joan, whose mother demonstrated the aforementioned phenomenon quite well. I saw the girl in the psychiatric clinic where she was referred because she had been "gang raped" by approximately 14 or 15 boys. The girl and her mother were not exactly sure how many boys it was, but it was in that range. This took place in the girl's bedroom while her parents were away one evening. On gaining further details it was clear that there was absolutely no forced entry, either into the girl's home or into her vagina. In fact, the girl had invited a few boys to come over and "have some fun" and they were even asked to bring along some friends.

When getting background history I learned from the mother that she always considered it important to impress upon her daughter the dangers of sex. Accordingly, from the time Joan was five or six she began to lecture her on how sinful sex was and the terrible things that could happen as a result of it—including pregnancy and sexually transmitted diseases. (In those days they were called venereal diseases.) However, the mother also related how she appreciated that teenage girls need "privacy." Accordingly, starting at about the age of 12, when a boy would come to the home to visit Joan, the mother would allow Joan and her friend to go into the bedroom and even close the door. But she insisted that the door not be locked. Periodically, without advance warning, the mother would charge into the room. Not surprisingly, she would often find the youngsters at various levels of disrobing, would then chide them for what they were doing, and insist they put their clothing back on and stop fooling around. She would then close the door because she knew she could then "trust" her daughter not to do it again. Of course, this trust did not extend more than 15 minutes, at which time the same scenario was repeated.

Obviously, with this programming, it was no surprise that this girl was "gang raped." This vignette is an excellent demonstration of the mother's utilization of this girl for vicarious gratification of her own frustrated sexual needs. The mother set up a situation that would insure that she would gain the gratifications she desired, namely, observing her daughter enagaged in various sexual acts. In addition, the mechanism of reaction formation was utilized in that by lecturing her daughter on the evils of sex, and reprimanding her when so engaged, she could assuage the guilt she felt over what she was doing.

The next example of this phenomenon that I present is an unusual one (as the reader will soon come to see), in that it involves a personal and professional experience of mine—combined into one person. The story begins in high school when I dated briefly a girl who attended the same school. I was 17 and Virginia (a not inappropriate pseudonym as the reader shall soon appreciate) was 16. During our first date she informed me—in very emphatic terms— that she had every intention of being a virgin when she got married. It is important to appreciate that this took place in the late 1940s when such was the official position of most girls whom I dated. Such professions, therefore, would not expose the individual to the kind of ridicule that they might in many circles these days. As the evening progressed I was surprised by how readily she brought up the subject of her virginity and how frequently she mentioned it. At the end of the second date her mother called me into the bedroom for a private conference. There she told me that I seemed to be a nice young man; however, I should know that her daughter had every intention of being a virgin when she got married, and Virginia had the mother's full support on this resolution. When she was sure that I had gotten that message, she dismissed me from the room.

Throughout the third and fourth dates it became apparent that Virginia was obsessed with this virtuous goal and it became clear that, unlike her girlfriends, she really meant it. Her peers, although they would occasionally profess such intentions, generally showed some flexibility with regard to this resolve and engaged in a variety of activities which led me to the conclusion (and hope) that they might not last long regarding their commitment to this principle. I, at that point, hoped (desperately) that I would *not* be a virgin when I got married—especially because I planned to go to college, then medical school, then internship, and then residency—training that might last until the time I was around 30. As I saw it, I was 17 and already considering myself somewhat retarded regarding "how far" I had gone—if I could believe my friends (who, of course, would never lie about such matters). As far as I was concerned the sooner I lost my virginity the better, and so Virginia and I parted ways. Clearly, Virginia and I had "irreconcilable differences."

We then went down our separate paths in life. Every few years, when the subject of compulsive commitment to the state of virginity would come up, I thought of Virginia and wondered whether she had gotten married and, if not, whether she was still a virgin. The answer came about 30 years after graduation from high school. I received a telephone call in my office one day from a woman who asked me if I would see her 16-year-old daughter on an emergency basis. She described the situation as being an urgent one because during the previous weekend, while she and her husband were away on vacation, her daughter had a "sex orgy" in the house with some of her friends. Worse yet, the male participants in this orgy were said to have been black and Hispanic (the family was Jewish). Last, she had good reason to believe that this all took place under the influence of drugs. I informed the mother of my usual practice of seeing the youngster and both parents in a two-hour consultation, during which time I see the three in varying combinations, as warranted. And so an appointment was made.

I can still remember my astonishment when I walked into the waiting room that day and saw not one, but two Virginias. The older Virginia was still named Virginia. (I had not linked the mother's name with my former high school date, especially because her last name was now different.) Although clearly 30 years older, I immediately recognized her as the girl I had dated in high school. Her daughter, whom I will call Sally, could have been a clone of the girl I had dated. After the initial introduction I informed the parents that it was my usual procedure to see teenagers first and then bring the parents into my office subsequently. However, I thought it important that we have a little chat before my interview with their daughter. I first asked the mother if she remembered me. She looked at me, somewhat quizzically, and replied that she did not. I asked if she had any recollection of ever having seen me at any point in her life, especially during the teen period. Again, she emphatically stated that I was totally unfamiliar to her and that she was quite sure she had never seen me. I then informed her that we had dated briefly while in high school. She was incredulous. She agreed that she had indeed attended the high school I named, but insisted she had not dated me. In order to provide her with further "evidence," I mentioned the names of a number of people whom we knew in common. She remembered some of them, but still insisted that she had no recollection of me. I decided not to pursue the matter further in the waiting room and came to the initial conclusion that she had probably blotted out of her awareness "sex maniacs" such as myself.

I then went into the consultation room with Sally. After sitting down, I had the feeling that a time machine had transformed Virginia back to the way she was 30 years previously — so uncanny was the similarity between the daughter and mother. The girl was a clone of her mother. It was as if she had inherited only the genes of her mother and none from her father. Perhaps, I thought, her mother was indeed a virgin when she got married and, not only that, was a virgin when she conceived, and I was dealing here with an immaculate conception. And, I even wondered whether Virginia might *still* be a virgin. Sally interrupted my musings and probably did so in part because of the strange expression I must have had on my face as I looked at her. "Doctor Gardner," she said, "my mother is a nut! As long as I can remember, she's given me this shit about being a virgin when I get married. As far back as I can remember she's been telling me about how proud she is of the fact she was a virgin when she got married, and that her grandmother was a virgin when *she* got married, and that she has every intention of me being a virgin when I get married. And my father's bought that crap. He's always told me about how proud he is of the fact that my mother was a virgin when they got married. I've often said to him: 'maybe no one else wanted her.'" As she spoke I kept thinking: "Incredible, I can't believe it. Maybe it's true what they say about truth being stranger than fiction."

The daughter then continued: "I assume she told you a story about a sex orgy that I supposedly had with black and Puerto Rican drug addicts. This is more of her crap. The woman's off the wall. What really happened was this: My girlfriend and I went out on a double date. Her boyfriend is black. He's a great kid. He's one of the best students in the class. In fact, I think I like him more than I like the boy I was going out with, but she doesn't know that. Anyway, after the movie we went back to the house. I know I promised my mother that I wouldn't bring anybody back, but what the hell! There was nothing illegal about what we were doing. Then the four of us shared *one joint*. That was it. One joint she turns into drug addiction! It was the second time I did it and I really didn't even enjoy it. My boyfriend and I went into the bedroom and fooled around a bit. I'm still a virgin and it's lucky that I still have sexual feelings. With a mother like her, it wouldn't be surprising if I ended up frigid or something like that. There's no way I'm going to be a virgin when I get married, but I'm not ready for it yet. It's crazy to marry someone that you haven't gone to bed with. I don't know where she's coming from. That's the whole story. I'm not lying to you."

There was nothing in the girl's story, either in the way she told it or about the facts that she had presented, that led me to believe that she was not being honest. Furthermore, I had "background information" that made her story quite credible. Inquiries into other aspects of Sally's life revealed no evidence of psychopathology. She was doing well in school, had many friends, and was not causing her parents difficulties at home in other areas. Apparently, she had grown up in a fairly healthy way in spite of her mother's obsession. I suspect that this was due to the influence of peers and society at large, a society in which more permissive attitudes toward sex served to counterbalance the puritanical indoctrination of her mother.

I then brought the parents in and the girl confronted them directly with the disparity between what she claimed happened and that which her mother fantasized. It was clear that the mother's renditions were fantasy and a reflection of her own problems in this area. In the course of the interview Virginia—not surprisingly—told me that she had always vowed that she would be a virgin when she got married (apparently thinking that this was news to me) and that she had always encouraged her daughter to follow in her footsteps in this regard. Virginia's husband then stated: "I'm in full agreement with my wife. I was very impressed on our first date with the fact that she felt so strongly about being a virgin when she got married. That was one of my main attractions to her." And then Virginia continued: "Yes, I knew that my husband really respected me. He never made advances like the other boys. He never pushed for sex like the others." All I could say to myself while listening to this was: "It takes one to marry one" and "For every man there's a woman."

Near the end of the interview I informed the parents that I did not consider their daughter to be in need of treatment. I recognized that a direct statement to the mother that it was she (and also the father) who needed therapy would not have worked at that moment. Accordingly, I recommended family counselling in the hope that the mother might ultimately become a patient herself. The mother was receptive to this idea and was quite astonished when I told her that it would not be possible for me to serve as the therapist. She was surprised by my statement and asked me why. When I told her that our past relationship precluded my having the kind of objectivity necessary for successful treatment, she replied, "What relationship?" I told her again that it was my firm belief that we did indeed have a relationship in the past, and that as long as *I* believed that (even if it were only a fantasy) my serving effectively as a therapist was not possible. Once again, she was unconvinced. I was not going to argue with her on this point. Also, I told her that even if there had been no previous relationship between us, I would have recommended another therapist anyway—because of my belief that in this situation a female therapist was warranted. I informed her that I believed she might be more receptive to comments about her daughter's sexuality if they came from a woman. She agreed that this would probably be the case, because both she and her husband were firmly convinced that all men—even psychiatrists—were obsessed with sex (with the exception of Virginia's husband, of course). Accordingly, I referred the family to a female colleague with whom they lasted about two sessions. My colleague informed me that the mother left claiming she would have no further involvement with therapy because all psychiatrists (regardless of sex) were obsessed with sex and she would have to find another way to insure that her daughter would be a virgin when she got married.

This vignette is presented as an example of a situation in which a parent's pathological attitudes about sex could contribute to psychopathology in an adolescent. Fortunately for Sally she somehow avoided developing psychopathological reactions to her mother's attempts to indoctrinate her. The most likely outcome for Sally would have been some identification with her mother's obsession, which she might have transmitted down yet another generation. However, as mentioned, I suspect that the more sexually free environment in which she grew up probably served to counterbalance her mother's influence and put her on a more reasonable course. Another possible outcome of such indoctrination could have been sexual promiscuity. Certainly the mother's preoccupation with sex provided her with fantasy gratifications; however, she utilized the mechanism of reaction formation to assuage the guilt she felt over her sexual cravings. Each time she told herself she would not have sex until she got married, she had to have some kind of sexual fantasy—which she ostensibly was not going to indulge in. The fantasy about Sally's being a virgin until she (Sally) got married must have involved fantasies about Sally's sexuality. Under these circumstances it would have been reasonable that Sally might have acted out her mother's unconscious wishes. We do not know more than a fraction of those factors that determine the way in which psychopathology will develop and the factors that prevent its occuring. My hope is that Sally has finally interrupted the traditional psychopathology of her family heritage.

Now to another example of how pathological sexual attitudes in a parent can produce pathological sexual behavior in an adolescent. Many years ago, while I was serving as a psychiatrist in the military, a colonel once came to me, quite depressed, claiming that this was the most painful and humiliating day of his life. The story, he stated, began 17 years previously when his wife gave birth to their oldest, a boy: "The obstetrician came out of the delivery room and told me that my wife had just given birth to a boy and that both she and the child were doing fine. The first thought that came to my mind was, 'The thing I fear most is that this boy will grow up to be a homosexual. I hope I never live to see that day.' And so, in order to prevent that terrible thing from happening, I bought him these porno books when he was three and four years old. I bought both homosexual and heterosexual porno books. I showed him the pictures in each and explained to him how the things that the men were doing to each other were *bad*, and how the things the men and women were doing together were *good*. When he was 13 years old, and started to mature physically, I told him that he never had to worry about sexual frustration, because I was going to take him to a 'nice lady' who was going to teach him about sex. So I took him to a house of prostitution where he had his first experience with a woman. I told him that anytime he wanted money to go back I would give it to him. And last night, Doctor, the thing I was most terrified of, occurred. The military police came and informed me that they had found him in bed with a sergeant engaged in homosexual activities."

This boy was almost destined to become homosexual, so great were his father's unconscious pressures on him to go in this direction. The boy's compliance was in part related to his recognition, at some level, that a homosexual was exactly what his father wanted him to be. With such programming, with such inculcation of homosexual imagery, with so many warnings to stay away, the child could not but be tempted. This father, although he had never engaged in a homosexual act himself (in fact, he exhibited disgust and anger toward anyone who had), was a man who basically had strong homosexual inclinations that he could not admit to himself. His preoccupation with the fantasy that his son might become a homosexual was basically the wish that he do so—disguised as a fear. The image that appears in a person's mind is the most important manifestation of his or her genuine wish. The words that one conjures up in association with the image can serve to deny the wish's true intent. The thought "I hope he doesn't grow up to become a homosexual" reflected the father's basic wish that the boy do so—to satisfy vicariously, through his son, his own unconscious wish to become one. Putting the desire in the negative, or in the form of a fear, served to lessen guilt over unconscious awareness of the basic wish. The boy was driven to comply with his father's wish, and allowing disclosure was most probably his way of communicating his compliance. I obtained some verification of this subsequently when I learned that the father wanted exact details of the nature of the boy's homosexual involvement. It was clear that he was then gaining vicarious gratification from these explanations.

The Divorce Situation

Parents who are actively embroiled in divorce conflicts may consciously and unconsciously sanction pathological behavior in their children. One of the more common types of pathological behavior engendered in children by divorce is the utilization of the youngster as an ally and as a weapon in the divorce war. Both parents try to enlist the aid of all the "troops" they can recruit, and children may serve as the central warriors. Elsewhere (1976) I have described in detail this phenomenon as well as a wide variety of other pathological reactions that children may develop in the divorce situation. Here, I focus on a syndrome that may develop in the course of custody litigation. Again, there are a large variety of disorders that may develop in children in the course of such litigation and I have described these in detail elsewhere (1986b). The syndrome I describe here is selected as a good example of overt and covert parental sanction of a child's symptomatology. Although the focus here is on the child, in whom the disorder exhibits itself in the most blatant fashion, much of what I describe here is also applicable to the adolescent.

Clinical Manifestations of the Parental Alienation Syndrome
Although this syndrome certainly existed in the past, it is occurring with such increasing frequency at this point that it deserves a special name. The term I prefer to use is *parental alienation syndrome*. I have introduced this term to refer to a disturbance in which children are obsessed with deprecation and criticism of a parent—denigration that is unjustified and/or exaggerated. With rare exception, the disorder arises in the context of a custody dispute, especially when the custody conflict is being litigated. The notion that such children are merely "brainwashed" is narrow. The term brainwashing implies that one parent is systematically and consciously programming the child to denigrate the other parent. The concept of the parental alienation syndrome includes the brainwashing component but is much broader. It encompasses not only conscious but subconscious and unconscious factors within the parent that contribute to the child's alienation. Furthermore (and this is extremely important), it includes factors that arise within the child—independent of the parental contributions—that contribute to the development of the syndrome.

Typically the child is obsessed with "hatred" of a parent. The word *hatred* is placed in quotes because there are still many tender and loving feelings felt toward the allegedly despised parent which are not permitted expression. These children speak of the hated parent with every vilification and profanity in their vocabulary, without embarrassment or guilt. The vilification of the parent often has the quality of a litany. After only minimal prompting by a lawyer, judge, probation officer, mental health professional, or other person involved in the litigation, the record will be turned on and the command performance provided. Not only is there the rehearsed quality to the speech but one often hears phraseology that is identical to that used by the "loved" parent. Again, the word *loved* is placed in quotations because hostility toward and fear of that parent may similarly be unexpressed.

Even years after they have taken place, the child may justify the alienation with memories of minor altercations experienced in the relationship with the hated parent. These are usually trivial and are exeriences that most children quickly forget, e.g., "He always used to speak very loud when he told me to brush my teeth," "She used to say to me 'Don't interrupt'," and "He used to make a lot of noise when he chewed at the table." When these children are asked to give more compelling reasons for the hatred, they are unable to provide them. Frequently, the loved parent will agree with the child that these professed reasons justify the ongoing animosity.

The professions of hatred are most intense when the children and the loved parent together are in the presence of the alienated one. However, when the child is alone with the allegedly hated parent, he or she may exhibit anything from hatred to neutrality to expressions of affection. Often, when these children are with the hated parent, they will let their guard down and start to enjoy themselves. Then, almost as if they have realized that they are doing something "wrong," they will suddenly stiffen up and resume their expressions of withdrawal and animosity. Another maneuver commonly utilized by these children is to profess affection to one parent and to ask that parent to swear that he or she will not reveal the professions of love to the other parent. And the same statement is made to the other parent. In this way these children "cover their tracks" and avoid thereby the disclosure of their schemes. Such children may find family interviews with therapists extremely anxiety provoking, because of the fear that their manipulations and maneuvers will be divulged.

The hatred of the parent often extends to include that parent's complete extended family. Cousins, aunts, uncles, and grandparents, with whom the child previously may have had loving relationships, are now viewed as similarly obnoxious. Greeting cards are not reciprocated. Presents sent to the child's home are refused, remain unopened, or even destroyed (generally in the presence of the loved parent). When the hated parent's relatives call on the telephone, the child will respond with angry vilifications or quickly hang up on the caller. (These responses are more likely to occur if the loved parent is within hearing distance of the conversation.)

With regard to the hatred of the relatives, the child is even less capable of providing justifications for the animosity. The rage of these children is so great that they become completely oblivious to the privations they are causing themselves. Again, the loved parent is typically unconcerned with the untoward psychological effects on the child of the rejection of these relatives.

Another symptom of the parental alienation syndrome is complete lack of ambivalence. All human relationships are ambivalent, and parent-child relationships are no exception. The hated parent is viewed as "all bad" and the loved parent is "all good." The hated parent may have been greatly dedicated to the child's upbringing, and a deep bond may have been created over many years. The hated parent may produce photos that demonstrate clearly a joyful and deep relationship in which there was significant affection, tenderness, and mutual pleasure. But all these experiences appear to have been obliterated from the child's memory. When these children are shown photos of enjoyable events with the hated parent, they usually rationalize the experiences as having been forgotten, nonexistent, or feigned: "I really hated being with him then. I just smiled in the picture because he made me. He said he'd hit me if I didn't smile." This element of complete lack of ambivalence is a typical manifestation of the parental alienation syndrome and should make one dubious about the depth of the professed animosity.

The child may exhibit a guiltless disregard for the feelings of the hated parent. There will be a complete absence of gratitude for gifts, support payments, and other manifestations of the hated parent's continued involvement and affection. Often these children will want to be certain that the alienated parent continues to provide support payments, but at the same time adamantly refuse to visit. Commonly they will say that they *never* want to see the hated parent again, or not until their late teens or early twenties. To such a child I might say: "So you want your father to continue paying for all your food, clothing, rent, and education—even private high school and college—and yet you still don't want to see him at all, ever again. Is that right?" Such a child might respond: "That's right. He doesn't deserve to see me. He's mean and paying all that money is a good punishment for him." And the child's mother may smugly agree that the child's position is completely justifiable.

Those who have never seen such children may consider this description a caricature. Those who have seen them will recognize the description immediately, although some children may not manifest all the symptoms. The parental alienation syndrome is becoming increasingly common and there is good reason to predict that it will become even more common in the immediate future if custody conflicts become even more prevalent. It is seen in younger children and adolescents. Younger children, however, are likely to develop more primitive and naive complaints than adolescents, but in both cases fabrications and exaggerations are characteristic. At this point I will discuss the pathogenesis of this disorder, with particular emphasis on three contributing factors: parental "brainwashing," the child's own contributions, and situational factors.

"Brainwashing" By brainwashing I refer to an active and conscious attempt on a parent's part to deliberately bring about the alienation of the child from the other parent. Often the brainwashing is overt and obvious. The loved parent embarks upon an unrelenting campaign of denigration that may last for years. A mother, for example, whose divorce was the result of marital problems that contributed to her husband's seeking the affection of another woman, may continually vilify the father to her children with such terms as "adulterer," "philanderer," and "abandoner." Similarly, she may refer to the father's new woman friend as a "slut," "whore," and "home-breaker." No attention is given to the problems in the marriage, especially such a mother's problem(s) that may have contributed to the husband's new involvement.

At times the criticisms may even be delusional, but the child is brought to believe entirely the validity of the accusations. The child may thereby come to view the noncustodial parent as the incarnation of all the evil that has ever existed on earth. Often the infrequency of visits or lack of contact with the hated parent facilitates the child's accepting completely the loved parent's criticisms. There is little or no opportunity to correct the distortions by actual experiences.

A mother may complain so bitterly about her financial restrictions that she will lead the children to believe that they may actually go without food, clothing, and shelter, and that they may very well freeze and/or starve to death. I have seen extremely wealthy and extravagant women utilize this maneuver—to the extent that their children have come to believe that because of their father's stinginess they are ever on the verge of starvation. There are mothers who, when talking to the children about their husbands' having left the home, will make such statements as, "Your father's abandoned us." In most cases the father has left the mother and has not lost any affection for the children. Clumping the children together with herself (by using the word "us" rather than "me") promulgates the notion that they too have been rejected.

There are parents who are quite creative in their brainwashing maneuvers. A father calls the home to speak to his son. The mother answers the telephone in the son's room. The father simply asks if he can speak with his son. The mother remains silent. Again, the father asks to speak with his son. Still the mother remains silent. After another minute or two of the father's pleading and the mother's stony silence, the mother (with the boy right next to her) says: "I'm glad he can't hear what you're saying right now" or "If he heard what you just said, I'm sure he would never speak with you again." When the father finally speaks with the boy, and explains that he had said absolutely nothing that was critical, the boy may be incredulous. The result is that the father becomes very fearful of calling his son, lest he again be trapped in this way. The father then is accused by the mother of showing no interest in his boy. A related maneuver is for the mother to say to the calling father after such a scenario (again when the boy is within earshot): "That's *your* opinion. In *my* opinion he's a *very fine boy.*" The implication here is that the father has made some scathing criticism, and that the mother is defending the child.

These attempts to denigrate a parent are conscious and deliberate. There are, however, other ways of programming children that can be equally, if not more, effective, but which do not involve the parent actually recognizing what is going on. In this way the parent can profess innocence of brainwashing propensities. A parent may profess being a strong subscriber to the common advice: "Never criticize the other parent to the child." A mother may use this advice with comments such as: "There are things I could say about your father that would make your hair stand on end, but I'm not the kind of a person who criticizes a parent to his children." Such a comment engenders far more fear, distrust, and even hatred than would the presentation of an actual list of the father's alleged defects. The parent who expresses neutrality regarding visitation is essentially communicating criticism of the noncustodial parent. The healthy parent appreciates how vital is the children's ongoing involvement with the noncustodial parent and does not accept inconsequential and frivolous reasons for not visiting. The "neutrality" essentially communicates to the child the message that the noncustodial parent cannot provide enough affection, attention, and other desirable input to make a missed visitation a loss of any consequence.

Related to the neutrality maneuver is the one in which the parent repeatedly insists that *the child* be the one to make the decision regarding visitation. Such a child generally knows that the parent basically does not want the visitation and so the child then professes the strong opinion that he or she does not wish to visit. Such a mother might say after a child refuses: "I respect your strength in standing up for your rights. If we have to go to court to defend you we'll do it. I'm not going to let him push *you* around. *You* have *your* right to say no, and you can count on my full support."

A common way in which a parent will contribute to the alienation is to view as "harassments" the attempts on the part of the hated parent to make contact with the children. The alienated parent expresses interest by telephone calls, attempts at visitation, the sending of presents, etc. These overtures are referred to as "harassments" and the children themselves come to view them similarly. In frustration, the parent increases efforts to contact the children, thereby increasing the likelihood that the attempts will be viewed as nuisances. A related maneuver involves a mother's saying to a calling father (with the child within earshot): "If you keep up this pressure to see him we're going to have one of those teenage suicides on our hands." If this is said enough times, the child learns about a maneuver for avoiding visitations with the father, thereby complying with mother's wishes. The next step is for the child to threaten suicide if the father attempts to visit, to which the mother can then say to the father: "He keeps saying that he'll kill himself if he has to visit you."

Factors That Originate Within the Child   Of course, a parent may use the child's contribution to promulgate the alienation and "get mileage out of" this factor, but it is a contribution that originates from psychopathological factors within the child. An important contributing element stems from the child's fear of alienating the preferred parent. The hated parent is only ostensibly hated; there is still much love. But the loved parent may be feared much more than loved. The fear may be that of losing the love of the preferred parent. In the usual situation it is the father who has left the home. He has thereby provided for himself the reputation of being the one who rejects and abandons. No matter how justified his leaving the home, the children will generally view him as the abandoner. Having already been abandoned by one parent the children are not going to risk abandonment by the second. Accordingly, they may fear expressing resentment to the remaining parent (usually the mother) and will often take her position in any conflict with the father.

I believe the courts have not been paying enough attention to the formidable influence of the early life influences on the child's subsequent psychological status. Early life influences play an important role in the formation of the child's psychological bond to the parent who was the primary caretaker during the earliest years. Courts have been giving too much weight to present-day involvement and ignoring the residual contributions of early bonding to present experiences. Mothers have been much more often the primary custodial parents during the child-rearing process. This produces a bond between the two that results in strong attachment cravings when there is a rupture of the relationship. Accordingly, when there is a threatened disruption of this relationship by a "sex-blind" judge or joint-custodial mandate, mother and child fight it vigorously. Commonly, the mother brainwashes the child and uses him or her as a weapon to sabotage the father's attempts to gain primary custody. And the children develop their own scenarios, as well, in an attempt to preserve this bond. I believe that residua of the early influences are playing an important role in the attempts on the part of both parties to maintain the attachment bond. Many of the preposterous, naive, and absurd complaints described above in the initial description of the syndrome are examples of the kinds of contributions and scenarios children create by themselves. These include such complaints as they only smiled for a happy, family photograph because their father has threatened to hit them, that they hate all members of their father's extended family, that they really want to throw his presents in the garbage, that they never want to see him again in their whole lives, etc.

Situational Factors   Often situational factors are conducive to the development of the disorder. Most parents in a custody conflict know that time is on the side of the custodial parent. They appreciate that the longer the child remains with a particular parent, the greater the likelihood the child will fear and resist moving to the home of the other. One way for a child to deal with this fear is to denigrate the noncustodial parent with criticisms that justify the child's remaining in the custodial home. For example, a child's parent dies and the grandparents take over the care of the child. Although at first the surviving spouse may welcome their involvement, there are many cases in which the grandparents subsequently litigate for custody of the child. The child may then develop formidable resentment against the remaining parent in order to insure that he or she will remain with the grandparents, the people whom the child has come to view as preferable parents.

In one case I was involved with, two girls developed this disorder after their mother, with whom they were living, met a man who lived in Colorado. The mother then decided to move there with the two girls. The father brought the mother to court in an attempt to restrain her from moving out of the state with the children. Whereas previously there had been a good relationship with their father, the girls gradually developed increasing hatred of him as their mother became progressively embroiled in the litigation. It was clear that the disorder would not have arisen had the mother not met a man who lived in Colorado, a man whom she wished to marry.

We are now observing another phenomenon that is contributing to the development of the parental alienation syndrome: the widespread attention being given to the sexual abuse of children by parents. Heretofore, the consensus among those who worked with sexually-abused children was that it was extremely rare for a child to fabricate sexual abuse. This is no longer the case. A child's accusation of a parent's sexual abuse can now be a powerful weapon in the alienation campaign. A vengeful parent may exaggerate a nonexistent or inconsequential sexual contact and build up a case for sexual abuse—even to the point of reporting the alleged child abuser to investigatory authorities and taking legal action. And the child, in order to ingratiate him- or herself with the litigious parent, may go along with the scheme.

The argument previously given to support the position that false accusations of sexual abuse by children are extremely rare was that sexual encounters with adults were basically outside the child's scheme of things. Accordingly, having no specific experience with sex abuse, the child was not likely to describe in detail sexual encounters with adults. This is no longer the situation. We are living at a time when sex abuse is discussed on television, in newspapers, magazines, and even in school prevention programs. There is hardly a child who is not bombarded with information about the details of sexual abuse. Accordingly, it is no longer true that the child does not possess the information to make a credible accusation. Children who are looking for excuses for vilification and/or ammunition for alienation now have a wealth of information for the creation of their sexual scenarios. And there are even situations in which there has been no particular sex-abuse indoctrination or prompting by a parent; the child him- or herself originates the complaint.

It is important for mental health professionals who are evaluating children who allege sex abuse to inquire as to whether the parents are involved in a custody conflict. If so, they should consider the possibility that the allegation has been fabricated. I am not claiming that bona fide sex abuse does not take place in families in which there is a custody conflict; I am only stating that the possibility of fabrication is increased in this situation. One of the ways of differentiating between the child who is fabricating and the one who has genuinely been abused is to observe closely the way in which the child makes the accusation. Children who have genuinely been abused are often fearful of revealing the facts. Often they have been warned by the abuser that there will be terrible consequences if the sexual encounters are divulged. They tend to be anxious, tense, timid, and shy. They may fear encounters with other adults who are of the same sex as the abuser, anticipating similar exploitation and threats. In contrast, the child who fabricates sex abuse presents with an entirely different picture. Most often these children are quite comfortable with their accusations and have prepared little speeches, which they freely provide to attorneys, mental health professionals, judges, and anyone else who will listen. Their litany should be a clue that they are fabricating.

Another way of finding out whether the child is telling the truth is to place the child and the accused parent in the same room. The adversary system does not allow itself this important method for obtaining information that could be useful to it in determining "the truth." When the accused and the accuser are in the same room together, with the opportunity for an "eyeball-to-eyeball confrontation," there is a much greater likelihood that the two individuals will be honest with one another. After all, they were both allegedly there. They know better than anyone else the details of the alleged encounter and each one is likely to pick up the other's fabrications in the most sensitive way. Of course, the younger the child, the less the likelihood he or she will be able to engage effectively in such confrontations, but they can still be useful. Last, mothers of fabricating children relish the accusation and deny conflicting evidence. Mothers of children who are genuinely abused commonly deny the abuse or react with horror and grief. Elsewhere (1987a and 1987c) I discuss in greater detail these differentiating criteria. Particularly useful in this regard is my *Sex Abuse Legitimacy Scale (SAL Scale)* (1987d).

Concluding Comments on the Parental Alienation Syndrome
The implementation of the presumption that children do best when placed with the parent who is most involved in child rearing, especially during the formative years, would reduce significantly the custody litigation that we are presently witnessing. It would result in many mothers' automatically being awarded custody. It would not preclude, however, fathers' obtaining custody because there would be some fathers who would easily satisfy this important criterion for primary custodial assignment. The implementation of this presumption would still allow those parents (whether male or female) who were only secondarily involved in the child's rearing to still have the opportunity to seek and gain custody. Such parents would, however, have to provide compelling evidence that the primary custodial parent's child-rearing input was significantly compromised and their own contributions so formidable that they should more justifiably be designated the primary custodial parent.

Elsewhere (1986b, 1987a, 1987c, 1987d), I discuss these aspects of the disorder in greater detail.

PARENTAL OVERPROTECTION

Children who are overprotected by their parents are likely to become overdependent and, when older, less equipped to function independently at an age-appropriate level. I believe that if one compares adolescents today with those who grew up prior to the 20th century, we would have to say the vast majority are over-protected. Prior to the early part of this century, when the child labor laws were passed in most states, there was no age limit below which children could not be employed. Furthermore, because of the absence of welfare, labor unions, and other social benefits, if family members did not work they might not indeed survive. Although things became easier for children in the 1920s, they once again suffered privations in the 1930s—during the Great Depression. During World War II there was little time and money available for the indulgence of children. It was in the 1950s that we entered into an era of ever-increasing affluence. Many parents today, who suffered privations in their youth, have tried to compensate and give their children the things they did not enjoy in their own childhood. Sometimes they do this to the point of overindulgence. Moreover, we are living in a child-oriented society in which the importance of proper child care has been emphasized—often inordinately so.

   In this section I describe youngsters who are more overprotected than the average, who will become thereby more overdependent than the average, and whose overindulgence then serves as a foundation for the development of psychopathology. Because parental overprotectiveness generally manifests itself most blatantly in the earliest years of a child's life, I will discuss in detail its manifestations and psychodynamics in childhood. However, residua of these influences certainly manifest themselves in the adolescent period and even later. In my discussion of parental overprotectiveness I will be making much more reference to mothers than fathers. I do not believe that this emphasis is a reflection of any sexism on my part; rather, it relates to the fact that at this time mothers, more often than fathers, are the primary caretakers and therefore the ones who are more likely to be overprotective of their children. I am not claiming that this is "good," only that this is the situation that prevails at this time.

Overinvestment in the
Child's Life

There are mothers who are overprotective as a way of compensating for basic feelings of maternal inadequacy. By becoming "super-mothers" they can protect themselves from the basic feelings of incompetence that they unconsciously feel. Their own mothers may have been poor models for mothering, and so they have not acquired techniques that will insure their functioning adequately as mothers themselves. Many such mothers denigrate the maternal capacity of other mothers and view them as neglectful or incompetent. The healthy mother recognizes that she cannot devote herself 100 percent to her child's welfare and appreciates that there will be certain times when the care of the child must be entrusted to others. She accepts the fact that there will be times when, in spite of her vigilance, she will not be able to give uninterrupted attention to her child. Overprotective mothers may view these normal lapses and interruptions in mothering as manifestations of ineptitude.

Some mothers' lives are so limited that their total feelings of usefulness are derived from their children; they may have little if any other involvements that provide them with meaningful gratifications. Such mothers may be threatened by maturation of their children, whose ultimate independence would deprive these mothers of their primary source of satisfaction in life. Such mothers may utilize a wide variety of excuses to retard their children in their emotional growth and development. They may not permit their children to ride their bicycles away from the home, cross the street alone, or venture far from the home when others their age are doing so. Such mothers may view the neighborhood as far more dangerous than do other parents. They may not consider their children old enough for overnight visits, sleep-away camp, or staying at home alone—at ages when other children are doing these things.

The healthy mother has other sources of gratification and, therefore, need not retard her children in their development in order to maintain a sense of usefulness. Many women in ghettos, women without adequate education, and mothers without husbands, may have many more children than they can adequately provide for—both economically and psychologically. Yet they continue to bear them, in part because of their dread of the time when their youngest will be out of the house. When this time comes, they fear they will then be of no use to anyone. This is one of the reasons why such women may be particularly lax when using contraceptive measures. But the syndrome is by no means confined to the socio-economically deprived. There are women from every stratum of life who find themselves significantly depressed when their youngest children go out on their own. Some of these women have had deficient relationships with their husbands and have used their children to make their lives more rewarding. The "involutional depression" (a deep depression generally occurring in the forties or fifties) has many contributing factors. One is the feeling of uselessness that is experienced by people who have been so extensively devoted to their children that they have no other satisfactions to turn to when their youngsters grow up and become independent of them. Treatment of such women is predictably futile if it does not help these patients provide themselves with new and meaningful sources of gratification.

Parents' anxiety over their grown children's impending separation may be clearly seen in many parental maneuvers. Such parents may find fault with every prospective marital partner. They may engender guilt in a youngster who is preparing to leave the home: "How can you leave your poor old mother? After all the sacrifices I've made for you, how can you do this to me?" Or, they may inculcate the notion that the ideal child is the one who is continually concerned with his or her parents' welfare and that marrying is an abnegation of this responsibility.

The husbands of these overinvested mothers are often passive. They generally view the mother as a "super-mother" and are unaware of the depth and psychopathological nature of the relationship between the mother and the overprotected child. They generally support the mother's rationalization that other mothers are neglectful. They usually subscribe to the traditional view that the mother should be in complete control of child rearing and that fathers are the breadwinners. There is usually little conflict between the parents with regard to child rearing because the father typically submits to the mother's "authority" in this area. He may rationalize such submission by subscribing to the "united front" theory, which states that it is very bad for a child to observe parents disagreeing. By complying with this dictum, he justifies submitting to the mother's will and passively accepts the mother's opinions regarding what is best for the child. Sexual inhibition problems in the parents may contribute. These "super-mothers" may be so invested in their children that they have little investment in other activities, such as sex. And their passive-dependent husbands may relate to their wives in a mother-son pattern in which sex has little place. The mothers may be threatened by a sexual relationship with an adult male, but may be more comfortable with the milder sexuality of the mother-son relationship. In such situations the male child is used by the mother as a sexual-sensual surrogate. The processes by which this arrangement takes place are usually unconscious.

Fear of the Child's Anger

There are people who subscribe to the dictum: "If someone is angry at me, I must be terrible. I must, therefore, do everything possible to avoid annoying anyone." Such people do not seem to be aware that, no matter how hard we try, there will still be those who will dislike us. In their attempt to be loved by everyone, such people are ever vigilant to avoid saying or doing anything that might alienate. These people live by the dictum: "If the situation is such that someone has to end up angry, I'd rather it be the one than the other person." They go through life passive, friendly, and compliant – but inwardly hating themselves. They are not concerned with the appropriateness of the other person's anger or with the distortions that may have occasioned it; only that angry interchanges are to be avoided if one is to protect oneself from the anger of others and preserve one's self-respect.

Some people in this category are even threatened by the anger of their children and do not seem to appreciate that much of a child's anger is inappropriate and irrational. They are so conditioned to preventing or avoiding anger that they automatically react to their children's anger by doing everything possible to prevent or interrupt it. Also, they may consider the child's anger to be a reflection of some parental impairment on their part—subscribing to the dictum that the good parent never frustrates the child and has a child who is always "happy." The children of such parents become spoiled and overindulged, because they quickly learn the manipulative value of their temper outbursts. With a screaming tantrum the child can get just about anything he or she wants. Such children, clearly, grow up ill- equipped to function in the adult world—unless they find someone who will similarly indulge them, and some do.

Some parents with anger inhibition problems harbor residua of their childhood belief that anger can destroy. Their overprotection serves to eliminate all overt expression of the child's anger. They may view the child's expression of anger to be a dangerous phenomenon and may not be able to conceive of love and anger as coexisting. They may be significantly impaired in providing proper disciplinary and punitive measures because of their fear of the child's angry response. The child incorporates these parental attitudes—a process that contributes to the child's suppression and repression of hostility. When the parents do everything possible to prevent and/or interrupt the child's anger, the youngster gets the message that angry expression is dangerous and such feelings should be suppressed or repressed, if at all possible. The foundation is thereby laid for the development in the child of anger inhibition problems and the host of symptoms that can derive therefrom, e.g., phobias, obsessions, compulsions, regression, and even paranoid projection of anger.

Use of the Child for Vicarious Gratification of the Parent's Frustrated Dependency Cravings

Many overprotective mothers are basically dependent adults. Many are still quite dependent on their own parents and inwardly crave to revert to the infantile role and gratify thereby their dependency cravings. Because this would be socially stigmatizing, these desires cannot generally be realized overtly. However, they can be gratified vicariously, i.e., by such mothers' psychologically projecting themselves into the position of others who are enjoying such dependency satisfactions. In many cases a mother may gratify these dependency cravings by projecting herself psychologically into the position of her child. Each time she ministers to the child, she is vicariously gratifying her own dependency needs. She is psychologically giving to her projected self. Each time she indulges and infantilizes the child, she vicariously gratifies her own desire to be the recipient of such indulgence. This is a common mechanism. It is at the root of compulsive benevolence. Many saint-like individuals are not as altruistic as they may appear. Although society may certainly derive great benefits from their benevolence, less than holy contributing factors are often present. Vicarious gratification of dependency is one of them.

Coolidge et al. (1962) described a related phenomenon in these mothers. Specifically, they fear that they will never be able to give enough to their children and are excessively guilty over minor child-rearing lapses. The authors believe that the mother's view that she can never give enough to her children relates to her identification with the child and her own dependency needs. Psychologically, she has projected herself out onto the child and her belief that the child never has enough is based on her basic belief that she herself can never have enough. In short, she projects onto the child her own insatiable dependency cravings.

Exaggerated Reactions to the Child's Physical Illnesses

One way in which a parent can compensate for feelings of inadequacy about parenting capacity is to be excessively cautious about exposing the child to potential infection and other situations that might bring about physical illness. Such parents can then look upon other parents as being neglectful and thereby feel superior. A common example of this phenomenon is the parent who views the child to be particularly vulnerable to infectious diseases such as colds. There are two common myths that contribute to the concerns of parents and entrench this manifestation of overprotection. The first is that one can catch a cold by exposing oneself to cold air without the protection of warm clothing. There are, unfortunately, even physicians who subscribe to this theory. It is indeed unfortunate that the name of the disease "the common cold" (or simply "cold") is the same as the word to describe a state of relatively low temperature. The first use refers to a disease caused by a virus and is characterized by nasal congestion and sneezing. It is rarely accompanied by fever (although at times one may feel a little "chilly"). The second use of the word refers to the temperature of an object or place. Most important, it has never been demonstrated (to the best of my knowledge) that there is a cause and effect relationship between the two. In other words, one does not "catch a cold" from cold air. One gets a cold by being infected with a particular virus. This can only occur if one ingests, inhales, or otherwise introduces into the body the particular virus (or, more accurately, one of the class of viruses) known to cause the disorder at a time when the body defenses cannot successfully fight it. (I will elaborate on this point in greater detail in my discussion of myth number two.) These viruses do not have wings, and they do not fly around like bats in the night air. They are much more comfortable in the nasal passages of our friends and relatives, and one is much more likely to come in contact with them by someone's sneezing in one's face. Exposure to the cold (whether indoors or outdoors) does not give us a cold—at worst it only may make us a little more uncomfortable and chilly if we already have a cold in the first place. Exposure to cold has no effect on the duration of the illness. There is an old medical adage that states this quite well: "A cold, if untreated, lasts a week; if treated, it will last seven days."

What I have just said is well appreciated by most physicians and is standard medical knowledge. Yet it is very hard to convince even well-educated and otherwise intelligent parents of this simple truth. Extensive studies by the U.S. Army have demonstrated that the incidence of colds is no greater among men out on winter maneuvers (with all its cold, mud, rain, sleet, etc.) than among those who remain in the warm barracks. Quoting these studies to overprotective parents has generally been a waste of words, so deeply ingrained is this myth. Parents who can rise above their misconception on this matter, and allow their children more freedom and flexibility of exposure, will have children who are not only psychologically healthier than they were before but, for reasons that I will now present, physically healthier as well.

The second myth is that the most important factor in determining whether an individual will contract a disease is exposure to it. If this were the case, our hospital beds would be filled with doctors, and there would be no room for anyone else. Practically everyone has wondered, at some time or other, why it is that doctors don't get sick very often, that they seem to be less susceptible than others to catching diseases from their patients. The answers to this question are simple—and well known among most physicians. First, physicians as a group are not the kinds of people who quickly take to bed when they get sick. If for no other reason, their livelihood depends on their being up and about. Not too many people are going to seek medical advice from a doctor who is sick in bed. Second, there are many mechanisms in the body (such as serum antibodies and white blood cells) that serve to fight off invading germs, and these defense mechanisms are strengthened by exposure to the organisms that produce disease. Each time we are exposed to disease-producing organisms, the body intensifies its production of antibodies and other disease-fighting agents. After we have successfully fought off the germ, these defense mechanisms remain for varying periods of time and serve to protect us from future infection. Sometimes we have contracted a disease and may not even be aware of it because the symptoms are so mild. Even when we have had such "sub-clinical" cases of the disorder, we have built up our protective mechanisms.

We do children a service then when we expose them—to a reasonable degree—to the variety of infections they may encounter. We thereby enable them to acquire many "sub-clinical" infections that serve to protect them from the numerous reexposures they will inevitably encounter. Parents who try to protect their children from exposure to germs (and this is difficult to do, so ubiquitous are the organisms) deprive their children of the opportunity to build up their immunity and this may result in their becoming more sick after exposure to germs than they would have been had they been allowed the usual exposures. Although some children are constitutionally very susceptible to infection, most who are considered to be in this category do not differ from others in their germ-resisting mechanisms. They are different from other children by having parents with phobias and germ preoccupations.

This type of overprotectiveness may bring about the very disorders such parents are ostensibly trying to avoid. Frequent references to sickness provide children with preoccupations they might not have otherwise entertained and introduce modes of behavior that might not have entered so readily into the child's

scheme of things. The sickness adaptation enters the child's repertoire and thereby increases the likelihood that he or she will feign or
exaggerate illness (either consciously or unconsciously) to gain
certain pathological gratifications. Bombarding the child with the
possibility that something terrible will happen is one of the most
effective ways of bringing about the feared occurrence. And the
illnesses so engendered may be reinforced by indulgent treatment
when the child becomes ill (either in reality or psychosomatically).
The child is put to bed, fed three meals a day, entertained, and
given sympathy and understanding. Such parents may subscribe
strictly to the rule that a child is not to return to school until after
three days in the afebrile state. Even though the pediatrician may
advise the parent that such precautionary measures are excessive,
the parent will not accept the advice and will continue to indulge the
youngster.

The parent who frequently visualizes a child to be ill (or on the
verge of an illness) – when there is no evidence for sickness or real
danger of such – reveals a basic wish that the child be sick. There are
many reasons why such a mother might want a child to be ill. The
sick child can enable the mother to satisfy vicariously her own
dependency needs, because each time she unconsciously ministers
to the sick child she is ministering to her own projected self. In
addition, taking care of the helpless child provides her with an
enhanced sense of usefulness and may thereby provide her with an
opportunity to prove her competence as a parent. This is especially
likely for the parent with feelings of parental inadequacy.

Visualizing or anticipating a child's illness can serve as an
outlet for parental hostility. All relationships are ambivalent, and in
even the most loving relationship there is some hostility. Living in
close proximity with another person must, by the very nature of
living, at times frustrate us. And this is especially the case with
children who may cause us more frustration and inconvenience
than many adults. Infants get up at all hours of the night, wet, soil,
make irrational demands, need our constant surveillance, etc.
Accordingly, they inevitably produce angry feelings in us and, at
times, the thought that we would have been better off without
them. Some parents, however, feel very guilty about such thoughts
and believe that some fine folks somewhere have no such ambivalence – but have only loving feelings toward their children. Because
such hostility may not be admitted comfortably to conscious aware-

ness, it is repressed and may be released via a variety of disguise mechanisms—one of which is to imagine that the child is physically ill. Each time a visual image of the child's illness appears, the wish that the child be sick is thereby gratified. However, the guilt over this wish is assuaged and/or alleviated by the associated fear that the illness will occur. In association with such fantasies, the parent is basically saying: "It is not that I *wish* my child to be ill; it is only that I *fear* that the child will be sick." I am not claiming that such parents *really* wish their children ill. Generally, their hostility is not that extreme and the loving components are still the major ones. What I am saying is that they are *ambivalent* toward their children and that they are too guilty to express openly their hostilities. The illness image is the symbolic expression of hostility toward the child; converting the wish into a fear serves to reduce and possibly eliminate guilt over such hostile expression.

There is often a realistic element in this type of overprotection. Children do get sick, automobile accidents do occur, and certain neighborhoods are indeed dangerous; it is neglectful to deny this. Overprotective parents, however, can be identified by the *degree* of precaution they exercise. Their exaggerated concerns and precautions—above and beyond what is reasonable—distinguish them from other parents and are the criteria by which one can ascertain whether such worries are inappropriate and harmful to the child. Children in such families may not only fulfill such parental wishes and become sick (thereby complying with their parents' psychopathological desires), but utilize the parents' fears to their own advantage. They may feign physical symptoms in order to avoid unpleasant tasks and obligations, and the parents may comply because the child's illness provides them with the aforementioned gratifications. The stage is then set for the development by the youngsters of a variety of psychopathological mechanisms that involve utilization of physical symptoms.

Exaggerated Protection of the Youngster from the Inevitable Pains and Discomforts of Life

Many parents, with the justification that they are protecting their children from psychological trauma, lie or evade rather than answer directly certain children's questions. Most parents no longer give the old stork story when a child asks questions about his or her origin, but many still couch their responses with euphemisms or other patent prevarications. Many are careful to avoid discussing in front of a child the impending death of a person well-known to and possibly even loved by the child. When the child is finally told, only he or she is shocked by the news. Everyone else has had the time to slowly accustom themselves to the loss. The child may then be told that the deceased is now "living in heaven" and leading a very enjoyable life—even when the parent has absolutely no belief in an afterlife. Children may not be told about an impending divorce until the actual day of separation. Again, they are thereby deprived of the opportunity to desensitize themselves in advance to the trauma. Similarly, a child may not be told about a hospitalization until the actual day that he or she is to go. And then the child may be told all sorts of absurd things about its purpose, for example, that there will be no pain, and even that there will be no operation—when the parent knows well that this is not the case.

In all of these examples the parents operate under the misguided notion that the disclosure of the unpleasant news will be psychologically deleterious to their children. Actually, children are far less fragile in this regard than most parents appreciate. Most are able to tolerate well all of the aforementioned painful situations. What they are not able to handle (and they do not differ very much from adults in this regard) is the anxiety that comes from being kept in ignorance. The child usually senses that something "bad" is taking place. When children's questions are unanswered, avoided, or responded to euphemistically, they sense the duplicity. They know that they are not being given the full story and may then only think the worst. From the child's vantage point, the issue is one that is "too terrible to talk about." Then, he or she may become preoccupied with a variety of fearful fantasies—fantasies far more horrible than the event that is not being disclosed. Such children would adapt far better to the trauma if they were given direct and honest explanations—at a level commensurate with their age and ability to understand.

Parents who lie in the ways I have just described are doing their children a serious disservice. Under the guise of protecting them from pain, they are causing them more problems than the children would have had were they told the truth. They are causing their children to lose trust in their parents and this cannot but be psychologicaly detrimental. If a child's parents cannot be relied upon to tell him or her the truth, who then can be believed? This problem may become worsened when the child's lack of trust extends to the teacher — resulting in a compromise of the youngster's ability to learn in the classroom. In addition, such parental duplicity squelches the child's natural curiosity. If important questions are continually avoided or unanswered, curiosity is dampened. And by the time such children reach school, they may have lost the interest in and the hope of learning anything from anyone.

Material Indulgence of the Youngster

Parents who have suffered a variety of privations in their own childhood may wish to compensate for their own deprivations by providing their children with the benefits they could not or did not enjoy. Such parents may commonly say: "I want to give them everything I didn't have when I was a child." By identifying themselves with their children and by observing *their* gratifications the parents partially achieve similar gratifications themselves. An uneducated parent, for example, may be willing to suffer significant sacrifices in order for a child to have a college education. And parents who were economically deprived during their childhood can, through their childrens' successes, vicariously compensate for their own earlier privations. Such experiences are ubiquitous and generally healthy. They are beneficial to both the child and the parent. They are, in part, responsible for human progress. Knowing that their parents derive so much pleasure from their accomplishments may serve as a strong impetus for children to succeed; and the parents' frustrations can be lessened through such vicarious satisfactions. The mechanism becomes abnormal, however, when it is used to excess, e.g., via indulgence of the youngster, especially material indulgence. This may be associated with an exhibitionistic aspect in which the children are used to compete with the neighbors' children with regard to who has the most expensive clothing, vacations, summer camps, college, etc. The children thereby develop pathological values and dependency problems in which they become ill-equipped to suffer the discomforts and privations necessary to tolerate if one is to achieve goals on one's own.

A related disorder is one that I refer to as *The rich-man's son syndrome*. In this disorder in parent-child relations the child is indulged as an extension of the parents' own self-indulgence or as a means of exhibiting the parents' wealth. This is well described in the anecdote about the rich lady and her son who pull up in their chauffeured limousine to the front entrance of an ultra-expensive hotel. As the doorman assists the chauffeur in putting the son in his wheelchair, he comments to the mother, "I'm sorry your son can't walk, Ma'am." To which she replies, "Of course, he can walk. But thank God he doesn't *have* to." The story demonstrates beautifully the principle of the child's being indulged for the parent's own glorification. The effects of this kind of abuse can be devastating.

I recall an 11-year-old boy who was brought to me because he lacked motivation in school. Although basically bright, he was doing very poorly. His father, in his mid-thirties, worked in the business of the paternal grandfather, who was a multi-millionaire. The boy stated that he knew that it didn't make any difference whether or not he did well in school because, no matter what happened, he would ultimately go into the family business. The boy's father had been asked to leave a series of prep schools because of poor academic performance as well as refusal to comply with the school's routines and regulations. Although he had progressive difficulty gaining admission to other schools, his father's donations ultimately resulted in his acceptance. His experiences in college (more accurately colleges) were similar. After graduation he entered his father's business, where he had little involvement. There, he was treated with the deference due the boss's son, but he was not basically respected. The patient's mother, a very good-looking woman, married her husband primarily for his money. Both were waiting for the paternal grandfather to die in order to inherit his fortune.

From early childhood, the father had had a recurring dream in which he was drowning. But just as he was about to suffocate, he would suddenly realize that he could breathe under water. The dream clearly reflected his life situation: no matter how overwhelmed he might become over the repercussions of his laxity, and no matter how oppressive life became for him because of his failure to effectively fulfill his obligations, he would suffer no consequences. At the last moment some magic force (his father, of course) would enable him to survive. The father had many problems. He drank in excess and would have violent outbursts when inebriated (during which he would beat his wife). He was chronically agitated and flittered from pleasure to pleasure in an attempt to gain some gratification from what was basically a very ungratifying life. The boy was already following in his father's pattern. He was deprived of nothing material and took at his whim. He had no motivation for change or treatment, and my attempts to engage him in therapy met with failure.

To want one's children to have some of the things one was deprived of in childhood is reasonable. However, to give children the idea that the primary purpose of those around them is to satisfy their every whim ill-prepares them to function adequately in reality. Such indulgence deprives them of the ego-enhancing sense of mastery that can only come from striving and accomplishing on their own. Many parents who grew up in the Great Depression tried to compensate for their own childhood frustrations by giving their children "everything they didn't have." A sad mistake. They would have done far better had they *given* their children a little privation (still possible in the midst of affluence) and prevented their the-world-owes-me-a-living attitude that is one of the effects of this well-meaning, but misguided, indulgence. The child who is overindulged with material things in order to make him or her happy brings to mind James Thurber's comment: "The world is so full of a number of things, I am sure we should all be happy as kings. And you know how happy kings are."

Parental Overvaluation of the Child

A moderate degree of parental overvaluation is normal and healthy. Parents who do not distort slightly in the positive direction regarding their children's attributes are usually somewhat deficient in providing affection. Parents who harbor absolutely no delusions about their children, who see their liabilities quite accurately, and who do not at all overestimate their children's assets, are depriving their children of a vital stimulus to growth and development.

Children require praise, reward, and other forms of positive reinforcement for their accomplishments if they are to be motivated to
repeat them and pursue other goals. Such encouragement, by the
very nature of the child's immaturity, requires a certain amount of
exaggeration and overvaluation by the parent.

For example, a four-year-old boy comes home from nursery
school with a Mother's Day card that, by most adults' artistic
standards, is certainly not extraordinary. However, the child's pride
in presenting it, the feeling of mastery he enjoys over having made
it, is clearly present. The healthy parent responds to these additional feelings on the child's part. The healthy parent is filled with
pleasure in response to the child's joy and responds with enthusiasm. These "vibrations," which are transmitted by the child as he
proudly shows his parents his Mother's Day card, contribute to the
parents' overvaluation and enthusiastic response and they exclaim,
"That's beautiful!" Intellectually, they know that the card is not
beautiful. What is beautiful is the total situation: the child's vibrations and the parents' responding resonations. These contribute to
the parents' belief that the card is "beautiful." The parent who does
not respond with such resonance is deficient in the ability to provide
the child with meaningful affection, and this particular defect on the
parent's part may play a role in lessening the child's motivation for
further creative endeavors.

There are parents, however, who go too far in this regard and
their exaggerations can justifiably be called delusions—so divorced
are they from reality. Such parents cannot permit themselves to
view accurately their children's deficits and they exaggerate their
children's assets to an inordinate degree. Because our children are
the psychological extensions of ourselves, we can enhance our
feelings of self-worth through their accomplishments. However,
there are parents whose need for this particular mode of ego-
enhancement is excessive. They have few if any other ways of
gaining a feeling of self-worth and so may develop delusions about
their children that go far beyond the normal parental exaggerations.
Such parents may then view a child as a genius or a prodigy, and
they may view others who do not show proper appreciation of the
child's unusual abilities as blind, jealous, etc. Youngsters who grow
up in such a setting may not develop an accurate image of
themselves, may select unreasonably high goals, and may lead a life

of considerable frustration. In addition, they may take a very jaundiced view of people around them and believe that they are ignorant, hostile, and unappreciative of their talents – not a situation conducive to the formation of meaningful friendships and success in life.

Engendering in the Youngster Excessive Fear of the World

There are parents (especially mothers) whose whole lifestyle is pervaded by a morbid fear that dangerous things are taking place in the world around them. These mothers are likely to engender in their children separation anxieties and a wide variety of phobic responses, especially a separation anxiety disorder. More than anything else, these mothers are overprotective. They do not allow their children to ride bicycles on streets where peers are being trusted to do so or to swim in deep water when other children their age are permitted. Running errands to distant neighborhoods is not allowed. Summer camp may be unthinkable. The mothers may consider parents who send their children off to such camps to be neglectful: "Parents who send their kids to summer camp just want to get rid of them. I would never do such a thing to *my* child." Or they may rationalize never having sent the child off to summer camp: "He (she) never asked to go." Day camps, however, may be permitted. Some of the children with separation anxiety disorder may not even be able to tolerate this degree of separation, but others can. I suspect that those children who do go are less threatened by the day-camp situation, because it is so filled with fun and games that they may be distracted from their phobic preoccupations.

These are the mothers who are forever peeking out the window to make sure that everything is all right in the street. They may not permit their children to play at such distance that they cannot easily be seen or heard. Even going around the corner may be too threatening. Some are given even less freedom because of dangers that are seen to exist in the neighborhood. Although there are certainly dangerous neighborhoods, other children are allowed to play, and the restrictions and warnings they are provided are far fewer than those given to the child with a separation anxiety disorder.

There may be a general atmosphere of secretiveness in the home which, in subtle ways, is a manifestation of the maternal overprotectiveness. The child may not be told about disturbing events that occur in the family, such as serious illness, divorce, or job loss. The child is viewed as not being able to handle such upsetting news and a conspiracy of silence may be entered into between the mother and other family members in order to protect the child.

The basic message that such mothers are giving to their children is this: "The world is a dangerous place and only I can protect you from the calamities that may befall you if you venture forth into it. If you always stay by my side, you will be protected from these dangers and all will be well with you. If you go forth without me, terrible things may happen to you. In fact you may even die!" This is the common element that lies beneath all of the aforementioned overprotective maneuvers. The child is repeatedly being told: "Watch out for this! Beware of that! Be careful of this! Stay away from that!" The child is being programmed with the message that there are dangers all around. These children are consistently being told that mother can be relied upon to protect them from these dangers. An important reason why such children fear going to school is that, for the first time, there is an enforced separation from the mother. Although the school doors are not actually locked, there is formidable social pressure for the child to remain there. The child who wants to go home is viewed as infantile, still "a baby," and is likely to suffer social stigma. In the school situation such children are captive. They are exposed to the dangers they have been taught await them when not under mother's protection. And they cannot readily run home to reassure themselves that their mothers are not suffering some calamity if this is one of their concerns.

Most often, the fear of school does not exist in isolation. Refusal is a common concomitant. Generally, the younger the child the greater is the fear element. And the older the child, the greater is the refusal element. But even the younger, panicky child will usually exhibit a refusal element. An adolescent is more likely to present as school refusal; he or she may even rationalize what is actually fear with professions of refusal. If the adolescent stays at home when not in school, then the fear element is probably dominant. However, if the adolescent spends time with friends outside the home, then the disorder should more properly be referred to as a school refusal problem or truancy. In the latter case, the term *school phobia*, or *separation anxiety disorder*, is not appropriate in that the child is not exhibiting the characteristic dependent tie to the mother.

When leaving the home in the morning the child frequently complains of a variety of *physical symptoms:* headache, nausea, vomiting, diarrhea, fever, stomachache, low-grade fever, etc. These symptoms are usually physiological concomitants of the fear and/or anxiety. Typically they are indulged by the mother, and it is difficult, if not impossible, to convince her that no physical disease is usually present. She may accuse the physician who advises her to ignore or not to indulge these symptoms of being insensitive and even deficient as a doctor for taking such a blasé attitude toward physical illness. She may also justify keeping the child home on the grounds that she doesn't wish to expose the other children in the classroom to possible communicable disease.

Children with a separation anxiety disorder will often exhibit a wide variety of other fears. They may fear visiting other children's homes when unaccompanied by their mothers. Overnight visits may be impossible. Sleep-away camp is often unthinkable, and even summer day camps may be out of the question. These children are often afraid of the dark and will insist upon night-lights in their bedrooms. All children linger at bedtime and find a variety of excuses for keeping parents close by to help assuage the "separation anxiety" they experience before going to sleep. These children exhibit even more fears of such nighttime "separation."

Children with separation anxiety disorder may be afraid to go on errands in the neighborhood when other children their age are eager for such growth experiences. They may be afraid to stay in their rooms alone or venture alone into remote parts of their own homes, such as the attic or the basement. Many young children are afraid of dogs and other animals. These children persist in exhibiting such fears beyond the age when most children no longer manifest them. Many children, especially younger ones, are fearful when their parents go out for an evening. But these children are even more fearful of being left with babysitters and dread the prospect of their parents going out for an evening. They are usually more fearful of new situations than other children their age. And a whole list of other fears may be present, such as fear of monsters, muggers, strangers, plane travel, and dying.

In addition to the aforementioned fears, other personality difficulties are often present. These children tend to be demanding, coercive, and manipulative. This is especially the case with regard to the school situation. Upon being cajoled or pressured into going to school, a child may state, "If you make me go to school, I'll jump out of the window." Unfortunately, the parents of these children tend to take such threats more seriously than is warranted. There is a grandiosity to these children that relates to the pampering and indulgence their parents provide. Often they act as if they were the masters and their parents the slaves. Coolidge et al. (1962) emphasize these children's exaggerated sense of infantile omnipotence. Leventhal and Sills (1964) propose that a central personality characteristic of these children is their grandiose and unrealistic self-image. They too consider this to relate to the narcissism and feelings of omnipotence engendered by the parental overprotectiveness. They describe how these children's aggrandized self-image is threatened in the more egalitarian school situation, so they thereby crave to retreat home where their narcissistic gratifications can be indulged.

The mothers of these children are often phobic themselves. They may be agoraphobic, e.g., they may be afraid to drive in open places, or even drive at all. They may be afraid of crowds or airplanes. They may be afraid to travel alone and are thus tied down to their homes. Some are claustrophobics. Such mothers serve as models for their children's phobias. It is by identification with the parental model that we see another contributing factor. Eisenberg (1958) emphasizes the mother's communication of her anxiety to the child. It is not so much by word as through gestures, attitudes, and facial expressions. The mother fears the cold, impersonal attitude of the school, and she serves as a model for such fear for her child. In addition, the mother's very life style reiterates the basic message that the world is a dangerous place. The mother sees dangers where others do not, or she exaggerates dangers that others consider to be mild.

As was true of other types of overprotectiveness thus far described in this section, the fathers of children with separation anxiety disorder tend to be passive in their relationships with their wives. They tend to view their wives' overprotectiveness as a parental asset. Some will consider the mother to be the expert in the home, and they view themselves to be the experts in the workplace. Accordingly, they bow to her authority. However, they may not only defer to her in the child-rearing realm, but in other areas as well. Basically, many of these men are dependent individuals themselves and gratify their longings for a passive-dependent relationship in their marriages. The weakness of such fathers makes them poor models for identification and does not engender in their children a sense of security. This further contributes to their youngsters' separation anxieties and feelings of vulnerability in their relationship with a world that they have come to view as hostile and dangerous.

The Complementary Psychodynamic Patterns of the Mother and Child   At this point I present what I consider to be a central psychodynamic pattern in the etiology of the separation anxiety disorder. To the best of my knowledge, this formulation has not been presented elsewhere, (with the exception of my own previous publication, 1984). It comes from my observations of these children and their parents over many years. As is true for all psychodynamic formulations, it is a speculation. However, it is a speculation that I believe warrants serious consideration when one attempts to understand what is going on with these children and their families.

To understand better this somewhat complex formulation, it is best to begin with the mother. I present here what I consider to be a typical picture, a composite of many mothers I have seen whose children exhibit a pathological degree of separation anxiety. As mentioned, she is often a dependent person, still dependent on the maternal grandmother. Consciously or unconsciously, she did not wish to leave the home of the maternal grandmother, but submitted to social pressures to leave home and marry. However, she did so with a neurotic compromise in that she still maintains her dependent tie to the maternal grandmother. She may live close to the maternal grandmother or, if not, she still maintains very strong and frequent ties. Not only did she basically not wish to marry, but, in addition, she did not wish to assume the role of child rearer. Basically, she wished to remain a child in the home of her own mother. Accordingly, she resents the burden of raising her child and is basically angry at him or her. (Coolidge et al., emphasized this factor in the etiology of this disorder.) She cannot allow herself to accept these unloving feelings because of the guilt they would evoke in her. She deals with her hostility toward the child by reaction formation. Each time she envisions some calamity befalling the child, she gratifies in fantasy her basic wish that the child die. But she is too guilty to accept the fact that she harbors such death wishes within herself and so transforms the wish into a fear (an extremely common mechanism). It is not, then, that she *wishes* the child to be harmed, but that she *fears* that the child would be harmed. To fear a child's death is socially acceptable; to wish it is not. But the fantasy provides partial gratification of the wish, whether or not she views it as a wish or a fear. She tries to keep the child constantly at her side in order to reassure herself that her hostile wishes have not been fulfilled. Accordingly, she is forever peeking out the window to make sure that the child is fine and fears his or her going around the corner because from that vantage point she cannot reassure herself that the child has not been harmed. It is around the corner especially that the child may be hit by a car, mugged, raped, etc. In school, as well, she is deprived of such reassurance.

It is important to appreciate that when I say these mothers harbor death wishes toward the child, I am not saying that they actually wish the child to be dead. Our unconscious minds utilize primitive mechanisms to represent thoughts and feelings, mechanisms that often "exaggerate to make a point." Visualizing the child as dead is a way of symbolically representing the hostility the mother harbors toward the child. It must also be appreciated that the mother's "death wishes" are really only one aspect of her feelings toward the child. Like all human relations, the mother-child relationship is ambivalent. Deep loving feelings are present as well, and the mother of a school-phobic child would generally be devastated if her child were to die—the intense hostility notwithstanding.

The anger they originally felt at the prospect of rearing a child becomes intensified over the years as the demands on these mothers increase. She becomes increasingly angry at the child because of the drainage of her energy and increasingly guilty over the direct expression of such resentment. Accordingly, there is a build-up of the reaction formation mechanism that serves, as mentioned, to allow for a fantasized expression of hostility without concomitant feelings of guilt.

Interestingly, an almost identical psychodynamic pattern develops in the child. The child is basically angry at the mother for a number of reasons. Being kept from activities that other children enjoy produces social stigmatization. Other mothers are allowing their children to venture forth into areas in the community where these children are prohibited from entering. Being made more infantile is a source of anger for the child. The children's excessive dependency on the mother is a source of frustration and irritation. The basic impairments in the mother's capacity to be a parent (more of which will be discussed later) are a source of deprivation for them. So deprived, these children become angry. They are not getting the same degree of healthy attention and affection as are children being reared in more stable homes. However, they cannot directly express this anger. They are much too fearful of doing that. They are much too dependent on their mothers to allow such expression. After all, she is their protector from the dangers that await to befall them "out there." If resentment were to be expressed openly toward her they might lose her and then be exposed to the malevolent forces that ever await to pounce on unprotected children. So they must repress and suppress their hostility. And the children too come to deal with their hostility in the same way as their mothers. Specifically, they use repression, reaction formation, and fantasized gratification. Each time they envision calamity befalling the mother, they satisfy in fantasy their own hostile wishes toward her. By turning the wish into a fear, they assuage their guilt. They must be ever at their mother's side in order to reassure themselves that their hostile wishes have not been fulfilled. In this way, mother and child develop very similar psychodynamic patterns.

In this situation other difficulties develop that contribute to the entrenchment of the pathological tie. The parasite and the host ultimately come to hate one another. The host comes to hate the parasite because its blood is being sucked. And the parasite grows to hate the host because it is ever dependent on the host and, at the whim of the host, may be "flicked off" and then may die. Although the host gains the gratification of benevolence, altruism, and other ego-enhancing feelings, the basic resentment may counterbalance these benefits. Although the parasite may gain the gratifications of a "free meal," there is a precariousness to the situation that compromises this gratification. Being at the mercy of another person is not only ego debasing but frightening. And the frustrations associated with being in such a situation may ultimately produce resentment. The mother-child relationship in the separation anxiety disorder is basically a host-parasite one. And the anger so engendered in each feeds back into the aforementioned psychodynamic patterns. It becomes an additional source of anger that cannot be allowed expression in conscious awareness. It contributes thereby to an entrenchment of the repression, fantasized wish gratification, and reaction formation.

In short then the mother and child exhibit complementary psychopathology. However, more than complementing one another, the psychopathology is almost identical. It is almost as if the child's psychopathology is a rubber stamp of the mother's. Accordingly, a therapeutic approach that focuses on the child primarily, if not exclusively, is not likely to be successful. The forces in the mother that contribute to the maintenance of the pathological tie are great and are not likely to be altered significantly by a therapeutic program restricted to working with the child alone.

It is important for the reader to appreciate that what I describe as "new" in this formulation is the basic similarity between the psychodynamic patterns of the mother and child. The mechanisms of repression, fantasized gratification, and reaction formation are well-known mechanisms and have been described in a wide variety of psychogenic disorders. In addition, it is important to reiterate that when I say "death wish" here I do not believe that the mother really wants the child to die. In fact, were the child to die, it might very well be the greatest tragedy ever to befall the mother (and, obviously, the child). Rather, I am referring to the primitive unconscious impulses that exist within all of us. All human relationships are ambivalent. All have a combination of hostile wishes and loving feelings. And the hostility, on occasion, can become formidable – to the point where there may be transient wishes that the other person be removed. When all is balanced out, the mother basically does not want the child dead. The death wish is a primitive expression of the intense hostile feelings that may exist in all relationships and which exist to a greater degree in both the mother and child when a separation anxiety disorder is present.

Separation Anxieties in the Adolescent   The separation anxiety disorder is most often diagnosed in the prepubertal years. It is unrealistic, however, to expect that such programming is going to reduce itself significantly in the adolescent period. Although some reduction may inevitably accompany the child's physical growth and development, with its accompanying autonomy, residua of the early separation anxieties are likely to manifest themselves in the teen period. The refusal element may be more apparent than the phobic in such adolescents. If, when absent from school, the youngster stays at home, then it is likely that dependency on an overprotective mother is the central theme. If, however, the youngster does not go home when out of school, but rather stays with peers, it is likely that the problem does not warrant the term separation anxiety disorder. Furthermore, the adolescent is generally more embarrassed to exhibit fearful symptoms than the younger child. In fact, I have often been surprised about how little shame many young school-phobic children have over their symptoms. In their states of panic they may give forth blood-curdling shrieks that cause teachers to run out of their classrooms wondering who is being murdered. And yet, most often they are not generally humiliated by these displays. The adolescent is much more likely to cover up fearful feelings and utilize refusal as the ostensible reason for not going to school.

Another factor in the adolescent separation anxiety disorder relates to the adolescent's appreciation that adult independence is close. The younger child tends to view adulthood as millions of years away. It is so remote that for all practical purposes it can be ignored. Adolescents cannot utilize such denial mechanisms. They have the bodies of adults and are capable of procreation. They may even be physically taller and stronger than both parents. Such a situation may be very frightening, especially if they are ill equipped to deal with life at an age-appropriate level—as is often the case with school-phobic youngsters. In response, adolescents may regress and entrench the dependent tie with the mother to provide protection from venturing forth into a more demanding and less benevolent world. However, one rarely sees a separation anxiety disorder beginning in adolescence. Even when the overt symptomatology does manifest itself in adolescence, there have generally been many factors (such as those described above) that have contributed during earlier years. Some precipitating symptom may have brought the whole complex to a head, but there is generally a wealth of contributing factors that have antedated the appearance of the phobic symptoms.

Adolescent separation anxieties may manifest themselves at the time the youngster is applying to college. Procrastination in filling out applications is a common problem for these youngsters. In some cases the parents are ever on the youngster's back to get these in on time; in other cases (especially when the parents are significantly overprotective) they do not concern themselves with the application deadlines and thereby join the youngster in the neglect that will reduce the likelihood that he or she will go off to college. If such youngsters do go to college they may only attend those in their immediate area. These are the youngsters who have the greatest difficulty adjusting during their freshman year. They will rationalize frequent returns to their home by complaining about their roommates, the faculty, or a wide variety of other discomforts and inconveniences they suffer at school. They may justify returning home with the complaint that the kids in their college are primarily involved in sex, drugs, and drinking. Therapists do well not to be taken in by this latter complaint. Student preoccupations with sex, drugs, and drinking are to be found in practically every college—including the most prestigious. Healthy youngsters do not leave school because of the ubiquity of such patterns of behavior. Overprotective parents can be relied upon to agree quickly with the youngster that removal from the institution is warranted. Some of these youngsters may actually fail in school in order to return home. Many then quit college altogether, remain at home, and may ultimately get a job close to the parental household. And some may stay at home for years, not working, and supply an endless series of rationalizations for their failure to leave home.

ENGENDERING THE YOUNGSTER'S OVERVALUATION OF THE PARENT

It is important to differentiate between true respect of a parent, which is engendered in a child in response to genuinely admirable qualities that a parent exhibits, and specious respect, in which the child merely acts as if there were respect or refrains from verbalizing disrespectful thoughts. The parent who does not genuinely earn the first may resort to trying to get the second—that being better than nothing. The parent who says, "All I want is respect" is, in the very process of making the statement, losing it. In order to compensate for the lack of real admiration they detect in their children, they pathetically try to obtain respect by demanding it ("I want you to show respect around here"), or by evoking guilt ("What a terrible thing to say to a parent"). Such maneuvers can only cause the child to *lose* respect for his or her parent. How can the child respect a parent who asks to be lied to—either through coercion or by causing guilt?

In the healthy situation, the child truly admires many qualities in the parents and genuinely respects them in response to attributes exhibited by the parent and appreciated by the child, not to some nebulous inner quality. I am not an adherent of the philosophy that holds that true love ignores and transcends the loved one's deficiencies—no matter how alienating they may be. Rather, love is a response to readily observable attributes that far outweigh the loved one's deficiencies. When the latter outweigh the former, the terms *love* and *respect* have little applicability.

Parents who believe that they have to present a perfect image to their children try to hide their deficiencies with the rationalization: "I wouldn't want him (her) to lose respect for me." This is an excellent way to lose a child's respect because most children, as they grow older, inevitably discover their parents' deficiencies and the parents' duplicity in hiding their faults lessens the child's respect.

Healthy parents recognize that they have both assets and liabilities. It is hoped that the former will outweigh the latter so that the child will profit far more than suffer from the relationship with the parent. Such parents can tolerate the revelation of deficiencies because they are more than counterbalanced by their assets. Admitting one's defects (in situations where their revelation is reasonable and appropriate) truly gains the respect of the child. The child respects the honesty and the strength of character intrinsic to such admission and acquires realistic ideas about what the parents are really like, namely, that they are not perfect, but rather a composite of both admirable and alienating qualities.

Children who grow up with the notion that their parents are perfect will often have trouble in their future relationships with others, whom they may similarly expect to be perfect. Accordingly, they will inevitably be disillusioned and frustrated as each human being they encounter proves to be fallible. They may spend their lives in the futile quest for the perfect mate or be unable to adjust to marriage, where the acceptance of deficiencies in the mate is vital to survival. In work situations, they may be deprived of satisfaction because they are unable to accept fallible superiors and colleagues, and their continual disappointment and dissatisfaction with other relationships as well may result in significant loneliness.

The younger the child, the more likely he or she will be blind to parents' defects. The very young child, in the early years of the identification process, tends to accept everything parents do and say as gospel. Parental distortions about reality become the child's. Although some parental misconceptions are often rectified as the child grows older (for example, their prejudices and superstitions), others may not be (for example, "It's bad to be angry" and "Sex is evil"). Many things occur in psychotherapy. But one process that is central to the treatment of all patients, regardless of age, is the correction of the distortions about life that they have acquired from their parents. In my work with children there invariably comes a point, usually quite early in treatment, when I will tell the parents, in the presence of the child, that their approach to or ideas on a certain subject are, in my opinion, misguided, false, etc. Many parents become fearful that such confrontations will undermine their child's respect for them. This has not been my experience. Rather, the child generally welcomes these conversations and the accompanying atmosphere of openness and honesty. The child gets a more accurate view of the world, which cannot but be therapeutic; indeed, his or her respect for the parents is increased because, by admitting their defects, they are acting in a more respectable manner. I do not, in such situations, insist on the parents' revealing their every fault—only those that directly pertain to the child and come up naturally in the context of the child's therapy. The parents' lives need not be an open book to the child; they have a right to their privacies. For example, a father's impotency or a mother's frigidity are not problems that would generally come up in interviews in which the child is present.

I once treated a child who had a school phobia as well as many other fears, such as ghosts and visiting the homes of other children. The child's father was afraid to fly in airplanes, and the mother was claustrophobic. Both were overprotective and feared letting the child cross the street alone, ride her bike, and swim in deep water — when other children her age were doing so. The parents' own fears plus their admonitions to the child regarding neighborhood activities made her world a dangerous place indeed. The parents were able to follow my advice to let the patient engage in the same activities as her peers and this was helpful in reducing some of her phobias. However, their own phobias were of many years' duration and were deep-seated. I could not, therefore, remove significantly this contributing element to the child's phobias. In order to reduce its effects on her, I advised the parents to discuss their phobias with the patient. I encouraged them to communicate to her their realization that their fears were exaggerated and unrealistic as well as their helplessness to change themselves in spite of their wishes to do so. I considered it important for the patient to hear directly from them that their thinking was distorted.

The parents were hesitant to follow my advice, lest the child lose respect for them. I convinced them that it was important for the child's therapy for her to gain an accurate view of the world and that they were contributing to her distortions by not confronting her with their awareness that they themselves had symptoms that were, in part, the result of false notions about reality. Furthermore, I convinced them that their daughter was already aware of their phobias and that the very process of their hiding them from her was causing her to lose respect for them. They hesitantly agreed to follow my advice, and their doing so, I believe, played a role in the child's improvement. It is important for the reader to appreciate that all psychiatric symptoms are complex and are not merely the result of distorted ideas about reality. But the correction of false notions is a central and vital aspect of psychiatric treatment.

A common pronouncement of parents to children is: "Mother knows best" or "Father knows best." If believed by the child, this kind of remark tends to provide him or her with a distorted view of parental assets. If disbelieved, it lessens the child's respect for the parent because of the intrinsic duplicity of the statement. This kind of comment, however, has additional implications. Generally, parents who profess it mean well and hope that their children's adherence to the principle will serve them well. It is usually true that when there is a difference of opinion between a mother and an infant or very young child, the mother's position is the more prudent one. However, some parents continue to imbue this concept into their children long after it is appropriate. As a result, the children may continue to rely excessively on their parents' advice, beyond the age when they should be making many decisions on their own. They may continue to the point where their own opinions about what is best for themselves should, at least, be given serious consideration and may, indeed, be better-advised than those of the parents. In addition to fostering dependency, such comments also tend to undermine the child's self-esteem. Implied in the notion that mother is always smarter, is the idea that the child is always dumber. Resentment toward the parent inevitably arises in response to such implications, and continual advice from an omniscient parent cannot but lower the child's self-esteem even further.

For the very young child, absolute decisions by the parents are most often necessary. The child cannot appreciate the subtleties, shades of meaning, or the arguments for and against a particular decision. Even for controversial subjects, such as whether or not to allow thumb-sucking and pacifiers, the parent should weigh the pros and cons, come to a decision, and then follow through with the chosen approach. Benevolent despotism, I believe, is the best form of government for children and other primitive peoples. As children grow older, however, they can appreciate more of the complexities of life and should be told, in a controversial situation, whether or not their parents are certain about their decision. If *some* course of action is warranted, it is best taken, even if ambivalently; but the parents' lack of certainty should be communicated to the child without shame or hesitation. For example, "We don't know whether you'll be better off at Camp A or Camp B. They're different kinds of camps. Let's try Camp A this summer. If it doesn't work out, we'll try Camp B next summer." Such an approach helps the child appreciate that parents are fallible and not omniscient. It does not undermine respect because, as already mentioned, admitting occasional deficiencies and fallibilities enhances, rather than detracts from, the child's respect for a parent.

In the adolescent period, as discussed in detail in Chapter One, youngsters need to view their parents as backward, old-fashioned, pig-headed, etc. This makes it easier for them to leave their homes and go off into a world which, in reality, is never going to treat them with as much love, tolerance, and willingness to sacrifice as their parents. Perfect parents make it more difficult for the adolescent to find flaws. Denigration of the parents also serves the purpose of helping the adolescent compensate for feelings of low self-worth. Although adolescents may profess superiority over their parents, the reality is that adolescents are not capable of independent functioning in our complex industrialized society and so their feelings of independence and superiority have delusional elements. If, however, the adolescent does indeed have certain areas of proficiency that the parents do not genuinely possess, then an extremely salutary situation is present. For example, many adolescents today know more about computers than their parents. When they have the opportunity to give meaningful information and assistance in this area to a parent, they are being provided with a salubrious experience. Under such circumstances there is less need for the youngster to resort to compensatory delusional superiority. In addition, there will be less need to view the parents as having outlandish deficits (as imbeciles, village idiots, and anachronisms of the Middle Ages) because they have real "deficiencies" that the adolescent does not possess.

SEXUAL PROBLEMS

With the exception of sex abuse, sexual problems are not generally common prior to the age of puberty. My experience has been that a sexual explanation is rarely applicable when attempting to understand the psychiatric difficulties of children below the pubertal period. In adolescence and thereafter, sexual issues may be central elements in the formation and perpetuation of a patient's psychopathology. Although I believe that Freud gave too much attention to sexual factors—and thereby neglected other important elements in the development and perpetuation of psychopathology—the sexual factor is still an important one. In order for the reader to understand better my views on the sexual difficulties of adolescents, I will first present my understanding of the Oedipus complex because it so frequently is brought in when discussing sexual problems—at any age. An understanding of my views on this issue will place the reader in a better position to appreciate my opinions on the other sexual problems of adolescence to be discussed in this section. I will give particular attention to the sexual problems that may arise in stepfamilies and to homosexuality. Although other sexual difficulties certainly may appear in adolescence, the ones that I focus on here are those with which I have had the greatest experience.

Oedipal Problems

Freud's Theory of the Oedipus Complex   Freud described the Oedipus complex as a normal childhood psychological phenomenon in which the boy or girl, between the ages of three and five, exhibits sexual-possessive fantasies toward the opposite-sexed parent and simultaneously views the same-sexed parent as a rival. The boy anticipates that his father will castrate him for his incestuous designs on his mother, and the girl is said to fantasize that she once did indeed have a penis but lost it or it was cut off. Freud's theory of the Oedipus complex was derived from the analysis of adult patients—most of whom Freud considered neurotic and some of whom we would today consider psychotic. To the best of my knowledge, Freud only published one article on the treatment of a child, the case of Little Hans (1909), and even here Freud was not the therapist. Rather, the boy's father treated him with Freud serving as the supervisor. In the three-and-a-half month course of treatment, Freud saw the boy only once. Freud believed that Hans' treatment confirmed his theories of infantile sexuality and the Oedipus and castration complexes. Furthermore, Freud believed that sexual attraction toward the opposite-sexed parent and jealous rivalry with the same-sexed parent appeared universally in children between the ages of about three and five.

Freud's Theory of the Resolution of the Oedipus Complex   Freud believed that the healthy child resolves the Oedipus complex at about five years of age and then enters into a six-year period of relative sexual quiesence—the latency period. According to Freud, the resolution of the Oedipus complex comes about partly via natural developmental processes. He compared oedipal resolution to the loss of the milk teeth and the growth of the permanent teeth. In addition, he believed that natural psychobiological processes also contributed to the resolution, specifically that the boy's fear that his father would castrate him contributed to the development of his superego and subsequent suppression and repression of sexual fantasies toward the mother (S. Freud, 1924). By psychologically identifying with his father's superego, the boy incorporates his father's dictates against incest and thereby inhibits expression of his sexual designs on his mother. He thereby protects himself from his father's castrating him. He simultaneously carries down other elements of his father's superego and thereby incorporates other family and social rules. Freud held that the therapist's role in helping children alleviate oedipal problems was to foster resignation in the boy that he cannot gratify his sexual-possessive cravings toward his mother. However, he is consoled with the hope that someday he will get a suitable substitute, someone "as wonderful, beautiful, etc." as his mother. In short, the boy is asked to forestall gratification in this area for many years. Last, Freud believed that the failure to resolve the Oedipus complex successfully was a central contributing factor in *all* neuroses.

The Author's View of the Oedipus Complex   My own experience over the 30 years that I have worked intensively with children is that only a small fraction, less than two percent of all patients I have seen (regardless of age), exhibit oedipal problems or problems that are most readily understood as being oedipally derived or related. The remainder have difficulties that are unrelated (or only remotely related) to oedipal difficulties. And when oedipal problems are present, there are usually specific factors in the family constellation that directly contribute to the development of such. They do not arise naturally, as Freud would have us believe, but are the result of very specific family patterns that are conducive to the development of such symptomatology.

To elaborate: I believe there is a biological sexual instinct that attracts every human being to members of the opposite sex. From birth to puberty this drive is not particularly strong. Although weak and poorly formulated during the prepubertal period, it nevertheless exhibits itself through behavior that I consider manifestations of *oedipal interest*. A normal boy may speak on occasion of wishing to marry his mother and get rid of his father. These comments may even have a mildly sexual component such as "and then Mommy and I will sleep in bed together." I believe that the possessive, more than the genital-sexual, interest predominates here. The child is primarily interested in a little more affection and attention undiluted by a rival. I am not claiming, however, that there is absolutely no sexual interest at all during these early years. Such interest does exist, in mild form, and is likely to express itself toward the opposite-sexed parent, the individual with whom the child is most familiar and with whom the child feels safest. The child then has to be taught about the incest taboo: that one cannot touch parents in certain places, see the opposite-sexed parent undressed, kiss with the tongue, and engage in a variety of mildly sexual activities. To label these manifestations an Oedipal complex is to imply that they are possibly pathological and that they play an important role in the child's life. Rather, I consider them relatively unimportant phenomena in normal development, neither warranting any special label nor having any particular pathological significance. However, like all forms of behavior, they have the *potential* for becoming exaggerated and may contribute thereby to the development of psychopathological processes.

In a setting where the child is not receiving the affection, nurture, support, interest, guidance, protection, and generalized physical gratifications (such as stroking, warmth, and rocking) necessary for healthy growth and development, he or she may become obsessed with obtaining such satisfactions and develop one or more of a wide variety of symptoms in an attempt to deal with such frustrations. One *possible* constellation of symptoms are the kinds of sexual urges, preoccupations, and fantasies that Freud referred to as oedipal. The instinctive sexual urges, which are normally mild and relatively dormant, have the *potential* for intensive expression even as early as birth. Getting little gratification from the parents, the child may develop a host of fantasies in which frustrated love is requited and the rival is removed. Such fantasies follow the principle that the more one is deprived, the more one craves, and the more jealous one becomes of those who have what one desires. When this deprivational element *is combined with* specific oedipal-inducing factors (to be discussed below), then a symptom complex may exhibit itself that can appropriately be called oedipal in the classical sense. The foundation for the development of neurosis is formed not, as Freud would say, through the failure to resolve successfully one's sexual frustrations regarding the parent of the opposite sex, but through the failure to come to terms with the more basic deprivations from which the child is suffering.

But other specific factors must *also* be operative in order that oedipal paradigm symptomatology be selected. It is not simply the aforementioned deprivations. Among these other factors that channel the adaptation in the oedipal direction, I believe that the most common for the boy are sexual seductivity by the mother and/or castration threats (or the equivalent) by the father. It is important for the reader to note that the oedipal paradigm includes two phenomena: 1) sexual attraction toward the opposite-sexed parent and 2) fear of retaliation by the same-sexed parent. Although the latter is considered to be caused by the former, this is not necessarily the case. A boy, for example, might be threatened with castration without there necessarily being any kind of sexual seductivity on his mother's part. A boy might be threatened that his penis will be cut off if he plays with it, and this threat might be made in a situation where there is no seductivity on the mother's part. (This is exactly what took place in little Hans' case, Gardner, 1972). Or there might be maternal seductivity without any retaliatory threats by the father. When either one or both of these processes are operative—on a preexisting foundation of parental deprivation—then, I believe, there is the greatest likelihood that symptoms will arise that can justifiably be referred to as oedipal. Of course, one might ascribe "unconscious" oedipal factors to a wide variety of symptoms. Psychoanalysts are famous for their ingenuity in creating a series of links between a symptom and the Oedipus complex—and these linkages range from the plausible to the preposterous. Here I confine myself to the phenomenological definition, one based on observable or accurately reported symptoms and/or behavior.

My discussion focuses here primarily on boys. I do not believe that this reflects any bias on my part; rather, it relates to the fact that Freud himself elaborated much more on oedipal manifestations in the boy and had great difficulty applying oedipal theory to girls. (It is beyond the purpose of this book to speculate on the reasons for this.) It is also important to differentiate between *sexual seductivity* and *sex abuse*. Oedipal problems may arise when there is sexual seductivity, but not when there has been actual sex abuse. When there is sexual titillation, the child develops cravings that cannot be gratified, and symptoms may then emerge which are designed to deal with these frustrations and deprivations. In sex abuse, there is usually no sexual frustration and an entirely different constellation of symptoms may emerge, such as symptoms related to distrust, fear of disclosure of the sexual activity, and generalized fear of involvement with adults who are of the same sex as the abusing parent (Gardner, 1987a, 1987c, 1987d).

The Author's Approach to the Alleviation of Oedipal Problems   Freud used the term "resolution" to refer to the passing of the Oedipus complex between the ages of five-and-a-half and six. I prefer to use the term *alleviation* because I do not believe that oedipal involvements and interests are ever completely resolved. At best, oedipal problems can be alleviated. In fact, I generally go further and use the term alleviation to refer to the therapeutic aim of just about all psychogenic symptomatology. Considering the present state of our knowledge (perhaps the word ignorance would be preferable here), it is premature to use such strong words such as *resolution* and *cure*.

My therapeutic approach to the alleviation of oedipal problems reflects my concept of the Oedipus complex itself. The problems to be alleviated relate to the general problem of emotional deprivation *and* parental seduction and/or threats of castration. When addressing myself to the deprivational element I consider the improvement in the parent-child relationship crucial to the alleviation of oedipal problems in children. An attempt is made to improve the boy's relationship with his mother so that he will obtain the gratifications that are due in childhood and will be less obsessed with gaining them in psychopathological ways. A similar approach is used with girls exhibiting oedipal problems in their relationships with their fathers. In addition, such children are helped to accept the fact that they cannot completely possess either of their parents and that the affection and attention of each of them must be *shared* with other members of the family. This sharing concept is an important one to impart. The child must be helped to appreciate that no one can possess another person completely: The father shares the mother with the children; the mother shares the father with the children; and the child has no choice but to share the mother and father with the siblings. In the context of such sharing, children must be reassured that although they might not get as much as they want, they will still get something. In addition, they must be helped to gain gratifications from others during the present time. Whatever deficiencies may exist in the parent-child relationship can be compensated for to some degree by satisfactions in other relationships.

It is a well-known therapeutic principle that if one is going to take something away from a patient, one does well to provide substitute gratifications at that time, i.e., gratifications which are healthier and more adaptive. My approach does not involve suggesting to the child (as does Freud's) that he wait until adulthood. To wait for his possessive gratifications may appear to consume an endless number of years. Rather, he is told that he has the potential to gain some of these satisfactions in the present, and he is given the hope that as he grows older he will have greater autonomy to acquire the more exclusive type of possessive relationship enjoyed by his father.

I attempt to ascertain whether there has been parental seduction. If so, I inform the parents of my opinion that their behavior is seductive and strongly recommend that they refrain from such activities. At times they are consciously aware of the process and, at other times, they are not. In the latter situation, it may be very difficult to impress upon them the seductive elements in their behavior. I also try to learn whether there have been castration threats, overt or covert. Again, if present, I do everything to discourage them. Elsewhere (1975, 1986a) I have presented details of my clinical approach to the treatment of oedipal problems.

Oedipal Problems in Adolescence   The Freudian theory holds that there is a reactivation of the Oedipus complex in the early post-pubertal period. I personally have never observed this in my extensive work with adolescents. I am not simply referring to clinical and phenomenological manifestations; rather, I am referring to unconscious processes as assessed by projective tests and dream analysis. I am not claiming that I never see Oedipal problems during the post-pubertal period. Rather, I am saying that there does not appear to be any increased frequency during this phase when it is compared to other phases of life.

The therapeutic approaches described above are applicable to younger children as well as adolescents. There is one extremely important difference, however, between the therapeutic approaches to adolescents and those which I utilize with younger children. Specifically, as mentioned above, younger children must be given the *hope* that someday they will be able to get their possessive-sexual gratifications from others. The substitutes that they can reasonably be encouraged to avail themselves of during the prepubertal period are generally those of some physical caressing with mother and possibly a reasonable degree of physical contact with others. For the healthy child, this generally suffices. If the child is so charged up sexually that more is desired, it is likely that other factors are operative—such as sex abuse or an unusual degree of titillation. Even when this is the case one cannot reasonably recommend to a prepubertal child that he or she get sexual gratifications from peers. One can't suggest that the little boy play "You show me yours and I'll show you mine" with the little girl next door or take her to a secret place where they can enjoy mutual genital stimulation. Our society generally views such behavior as undesirable, and the parents of the young child who has been selected for such activities is likely to be quite upset (with justification) over such a recommendation.

In the adolescent period, however, such opportunities can be reasonably encouraged and there is a likelihood of varying degrees of gratification. Obviously, the further along the adolescent path the patient is, the greater the chance that such satisfactions will be available and enjoyed. It is important, however, for the therapist to impress upon the youngster that the best and most meaningful sex comes in the context of a relationship; however, I would not take this caveat so far as to condemn occasional transient sexual activities. Last, when Oedipal problems are present in adolescence they are likely to have been present during previous years. Accordingly, they are more likely to be deeply entrenched and therefore less likely to be alleviated. However, the prognosis is still better than that of the patient who is first seen during adulthood—by which time there has been a longer period of entrenchment.

Sexual Problems in the Stepfamily

I will begin my discussion of sexual problems in stepfamilies with some *speculations* on the origins of the incest taboo. It is reasonable to speculate that in the distant past, long before humans learned to record their experiences in writing, men and women began to appreciate that sexual relations among members of the same family tended to have a disruptive effect on family life. In fact, the jealousies, rivalries, and hostilities that such activity could result in might destroy completely the family's ability to function together as a cooperative unit. It was probably also appreciated (again this is speculative) that a coherent family produced the most stable, reliable, hard-working, and effective children. Such children then were not only more likely to produce coherent families themselves, but were more likely to contribute to the success and advancement of the society. In short, it was probably recognized that the survival of a civilized society depended upon a stable family life, and that free sexual access of the family members to one another could be a disruptive influence on family stability. Accordingly, incest taboos were created—not out of some higher moral or ethical principle, I believe, but from the practical observation that the very survival of the society depended upon them.

Our sexual hormones, however, know nothing of incest taboos. They hedonistically produce sexual cravings with little concern for whether the object that may potentially provide release happens to be a relative. We have to learn that certain people are "off limits." Lower animals learn no such restrictions. Keep a mother rat in a cage with her brood and her sons do not hesitate to copulate with her when they become sexually mature. The rats seem to suffer no guilt (like poor Oedipus did) over the fact that they may be fathers to their own brothers and sisters. But even with this long-standing history, the incest taboo is a shaky one. Even in the relatively stable, intact home the children tend not to be too strong in their adherence to the principle. In early childhood, especially, children may be quite obvious about their physical desires toward the opposite-sexed parent. Although such desires may not be specifically for heterosexual intercourse, they do include various other kinds of heterosexual activities, e.g., erotic play and the observation of undressing and toilet functions. And if there is parental seduction, then the child's sexual cravings are likely to be intensified.

In the adolescent period, when sexual desires become markedly intensified, sexual urges toward parents may become particularly strong. In childhood the likelihood of reciprocal sexual interest by the opposite-sexed parent is small (but certainly not nonexistent—as evidenced by the ubiquity of child sex abuse). In adolescence reciprocal interest by an opposite-sexed parent may be significant, because the adolescent's sexual development can be a source of strong sexual stimulation to the parent. The youngster's attraction to the parent, then, becomes even harder for the adolescent to handle—intensified as it is by the parental stimulation. It is quite common for such mutual attractions to be repressed by both parents and children. Like most repressed impulses, however, they often find release via symbolic and other forms of disguised expression.

For example, an adolescent girl may complain how "disgusting" her father is when he engages in everyday physical functions. She may become "nauseated" by his chewing at the dinner table, the sounds of his brushing his teeth and gargling, or even by an occasional burp or belch. Such disgust generally covers up and serves to repress from conscious awareness the sexual titillation that results from such primitive physical expression. Although one may not immediately consider the aforementioned activities to be typically sexually arousing, they, like sex, are manifestations of primitive animal functioning. And this may suggest sexual activity to a teenage daughter, who generally has no closer access to her father's more directly sexual forms of animal functioning. The young woman who becomes anxious when eating dinner with a date (sometimes to the point of being panicked) is often afraid of the sexuality implied by the primitive eating function. Or father and adolescent daughter may cover up their sexual attraction to one another by frequent bickering. Angry interchange can hide underlying loving feelings and serve to distract the individuals in conflict from their loving feelings that press for release. And all this may occur in the normal, intact home.

In the stepfamily the incest taboo is usually less strong on the part of both the children and the adults. Neither have had years of living together during which time there has been ample opportunity for indoctrination to the incest taboo (both directly and subtly). Also, years of familiarization lessen the novelty that enhances sexual stimulation. Stepparents and stepchildren are very "new" to one another and are thereby more likely to be sexually stimulated by one another. Accordingly, the situation becomes much "hotter" and more highly charged, and the maneuvers to decompress it more formidable. Violent arguments between stepfather and stepdaughter (as well as stepmother and stepson) are one of the more common ways in which both may protect themselves from their sexual feelings. In addition, the child, before separation, may have resigned him- or herself to the fact that the parents' bond is unbreakable and oedipal cravings futile. When the parents do break up, and a newcomer replaces one of them, the child is less likely to view the marital relationship as inviolable. A boy living alone with his mother may consider the arrangement a fulfillment of oedipal fantasies. The appearance of a stepfather on the scene robs him of the total possession of his mother that he considered himself to have had. Accordingly, the oedipal rivalry and hostility may become very intense. And a girl living with her divorced father may have similar reactions to her new stepmother. Prior to the separation the child had to come to terms with *one* rival for the affection of the opposite-sexed parent. Now that that one has been displaced, a second rival has appeared on the scene. It is as if after David subdues Goliath, a second giant suddenly appears from behind a mountain. And the child may wonder how many more giants there are behind it. Sometimes the sexual titillation, rivalries, guilt, frustration, and hostility produced by the sexual feelings between a teenaged stepchild and the opposite-sexed stepparent can become so intense that the youngster's leaving the home (to live with the other parent or go to boarding school, for example) may be the only viable solution to the problem.

Myra's situation provides a good example of how disruptive of a second marriage an adolescent's sexual rivalries can be. Myra was 16 when her parents separated because her father was having an affair with Gail, a 25-year-old woman. Following the separation Myra and her two brothers lived with her father, because her mother did not feel that she could cope with raising the three children herself. One year later her father married Gail, who had never been married before. And Gail moved into the home.

Gail was much closer in age to Myra than she was to Myra's

father, who was about 50 at the time. In addition, Gail claimed that she would prefer to be a "friend" to Myra, rather than a mother. In fact, it was quite apparent that Gail was so immature a person herself that it would have been impossible for her to have assumed a maternal role to an infant, let alone to a 17-year-old girl. Gail was demanding of her husband, kittenish, self-indulgent, and severely materialistic. She thought about little other than clothing, jewelry, cosmetics, and decorating her new home. Myra ostensibly welcomed Gail's decision that she would be a friend rather than a mother to her, but in my work with her it became apparent that she was disappointed in Gail because she was being deprived of the guidance and protection that she still basically wanted—even though she could not openly admit this. Soon after Gail moved in, she and Myra began lending one another clothing; they confided in one another (even about personal matters between Gail and Myra's father); and they often enjoyed passing as sisters.

The honeymoon, however, for all three was short-lived. Myra began to complain that her father took his wife's side over hers whenever there were differences of opinion. Myra resented bitterly when her father and Gail would go out on a Saturday night and couldn't understand why she couldn't go along—especially because she and Gail were such good friends. On a few occasions, Myra knocked on the master bedroom door and was told to go away with reasons such as "we're busy" or "we're resting." Myra was convinced they were having sexual intercourse and bitterly complained that it was vulgar of them to make love during the day. "They're just like animals," she complained, "and have no sensitivity to the feeings of others." Within two months of the father's second marriage, bitter fighting between Gail, Myra, and her father became almost incessant. Hardly an issue did not become blown up into a major battle. It was quite clear that Myra was furious at her father for choosing a "peer" over her for a wife. And she was jealous of Gail's intimacy with her father, a jealousy that was made worse by Gail's flaunting to Myra her relationship with her husband under the guise of divulging intimacies to a close friend.

It became apparent to me very early in my work that all three would probably require years of intensive therapy if there were to be any possibility of their dealing successfully with this problem. Myra was in her third year of high school at the time of the marriage and I decided that her being out of the home would probably be the most expedient way of decompressing the situation. Although this would involve her "losing" her father such a short time after she had "lost" her mother, I believed that the pains of such separations would be less than those she was suffering in this intolerable situation. Accordingly, I raised the question of Myra's going off to boarding school. Although each of the members of what had psychologically become a *ménage à trois* had mixed feelings about the recommendation, all finally agreed that it would probably be best for all concerned—which it proved to be. Although Myra's example is an extreme one, the basic rivalries exhibited in her situation are common, even though they generally manifest themselves in less dramatic and traumatic ways.

Another situation in which sexual tensions commonly arise is the one in which a man marries a divorced woman who has a teenaged daughter. In such cases there is often a greater degree of sexual expression and awareness than may occur between a father and his natural daughter. Sometimes these sexual needs are gratified through seductivity on one or both sides, although usually one or both parties will suppress such threatening feelings. Overtly, the relationship often appears to be a hostile one and they rarely have a nice thing to say to one another. However, their ongoing feelings of anger and irritation are manifestations of their deep involvement, and by considering themselves to be irritated by one another they can assuage the guilt they would feel were they to come to terms with their genuine feelings. In some cases the stepfather may be excessively concerned that his adolescent stepdaughter is dressing too seductively. He may become particularly upset when she wears tight sweaters or low-cut blouses, and fights will ensue over whether or not she should be permitted to leave the house "so exposed." Actually, the stepfather in such situations is usually unconsciously jealous of the opportunities other men have with his stepdaughter that he does not enjoy. In essence he is operating on the principle: "If I can't have her, then nobody else is going to have her either."

A boy whose father has left the home may be unconsciously unreceptive to sharing his mother with a substitute father. The hostility toward the stepfather in such cases may sometimes become quite fierce, although generally the healthy child does not react so violently to the appearance of a stepfather. If his relationship with his natural mother and father had been good, he would not be so threatened by the prospect of sharing his mother's affection with his stepfather. He would be secure enough in his relationship with his mother to know that he can still get meaningful affection at the same time that she is involved with another person. If his relationship with his parents had been poor and there was insecurity regarding whether affection would be forthcoming, the son may become excessively possessive of his mother and intensely threatened by his stepfather.

Then there is the situation in which a teenaged boy is living with his father and the latter marries a young woman, possibly closer in age to the boy himself than to the father. Even if the father's young new wife is totally uninterested in the boy and has little if any sexual attraction toward him, the likelihood is that the boy is going to find the experience titillating. On occasion, the boy's attraction is overt and conscious. More often it is primarily unconscious, with only fleeting and transient sexual thoughts toward the stepmother. Often, the stimulation is great and it may be dealt with through hostility. By constantly finding fault with the stepmother and seizing upon every excuse for an altercation, the young man can distract himself from his sexual attraction and preoccupy himself with less threatening thoughts and feelings.

Because of the weakened incest taboo that exists in families in which a teenaged youngster is living with an opposite-sexed step-parent a highly charged situation exists. The idea that therapy may bring about an alleviation of such tensions is often naive and even grandiose on the part of the therapist. A therapeutic goal of alleviating such tensions must ignore the power of our hormones as well as the conditioning of a highly sexually oriented society. But even those who have conviction that therapy can be useful in such situations will generally agree that the goal of such decompression is not likely to be achieved in a short period. By this time the youngster would have been out of the house anyway, and so one cannot be sure that the improvement in the relationship between the teenaged youngster and the stepparent was an outcome of the therapy, or simply the result of the youngster's leaving the home.

Homosexuality

The Question of the Etiology of Homosexuality Now to the difficult and controversial subject of homosexuality. No one can say that he or she knows with certainty the etiology of homosexuality. Some claim it is a normal variation in the human repertoire. Others consider it a definite form of psychopathology. Still others would say that both genetic and psychological environmental factors may be operative to varying degrees and that individuals differ regarding the contribution of each of these factors. The subject, unfortunately, often generates strong emotional reactions that are likely to becloud objectivity. For example, if in a conference on the etiology of schizophrenia, an authority believes personally that it is organic in etiology, even those who disagree are not likely to get too heated in their refutations. Similarly, those who claim the disorder to be psychogenic are not likely to raise the blood pressures of those who disagree with them. Last, those who claim it results from a combination of both organic and psychogenic factors are not likely to be vilified by those who disagree. Similar calmness is seen when one talks about organicity vs. psychogenicity for such disorders as migraine headaches, ulcerative colitis, peptic ulcers, hypertension, etc.

But if one says publicly in the 1980s that homosexuality is a psychological disorder, the speaker may be pelted with rocks and, if well known, may be the subject of public demonstrations, angry editorials in newspapers, and heated diatribes. Even in university and academic settings, where differences of opinion are supposedly given equal opportunity for expression, those who hold that homosexuality is a psychological disorder may find themselves ostracized. I believe that such intense emotional reactions may be related to reaction formation on the part of those who respond with such strong feelings. Certainly, their anger and condemnation are the hallmark of reaction formation and suggest that it is psychologically threatening for many to accept the possibility that homosexuality may be psychogenic. (Similarly, it may be psychologically threatening to some to consider it organic.)

The position taken by most mental health professionals in the 1970s and 1980s is that homosexuality is a normal human variation and not a form of psychopathology. This is not my view. I recognize that my position on this point is atypical and unpopular; it is nevertheless my belief. To elaborate: I consider there to be a continuum with strong heterosexuality on one end and strong homosexuality on the other. No individual, no matter how strongly heterosexual, is free from homosexual tendencies. Similarly, no homosexual individual, no matter how strongly homosexual, is free from heterosexual inclinations. All individuals, therefore, are at some point between the two ends of this continuum. Although homosexuality is seen in lower animals, it generally manifests itself when heterosexual outlets are not available or as a transient phenomenon. To assume that there are human beings in whom it is the inborn preferential orientation requires the assumption that mankind has departed markedly from the evolutionary pattern. In addition, one must then believe in the existence of a natural sexual variant without the goal of direct or indirect species procreation— another evolutionary innovation, to say the least.

I believe that the person who is an obligatory homosexual, who cannot or who has no desire to function heterosexually (especially when such opportunities are available), is suffering with a psychiatric disorder that is primarily, if not exclusively, environmentally induced—although there still may be a small genetic (or constitutional) contributing factor. Such an individual has a problem that might readily be classified in many cases as a kind of phobia or inhibition. Specifically, this person is so fearful of or inhibited from functioning sexually with a member of the opposite sex that he or she *cannot* do so, even when opportunities are available and the heterosexual partner is desirous of such an involvement. I will discuss in the next section what I consider to be the more common factors that contribute to the development of an obligatory homosexual orientation. Such an individual might be viewed as similar to the person with other kinds of phobia, such as agoraphobia or claustrophobia. There may very well be a genetic predisposition in that the individual has a very low threshold for elicitation of the flight reaction. Environmental factors that engender phobic responses become superimposed upon this genetically determined foundation and the clinical phobia manifests itself.

The fact that a genetic component may be operative does not warrant our declassifying the phenomenon from the list of psychiatric disorders. And this is what has happened with homosexuality. I believe that political factors much more than psychiatric, have played a role in its removal from the list of disorders. It would be an error for the reader to conclude that my position regarding the etiology of homosexuality should justify any infringement on the civil rights of such persons. In fact, I am a strong proponent of the position that one's private sexual orientation should in no way be considered for job placement, advancement, and/or a variety of other rights and privileges—as long as the individual's sexual behavior does not impinge upon the rights and freedom of others. This principle should apply equally to both homosexuals and heterosexuals.

My views are less firm with regard to the possible psychopathology of people who are bisexual or are non-obligatory homosexuals. Such individuals appear to work on the principle: If it feels good I'll do it—regardless of the sex of my partner. Such persons may enjoy homosexual activities, even when heterosexual opportunities are available. Although I am less firm in my belief that bisexuals are suffering with psychopathology, I suspect that many (but not necessarily all) are. Lastly, because of the homosexual potential in even the strongest heterosexuals, I would not consider pathological a rare homosexual act on the part of a heterosexual person. This would especially be the case when heterosexual opportunity is not available. The inborn homosexual *capacity* allows for sexual gratification in a heterosexual when heterosexual gratification is not available. It provides a vehicle for the release of pent-up sexual tensions in a situation where such release would be difficult or impossible. Accordingly, homosexuality serves a function in certain situations. As an alternative mode of sexual release one could even argue that it is superior to masturbation because it involves human interaction rather than narcissistic self-gratification.

It is important for the reader to appreciate that I am not claiming to know with certainty that the above theory is correct. It is the view I hold at this time on the basis of my present understanding of human sexual behavior. It behooves the examiner to have an opinion on this issue if he or she is to be providing recommendations regarding the treatment of people who present with homosexual urges and are considering treatment. One cannot wait for all the information to come in (it may take hundreds of years). A mother brings a four-year-old boy for consultation because he is preoccupied with dressing in her clothing and has been exhibiting effeminate gestures. One therapist might take the position that the child's behavior is normal and/or the child is an individual who is genetically programmed to be homosexual. Accordingly, that therapist would not recommend treatment. Another therapist might consider the child to be exhibiting pathological manifestations and would recommend therapy. (I consider myself to be in the latter category.) A 14-year-old boy asks his parents to bring him to therapy because of homosexual preoccupations. One therapist may consider the boy's thoughts to be inevitable concomitants of a normal homosexual variation and might treat the youngster to help him to become more comfortable with his homosexuality. Another therapist (include me again in this group) considers the boy to be exhibiting pathological manifestations and recommends treatment for the alleviation of the homosexual tendencies. Obviously, the position the therapist takes in each of these situations may have an important effect on the total course of these youngsters' future lives. Accordingly, we *must* make recommendations, recognizing that they have been made on the basis of *hypotheses* regarding the etiology and significance of homosexuality.

Although I believe that the obligatory homosexual is suffering with a psychiatric disorder, this should not be interpreted to mean that I believe that an obligatory homosexual (or any other kind of homosexual for that matter) should be deprived of his or her civil rights. One's private sexual life should not be a factor in determining job opportunities, career choice, and so on. If a homosexual's proclivities interfere with job functioning, then that must be taken into consideration. But this same principle holds with heterosexuals. If a homosexual man has a job as an elementary teacher and encourages homosexual activities among his students, then one should limit his opportunities for such inculcation. But the same principle holds if a heterosexual teacher were to engage in similar behavior.

In addition, I consider the average male obligatory homosexual to be suffering with more psychological difficulties than the average female obligatory homosexual. This may come as a surprising statement to many readers, and I have not seen anything in the literature supporting such a statement. What I say here is my own opinion supported, I believe, by these arguments: With rare exception, the primary sexual object for both males and females is the mother. She has carried the child within her own body for nine months, has suffered the pains of its delivery, and has the capacity to feed it from her own body (although she may not choose to do so). The average healthy father, no matter how deeply involved with his newborn infant, is not as likely to have as strong a tie with the *newborn* child as the average healthy mother.

In our society, where the mother is still the primary caretaking parent in most families (recent changes in the pattern notwithstanding), the earliest primary attachment for infants of both sexes is the mother. In the normal development of the boy, he transfers his affection from his mother to girl friends and ultimately to other adult females. The progression is a relatively smooth one for the average healthy boy and does not involve the kind of shift required of the female. The girl, in contrast, must transfer her sexual involvement from a female (her mother) to male figures: boy friends and then adult males. It is reasonable to assume that residua of the attraction to the mother are likely to be present at subsequent levels of development. One confirmation of such residual attraction is the fact that many more heterosexual women are physically attracted to the naked female body than heterosexual men are to the naked male body. Many more heterosexual women purchase magazines depicting naked women than heterosexual men purchase magazines depicting naked men. (The latter are primarily purchased by homosexual males.) For a woman to become a lesbian involves a fixation at an earlier level of development: the level at which she was attracted to her primary sexual object, the mother. Her subsequent lovers are in the same mold, so to speak, and are readily understandable. Blocked from heterosexual gratification by internal psychological and/or external situational factors, it is reasonable that she may be fixated at or regress to an earlier level—but along the track of sexual attraction to a female.

The male homosexual, in contrast, has a much more complex course toward his resultant homosexual orientation. He must abrogate mother and all her derivative surrogates. He must shift toward an intense sexual involvement with a father surrogate without any continuity with his previous psychobiological track. The psychological processes involved in such a path are complex and extremely powerful. The distortions of thinking necessary to effect such a transfer are profound. It is for these reasons that I consider the obligatory male homsexual to have deeper psychopathology than the obligatory female homosexual.

Common Psychodynamic Patterns That Contribute to the Development of Male Homosexuality   It is not my purpose here to present a lengthy discussion of the various psychological factors that have been considered of etiological significance in the development of male homosexuality. Rather, I will describe those factors I have found to be operative in the patients whom I have seen over the years who have presented with this symptom. My experience with male homosexuals has been much greater than that with lesbians; accordingly, I will have more to say about the male homosexual's psychodynamics. I have seen a number of boys whose parents have brought them to me at the ages of three to four because of effeminate characteristics. I have seen boys at the elementary school level who are brought to treatment because they are teased by their classmates with epithets such as "fag" and "gay." I have seen adolescents who initiated the request for treatment because of disturbing homosexual inclinations. (Those who have not been disturbed by these, of course, have not sought therapy.) And I have seen men in their 20s and 30s who have come for therapy for their homosexuality.

I believe that an important factor operative in the development of the homosexual symptom is the craving for the love of a father. In over 30 years of experience as a psychiatrist I have not once seen a male homosexual who has had what I consider to have been a strong, healthy relationship with his father in childhood. Although there may be exceptions to this, I have not yet seen them. Furthermore, a number of male homosexual men have told me that they themselves have never met a homosexual man who had a good relationship with his father. What is often lacking is the traditional father-son relationship in which the "two guys together" do things as a team. Homosexual men have not had the experience of joining together with their fathers and engaging in a variety of activities with a sense of camaraderie. They do not have fathers who proudly show off their sons. I do not believe it is necessary that these activities be "male" or "macho" such as sports and other traditionally male activities. They could involve intellectual, artistic, and creative interests. What is important is that the two together be "buddies" and that there be a sense of pride in each other. The father enjoys showing off the son and the son is proud of his father—and thereby identifies with him and emulates him. I believe that boys who have had this experience *over time* in their childhood *can't* become homosexuals. This may sound like a very strong statement, but I believe it to be the case. The obsessive quest for the love of a man is basically a quest for the love of the father who never gave it, or who gave very little. Commonly, obligatory homosexual men search the world in an endless hunt for the man who will love them, and they equate sex with affection. But the quest is futile, because what they get (sex) is only a *symbol* for what they want (love). It is not the real thing and so it does not give them what they are really looking for. This is one of the important factors in the compulsive promiscuity of many homosexual men. I. Bieber (1962), who studied and treated homosexuals intensively for over 50 years, has come to the same conclusion. In a lecture of his that I attended in the late 1970s he stated: "I have never seen a male homosexual who had a good relationship with his father. If a man had a good father-son relationship in childhood, it is impossible for him to become a homosexual."

There are many different types of father-son impairments that may result in this deprivation. In some cases the fathers are absent, or almost entirely so. I am not claiming that the absence of a father automatically dooms a boy to become a homosexual. I am only claiming that the situation increases the likelihood that the boy will develop a homosexual problem. I believe that the ever increasing divorce rate in the last 30 years has contributed to the increasing prevalence of homosexuality. More and more boys are being brought up in homes without fathers and this, I believe, increases the likelihood that they will become homosexual. Homosexuality increased in Germany after World War II—during which almost a whole generation of German men were killed. I believe this is the most reasonable explanation for the post-war rise in homosexuality in Germany.

Fathers who are present but rejecting, denigrating, and abusive are not likely to have the aforementioned healthy relationship that will prevent the development of homosexuality. Sometimes the weakness of the father-son bond can be subtle. I once saw a homosexual adolescent youngster whose father was a mortician. The family lived above the funeral home and although described as present and available for his son, he was psychologically extremely remote. First, the kind of person who becomes a mortician is generally one who must have significant inhibition in the expression of feelings in that someone who is more emotional could not tolerate the daily emotional strains of this profession. And the same emotional inhibition reflected itself in the father's inability to serve as a confidante, comrade, and meaningful "friend" of his son. The only father-son activities they did engage in occurred in adolescence when the boy was old enough to assist his father in the funeral home. Furthermore, during the father's absences (both physical and emotional) the boy spent significant time with his mother, maternal grandmother, maternal aunt, and paternal aunts. The aunts were unmarried, doted over the boy, and he could have been considered a substitute son for them. He was basically brought up by women with whom he had identified to a significant degree.

I once saw a three-year-old boy whose parents brought him because of effeminate gestures and frequent attempts to put on his mother's clothing. One of his greatest pleasures was to sit with his mother and her women friends and chat. His father was a hairdresser as was his paternal grandfather and three uncles. (Homosexuality was denied in the hairdressers as well as any other members of the family.) The father worked six days a week and relaxed on the seventh. The boy would frequently go to his father's shop on afternoons and all day Saturday to watch his father work. On Sunday the father was "too exhausted" to spend significant time with the boy. I believe that in this case the boy was not only being deprived of a strong relationship with his father (his presence notwithstanding) but was identifying with females whom he observed received significant attention from his father.

A 14-year-old boy asked his parents to bring him to therapy because of strong homosexual fantasies. His father was an extremely domineering, controlling individual who always presented with a facade of reasonableness. However, in any discussion in which differences of opinion were expressed, he maintained a rock-like rigidity. The patient's mother was passive and submissive in her relationship with the father. Neither parent had much capacity to get involved emotionally with the patient and his older sister, then 17. During his initial evaluation, he described very early recollections of his scratching at the locked door of his parents' bedroom every Sunday morning. His parents viewed his attempts to crawl into bed with them on weekend mornings to be an intrusion into their privacy and had absolutely no appreciation of the family joys that such cuddling and horse playing can provide. Early in treatment the patient described this repetitious dream:

> My family and I were in a car going up the driveway to my school. There was a little shack next to the school. I went into the shack. There was a hand there in a white glove. It was a mechanical hand. I had to be very quiet. It was very dangerous, so I couldn't make any noise. Once I sneezed and the hand went over my mouth.

On analysis we learned that the little shack, next to the school, represented the patient's view of himself as isolated from the mainstream of his peers and possibly his family as well. The mechanical hand, covered by a white glove, represented his father who did not allow the patient to express his genuine thoughts and feelings. Even the sneeze, which the patient could not control, was suppressed by the white-gloved hand. The dream was a statement of the great pressure for expression of the patient's repressed thoughts and feelings. Viewing his father as a mechanical hand in a white glove was a statement of the patient's belief that his father was machine-like rather than human. The white glove implies sterility and cover-up of "blackness" and other undesirable personality qualities. It also symbolized the father's veneer of reasonableness to disguise inhumane (mechanical) qualities.

There are a variety of other mechanisms that may be operative in producing a homosexual orientation in a son. The father consciously or unconsciously may wish that his son either be homosexual or a woman, and the youngster complies with the father's wishes—again, consciously or unconsciously. Earlier in this chapter I described this phenomenon in the case of the army Colonel who "feared" over many years that his son would become a homosexual and did everything possible to prevent this from taking place. Sometimes the fathers of homosexual men are jealous of their sons' close relationships with their wives and this rivalry *contributes* to their hostility and rejection of their sons.

Another important factor which I have found to be operative in male homosexuality is the reaction formation to hostility that is often beneath the homosexual's obsessive love of men. Like most obsessions, the obsession with the love of a man is often a way of denying a basic hatred. Considering the poor relationships male homosexuals have had with their fathers in youth, it is more reasonable to predict that homosexual men would be antagonistic toward other males rather than be loving of them. I believe that many homosexuals deal with their anger by reaction formation. However, the hostility may still express itself in the context of the jealous rivalries that they often have in their relationships with one another. Taunting lovers with other lovers is a common phenomenon. Flirting with others in the presence of a lover is commonplace. Although there are certainly homosexual relationships that are benevolent, many are extremely malevolent—relationships in which the "lovers" treat one another quite sadistically.

In the late 1950s, during my residency days, I once spent a two-week vacation period working as a general physician at a homosexual community on Fire Island near New York City. I learned much about homosexuality during that two-week period. Most striking was the hostility these men exhibited toward one another. Although typically well mannered, gracious, and quite well groomed, when inebriated they were capable of extremely brutal behavior toward one another. In fact, the main kind of medical treatment I provided was treatment of various physical traumas that they inflicted upon one another. In restaurants and bars they thought nothing of flirting with one another's "dates." Although heterosexual men and women may have some attraction to their friends' dates, they generally suppress these out of a sense of loyalty to their friends. This was not the case among these men.

I recall being invited to a dinner party by a homosexual couple. Within minutes of my arrival it was quite apparent that one of the couple (whom I will call Ralph) was the dominant and assertive one and the other (whom I will call Paul) was the passive and submissive one. Ralph ordered Paul around as if he were a slave, and Paul did everything possible to ingratiate himself to Ralph. Ralph treated Paul with scorn, and Paul seemed not to notice how much he was being denigrated. When we sat down to eat, Ralph sat at the head of the table, while Paul was in the kitchen preparing to serve the meal. Paul served Ralph first. Ralph tasted the food, spit it in Paul's face, and picked up the plate and emptied its contents on Paul's head. He screamed: "What kind of shit do you think this is?" Paul then began crying, begging Ralph for forgiveness. Although I am sure that such a scene could take place with a heterosexual couple, I consider it far less likely. These men presented themselves as "lovers"; I think they would have been more honest if they had presented themselves as "haters." It is not difficult for me to understand why murder of the homosexual lover is not uncommon.

Another factor I have found operative in many homosexuals is the narcissistic one. A heterosexual man is attracted to someone who is quite different from himself; the homosexual man, in contrast, is attracted to someone who looks like himself. It is not uncommon for homosexuals to become sexually aroused when looking at themselves in the mirror, and I had one patient who actually masturbated when looking at himself in the mirror. He told me that this was a fairly common practice among homosexuals.

Interestingly, most homosexual men have good relationships with women. Although they may have little if any sexual desires toward women, and although they may be fearful of sexual encounters with them, they are not fearful of women in general. In fact, they often get along quite well with women because they share the same interests. They can discuss at length clothing styles, hair styles, furniture, home-making, and other topics that are usually of interest to women. This is one of the reasons why homosexuals are overrepresented in the hairdresser population. The average man would find intolerable even the prospect of spending many hours each day talking with women about the topics women discuss in their beauty parlors. This comfort with and enjoyment of women as friends often stems from a close and sometimes seductive relationship with their mothers. Many were "Mama's boys" in their childhood and even as adults are quite interested in their mothers and treat them quite well. It is not uncommon for homosexual men to ask each other about how their mothers are; however, it is far less common for them to ask each other how their fathers are. Many of the mothers of boys who become homosexual had poor relationships with their husbands and turned to their sons for a compensatory relationship. Commonly their sons became their confidantes. Often the sexual relationship between the parents is a poor one, and the mother turns to the son for some kind of physical gratification — although not generally overtly sexual. This, however, is often enough to satisfy her needs. The son may also have been titillated by this special relationship with his mother and may gravitate toward men as a way of avoiding heterosexual relationships because of their incestuous connotations. The titillation by the mother may also evoke resentment toward women in general. The homosexual orientation then becomes a statement of the homosexual male's total sexual rejection of women.

The mothers of these men are often overprotective, domineering, and interfere with the youngsters' developing strong ties with girls in the dating period. Subsequently they do whatever they possibly can to disrupt their sons' relationships with women who are potential candidates for marriage. In fact, the mother may have actually encouraged the homosexuality (most often unconsciously) because of her appreciation that a homosexual son is less likely to marry and leave her. Some mothers of homosexual men had conscious or unconscious wishes that the child be a daughter and the boy's homosexual orientation is, in part, an attempt to gratify the mother's wish. The mother's position as the primary authority and disciplinarian in the family may result in the son's view of women as harsh, hostile, and as individuals who are to be feared or avoided for intimate relationships.

For some homosexual men, an important contributing factor has been homosexual seduction in the prepubertal or pubertal years. Some of these men, I suspect, would not have developed along the homosexual route had it not been for this (or these) early encounter(s). It is as if the homosexual encounter caused them to "switch tracks." Because of their lack of sexual experience they came to view homosexuality as a source of intense pleasure and had no appreciation that heterosexuality was also a pleasurable option. And residua of this early distortion seem to have played a role in their subsequent gravitation toward homosexuality.

I am not claiming to have presented a comprehensive statement of all the psychodynamic mechanisms operative in producing male homosexuality. Rather, I have described what I have found to be some of the more important mechanisms that contribute to the development of this form of psychopathology. I. Bieber (1962) and L. Hatterer (1970) are both proponents of the view that homosexuality is primarily, if not exclusively, a psychogenic disturbance and have described in detail their studies in this area. L.C. Kolb and

H.K.H. Brodie (1982) make reference to a number of studies of identical twin pairs in which one member became heterosexual and the other homosexual. These studies lend support to the theory that the genetic loading in homosexuality may be minimal and that it is primarily a psychogenic disorder.

Common Psychodynamic Patterns That Contribute to the Development of Female Homosexuality   As mentioned, I have had less experience with female homosexuality and would prefer not to merely report here the experiences of others. In my discussion of the etiological factors operative in bringing about male homosexuality, I mentioned my experiences with consultations and therapy of homosexuality in childhood and adolescence. In contrast, I cannot recall parents ever having brought a pre-school girl to me because of masculine tendencies. Nor have I had any experiences with girls at the elementary-school level being brought to treatment because of this complaint. I have, however, seen adolescent girls who are disturbed by their homosexuality (again, those who are not upset by it do not come for therapy). And I have seen a few young adult women in whom homosexuality has been a presenting complaint; however, as mentioned, my experience with such women is limited. One reason for this, I suspect, is that such women are more likely to go to a female therapist. In addition, in recent years, both male and female homosexual adults are less likely to view their homosexuality as a manifestation of psychopathology, because of the view held by many mental health professionals today that such behavior is not a psychopathological manifestation.

However, in the course of my custody evaluations (Gardner, 1982 and 1986b) I have had many occasions to evaluate both male and female homosexual parents. Some of the women I have seen who are homosexuals have become so after varying degrees of involvement in heterosexual life. Often they have turned to homosexuality because of their disillusionment with men. Some considered themselves heterosexual in their earlier years but, after many rejections and disappointments, turned to homosexuality for sexual gratification as well as satisfaction of their needs for emotional involvements with other people. A common statement made by homosexual women is that women make much more sensitive lovers than men. They describe most men as being concerned only with their own needs and as losing interest entirely after they have had their own satisfactions. Women, in contrast, are described as being far more sensitive and empathic lovers who are more concerned with the needs of the partner. Whereas one can say with a high degree of certainty that homosexual men have had poor relationships with their fathers, I cannot make the same statement about homosexual women having had poor relationships with their mothers. Some have actually had good relationships with their mothers and are not turning to other women as part of a life-long campaign to extract love from a female. This may be an explanation of why lesbian relationships are more likely to be deep and ongoing than male homosexual relationships.

A powerful anger element, however, is frequently operative in lesbianism. Whereas in male homosexuality the anger is dealt with by reaction formation and obsessive love of men, in female homosexuality the anger is the result of disappointment with and rejections by men. Accordingly, the love of women is not particularly sought as a way of suppressing and repressing underlying hatred of them. Lesbians hate men and love women. Male homosexuals are friendly with and like women, but their love of men is often a reaction formation to underlying hatred. Accordingly, they are much worse off because there is less of a likelihood that they will have bona fide loving relationships with either sex.

Other factors may be operative in bringing about female homosexuality. A woman may find lesbianism attractive because of fears of heterosexual involvements. Some homosexual women basically would have preferred to be men and such women may gratify these desires (at least in part) by acquiring male gestures, wearing male clothing, and using dildos in sexual acts in which they portray the role of a male. Some have identified with homosexual mothers. Just as some male homosexuals are obsessively involved with loving men as a reaction formation to an underlying hatred of men, there are female homosexuals who are enraged at women and their homosexuality is a reflection of their dealing with this by reaction formation. Some have indeed been rejected by their mothers and are looking for mother love from another woman. Some rival with a male for the love of a female as a manifestation of an Electra complex. Some have parents who basically wanted a boy, encouraged them to be tomboys when younger, and may have even encouraged their becoming "dykes." An overprotective mother may contribute to a daughter's homosexuality in order to discourage marriage and keep her in the home. A father who is threatened by his daughter's heterosexuality may also encourage her homosexuality. Just as a seductive mother may contribute to a boy's development of homosexuality, a seductive father may similarly contribute to a girl's development of lesbianism. In both cases the opposite-sexed partner comes to be viewed as titillating, but not gratifying, and therefore a source of frustration. A woman who was rejected by her mother in childhood may assume a male identity in order to attract mother and derivative females, just as she observed father to attract her mother.

Considerations Regarding the Treatment of Homosexual Adolescents   It is not my purpose here to discuss at length the psychotherapy of adolescent homosexuals. Furthermore, my experience in this area is not vast enough for me to be able to present myself as an expert in this area. However, I certainly have had some experience in the treatment of these youngsters, and there are some statements I can make that I believe might be of interest and help to those who are treating them.

First, when the teenage homosexual boy comes for treatment the therapist does well to warn the youngster that an important determinant of whether or not he will be able to switch to the heterosexual track will be his ability to avoid entering into an active homosexual life. The youngster may be greatly tempted to do so because of the high likelihood that there will be little sexual frustration and frequent success. When a young teenage boy walks into a gay bar, the likelihood of his being rejected is extremely small. But even if he is rejected in the first and second encounters, it is not likely that he will continually be spurned. This is in sharp contrast to the situation for the adolescent boy in the heterosexual scene where, sexual revolution notwithstanding, the youngster is not likely to enjoy immediate success with a high degree of predictability. The heterosexual youngster, then, must have the ego-strength to tolerate rejections and recognize that they do not necessarily mean that he has significant deficiencies. Rather, he must be able to appreciate that he cannot be attractive to everyone and that a significant percentage of girls will not find him particularly desirable. However, he must have the self-confidence to move on to other girls and recognize that after a certain number of overtures he is likely to achieve some kind of successful involvement. During the course of his quest he must have a thick enough skin to tolerate occasional rejections. A homosexual youngster may not have the fortitude for such rejections and his "thin skin" results in his gravitating toward homosexual bars (or other places with a high density of homosexuals) where he is far less likely to suffer such rejections. Once in that scene he is also far less likely to go back to the heterosexual track.

In the last few years, with the increasing spread of AIDS, homosexuals have reduced significantly their frequenting gay bars, bath houses, and other places where they go for sexual encounters. Accordingly, this danger for the homosexual adolescent has lessened. However, these youngsters are still viewed as "luscious fruits" by older homosexuals and are likely to be lured into homosexual encounters by them. One or two such encounters may tip the balance significantly in the homosexual direction. As mentioned, the power of these early encounters cannot be underestimated. I have seen a few homosexual males who claim that their introduction to homosexuality took place around ages four to six when they were sexually seduced. Although other factors were certainly operative, the seduction somehow "locked" the youngster into a homosexual track.

The therapy of such youngsters must involve attempts on the therapist's part to encourage dating. Therapy is not likely to be successful as an intellectual pursuit; rather, it must be combined with actual experiences in the heterosexual realm which can be discussed in the treatment process. It is important for the therapist to appreciate that such heterosexual encounters are only a small part of the treatment. There are homosexual men who have married in an attempt to cure their homosexuality and have been unsuccessful. The youngster who is ambivalent about homosexuality and who has definite heterosexual desires as well is more likely to be helped by heterosexual encounters. Others may be frightened by them, so much so that they may withdraw from treatment.

Although there may be some exceptions, I think it is preferable for a homosexual boy to have a male therapist. As mentioned, difficulties in the relationship with the father have most often been a central factor in the development of the homosexuality. Providing such youngsters with a relationship with a therapist who is warm and understanding may help to counteract the privations the youngster has suffered in his relationship with his father. Whereas the homosexual youngster equates sexual encounters w.ch love, in proper therapy no such gratification will be provided. Rather, the therapist provides something closer to what the youngster has been deprived of, namely, a warm, affectionate, and sensitive relationship.

If the youngster's treatment extends to the point where he goes off to college, then a new problem may arise in the treatment. Most colleges today have active gay communities which are not only quite overt about their homosexuality but involve themselves actively in various homosexual campus activities. They proselytize, seduce, and make every attempt to add to their numbers. This is a dangerous situation for the youngster who is ambivalent about homosexuality and trying to "go straight." Because I consider obligatory homosexuality to be a psychiatric disturbance, I view these groups to be a statement of misguided liberalism on campus. To me, it is as appropriate to have a homosexual club on a college campus as it is to have a club of drug addicts, people with character disorders, anorexia-bulemics, etc. If the latter clubs were formed with the recognition that we are dealing with a form of psychopathology and the groups' goal is to help one another with their problems ("self-help" groups), then I would have no difficulty supporting these organizations. However, the homosexual groups have no such philosophy. Rather, their goal is to promulgate, proselytize, educate people about homosexuality, and fight for their civil rights.

Although I have no objection to homosexuals' getting their civil rights, and although I also believe that a certain amount of education about homosexuality is useful, I believe that the kind of education these groups provide is erroneous and misguided, especially because it tries to educate others into believing that homosexuality is a normal, healthy human variation. A common maneuver for these proselytizers is to attempt to make "straight" youngsters feel embarrassed about their heterosexuality. They may try to get them to feel that they are not showing reasonable flexibility in their sexual options and that they are narrow minded. I believe that such need to convert others stems from an underlying insecurity about the stability of their homosexuality and follows the principle that "misery loves company." The more straight youngsters the homosexuals can convert, the more secure they believe they will be in their rationalization that their homosexuality is a normal human variant and not a form of psychopathology.

In recent years, many boys' colleges have gone coed, and many girls' colleges have gone coed as well. Furthermore, some formerly single-sexed colleges have merged to provide coeducation for their students. There are, however, certain girls' colleges that have remained all female. Not surprisingly, some of these have become attractive to homosexual girls. Heterosexual girls who attend such colleges, often because they may be quite prestigious, may then find themselves lured into a homosexual lifestyle. Some of these heterosexual girls had never entertained notions of homosexuality and, had they not been proselytized, would have proceeded along the heterosexual track. Accordingly, I consider these girls to have been corrupted. Many of these girls were not particularly successful in their relationships with boys and so became prime targets for conversion.

I recognize that the things I have just said about homosexuality on college campuses put me in a particularly unpopular position in the mid- to late 1980s. I suspect that there are many others on campuses who share my views, but who fear expressing them openly lest they subject themselves to public condemnation, picketing, and a variety of wild accusations. Although most universities pride themselves on being institutions where there is freedom of expression of ideas, there are still certain ideas not freely expressed—even in the most liberal and open universities. Criticism of homosexuality is one such example. Therapists treating college-bound homosexual youngsters do well to encourage them to avoid attending universities where militant gay groups are likely to have influence over their patients. Rather, they do well to encourage their applying only to schools where the gay community is either nonexistent or plays a limited role in college life. Admittedly, such places may be difficult to find, but they do exist.

Of course, the therapist must attempt to ascertain what the specific factors are that have contributed to that particular patient's homosexuality. Earlier in this section I have presented what I consider to be some of the more common contributory elements. The danger for the therapist is to assume that his or her patient automatically fits into one or more of the aforementioned categories. It is preferable to approach the situation with an open mind and to attempt to ascertain exactly which etiological and psychodynamic factors were operative in that particular patient's life situation. These are the issues that should be primarily dealt with in the treatment. The aforementioned recommendations are general ones and should be viewed more as external and facilitating factors in the therapy.

Other Sexual Problems of Adolescence

Therapists who treat adolescents will invariably be confronted with the problem of the adolescent's sexual behavior. As I will discuss in Vol. II (1999a), I do not believe that a therapist can conduct treatment without significant imposition of his or her own values on the patient. It is hoped that the values so promulgated will serve the patient well. And it is in the sexual realm, especially, that value judgements are likely to be transmitted. My own view is that it is normal and healthy for the adolescent to progress to increasing levels of sexual activity during the teenage period. Although one does well to try to get the adolescent to subscribe to certain principles regarding the superiority of sex in ongoing relationships over transient sex, one is not likely to be significantlly successful in pomulgating this notion with most adolescents. Boys, especially, need to prove themselves as "men" by having sexual relations. And girls, too, are increasingly viewing themselves as somehow inadequate if they are still virgins in their late teens. None of this may be particularly pathological in my opinion. What is pathological is the youngster who is so obsessed with sex—much more than the usual degree of preoccupation—that other functions are interfered with. If a girl believes that the greater the number of lovers she has the more attractive she is then she is likely to have problems. If she feels that no one will want her unless she provides sex, then her sexual behavior is likely to be pathological. Her feelings of inadequacy are likely to reveal themselves in other areas, and this lends confirmation to the view that her promiscuity has less to do with sex and more to do with a misguided attempt to compensate for such feelings of inadequacy. If a boy is merely using girls as objects, has little sensitivity to their feelings, and is compulisively trying to "lay" as many as he can in order to compensate for feelings of inadequacy, then this is pathological. Here too, feelings of low self-worth are likely to manifest themselves in other areas. This provides confirmation to the view that his compulsive sexuality is a form of pathological compensation.

Another pathological situation in the context of normal adolescent sexuality is the failure to use proper protection. As mentioned, adolescents suffer with delusions of invulnerability. A related phenomenon is the delusion that they can have sex without pregnancy and that somehow only others will get pregnant. At the time of this writing there is another reason for using contraception, namely, the increasing prevalence of sexually transmitted diseases. The most dreaded of these, of course, is acquired immune deficiency syndrome (AIDS). Many adolescents consider the use of condoms to be a sign of masculine inadequacy; unfortunately, their girl friends may go along with this. So we have two problems then that emerge from the adolescent's delusions of invulnerability: teenage pregnancy and sexually transmitted diseases. Because of these delusions, I have little faith in educational programs designed to get adolescents to be more reliable in the utilization of contraception. I am not claiming that such efforts are entirely futile, only that educators should recognize they have an "uphill fight" because of the power of adolescent denial mechanisms and their delusions of invulnerability. At the time of this writing the AIDS epidemic does not appear to have infiltrated to a significant degree into the college population. Considering the ubiquity of homosexuality and bisexuality on the college campus, and considering the freedom with which college students have multiple sexual partners, it is reasonable to predict that AIDS will start making its inroads into the college population (both homosexual and heterosexual) in the near future. When one adds delusions of invulnerability to the situation, the results are likely to be disastrous. Anything a therapist can do to encourage his patients to protect themselves from contracting AIDS (by judicious selection of partners and automatic utilization of condoms) may be lifesaving.

Occasionally, an adolescent girl will inform a therapist that she is pregnant and her parents do not know. If the therapist knows that the parents will deal with the problem in a sane way, he or she does well to do everything possible to insure that the parents learn of the pregnancy as early as possible. Such a girl has to be reassured that her parents are not going to react as horrendously as she may anticipate. Early disclosure is important because, for many families, abortion may be an option. However, the longer one waits, the less viable and the more psychologically traumatic this option becomes. In some cases the situation may warrant the therapist's not "respecting" the adolescent's confidentiality and revealing the fact of the pregnancy. As I have described elsewhere (1975, 1986a) the patient is not coming to the therapist for confidentiality; rather the patient is coming for treatment. To the degree that confidentiality serves the goals of the therapy, to that degree it should be respected. In contrast, to the degree that respecting the confidentiality is anti-therapeutic, to that degree it should not be respected. The reasons an adolescent gives for not disclosing a pregnancy to parents are, in most situations, pathological and the failure to get the parents involved is likely to cause the youngster far more trouble than early disclosure.

Another sexually related problem that one sees in early adolescence is that of stealing. I am not referring to stealing in general, but a specific kind of stealing that, I believe, is related to the youngster's emerging sexuality. I refer here to the practice among early adolescent girls of stealing certain items from department stores and novelty shops. Typically, the youngsters will steal such objects as lipstick, perfume, and scarves. Parents who learn about such thefts may be amazed and respond with comments such as, "I can't understand why she's stealing these things. We certainly can afford to buy these things for her." Often, the youngsters will steal these items, although they could well afford to purchase them from their allowances. If the parent offers to pay the youngster to buy them, the offer is often refused. I believe these thefts represent an attempt on the part of these adolescent girls to enhance their sexual attractiveness with the stolen items. They are operating on the principle that forbidden fruit is sweeter and that the perfume stolen from a department store is more likely to attract boys than that provided by a parent who, by virtue of old age and decrepitude, is viewed as sexless. Although it is obviously the same bottle of perfume, its having been stolen adds a certain allure to the scent.

Often the cure for this disorder is the youngster's being caught by a department store security guard and the parents' being informed that a recurrence will be reported to the police.

CONCLUDING COMMENTS

It has not been my purpose in this chapter to present all of the situations that might be conducive to adolescents developing psychopathology. Rather, I have described those environmental factors (both familial and social) that I have found to be frequently operative in my own experiences. I recognize that others have had different experiences and so would have provided a different presentation if they were in my place. Because many of these family and environmental factors are extensive and deep-seated, the therapist does well to have modest goals with regard to changing them. Furthermore, although the adolescent is only in his or her teens, the youngster has still been exposed to many of these influences for more than a decade and this too should produce some caution in the therapist regarding predicting therapeutic success.

THREE

THE INITIAL DIAGNOSTIC EVALUATION

My diagnostic evaluation is divided into two parts. The first is a two-hour consultation, during which I see the youngster and both parents in varying combinations. I refer to this section as *The Initial Diagnostic Evaluation*. If treatment is warranted then I will collect more extensive data, during which time I will see each parent once or twice, the youngster two or three times, and conduct a family interview if there are siblings old enough to contribute meaningfully to such a session. The second phase I refer to as *The Extended Diagnostic Evaluation*. In this chapter I will discuss the initial diagnostic evaluation and in the next the extended diagnostic evaluation. In both phases I am interested in assessing for both psychogenic and neurologically based disorders. However, in these two chapters I will only focus on the procedures I utilize for assessing psychogenic impairment. When a neurologically based learning disability is present or is suspected then further interviews and/or testing may be warranted. The reader interested in information about the tests I administer for youngsters with neurologically based learning disabilities might wish to refer to other publications of mine in this area (1979b, 1986a, 1987b).

WHO SHALL BE SEEN IN THE INITIAL CONSULTATION?

There are many ways to conduct the initial screening interview. Various combinations of patient and/or parent(s) in different sequences, with one or more interviewers, may be utilized. For example, the patient may be seen alone, the parent(s) alone, the patient and parent(s) together, or a total family interview may be held. There may be one interviewer for all or separate interviewers seeing one or more individuals at a time. Of all the possible approaches, I prefer the first interview to be conducted with the youngster and parents together, individually and in varying combinations—as warranted. All things considered, I believe this arrangement to have the greatest number of advantages and the fewest drawbacks as compared to the other commonly used methods. Moreover, I believe that the clinical interviews (and treatment) are preferably conducted by one person.

The three-person interview also provides the therapist with the opportunity to observe directly interactions between the parents and the patient. Seeing the parents alone in the initial interview deprives the therapist of first-hand observation of the patient. No matter how astute the parents may be in describing their youngster, they cannot provide the interviewer with as accurate a picture as the patient's actual presence can.

There are some who take great pains to keep the patient-therapist dyad completely separate from all therapeutic work and/or contact with the parents. From the outset, they will arrange for the parents to be counseled by a colleague, with whom there are occasional conferences. Proponents of this approach claim that the patient's relationship with the therapist will be diluted and contaminated by any contact the therapist may have with the parents. They hold that the patient must have the feeling of having the therapist all to him- or herself and the treatment will suffer without such exclusivity. There are some therapists who take this so far that they will have absolutely no contact at all with the parents at any time.

Many hold that such exclusivity is especially important for adolescents because of their special need for independence from their parents.

I have formidable criticisms of this approach. It deprives the therapist of the opportunity of seeing the parents first-hand. No matter how accurate the patient's description, he or she most often has distortions, which may be clarified via direct contact with the parents. And the colleague working with the parents is likely to have distortions about the youngster because information about him or her has been filtered through the parents. The patient's problems are inextricably involved with the family's, and the therapist, by isolating the dyad, removes it from the field within which the problems have arisen and taken place and within which they must be worked through. Furthermore, the arrangement precludes joint interviews with the parents that can be a valuable source of information about family dynamics and interpersonal relations. Nor does contact with the parents retard the adolescent's development of autonomy. Physical contact does not have to be equated with dependency. True independence need not preclude a close, mature relationship with one's parents.

I have not found that my relationships with my adolescent patients have suffered because of contact with parents (and these have varied from occasional interviews to actual simultaneous therapy with one of the parents, usually the mother). In fact, such contacts and involvements have most often deepened my relationship with the youngster. If the parents have respect for and faith enough in the therapist to consult him or her themselves, the youngster's involvement is likely to be enhanced. When the opposite is true, when there is little if any contact, the patient's commitment may become reduced.

There are some who hold quite strongly that the adolescent should be seen alone in the first interview, but they will work subsequently with the parents in varying degrees. They reason that such an approach communicates to the patient, from the very beginning, that *he* or *she* is the patient, and that this message is vital if subsequent work is to be successful. I do not consider this to be such an important consideration because, more often than not, I see the parents as equally deserving of my clinical attention. I prefer to communicate to all that they are each to be clinically evaluated and that the greatest concentration is yet to be determined—therefore, the three-person interview.

It is for these reasons that my initial two-hour interview is one to which all three parties are invited. During that time they are seen in any possible combination, either individually or jointly. I generally begin the interview, however, with the adolescent alone, and the parents join us subsequently. In this way, I provide the adolescent with a separate experience from the parents, which is important for youngsters of this age to have. however, the parents are still brought in, which gets across the message that I am going to involve them in the treatment as well. Some adolescents object strongly to parental involvement, usually as a manifestation of specious independence or as a way of preventing parental disclosures. There is rarely a good reason for the therapist to comply with the adolescent's request (and even demand) that the parents be excluded from the therapy. To comply with such a restriction will most likely compromise significantly the treatment.

THE INITIAL TELEPHONE CALL

Although one of my secretaries almost invariably answers my telephone, she makes no appointments—whether it be the first appointment or any other appointment in the total course of the treatment. When a person calls for an appointment, he or she is informed that I will be available to speak during certain call times when I can generally speak in a more leisurely manner. If the day is particularly tight (often the case), I will converse with the parent during the evening. I generally find a ten-minute conversation necessary before setting up the initial appointment. My purpose here is to get some information about the nature of the youngster's problems to place myself in a better position to deal with unexpected events that may occur during the initial consultation. Because of the unpredictability of adolescents, therapists who work with them must be prepared to deal with many more "surprises" than those who treat adults.

But there are other reasons for my acquiring more information before making the initial appointment. Sometimes, an appointment might not be necessary. A parent might call requesting a consultation regarding how to tell the children about an impending separation. In such cases I may refer the caller to my *The Parents Book About Divorce* (1977, 1979a) and suggest the section on telling children about an impending separation. I am careful, however, to reassure such callers that I am not turning them away; rather, I am trying to save them money in that the cost of the pocket edition of my book is far less than a consultation. I inform them also that if this does not prove sufficient, then I will be happy to set up an appointment for a consultation. On a number of occasions I have received calls from distraught parents at the time of a sudden death of a spouse, which was followed by a heated family argument regarding whether or not children should attend the funeral services and burial. Often I can provide meaningful advice in a short time, and no consultation is necessary.

Sometimes the symptoms described will be short-lived and the parent is not aware of the fact that all youngsters exhibit at times transient symptomatology such as tics, gastrointestinal complaints, or a wide variety of fears. On occasion, symptomatic reactions to parental divorce may be the reason for the parent's call. In many such situations I will advise the parents to wait awhile because such symptoms are predictable and are usually transient. The authors of *DSM-IV* are most appreciative of this phenomenon, and this is reflected in the stipulation that time considerations must be taken into account before many childhood diagnoses are warranted.

Some parents who anticipate custody litigation may call requesting therapy in the hope that they can then use the therapist as an advocate in the litigation. It behooves the therapist to "smell these out" over the telephone in order to avoid sticky and compromising situations. (I consider myself to have an excellent sense of smell in these situations.) If there is any doubt about such a caller's true motives, I will inform the individual that a decision must be made *before the first interview* as to whether my services are requested for the purpose of *litigation* or for *therapy*. I inform such callers that I am receptive to following either path and have significant experience in both realms; however, once one course is chosen I will not switch to the other and I will be asking that the appropriate document be signed—*again before the first interview*—which strictly confines me to a particular path. The reasons for my rigidity on this point relate to important legal issues (Gardner, 1982, 1986b).

On one occasion a mother called and, after telling me the presenting problems, told me that I would have to promise her something before she would make the first appointment. I immediately smelled something foul, but didn't know what it would be. She then told me that her child was adopted and that I must promise her that under no circumstances would I ever reveal this to him. I told her that I would make no such promise and that I cannot imagine the child's therapy proceeding without this topic being discussed at some point in the treatment. I reassured her that I would not scream the fact in the child's face as soon as he entered the room, but I would not agree to such a restriction throughout the whole course of treatment. She advised me that other doctors had agreed to this restriction. I advised her then to consult these other doctors and that I was giving her my position on the subject.

A common problem that can easily be obviated in the initial telephone call is the one in which a divorced mother sets up an appointment and informs the therapist that her former husband will be paying her bills and that the therapist should bill him directly. In response to such callers I generally respond that I will be happy to do so if her former husband will call me and tell me directly that he will be paying for my services. Often I will get the response that he is *required* to pay all medical bills as a stipulation of the divorce decree and that if I have trouble getting the money from him, I should sue him and she is sure the courts will order him to pay. Any therapist who is naive, gullible, or masochistic enough to accept a patient under these circumstances does not get my pity.

A mother will call asking for a consultation. I inform her that my usual procedure is to see both parents and the youngster, in varying combinations, during a two-hour consultation. The mother informs me that she is divorced, with the implication that that fact in itself is justification for my not involving her former husband in the consultation. I will generally then ask if the youngster's father still maintains some involvement with him or her. If the answer is in the affirmative, I then recommend that the mother consult with the father and invite him to join us for the first interview. I generally do this before a specific appointment is made. This insures that the mother will at least invite the father (who, of course, may or may not accept). My experience is that such involved fathers most often attend. The mother may argue that it would not be a good idea to have her former husband join us because "all we'll do is fight." My response to such a mother generally goes along these lines: "It is certainly not my goal to get you to fight. However, this I can tell you: I already know that as long as you and your husband cannot be in the same room together without fighting, your youngster will continue to have psychiatric problems. I cannot imagine helping your son (daughter) with his (her) problems, as long as there is such severe animosity between you and your ex-husband. I can tell you now that one of my goals in therapy will be to try to get the two of you to reduce your hostilities. If that wasn't one of my goals, I wouldn't be qualified to help your child. Also, although the fighting is certainly unpleasant, I will probably learn some important things from it that will be useful in your youngster's treatment." Here again I have most often been successful in getting both parties to attend the initial interview.

On occasion, the calling mother may respond to my request for the father's involvement with "My husband doesn't believe in psychiatry. He told me that if I want to take Wally to a psychiatrist, it's okay with him but he doesn't want to get involved." To which I will reply, "Please tell your husband that my experience has been that the more involvement I have on the part of both parents, the greater the likelihood the treatment will be successful. If your husband refuses to involve himself entirely, I will do the best I can, but please inform him that I'll be working under compromised circumstances." I call this: *The-ball-is-in-your-court-baby principle.* I basically say to the husband that the choice is his. If he wants me to conduct therapy under optimum circumstances, he will involve himself. If he doesn't do so, there will be less of a likelihood that the treatment will be successful, and he will have thereby contributed to its failure. Again, most often husbands appear when this message is transmitted to them. Doing everything reasonable to bring both parents into the initial interview establishes also a certain precedent, namely, that their involvement in the child's treatment is important and my urging them both to be present at the outset is a clear statement of this. I might say here parenthetically, for those readers in private practice, that those husbands who do not *believe in* psychiatry are not famous for their *paying for* psychiatry.

During this initial telephone conversation some parents ask my fee. Without hesitation I give my response. At the time of this writing my answer is this; "My fee for the initial two-hour consultation will be $300. My fee for the subsequent therapy ranges from a standard fee of $110 for a 45-minute session down to $80 for a 45-minute session. The exact fee will be determined at the time of the consultation on the basis of your financial situation and insurance coverage." I know of many therapists who refuse to discuss fees over the telephone. This is not only injudicious but alienating. It cannot but engender distrust on the patient's part. It is reasonable for a patient to conclude from such an answer that "I guess he's going to try to get as much as he can." And such a conclusion is warranted. The argument that the discussion may have psychoanalytic significance is not justified. The caller is not an analytic patient; he or she is just a parent who is entitled to know what the therapist charges.

Before closing the conversation, I inform the caller that I will be sending a questionnaire that I would like both parents to fill out. This questionnaire (Appendix II) is quite comprehensive and provides me with a significant amount of "upfront" information at the time of the initial consultation. I have found my questionnaire extremely valuable for the large majority of consultations. It provides the therapist with an immense amount of information in a few minutes, information that might take hours to obtain via direct questioning. It is useful in assessing for the presence of psychogenic disturbances as well as diagnosing youngsters who suffer with what I refer to as the *Group of Minimal Brain Dysfunction Syndromes (GMBDS)*. I prefer to use this term over MBD because MBD implies a single disease entity. Rather, we are dealing here with a group of syndromes. It is unreasonable to attempt to assess for both psychogenic problems and the presence of GMBDS in a single two-hour interview. In this book I will focus only on the psychogenic problems of adolescents. For a detailed discussion of the evaluation of their neurologically based psychiatric disorders, I refer the reader to my books on this subject (1979b, 1987b). The questionnaire helps the examiner determine which are the areas that should most appropriately be focused on in the initial consultation. It tells the examiner where the "smoke" is so that he or she can know where to look for the "fires." Accordingly, it should be referred to frequently in the course of the initial consultation. The reader who plans to use the questionnaire would do well to read my detailed discussion of its utilization (1986a).

Furthermore, the questionnaire has certain fringe benefits. It is detailed and thorough, thereby creating a good impression with many parents—even before the first interview. This "good impression" helps establish a sound relationship with the parents, which can ultimately contribute to the youngster's having a better relationship with the therapist. Furthermore, it provides examiners with a well-organized format on which to base their reports. When dictating a report the examiner merely peruses the questionnaire and dictates information directly from it. The organization is already there and the examiner is saved the trouble of thumbing through notes, shifting back and forth, etc.

Attached to the questionnaire is a face letter (Appendix I) which I consider to be quite important. For parents who have not asked about the fees, they are provided this information with the questionnaire so that there is no disappointment, incredulity, amazement, and other reactions that may result in nonpayment of the fees. It also informs the parents that they will have the obligation themselves to pay me and that I will not pursue third parties for payment. (Many patients feel no guilt over doctors' doing this.)

SPECIAL CONSIDERATIONS FOR THE ADOLESCENT WHO RESISTS COMING TO THE FIRST SESSION

On a few occasions an adolescent him- or herself has called to set up the initial appointment. The parents were aware of the telephone call and had agreed to pay for the treatment. In these situations it was not that the parents did not wish to have any involvement in the treatment; rather, they were told by the adolescent that their complete removal from the treatment would be a proviso of the youngster's going into therapy. Therapists who agree to such an arrangement are making a mistake. Although there may be very rare situations in which this is warranted, I personally have not yet seen one. With the exception of these circumstances, the restriction is best viewed as a cover-up maneuver, a mechanism for preventing the therapist from finding out important information about the patient. Accordingly, in these cases I asked the youngster why the parents were being prohibited from involvement in the treatment and I did not get a satisfactory answer. In each of the cases the answers involved "privacy," "It's none of their business what goes on in my treatment," and "I don't know, I just don't want them involved."

Many years ago, when I first started my practice, I received a call from a colleague who informed me that he was referring a 15-year-old girl who stated that she wanted to have treatment, but refused absolutely to have her parents involved. The parents agreed to pay for the therapy because of the girl's insistence that she would not see a therapist if they were to be involved. Reluctantly, the parents agreed. She came in the first session, gave me her name, address, and telephone number and said nothing else. It mattered not whether I was silent or reached out to her. In both cases she was mute. At the end of the session she paid me the $15 and made another appointment. During the second appointment I informed her that I was getting very bored and I would not continue with such sessions much longer. Again various approaches, including silences intermixed with overtures, proved futile. At the end of the second session I informed her that I would try *one* more session and that after that, if she still remained mute, I would terminate the treatment. The third session was spent in the same way. Following this session I called the parents and spoke with the father. He informed me that she had agreed to treatment only if he would give her $10 for each session that she attended. Accordingly, he was paying $25 a session, $15 to me and $10 to his daughter. From her point of view it was an easy ten bucks!

On a few occasions I have received calls from adolescents who wished to set up an appointment, but had not cleared this with their parents. From the purely ethical and legal point of view, it may be risky for the therapist to see such youngsters— especially if recommendations are made that the parents may interpret as not being in the family's best interests. From the therapeutic point of view, the youngsters have invariably not wanted their parents involved and the reasons given were not appropriate. From the financial point of view, making the appointment may be a bad idea because the youngster may not have given any consideration to the question of who is going to pay for the treatment. Accordingly, on each of these occasions I have questioned the adolescent further, asked for the reasons why the parents have not been informed, and recommended that he or she get back to me after the parents have been told of the call and then an appointment would be set up. (Needless to say I never heard from any of these youngsters again.)

On occasion, the calling parent will tell me that the adolescent absolutely refuses to come for treatment. I generally advise such parents to speak again with the youngster and present the meeting as a consultation, the purpose of which is to determine whether treatment is warranted. Sometimes this works, sometimes not. On occasion I have advised parents to inform the adolescent that if he or she doesn't come for the initial consultation as well as a few trial sessions then certain disciplinary measures will be implemented. Some therapists may be surprised that I will use such coercive tactics. Adolescents often need such coercion because it enables them to "save face." Under these circumstances they are not saying: "I am a sick person who needs a therapist." Rather, they are saying "I am a healthy person who is submitting to inordinate pressures by my all-powerful parents and it is judicious of me to come to these sessions in order not to suffer the consequences of my not doing so." Inwardly, they may know they need therapy and the coercion under these circumstances is good medicine. I am merely following here my principle: *Benevolent despotism is the best system of government for children and other primitive peoples.* I am not recommending that these maneuvers be utilized throughout the course of treatment; rather, I am only recommending that they be used during the early phase. In some cases the youngster will then become less defensive about the therapy and continue on his or her own. In other cases, the required number of sessions will be utilized and the adolescent will refuse to come again. On a number of occasions even these tactics haven't worked and the youngster still refuses to come — even to the first meeting. Under these circumstances I will generally see the parents a few times and provide advice regarding how to handle the patient. Although I generally am willing to continue the counseling as long as it proves useful, my experience has been that after a few sessions we reach the point of diminishing returns and the meetings no longer prove of value. There is just so long that one can treat a patient who isn't there.

THE INTERVIEW WITH THE
ADOLESCENT ALONE

As mentioned, I generally begin the initial two-hour consultation by seeing the adolescent alone. This is my practice for youngsters over the age of 13 or thereabouts. In these circumstances I go into the waiting room, introduce myself to both the parents and the youngster, and then invite the patient into the consultation room. I tell the parents that the youngster and I will be talking alone for a while and then the parents will join us a little later. Most parents appreciate at that point the importance of my starting off with the youngster and recognize that he or she may have to have this special time alone with me. Before leaving the waiting room with the youngster I get the aforementioned questionnaire from the parents. My experience has been that frequent reference to it during the course of the interview enriches the efficacy of the data-collection process — especially for youngsters who are shy, noncooperative, or uncommunicative.

Once the adolescent is in the room I begin with a casual discussion, the primary purpose of which is to make the youngster comfortable but which is general enough not to contaminate any "blank screen." Accordingly, I might ask the youngster if the family had any trouble finding the office and/or may make some comment about the weather or some other innocuous subject. Such interchanges also lessen anxiety by enabling the patient to view the therapist as a human being, similar to others, rather than some cold machine. From the outset one must consider the all-important relationship that one is trying to establish.

I then proceed to write down some basic data information: name, address, telephone number, age, grade, school, siblings, names and occupations of parents, etc. The purpose here is not simply to obtain this information for my files but, more importantly, to lessen the youngster's anxiety. The youngster cannot but be anxious about the interview, and providing the "right answers" to these questions is likely to lessen anxiety. If one had an instrument for measuring tension level, I believe that it would indicate a reduction of tension with each answer provided at this point.

When I was in training I was taught that the best first question to ask a new patient was something along these lines: "So what brings you to the clinic?" and "So tell me, what's the problem?" I believe this is just about the worst possible question to ask as the *initial* question in the *first* interview with a patient. To me, the therapist who does this is similar to the physician who begins a physical examination by examining first the patient's genitalia. There is a good reason why the doctor begins the examination with the eyes, nose, throat, neck and then works his or her way down to the more private parts. These "name, rank and serial number" type questions reduce anxiety and then make it easier for the patient to answer the more anxiety-provoking questions about the nature of the presenting problems. Although less than five minutes has passed, one has an entirely different patient after asking these factual questions. Accordingly, the kinds of answers one is then going to obtain will also be quite different. Answers given in a state of tension and anxiety are far more likely to be distorted than those given when an individual is calm.

I then proceed to the more specific questions about the presenting problems. On occasion, the youngster will respond that he or she has absolutely no problems at all and that the only reason for the visit is that the parents have coerced the patient to come to the session. I may then spend a few more minutes trying to ascertain what the problems might be. I might ask the youngster to tell me what he or she thinks the parents believe are the problems. If this inquiry also proves futile I will then ask the parents to join us and tell me what they consider the problems to be. Or I might refer to the questionnaire and ask the youngster to comment on what the parents consider to be problems.

An antisocial youngster may be extremely obstructionistic at this point and maintain a facade of arrogance. His or her primary attitude toward the examiner may be one of sneering condescension. All overtures of friendliness by the examiner are rejected. The patient denies any wrong-doing and considers the interview to be a total waste of his or her valuable time. Under these circumstances I generally do not waste significant time trying to engage such a youngster. Rather, I bring the parents in and invite their participation in the interview. In some cases the youngster may drop the facade; in others it is maintained throughout the course of the two-hour evaluation. Examiners do well to approach such situations with the attitude that it does not behoove them to be successful in engaging such a youngster; rather, it only behooves them to try. At the very worst the youngster will never become a patient. We did not create the pathology—it is often generations in the making—and it does not behoove us to cure anyone. In fact, vigorous efforts to do so may defeat the goals of the treatment—because pressures on such patients only enhance their obstructionism.

In Chapter One I described an antisocial adolescent who had previously been in treatment with another therapist. On entering the first session, he sneered: "You shrinks are all the same." He then glanced around the room and, while pointing to different objects, said: "The same stupid couches and those pictures of your crazy kids on the desk." Had I addressed myself to his hostility, I would have missed the point entirely and increased his defensiveness. Accordingly, I merely commented that he was perfectly right and that Dr. X and I did indeed have a number of things in common. He needed to see us as similar in order to be more relaxed, and my response served to help him be so.

Most often, in my interviews with prepubertal children, I will utilize a variety of projective techniques, diagnostic/therapeutic games, and other instruments that enable me to gain information about the patient. In the initial interview with the adolescent, however, I generally engage in "straight talk." I am primarily interested at this point in the clinical symptomatology, not in underlying psychodynamics. My main goal at this point is to collect enough information to make a recommendation regarding whether or not therapy is indicated. And, if therapy is warranted, I want to be in a position to say something about the nature and structure of the therapeutic process. The psychodynamics provide me with information regarding *why* a person has symptoms. It does not generally tell me *whether* treatment is warranted. Everyone has psychodynamics and not all psychodynamic patterns and processes warrant therapy. The primary, if not exclusive, determinant of whether therapy is warranted is the presence of symptoms and clinical behavior. In the extended evaluation I can spend time finding out *why* a person is exhibiting psychopathology.

This is an important point. Many psychologists quickly plunge into administering instruments that enable them to acquire information about underlying psychodynamics. I defy anyone to tell me whether or not a person requires therapy simply on the basis of psychodynamics. Even people who exhibit what is obviously severe pathology in their psychodynamic revelations may not necessarily be psychotherapeutic candidates. They may be too sick for psychiatric treatment and may have absolutely no insight into the fact that they have problems. Accordingly, they have little if any motivation to do anything about themselves. And for the less obvious cases, it is practically impossible to differentiate between the psychodynamic patterns of so-called "normal" people and those whom we label as having psychopathology. All the more reason then to focus on symptoms and clinical manifestations during the initial evaluative session. Later, however, once the patient is in treatment, we can certainly use such information to help us understand better the nature of the patient's problems. I am not claiming to be totally unconcerned with psychodynamics in the first interview. I certainly don't ignore such data if it "hits me in the face." Rather, I am only stating what one's priorities should be at that point.

After the initial period in which we may focus on nonthreatening material, I will usually ask the youngster to talk with me about anything that may be on his or her mind. The purpose here is to avoid going directly and quickly into the more anxiety-provoking areas related to the presenting problems. Accordingly, I may pose such introductory and vague questions as: "Now, what would you like to tell me?" or "So, what would you like to talk about?" Many adolescents at that point (especially older ones, over 16) will talk directly about their problems. The examiner does well to appreciate that even the youngster who chooses to talk about issues ostensibly unrelated to psychiatric difficulties may still be revealing them. Even younger adolescents are still aware that they are in a psychiatrist's office and so—consciously or unconsciously—are likely to think about issues related to the difficulties. Accordingly, the youngster's initial responses to these lead-in questions are likely to result in a discussion of the primary presenting problems. If not, I may then ask more specific and direct questions such as: "So why have your parents brought you to see me today?" or "As you know, your parents have indicated in this questionnaire what they consider to be your problems and difficulties. I'd like to hear from you directly what you consider them to be."

In the course of the conversation about the presenting problems, I try to get the youngster to provide me with specific details, actual examples, and elaborations. General statements and abstractions are of little value in understanding exactly what is going on with the youngster. For example, if the patient says, "I have trouble with friends," the examiner has only the vaguest idea about the problem. It is only after a detailed inquiry into the nature of the peer problems—with at least a few specific examples—that the examiner will have a clearer picture of the problem. And one should do this with each of the presenting problems. It is not the purpose here to conduct the kind of in-depth discussion that one would embark upon in a therapeutic session. Rather, the purpose is to get enough information to decide whether treatment is warranted.

Accordingly, in my initial interview with the adolescent, I generally devote the time completely to "straight talk." On rare occasions, however, I will spend a little time on projective material. I do this in situations where the youngster is telling me absolutely nothing about him- or herself, but still might be cooperative when such instruments are utilized. In other cases, the youngster has cooperated and I have learned, in a relatively short period, about the primary symptoms and so I may then wish to go on to learn something about underlying processes. For such youngsters I will generally start with the Draw-a-Person Test. The patient is given a blank sheet of paper and pencil and told: "Here's a pencil and piece of paper. I want you to draw a made-up person and then tell me a completely made-up, self-created story about that person."

From the universe of possible things a youngster can draw, selecting a person considerably narrows the child's options. However, there is still a universe of possible drawings and associations (a universe within a universe so to speak), and so the drawing is still fairly useful as a projective instrument. One should not ask the patient to draw a person of a specific sex because that may further narrow the possibilities and restrict associations. *After* the youngster has drawn a figure of a particular sex, one can then ask for one of the opposite sex. Generally, the age and sex of the figure drawn is revealing. If a boy, for example, draws a picture of a girl and pays significant attention to such details as eyelashes, coiffure, fingernails, jewelry, and other attributes generally of great concern to females in our society, one should consider the possibility that this boy has a sexual identification problem. This would especially be the case if most observers, not knowing the sex of the child, would consider it to have been drawn by a girl. If, however, a boy draws a picture of an older woman, it is likely that the mother or her surrogate is being depicted.

By looking at the picture, the therapist can sometimes learn some important things about the patient. However, the reader should be warned that such interpretations are highly speculative and inter-examiner reliability is quite low. This drawback notwithstanding, useful information can still be obtained. This is especially the case if speculations from projective material are substantiated by clinical assessment. Placing the feet of a figure flush against the bottom of the paper may connote feelings of instability with a need to anchor or secure the body to a stable place. Patients with marked feelings of inferiority are more likely to draw their picture in this way. Significant blackness, especially when drawn frenetically, sometimes symbolizes great anxiety and a view of people as threatening. This kind of picture is more frequently drawn by patients who are clinically anxious. Large shoulders and other accentuations of traditionally "macho" features may represent a boy's attempt to compensate for feelings of weakness. This is especially likely for the adolescent with feelings of masculine inadequacy. The way in which the youngster deals with breast outline may provide information about the patient's sexual feelings and attitudes. Family attitudes toward sexuality will often provide clues as to whether the examiner's interpretation in this area is valid. The way in which the patient draws the eyes may provide information in a number of areas. Those who are shy and prone to use denial mechanisms to a significant degree may draw a figure with the eyes averted. Staring eyes have generally been interpreted to connote suspiciousness and sometimes even paranoia. Again, the examiner does well to make such interpretations cautiously and to use clinical data for support or refutation of these speculations. Machover (1949, 1951, 1960) has written extensively on the psychological interpretation of children's drawings.

The examiner should try to get the patient to tell a story about the picture. One can begin the process by asking for specific information about the person depicted. Some examiners start with the general request that the patient tell a story, and then only resort to specific questions if the request is not or cannot be complied with. The therapist does well to *differentiate* between age-appropriate stereotyped stories (which are probably normal) and idiosyncratic ones. The latter provide the more meaningful information. But here again there is much speculation.

After drawing the first picture, the child should be asked to draw a picture of a person of the opposite sex. One should take care not to specify whether the picture should be of a child or an adult, lest the universe of possibilities be reduced. One might say, "Now that you've drawn a picture of a male, I want you to draw another picture. This time I want you to draw a female." After as much information as possible has been extracted from the pictures, the examiner should ask the patient to draw a picture of a family. Because of time limitations during the first interview, it is prudent not to require the patient to spend too much time on the details of the various family figures. Here, the therapist is primarily interested in the number and sexes of the figures chosen, their relationships with one another, and the story the youngster tells about the family. My experience has been that stories elicited from the family picture are generally less revealing than those from the individual pictures. More frequently one obtains stereotyped stories about family excursions or day-to-day activities. These are usually resistance stories and provide little if any psychodynamic information. Of course, at times, one does obtain rich and meaningful stories.

Another instrument that may provide useful psychodynamic information in the initial interview with an adolescent is a series of questions described by N.I. Kritzberg (1966). The youngster is asked the question: "If you could not be yourself and had to be changed into any human being in the history of the world whom would you choose? You can select any person, living or dead, past or present, real or fictional, well known or not well known. You have the whole range of humanity to choose from." After the patient responds, he or she is asked for the reason for that choice. Following this, the youngster is asked for his or her second and third choices, and the reasons why. Then the patient is asked what three persons he or she would *not* want to be, and the reasons why. Although there are no standard answers (and there probably never will be) that can enable the examiner to determine with certainty the relative degree of psychopathology exhibited by an answer, most examiners can develop a "feel" for whether a response is normal or abnormal. And the reasons for the various choices may be particularly useful in this regard. The greater the examiner's experience with this instrument, the more the likelihood he or she will be able to differentiate between the usual and common responses and those that are atypical and idiosyncratic. A common response such as George Washington or Abraham Lincoln is not likely to be too revealing. However, if one wants to be Adolf Hitler, then some useful information has been provided. The responses to the questions regarding which individuals the patient would *not* want to be may be more difficult to evaluate. Because one is already starting with the question who the patient would *not* want to be, one cannot quickly state that the response reveals reaction formation. In this section, the Adolph Hitler response would be normal. Here again the atypical response is more likely to be revealing. Furthermore, one does well to look for *themes*. If a repeated theme emerges from the six responses then it is more likely that pathological processes are operative.

At this point therapists should direct their attention to an issue that is second in importance only to the question of whether the patient is in need of treatment. They should ask themselves the simple question whether or not they *like* the youngster being evaluated: Can I relate well to him (her)? Does the youngster appear to be relating well to me? Have we established rapport? Is there some mutual emotional resonance? If the answers to these questions are for the most part *no*, and it does not appear that there is potential for improvement in the relationship, then the therapist should have serious reservations about treating the child. We *cannot* treat everyone. We should not expect ourselves to be able to establish a meaningful therapeutic relationship with all those who seek our help. If this is truly a "screening interview" we must not indiscriminately try to treat all those who need it. We must try to treat all those whom we think might profit from working with us. There is a vast difference.

Often one interviews an antisocial adolescent who is obnoxious from the first second of the interview and continues being obnoxious throughout its course. At no point does the youngster exhibit any manifestations of friendliness, motivation for treatment, cooperative attitude, or any of the other qualities that one hopes for in a patient. One might reason that all these alienating qualities are defensive and that beneath the scornful and arrogant facade is a loving and tender human being who is merely testing the therapist or is fearful of expressing these more human qualities. Also, one might reason that tensions in the initial interview result in the patient's appearing far sicker than he or she really is. Accordingly, one has to grant the patient the benefit of these considerations and not so quickly come to the conclusion that there is no possibility for a therapeutic relationship. However, if by the end of the interview one learns that this is the pattern with the parents, teachers, principal, and a wide variety of other individuals whom the youngster encounters, then it is extremely unlikely that the therapist is going to develop a more benevolent relationship with the patient. I cannot present specific criteria for making this discrimination, because the decision must be made primarily on the basis of the subjective feelings therapists have toward the patient and what they *surmise* the patient feels about them. If there is any possibility of the therapist's changing his or her opinion and ultimately developing a better relationship then, perhaps, other sessions should be offered. If these are absolutely refused by the patient, then the therapist need not feel that he or she was instrumental in rejecting prematurely a potential candidate for meaningful therapy.

In summary, I say this: Don't treat a child you don't like. If you cannot bring about a change in such antagonistic feelings, then recommend someone else. Generally, during the first interview I am able to come to a decision regarding this issue. If not, I may suggest a second (and sometimes a third) session. If by then I feel that there is hope for the formation of a therapeutic relationship with the youngster, I will suggest the full intensive workup. If not, I save everyone time, trouble, and money, and either refer to someone else or, if the youngster has already been given up as untreatable by a few previous therapists, I suggest no treatment at that time and discuss with the parents other recommendations.

INTERVIEWING THE YOUNGSTER
AND PARENTS TOGETHER

I will then invite the parents to join me with the adolescent. Again, I may begin this phase of the interview with some general relaxing questions in order to help the parents feel more comfortable. I might ask about whether they had trouble finding the office or whether they had difficulty because of the weather. Some parents, at this point, will make a humorous comment which may help to alleviate their anxiety. If they get a smile from the therapist, he or she becomes less menacing. It behooves the therapist, in this phase, to hear their message and comply with the parents' request for a friendly response. A poker face or austere, humorless mien will only increase anxiety and lessen the chances of obtaining accurate information. For example, as one family was taking seats, the father chose the larger, deeper chair and laughingly stated: "I hope I don't fall asleep in there. It looks so comfortable." The remark clearly revealed his desire to desensitize himself to his anxiety and avoid the anticipated threats of the interview. I smiled and replied: "I hope you don't. I usually find that I have a little more difficulty getting information from someone who's sleeping." The father laughed and then seemed more relaxed. I did not go into the sources of his anxiety nor did I psychoanalyze the remark. I responded at the exact level at which he was functioning and directed my attention to his true request. A well-selected humorous response is likely to do more to reduce anxiety at such a time than direct statements about how the interview is really not so bad. With my response he had the *living experience* that I was benevolent.

Many things can happen at this point and the therapist must be alert to appreciate their meaning and sufficiently flexible to alter the interview in order to derive the maximum benefit from what may occur. Therapists do well to appreciate, however, that the most likely reason for atypical comments and responses during this very early phase relate to the need to reduce the anxiety associated with the first screening interview.

I usually then turn to the parents and ask them to tell me what they consider the patient's problems to be. I generally look vaguely halfway between them, so as not to focus on one, but rather to determine if either tends to be more active and/or to dominate. Throughout the interview my position is that of the *ignorant interrogator*. I use the word ignorant here in the true sense of the word: someone who does not know. And I am interrogating continually in order to lessen my ignorance.

I go back and forth between patient and parents, ever clarifying, ever adding to my knowledge. If there are contradictions between what the youngster says and what the parents say (a common occurrence), I might say to the patient, "Now you say one thing and your parents say just the opposite. What about that? I don't understand. I'm confused." The question should be posed in the spirit of an honest, open desire to learn the truth and not with the implication that the therapist is trying to prove any particular person right or wrong. Such additional back-and-forth inquiry may result in agreement as to the presence or nature of a particular problem. If it does not, that line of inquiry should be abandoned for the time being, with a comment such as, "Well, it seems that you and your parents see it differently. Let's go on and talk about some of the other problems. Perhaps later I'll be able to get a clearer picture of what's going on."

Although some youngsters may suffer some embarrassment over their problems being discussed so openly, there are compensatory therapeutic benefits to be derived from such confrontation. They clarify the reasons for the patient's being in the therapist's office, and this serves to make the problems more ego-alien and more amenable to treatment. The therapist, a significant figure of authority, agrees that they are "problems" or "troubles" and by implication undesirable qualities without which the child would be better off. In addition, naming, labeling, and talking about unpleasant subjects reduces their anxiety-provoking potential. The patient often anticipates that revealing defects will result in scorn, punishment, derogation, and/or other unpleasant reactions from the therapist and/or parents. When the expected condemnation is not forthcoming, the patient has what F. Alexander and T. French (1946) and F. Alexander (1950) refer to as a "corrective emotional experience," and feelings of self-loathing and anxiety that surround the symptoms may be reduced. Generally, the advantages of the open discussion more than compensate for the patient's embarrassment. Those who avoid such confrontations deprive the patient of these benefits.

It is important to discuss also the youngster's assets, accomplishments, skills, and hobbies. This serves to counterbalance the ego-debasing material that has been thus far focused upon. By necessity, therapy must concern itself, either directly or indirectly, with the problems that have brought the patient to treatment. There is usually little in the symptoms that the child can be proud of and much that he or she is ashamed of. In the world beyond the consultation room, the problems may represent only a small fraction of the child's living experiences; in the consultation room, unfortunately, they occupy a significant percentage of the treatment time if the therapy is to be meaningful. In order to counterbalance this unfortunate but necessary emphasis, therapists do well to take every opportunity to focus on ego-enhancing material. If warranted, the therapist should compliment the patient on *meaningful* accomplishments. There is no place for gratuitous or feigned praise in therapy. Interest (only if genuine) should be expressed in any activity that is a source of gratification for the patient. This, too, can serve to enhance the relationship.

If the patient cannot think of any assets, I respond: "If you can't think of anything good about yourself, I'd say that that in itself is a problem." If the youngster still has trouble identifying admirable qualities, I enlist the aid of the parents. If they also cannot describe praiseworthy characteristics, it reflects deep inadequacy in their parental affection. I consider the healthy parent to distort *slightly* in the positive direction regarding a child's assets (Gardner, 1973a). The child who lacks such parental distortion is being deprived indeed. I am not referring to gross exaggereations which are clearly not manifestations of healthy parental attitudes. For example, to consider the mediocre piano player to be "talented" is healthy; to consider him or her a "prodigy" is a delusion, which can only create difficulty for the youngster in forming an accurate selfimage. Probably more important than what the parents *say* regarding the patient's laudable traits is their *feeling-tone* when presenting them.

Is there the smile of pride and the warm glance, which are the hallmarks of the loving parent, or are the positive qualities described in a perfunctory way, as if the parents felt it behooved them to "dig up something" to bolster the youngster's ego? Such considerations are vital to the determination of the depth of parental affection.

The concentration on assets may also reveal the pathological do-gooder, the "Momma's boy," and others with hypertrophied super-egos. The list of their assets is long. They dote over mother when she is not feeling well; they are clean, neat, bathed, and make their beds without being asked; they rarely fight with siblings; they get straight As in conduct; they may be teacher's favorite, and so on. Other mothers say to their children: "Why can't you be like Tommy?" This constellation of symptoms is often difficult to treat because it does not produce pain or discomfort for the youngster or the parents, but is rather a source of pride and ego-gratification. Nevertheless, it can reflect significant difficulties.

The information obtained during this phase of the interview is the most important for making the decision as to whether treatment will be necessary. The decision should be made on the basis of *symptoms*, not on psychodynamics. The therapist must not only know the appropriate levels at which normal behavior ends and the pathological begins, but must also appreciate that everyone has psychodynamics and that having psychodynamics is not the same as having psychopathology. Psychologists, especially, are prone to recommend therapy more on the basis of findings on the projective tests than on clinical symptoms. This is an error. The patient's psychodynamics tell us something about (but not *all* about) the mechanisms of symptom formation. But psychodynamics also tell us about the processes that contribute to the development of normal behavior as well. We should treat symptoms, not psychodynamics.

Conduct in the home is a poorer criterion of psychopathology than outside behavior. The home generally provides a more permissive atmosphere than the world at large. Inquiry into home life does not assess well the child's ability to inhibit the more primitive impulses and adjust appropriately to the demands of reality. Children generally recognize that parents are safe targets and convenient scapegoats for their pent-up hostilities. They appreciate that parents will tolerate much more abuse than anyone else.

When the patient has not acquired the skills and capacity to function properly in school or in relationships with friends, the presence of psychopathology is strongly implied. Good functioning in these two areas generally indicates that the youngster is not likely to be significantly disturbed. If not provided, I ask for information about these areas of functioning. The questionnaire (Appendix II) also provides information in these areas. How does the patient get along in school? What do the teachers say about his or her conduct? Does the youngster have a "best friend"? If so, how often do they see one another? Do other teenagers call on the patient? If so, how often? Is the patient invited to others' homes? Is the patient in the "ingroup," on the fringe, or is he or she a "loner"? Questions such as these are the most vital of the interview and provide the most meaningful data as to whether psychopathology is present.

One area of difficulty which I have not found helpful to dwell on at length is that of sibling rivalry. It is normally fierce, and to devote much time to its vicissitudes is wasteful because such inquiry adds little meaningful information. If the mother, for example, says that her son fights often with his brother, I will ask her how often. If the frequency is less than ten to fifteen fights a day and if there is no history of dangerous trauma being inflicted, I usually say something like: "That sounds par for the course. What other problems are there?" Of course, if the brother is having nightmares in which he screams out: "No, no, Jerry. Don't beat me!" then the rivalry is probably pathological. In contrast, the absence of overt manifestations of sibling rivalry suggests a family in which aggression is significantly inhibited.

At the same time that one is obtaining verbal accounts of the patient's difficulties with the back-and-forth inquiry, one should also attempt to stimulate and catalyze interaction among the members of the family. It is hoped that the exact kind of interaction which takes place in the home will be reproduced. It is the unwise interviewer who attempts to squelch or circumvent arguments between family members and tries to "cool things" when an argument threatens to erupt, because much of value can be learned from such encounters. Are feelings freely expressed or is the argument highly intellectualized? Who is dominant? Does the patient side with any particular person? Are there tears? If so, what effect do they have? The healthy family will be somewhat embarrassed and restrained in its arguments, whereas the sicker family will not be so self-conscious. The possible considerations are endless; it is a rich source of information indeed.

In the context of the family discussion it is important to look for the presence of laughter and humor. One or two humorous comments, mutually enjoyed by members of the family, speaks for a healthy element in their relationship—regardless of what pathology may be present. The ability to laugh is a vital ingredient to health, whereas the humorless family is usually a sick one. And the capacity to laugh at oneself indicates ego-strength, healthy insight, and makes one's foibles more bearable. Therapists who respond warmly, with a humorous comment at the right time, provide a setting that fosters these informative responses.

Of course, the therapist should not be party to pathological humor. The hail-fellow well met type, the back-slapping jokester whose humor is patently obsessive and defensive, should not be responded to in kind because to do so would only encourage the utilization of this ploy to avoid honesty. The parent who uses wit in the service of expressing hostility should not be encouraged by the therapist's laughing at his or her jokes. Sarcasm, verbal scapegoatism, the laughing ridicule should be noted mentally but certainly not joined by the therapist.

If, during the course of the parents' description of the presenting problems, the patient interrupts with comments such as "Don't tell him that," or "I told you never to tell him that," or "You promised me you wouldn't talk about that," one might react with surprise and say something like, "What! Keeping secrets from your *own* psychiatrist? Didn't you know that you're never supposed to keep secrets from a psychiatrist?" One might then reinforce this principle by asking the patient to think about television programs he or she has seen in which this fact has been demonstrated.

During the discussion of the presenting complaints it is important to observe the various parties. One should especially observe the patient's relationship with each of the parents. Glances and gestures, as well as vocal intonations, provide information about affection, respect, and other forms of involvement. Seat placement, physical contact, and direct statements to one another also give much information about the interpersonal relationships of the parties being interviewed. In fact, this aspect of the interview may be more important than the specific information about presenting problems that is ostensibly the focus.

At this point, one may proceed in a number of different ways. If the examiner suspects that there is much useful information that the parents can relate but have been hesitant to reveal in front of the patient, the youngster might be told, "Now I'm going to speak with your parents alone, so I'd appreciate your having a seat in the waiting room." To some youngsters this might be followed by, "I'll be speaking with them about things that are personal for them. If what they say relates directly to you, and should be your business, I'll call you back in." It is important for the reader to appreciate that I much prefer the atmosphere be one of an open pool of commun- ication in which all things pertinent to the patient are discussed freely with both parents and the youngster. Or, the interview with all three parties may be continued, if that appears to be the most judicious approach. But most often I do set aside some time to see the parents alone, especially because it provides me with the opportunity to learn about marital problems that might not so freely be discussed (often with justification) in front of the patient.

INTERVIEW WITH
THE PARENTS ALONE

When the parents are seen alone, they should be asked if there are other problems that they have hesitated to discuss in front of the patient. Often such reluctance is ill-advised, and the parents should be encouraged to discuss these issues with the patient (who is then brought back into the room). When this is not the case, and the parents are alone, one does well to get some information about the marital relationship. Time does not permit going into great detail at this point, but the therapist should attempt to get a general idea about its stability and whether significant problems are present. When making inquiries about the parental relationship, each side should be heard; however, in the initial interview, it may not be possible to come to any conclusions regarding which party exhibits the greater degree of pathology. The examiner merely wants to obtain a list of the main problems; an in-depth inquiry goes beyond the scope of the initial consultation.

On occasion, both parents will claim that they have a good marriage and that they love one another. There are two possibilities here: One is that this is true and the other is, of course, that the parents are denying (either consciously or unconsciously) impairments in their relationship. When presented with a "happy marriage," the examiner might respond with a comment like: "Every marriage has some problems; no marriage is perfect. There are times, I am sure, when the two of you have differences of opinion. Every marriage has its fights from time to time. What are the areas of difference in your marriage?" When presented in this way, the parents will generally become more comfortable about revealing areas of difficulty. Of course, there are marriages in which the partners never fight, but in such cases one or both generally suffers with a deep-seated anger-inhibition problem, and the "peace" they enjoy is paid for dearly with symptoms and/or character traits resulting from the pent-up hostility that inevitably arises in all human relationships. Sometimes parents who deny marital difficulties in the joint session will provide significant information about their marital problems in individual sessions. Of course, the therapist would then be negligent if he or she did not go into the reasons for the cover-up during the joint session.

It is desirable to get some idea about the depth and nature of psychopathology in each of the parents. The interviewer will often have already obtained some information along these lines from general observations. The level of tension in the initial interview is generally quite high from the outset. Strong emotions are evoked. In such an atmosphere it is likely that many forms of psychopathology will be revealed. This is especially so for such character traits as suspiciousness, dependency, volatility, low frustration tolerance, strong need to control and dominate, and seductivity. One of the easiest ways to obtain information about the parents' psychopathology is to ask whether either of them has ever been in treatment. If the answer is yes, the therapist should ask about the main problems for which the parent(s) has been or is in therapy. A person who is in relatively good psychological health usually will not hesitate to discuss the major reasons for seeking treatment. Significant secretiveness may, in itself, represent a problem. One should not, however, expect a person in therapy to reveal every secret or personal problem in the presence of the spouse, although it is reasonable to expect that the major issues will be comfortably discussed. Withholding from the spouse significant information about the therapy reflects a defect in a marital relationship—even if the therapist advised against such revelations to the spouse. Time only permits an outlining of the major problems for which the parent sought therapy; more detailed information can be gained in subsequent interviews.

Before closing the part of the initial interview in which the parents are seen without the patient, they should be invited to talk about anything else they consider important. If a presented issue appears to be significant, some time should be devoted to it—to a superficial degree—reserving detailed elaboration for subsequent sessions.

CRITERIA FOR DECIDING WHETHER
TREATMENT IS WARRANTED

Four areas of inquiry are useful in helping the examiner decide whether a youngster needs treatment. Before elaborating on these, it is important to emphasize that transient symptomatic manifestaions are extremely common in children and to a lesser extent in adolescents. Practically every youngster exhibits occasional tics, short-term phobic reactions, temper tantrums, occasional stealing episodes, lying, bribing, sleep difficulties, and so on. An example would be the youngster whose parents have recently announced that they are going to separate and then get a divorce. It is normal for such children to exhibit transient symptoms such as depression, impaired school curiosity and motivation, crying spells, psychosomatic complaints, withdrawal from friends, and antisocial behavior. The examiner should recognize this point and not quickly recommend therapy. Only when these symptoms persist more than a few months is treatment warranted.

Of course, some counseling with the parents may be useful during this period. It is often difficult to ascertain that level of symptomatology at which the normal frequency and intensity ends and the pathological begins. Also, it is only when atypical, inappropriate, or pathological behavior exhibits itself over time that one should consider therapy. It is difficult, if not impossible, to provide a sharp cutoff point regarding how long symptoms should be present before treatment is warranted, but a few months is certainly reasonable. This important consideration is taken into account in the latest diagnostic and statistical manual – *DSM-IV* (1994).

School

The school is the most important area of inquiry for determining whether or not a youngster requires therapy. The child is born a primitive infant. It is the role of parents, during the earliest years, to make every reasonable attempt to transform these primitive human beings into individuals capable of functioning in society. The school can be viewed as the first "testing ground" as to whether they have been successful in achieving this goal—to the degree required for functioning in nursery or kindergarten. It is there that children must restrain their primitive impulses most consistently and predictably. The home is a much more relaxed atmosphere and its toleration for atypical behavior much greater. In addition, parental denial of difficulties may also leave psychopathology undetected or unappreciated. In the school, however, the teacher can compare more objectively the youngster with others his or her own age and ascertain whether atypical behavior is manifesting itself.

There are two areas of inquiry that most sensitively assess school adaptation, namely, academic performance and behavior. if the patient is not reaching what the teachers reasonably consider to be his or her academic potential, then psychopathology may be present. In addition, one wants to know about the patient's relationships to teachers, especially with regard to cooperation, respect for the teachers' authority, and general willingness to comply reasonably with classroom routine. Inquiry into the patient's relationship with classmates is also important. Youngsters who are functioning well in these classroom areas are not likely to have serious psychopathology.

However, there are occasional patients with psychiatric difficulties who do well in school, both in the academic and behavioral areas. They may be over compliant and passive youngsters who are quite fearful of any manifestations of defiance or failure to follow usual routines. They may be viewed by the teachers as "a joy to have in the classroom" and may be an immense source of pride for their parents. Their "uptightness," however, will probably get them into trouble in some areas, especially when self-assertion is warranted. But these patients represent a small minority and the basic principle still holds, namely, that the youngster who is doing well in school in both the academic and behavioral realms is not likely to be suffering with significant psychopathology.

Neighborhood

The second important area to consider when deciding whether a youngster needs treatment is that of relationships with peers in the neighborhood. Whereas peers will not tolerate more atypical behavior than parents, they will tolerate more than the teachers. Accordingly, maintaining friendships does not require a degree of integration that successful school performance necessitates. In order to maintain good relationships with neighborhood friends, children must have learned to share, consider the rights of others, wait their turns, adhere to the rules of games, and they must have developed a wide variety of other interpersonal accommodations that will enable them to maintain friendships. The therapist does well to inquire as to whether the patient actively seeks friends and is sought by them. Does the patient invite others to the home and do other youngsters come to the home in order to spend time with the patient? One wants to know the *kinds* of youngsters the patient spends time with. Are they reasonably normal, healthy, and well-integrated children or are they in the fringe groups, the atypical, the antisocial, or those who have such personality disturbances that most of the youngsters do not want to involve themselves with them? If the latter is the case, then psychopathology may very well be present in the patient. But even this patient may be healthier than those who have no friends at all.

Home

Home behavior is the least valuable area for ascertaining whether or not psychopathology is present. There, the consequences of atypical behavior are the least (when compared to school and neighborhood certainly), and the mechanism of parental denial may also operate to compromise the parents' capacity to ascertain whether or not behavior is atypical. Children normally do not behave as well in their homes as they do in the homes of their peers and in school. They often follow the rules applicable to each situation, and the rules at home are generally most lax and the consequences for breaking them most lenient. It is well to assume that children "get away with as much as they can" in each situation.

Parents will often complain that a child does not cooperate at home regarding doing the usual chores and assisting in the household routine. For example, a mother may say that she has a hard time getting Billy to take out the garbage, and he always dawdles, finds excuses, or just flatly refuses to do it. My views on this are that there has probably never been a child, in the history of the world, who ever wanted to take out the garbage. In fact, even garbagemen generally don't like taking out garbage, although they are often paid quite well for these services (most often even more than the child's teachers)! It is the child who *wants* to take out the garbage who may be exhibiting difficulties. This is especially the case if the child wants to make sure that the garbage cans are completely clean, that not a speck of dirt remains in them, and that every coffee grain is completely removed. Obviously, such a child is suffering with moderately severe obsessive-compulsive symptomatology. I would go further and say that the child who does *not* occasionally exhibit uncooperative behavior probably has psychological difficulties.

I recall, as a student at The Bronx High School of Science, a teacher named Mr. Levinson who was the school disciplinarian. If a child was sassy to him he would often respond, "Who do you think you're speaking to? Your mudda?" Mr. Levinson recognized well that children are likely to be more disrespectful of their parents (especially their "muddas") than their teachers. A youngster who exhibits similar disrespect to teachers has not "learned the rules" and is thereby atypical. Parents, like siblings, serve well as scapegoats, as targets for much of the pent-up hostilities of the day that cannot safely be released elsewhere.

The repercussions for "unloading" one's pent-up anger on one's family are far less than for directing them toward their original sources. I am not stating that this is a "good" thing, nor am I recommending it. I am only stating that it is a widespread phenomenon and that examiners do well to appreciate it when assessing for the presence of psychopathology. It is extremely difficult, however, to differentiate between normal and pathological degrees of disrespectful and uncooperative behavior in the home. The level at which the normal ends and the pathological begins is very blurred. This is an extremely weak area of inquiry for determining whether or not a patient needs treatment. However, this area that should not be ignored entirely. If the youngster *rarely* cooperates, if sibling rivalry is so fierce that the fighting is almost incessant, if turmoil and conflict is the *modus vivendi* in the home, then psychopathology is probably present.

DSM-IV

If a youngster exhibits no difficulties in the three areas, school, neighborhood, and home, it is unlikely that a *DSM-IV* diagnosis will be applicable. On occasion, however, a patient will exhibit *DSM-IV* symptoms and still function well in the aforementioned three areas. This would be the case for a youngster with obsessions and/or compulsions that do not interfere significantly in daily life. Or, symptoms such as phobias, depression, and psychosomoatic complaints might be present without significant compromises in these three areas of functioning. The main reason for this is that many youngsters come to treatment with interpersonal, rather than intrapsychic, comflicts. The problems lie not so much *within* themselves but *between* themselves and significant figures in their environment, especially parents and teachers.

PRESENTING THE INITIAL
RECOMMENDATIONS

By this time about one-and-a-half hours to one-and-three-quarter hours of interviewing have taken place, and the examiner should generally have enough information to decide whether or not treatment is warranted. Although little information may have been obtained about the underlying psychodynamic factors that have brought about the presenting symptoms, it is the *symptoms* that should be focused upon when deciding whether or not therapy is warranted. This is an important point. All behavioral manifestations have psychodynamics. And sometimes the psychodynamic patterns include pathological adaptations. Treatment should only be recommended if the symptomatic manifestations are interfering *significantly* in the major areas of functioning. I have emphasized the word "significantly" because all individuals exhibit, at times, transient symptoms and even pathological manifestations that may be ongoing. Treatment should be recommended only when these interfere with the patient's ability to function in life to a significant degree. Only then is the time, effort, and expense of involvement in treatment warranted.

When Therapy Is Not Warranted

On occasion, I have concluded that treatment is not warranted. Sometimes the parents have been overly concerned about the youngster and have not appreciated that the behavioral manifestations that have been a source of concern are within the normal limits. Sometimes such parents may need some counseling themselves; other times they just need some reassurance. This is more often the case with first-born children. With subsequently born children the parents become more knowledgeable and less anxious and so are not as likely to seek unnecessary consultations. In some cases the patient has been "cured" between the time that the appointment was made and the time of the consultation. Merely informing the child that an appointment has been made may result in a significant reduction and even complete alleviation of symptomatology. It is as if the child reasoned: "I'd better stop this stuff right now. They've made an appointment with a psychiatrist, a shrink. They must think I'm crazy. I'll prove to them that I'm not crazy. No more crazy behavior." I refer to this as "threat therapy."

One could argue that treatment in such cases is still warranted because the underlying problems have not been resolved. Classical psychoanalysts, especially, would take this position. I generally do not embark on treatment or even continue therapy with anyone who is asymptomatic. The symptom gives me the "handle" for the therapeutic work. Our theories about psychodynamics are extremely theoretical and speculative. If the underlying processes that have originally caused the symptoms are still present to a significant degree, they will erupt once again and bring about symptoms once more. Then, I will be in a better position to treat. I have even had situations in which a parent will call me a few days before the initial consultation and state that since the youngster was informed of the appointment, the presenting symptoms have disappeared. I will express my pleasure and advise such a parent not to hesitate to call me again if the situation has changed. Sometimes a new appointment is set up in the future and sometimes not.

I generally take a conservative approach with regard to suggesting therapy. Recommending that the parents embark on the intensive evaluation (to be discussed in detail in the next chapter) is an expensive and exhausting proposition. I do not recommend it lightly. Furthermore, therapy may be extremely expensive and extended—even more reason to be cautious about recommending it. In spite of what I have said, the vast majority of youngsters who come for initial consultations do require treatment. One reason for this is that there may have been a long period of denial and refusal of treatment and, by the time the patient does come, things have built up to the point where treatment is definitely warranted. This is especially the case when a school has recommended therapy. Schools will generally tolerate significant degrees of atypical behavior before recommending treatment. By the time they do so, treatement is probably warranted.

When a Decision Regarding Therapy
Has Not Yet Been Made

There are times when the two-hour consultation does not prove adequate to make a final recommendation. On those occasions I will recommend one or more further sessions for data collection. I will not allow myself to be pressured into coming to conclusions and making recommendations in a specific period. When the parents are brought in, I tell them in a matter-of-fact way, without any embarrassment or apology, that the situation is a complex one and that I have not been able to come to any definite conclusion at that point. I then advise them what further data collection will be necessary. Sometimes one or two sessions with the patient and/or parents is all I anticipate will be required. On some occasions I will need more information from the teachers, and this is preferably done by speaking directly with them. Sometimes the patient has exhibited significant resistance during the initial session. Although psychiatric problems are present and warrant treatment, the resistance has been such that I cannot reasonably make a recommendation for therapy because there might be no patient to involve meaningfully in the process. Under these circumstances I may recommend one or two more sessions with the patient in the hope that I might then engage him or her. If this also proves unsuccessful, I discontinue my work with the youngster. I may provide some parental counseling, generally over a few sessions. On occasion, I might suggest that the patient might profit from some other modality or experience such as speech therapy, summer camp, organized recreational experiences, or treatment by a pediatrician or a neurologist. Under these circumstances, no further work with me is warranted.

When Psychotherapy Is Warranted

For most youngsters brought to consultation, psychotherapy is indicated. I then outline to the parents what I consider to be the major problems, at the manifest symptom level as well as the underlying family factors that may have contributed. I emphasize that these are my *initial* conclusions and that it is only with further experience with the family that I will be able to be more certain about the factors that are contributing to the youngster's difficulties. I advise them that it is going to be necessary for me to get to know each of them better if I am to work optimally with the patient. In order to do this I will need to see each of the parents once or twice individually to get background information from them. Following the individual interviews with each of the parents I will want to see them together because I will often get conflicting information about what is going on between them. If there are siblings old enough to contribute useful information, I will often recommend a family interview. I also advise them that I will want to see the patient two or three times more in order to collect more information from him or her. At times psychological tests will be indicated, and these will be administered concurrently with the intensive evaluation. I advise the parents that during the intensive evaluation I will be interviewing them as if they themselves were coming to me for a psychiatric evaluation. I then tell them that, when all the information is collected, I will review the material and present my findings and recommendations to them. I impress upon them the fact that I only recommend the intensive evaluation when treatment is warranted and that it serves as a foundation for my therapy. It is important for therapists to appreciate that the extended evaluation is not simply recommended for the purpose of data collection. Equally, if not more important, is its value in forming a relationship which serves as a foundation for therapy.

At this point it is important that the therapist invite the parents to ask any questions they may have about the proposal. They have to appreciate (if they do not already) that, in the private practice setting, the extended evaluation is expensive and time consuming but that it is the optimum way to proceed. My experience has been that many parents do not "hear" me at this point. They may have come with the idea that I will give them a recommendation and send them on their way and that is all that treatment involves. Although there was nothing in the face letter to my questionnaire (Addendum I) to suggest this, their wishes that this were the case or this misinformation about what treatment entails has led them to this conclusion. In such cases I try to impress upon the family that the youngster's problems are complex and that they cannot be understood very easily.

Some parents at this point will ask my opinion regarding how long the treatment will take. I hesitate to use words like always and never. However, I have no hesitation in advising therapists that they should *never* speculate on how long treatment will take. This is one of the most misguided things a therapist can do. One cannot know how successful one will be in engaging the child, nor can one predict how successful one will be with regard to involving the parents. One cannot predict how slowly or rapidly the difficulties will be alleviated; in fact, one cannot even know whether or not one will be successful at all. Often significant social and cultural factors were operative in bringing about the problems, factors completely beyond the therapist's control. Many patients' pathology has been transmitted down many generations. Accordingly, I firmly state to the parents that I cannot predict how long treatment will take and that it would be foolish on their part to put any circles on their calendars. I try to explain to them what I have just said about those factors that contribute to the unpredictability of the process. Such a statement also gets across the message that *their own participation* will play an important role in how rapidly or slowly therapy proceeds. I cannot emphasize this point strongly enough. If the parents view the treatment as a process involving their dropping their child off at the therapist's office, and then picking him or her up after a prescribed period of time, and then after X number of sessions, all will be well, they have a very misguided view of the process. Such a program may work well for many forms of medical treatment, but it is completely ill-suited to the treatment of psychiatric difficulties. The discussion at this time provides the therapist with an opportunity to get across this important point.

I emphasize to the parents that I would not be making a recommendation for the extended evaluation if I were not certain that treatment was indicated. However, at that point I may not be able to be more specific about exactly how I am going to proceed. I may say that I would anticipate one or two sessions per week (my usual frequency), but that I cannot say exactly who will be involved. Perhaps it will be primarily the youngster, perhaps primarily the parents, perhaps a combination of both. It will only be after I have had the opportunity to collect more data that I will be in a position to ascertain what the optimum therapeutic program will be. Here again, the examiner is foolish if he or she allows the parents to extract a specific statement regarding exactly what the therapeutic program will be. Of course, there are times when one can state it with certainty at that time and, under such circumstances, there should be no problem in doing so. My own usual procedure at this point, however, is to inform the parents that even after the evaluation, my proposed therapeutic program will be the one that seems most propitious *at that time*. It may be that new situations will arise that will warrant an alteration of the therapeutic program. Therapy is a slice of life. And like life, things are always happening that will warrant a change in one's plans.

Discussion of Fees

And now to the delicate subject of money. Although the face letter of my questionnaire (Addendum I) indicates my fee policy, the subject may still come up. This is especially the case if the parents wish to discuss with me the question of whether they should be given a fee lower than my standard. Whereas Freud's patients in Victorian Vienna were inhibited in discussing sex, most adult patients today reveal freely their sexual activities to their therapists—but are quite restrained when discussing financial matters. Some therapists may, indeed, share their patients' inhibitions in this area. The problem is complicated for the therapist treating adolescents because the person paying for the treatment is not the one receiving the treatment. The adult in therapy is available to discuss his or her reactions to the payment of fees; the parent of a youngster in therapy is often unavailable or unmotivated for such an inquiry. Accordingly, one cannot easily ask what the parents' income is. Even if one were to do so, and even if one were to obtain a figure, one is still not in a position to know exactly whether a fee reduction is warranted because gross income is only one part of the information needed to assess properly a person's capacity to pay one's fees. One must also know about expenses, debts, and other financial obligations. In many situations the therapist would have to have the expertise of an accountant to know whether or not a parent can afford the standard fee or whether a reduced fee is warranted. Even then, a question of family priorities must come into play, i.e., what the parents want to spend their money on, and the examiner is in no position to make decisions in that realm.

What I do then is to proceed as if the standard fee will be paid and ask the parents if they are clear on my policy of payment, namely, that payment is due at the time of each session and that my secretary will be available to assist with insurance forms and payments from third parties. It is important for the reader to appreciate that my policy of requiring payment for each session is the one that I utilize for parents of children in treatment, but I do not routinely use it for adults who are in therapy themselves. Asking a patient to pay for each session is essentially saying to the patient that there is no trust. Up until about five years ago I did indeed trust parents to pay each month for the treatment of their children. However, I believe that our society is becoming progressively more psychopathic and my former policy resulted in a significant percentage of defaulted payments. Accordingly, I have changed my policy and require parents to pay at the time of each session. This has not compromised my relationship with the child because he or she is generally oblivious to this aspect of the treatment. With adult patients, however, I have still maintained my original policy of their paying at the end of each month (or at some other mutually agreed-upon frequency). To require the adult to pay at the time of each session is essentially extending the "no trust" communication to the patient him- or herself. And this cannot but compromise the therapeutic relationship. If, however, a patient does exhibit difficulties in paying promptly, then I may very well, after therapeutic discussion, institute a policy of more frequent payments after each session. Under these circumstances, the patient has so acted that my distrust is warranted, and to trust a patient under these circumstances is not only naive and antitherapeutic but might be masochistic.

With regard to the question of a reduction to a lower level on my fee range (as originally described in the face letter of the questionnaire), I generally take a somewhat passive position when discussing this issue. It is preferable for the patient to step forth and make the request. And it also behooves the patient to present the information that supports his or her position. Otherwise, the examiner compromises him- or herself by becoming beholden to the parent to provide the information. In the context of such a discussion I might ask if the parents have insurance and exactly what coverage they have. (The face letter requests that this information be available at the time of the initial consultation.) If they cannot answer specifically these questions, then I reserve a decision until the information becomes available. If it is provided, but I still cannot ascertain whether a reduction is warranted, I might ask for other reasons why the parent believes a reduction would be appropriate. It is beyond the purposes of this book to go into the details of such discussions. The examiner must be aware that some parents pride themselves on their bargaining acumen, in the context of which guiltless duplicity is the rule. Others are ashamed to come forth with a statement of their difficulties in paying the higher fee. If the examiner suspects that such is the case, it behooves him or her to initiate the discussion of a lower fee. Some masochistic people may stay with the higher fee because of the self-destructive gratifications that paying it offers. Others may assess the value of the therapy with the level of the fee and would consider themselves to be getting less valuable treatment if they were to take a lower fee or even consider the therapist to be less adequate if he or she were to charge less. Some parents gain a sense of superiority from paying the "top fee." Some may be too passive to request a lower figure or may feel that the reduced-fee patients get inferior treatment. A divorcée, whose former husband is paying for the treatment, may welcome a high fee as another weapon against her former spouse.

What I have said thus far regarding fees relates to the initial fee at the outset of treatment. A fee may be reduced (even below my minimum) when a patient, in treatment for a significant period and committed to the process, suffers financial reverses which are not related to the patient's psychopathological processes (I use the term patient here to refer to an adult patient in treatment or the parents of a patient in therapy.) Under such circumstances I will discuss a reduction, but never to the point where no fee at all is charged. It may even be a few dollars taken from a welfare check, but I do not give "free therapy." If the patient is not willing to suffer some privations for the treatment, it is not likely to be meaningful. Patients who pay nothing for their therapy often (but not always) get exactly the value of what they are paying for.

The Question of Payment
For Missed Sessions

The question of charging for missed sessions is a difficult one. With adults, advance notice of cancellation varies from many months to no notice at all (the patient just doesn't show up). The reasons for missing can fluctuate from the most realistic (patient in the hospital) and appropriate (household emergency requiring the patient's presence) to the clearly psychopathological and/or acting out, e.g., "I forgot," "I overslept," or "I just didn't feel like coming." The intermediate situations are probably the most common, e.g., "I had a bad cold" or "My bursitis acted up." A physical illness may not be the patient's "fault," but psychological factors clearly play a role in the degree to which the patient is incapacitated.

Some therapists do not charge for missed sessions. This is a therapeutic error. Missing sessions and/or withholding fees may be among the most common ways in which patients act out with their therapists. Not charging for missed sessions may serve to encourage such behavior and thereby entrench pathology. One approach is not to charge when the therapist is able to fill the session. Some therapists charge if the session has not been filled *and* the absence was due to pathological behavior, e.g. "forgetting," or a voluntary decision that something else had priority, e.g., "an important business meeting." This approach has intrinsic defects which led me to abandon it after using it for a few years. Its main drawback is that it opens up the possibility of conflict between the therapist and patient regarding whether a particular reason for missing the session was pathological.

My policy is to charge my patients for *nonfilled* missed sessions *regardless of the reason for the absence.* Patients are informed that the time is reserved for them. They are told that if I am given advance notice, I can usually fill the hour. In such cases there is no obligation to pay for the session. In the treatment of children and adolescents, this approach is helpful. At one time I was a proponent of the "no fee for illness policy." I would be called by a mother who would inform me that her child was sick and could not keep an appointment. In the next session the child would tell me about the wonderful time she had at a birthday party on the afternoon of the missed session. What does the therapist do in such a situation? A mother is getting over "the flu" and can't bring the child. Another says that a sibling is sick and she can't get a babysitter. It was amazing how the frequency of such missed sessions diminished once I began charging. When describing my missed-session policy, I inform the parents that I have found that when a child has to miss a session, seeing one or both parents instead has often been helpful.

When telling parents about my missed-session policy, I emphasize the fact that there is *no specific cutoff point* to determine whether or not they will be charged. I emphasize that the more advance notice I have, the greater will be the likelihood of my filling the appointment and, conversely, the shorter the notice the less the likelihood of the session being filled. I strictly avoid mentioning any numbers, even in the negative sense. To do so is injudicious. For example, if I were to say, "I have *no* cutoff point, such as 24 hours. The determinant of whether you will be charged is purely whether or not I can fill the session." It is likely that that number 24 will be branded in that parent's brain as the cutoff figure. In fact, even though I studiously avoid mentioning numbers when presenting my policy, on a number of occasions parents have quoted me as giving the 24-hour figure, and have even sworn that they heard me say it. Recently, I have prepared a written statement of my missed-sessions policy (Appendix III) that the parents can refer to if there are any differences of opinion or misunderstandings regarding what they were told about my policy.

Although my missed-session policy may appear stringent, it emcompasses a benefit not enjoyed by patients of many psychoanalysts who pay for sessions missed when on vacations that do not coincide with the analyst's. When I say sessions missed for any reason whatsoever, I include vacations—at any time of the year—as a reason. The result has been that I have never charged a patient who has given me a week's notice or more. Although some readers may not consider me such a "big sport" on this point, there are thousands of patients of other psychoanalysts who have paid dearly for sessions missed when they take a vacation—even with a year's notice.

CONCLUDING COMMENTS

If, at the time of the final discussion, the parents express ambivalence or hesitation, the examiner does well to invite them to discuss further their reactions. At times, it is advisable to suggest that the parents think over what has been said, rather than make a decision at that point. This is a most judicious policy. Sometimes, a parent will have deep reservations but will not express them at the time of the consultation. Such a parent might even then accept subsequent appointments, only to cancel them on short notice. It is unreasonable to expect people to pay for cancelled sessions after they have indicated they wish to discontinue treatment entirely. In fact, it is probably unethical, in spite of the aforementioned verbal agreement. Accordingly, for the sake of the parents as well as the therapist, it is wise to invite ambivalent parents to think about their decision before making appointments.

For those who say they wish to go ahead, I generally set up three appointments: one for the adolescent, and one for each of the parents. Whereas my initial consultation is generally two hours, my subsequent sessions are generally 45 or 60 minutes, depending upon which appears to be most useful and judicious. Some patients (adults as well as children) use the full hour quite expeditiously; others find 45 minutes to be optimum. People who travel greater distances often prefer the full-hour session. One does well to clarify this issue before closing the initial session.

At this point, the reader may conclude that it is not likely I can accomplish all that has been discussed thus far in a two-hour consultation. This conclusion is not completely unwarranted. Actually, I have tried to cover many contingencies, all of which are not likely to come up with the same family. Accordingly, I generally am able to accomplish most of what has been presented here during the initial consultation. But, as mentioned, if I cannot, I have no hesitation requesting a third or even a fourth appointment.

FOUR

THE INTENSIVE
DIAGNOSTIC
EVALUATION

In the Greek language, the word *diagnosis* means *to know thoroughly* or *to know in depth*. Accordingly, when we use the term as a mere label we are not using it in the true spirit of its meaning. The initial two-hour consultation may enable us to provide a diagnosis in the superficial sense, but it does not enable us to provide a diagnosis in the full sense of the word. It is the purpose of this section to describe the techniques I utilize to provide a bona fide diagnosis, in accordance with the original meaning of the word.

This is being written at a time when shorter forms of treatment are increasingly in vogue. Many time-limited therapy programs provide a fixed number of sessions, ten or twelve not being uncommon. Considering the complexity of the problems with which we are dealing, it takes that number of sessions to understand what the basic problems are. The patients, therefore, are being discharged at just about the time the therapist is beginning to understand their problems in depth. To me such treatment can be compared to the surgical procedure in which the surgeon who opens the abdomen, isolates the source of disease, and then, without doing any further operative procedure or closing the abdomen, discharges the patient from the hospital. I am not claiming that therapy cannot possibly take ten or twelve sessions; I am only claiming that one can generally not predict in advance how long it will take, and it generally takes longer than that. Time-limited therapy is appealing to those who want quick solutions to complex problems. It is particularly attractive to administrators and those who are supporting treatment for large numbers of patients. Accordingly, I consider it most often to be a rip-off of the poor; rich people (unless they are naive) generally do not have to accept time-limited therapy.

Here I present what I consider to be the judicious kind of evaluation, one that enables the examiner to learn in depth what the patient's basic problems are. The evaluation here serves as a foundation for subsequent treatment. The knowledge so gained puts the therapist in the best position to proceed most effectively with the therapeutic program.

THE EVALUATION OF THE MOTHER

I generally find it useful to begin with an interview with the mother alone. My experience has been that, of the three parties, she is the one who is most likely to give me important background information. Often the youngster is the least capable of the three because of his or her immaturity and ignorance of the processes that may be contributing to the difficulties. Fathers, unfortunately, are often less receptive to "opening up." I believe this, in part, relates to the general pattern in our society that fathers are supposed to maintain a "macho" image and not admit weakness or deficiency. Discussing problems with a therapist is viewed by many fathers as being a sign of weakness. Another factor probably relates to the fact that, in the traditional home, the father is less likely to be knowledgeable about all the details involved in the child's life. He may also be more reluctant to admit difficulties in the marital relationship. Although these'reasons are speculative, I am convinced that my generalization is a valid one, namely, that fathers are less likely to provide me with important background information than mothers. Accordingly, I find it judicious to interview the mothers first in the intensive evaluation. However, I am not rigid with regard to this and, if scheduling of the child or father first is more readily acocmplished, I will certainly depart from this principle.

The Initial Inquiry

I generally begin the interview with the mother with an open-end question such as: "Is there anything special on your mind that you would like to say to me at this point, before I proceed with any questions?" The question is purposely vague and is designed to provide the mother with the greatest freedom to discuss any issue that she considers pertinent. I want to know here what is at the forefront of her mind, especially things that may be upsetting her, things that may be pressing for release. To ask a specific question at this point may deprive the examiner of this important information. Sometimes the mother's comments may suggest ambivalence for the intensive diagnostic program. It is important for the examiner to appreciate that bringing a child to treatment is generally viewed as an indication of the parents' failure to have raised a psychologically healthy child. The examiner's conclusion that treatment is warranted may then be viewed as confirmation that the parent is indeed deficient. In such cases I usually try to reassure the mother that I am convinced that she loves the child deeply and that, at every point, she did what she considered to be best for her child's healthy growth and development. I emphasize the point that her coming for treatment for the youngster and her willingness to make the sacrifices of time, money, and energy for the child's welfare, are a statement of parental strength and commitment. Comments along these lines sometimes reduce the parental feelings of failure. Of course, it is not proper for the therapist to make such a statement if it is untrue, and there is severe maternal deficiency. However, mothers willing to bring their children for treatment do not generally fall in that category.

If the mother has not offered any responses to my initial open-ended question, I will ask, "I'd like to know what reactions you had to our meeting last time." Or, if she has given no response along the lines just discussed, I might ask, "Are there any other reactions you had to our meeting last time?" In both cases, I direct my attention specifically to the two-hour consultation. This question also enables me to learn her feelings about the treatment, both positive and negative. It is crucial for the therapist to have a good relationship with the parents if an adolescent's therapy is to be successful. The answers to these questions at this point in the initial interview can provide information about the kind of relationship that is starting to develop between the mother and the therapist. It is the best opportunity for "nipping in the bud" difficulties that may already be starting to exhibit themselves.

I will then ask the mother what the youngster's reactions were to the interview. Here again there are a wide variety of responses. If the adolescent's reactions have been negative, I will try to ascertain what the issues were that caused the reactions. If positive, I will want to learn what things attracted the patient. If the mother states that she did not make inquiries in order to respect the patient's "privacy," I will impress upon her that my general therapeutic approach is to encourage all concerned parties to discuss the therapy as much as possible and she should err on the side of "invading the youngster's privacy." I do not recommend that she be intrusive here, only that she err on the side of being so and let the patient's own defenses and desire for privacy be the determinants of how much and how little he or she will reveal. Such "respect" for the patient's privacy often works against the aims of treatment in that it reduces the open communication that the therapist is trying to achieve in the family. Open communication among family members may be one of the most therapeutic experiences the therapist can provide. All too often psychological problems within families are the results of conspiracies of silence, suppressed and repressed thoughts and feelings, and other "skeletons in the closet." Therapy must open Pandora's boxes, and facilitating open communication is a step toward this goal.

The mother may, for example, say that the youngster told her something but made her promise not to divulge it to me. Here I will advise the mother that it was an error on her part to have agreed to keep a secret from me and that she would have done better to have said something like: "There must be no secrets from Dr. Gardner and I won't promise not to tell him." The mother may respond that if she were to say such a thing, the patient might not give her the information. My response to this is that it is better that the patient not provide the information than for her to be a participant in a conspiracy in which she and the child join forces to keep secrets from me. Also, I reassure her that important issues are likely to come out anyway and she need not fear that the nondivulged secret will compromise the treatment. (I will discuss this issue of confidentiality in more detail in Vol. II [1999a].)

I will then ask the mother what her husband's reactions were to the initial consultative interview. As mentioned, mothers are generally more candid to me than fathers, and so she might provide me with information about his reactions that the father himself might not so readily reveal. Often his comments relate to the financial aspects of the treatment, which may then open up a discussion again of the fee and the payment. If the husband has expressed negative reactions, I encourage the mother to tell her husband to state these directly to me. I use this as a point of departure to impress upon her that a common cause of disruption of treatment is parental discomfort regarding the expression of their grievances, disappointments, disagreements, and so on.

Inquiry into the Causes
Of the Child's Difficulties

Next I will make the following statement to the mother: "I know that you're coming here to get my opinion about why your youngster has problems. However, it's important for you to appreciate that, at this point, you probably know more about the reasons why your child has to come to therapy than I do. After all, you've lived with the child all his (her) life. You have been observer to thousands of events that I have not witnessed. Accordingly, I'm sure that you can provide me with very important information relevant to the question of why your child has difficulties." Most mothers will come up with some explanations at that point. And, interestingly, the issues they bring up are often extremely valuable and very much on point. Although she is not specifically trained in psychiatry or psychology, the mother's "guesses" are often valid explanations and provide the examiner with important information about the sources of the child's psychopathology.

I cannot emphasize this point strongly enough. Although the

mother may never have gone to graduate school, she knows the child better than the examiner and her hunches regarding why the child has difficulties (her denial mechanisms notwithstanding) may be better than the examiner's. If the mother cannot come up with any explanations, I will often urge her to "guess" or "speculate." I encourage her to do so with the advice that her guesses may still provide me with valuable leads as to what is going on with the child. Again, these "wild" guesses are often valuable sources of information.

Inquiry Regarding Parental Dealings with the Child

My purpose here is to get more specific information about the way in which the parents have raised the patient, with special focus on detrimental exposures and experiences. There are a number of ways of getting information in this area. I sometimes ask the mother to describe what she considers to be her strong points and weak points in the child-rearing realm. By presenting the question in this balanced way, one is likely to obtain information related to maternal weaknesses that the mother might otherwise have difficulty admitting. It is usually useful to ask questions in this area in such a way that guilt or embarrassment is reduced or obviated. For example, if the examiner were to ask: "Do you ever hit your child?" an accusatory finger is implied. But, if the examiner says: "All parents find, at times, that their backs are up against the wall and the child's behavior is so irritating that they feel that the only thing they can do is to give him (her) one. Then the child has a good cry, gets it out of his (her) system, and all is again well with the world. How often did you find this to be the case with your child?" Obviously, when the question is posed this way, the examiner is going to be in a better position to find out exactly how much (or how little) corporal punishment was utilized.

The same principle holds for questions in other areas. For example, if one says to a mother: "Did you like cuddling your child when he (she) was an infant?" the answer is likely to be yes in that the mother generally recognizes that not to have done so represents a parental deficiency. One is more likely to find out what really went on with a question such as: "When they're born, some babies love cuddling and others do not. How was Billy when he was born?" Actually, there is a small element of duplicity in this question. The realities are that there are indeed some babies who do not like cuddling when they are born, but they are relatively rare. They are mainly children born with serious physical illness, congenital defects, mental retardation, autism, and other severe disorders that manifest themselves at birth. Children who are not in these categories not only love to be cuddled at birth, but the deprivation of such may ultimately prove lethal. Because I know that Billy is in none of the aformentioned categories, I know that he would have wanted cuddling at the time of his birth. If his mother responds that he was not that kind of a child, it generally suggests that she herself had some deficiency in providing cuddling and her motivation for doing so was impaired.

One could ask the question: "Did you like to have Janie cuddle with you in the morning when she was a toddler?" Again, most mothers will say yes, even though the response may not be an honest one. However, if one asks: "Some children, when they're toddlers, love to come into their parents' bed, especially on weekends. How was Mary when she was that age?" By presenting the question in such a way that there are two categories of children, some who like cuddling and some who don't, it becomes easier for the mother to state that Mary was not in the cuddling category. Again, the implication here is that the deficiency lies in the child and not in the parent.

Another useful question: "What are your husband's feelings about the way you've raised Bobby? What does he consider your strong points to be and what does he consider your weak points to be?" It is generally easier for the mother to talk about deficiencies about herself if they originate from someone else because she has the opportunity to present disagreements if she wishes to do so. The examiner does well to review the list of the father's reported descriptions, both positive and negative.

An important area of inquiry to ascertain maternal capacity is the mother's involvement in school activities. In fact, this may be the most important realm if one is looking for manifestations of parental deprivation of affection. I first begin with an overall question about the mother's involvement in school activities and encourage her to provide me with an overall description. Following that, I ask specific questions that give me information about the mother's participation in the PTA, attendance at conferences with teachers, and involvement in the youngster's extracurricular activities such as school plays, recitals, sporting events, et cetera. The latter area is extremely important. The healthy involved mother finds attendance at such performances extremely gratifying. It is a grand moment when little Susie comes out on the stage dressed as Cinderella. Tears well up in the mother's eyes and her heart swells with pride. And the adolescent's parent beams with pride when the youngster appears on the stage. The parent who knows no such joy is not only missing out on some of life's greater moments but, for the purposes of the interview, has provided the examiner with important information regarding maternal capacity. In the context of this discussion, I ask the mother about the father's participation in school activities. Does *he* attend teacher conferences? Does *he* attend the school performances and does he exhibit joy and pride at them?

One wants to know about whom the child went to in the middle of the night when he or she woke up with nightmares, croup, or physical illness. One wants to find out about who takes the child to the pediatrician, especially during emergencies. Inquiry about what goes on during the evening, when both parents are home, is also important. One should inquire about homework and who helps the youngster with it. Does one parent do better than the other? One wants to know about parent's comfort with and patience with sitting on the floor playing childhood games, especially when the children were younger. One should inquire into who put the children to sleep at night, read them bedtime stories, and had more patience for dawdling.

A concept that I have found useful in assessing parental capacity is what I refer to as "Grandma's criteria" (Gardner, 1986b). These are the criteria Grandma's ghost would use if she were to be roaming invisibly around the house collecting data about parenting abilities. Because she doesn't have a Ph.D. in psychology she would be using more traditional criteria for assessing parental capacity, criteria related to the involvement of the parent in the everyday activities of the child-rearing process. Accordingly, the examiner does well to go through the course of a typical day with the mother, from the time the children wake up in the morning until the time they go to sleep at night, and find out exactly what each parent does with each of the children, especially the patient. One is particularly interested in who takes on the more unpleasant tasks and who has the greatest willingness to make sacrifices. Because she knows nothing about unconscious processes, Grandma will be focusing on these more valid criteria for assessing parental capacity.

The reader interested in more information about assessment of parental capacity does well to read pertinent material in my *Family Evaluation in Child Custody Litigation* (1982).

Description of the Marriage

I will then ask the mother the general question: "Tell me about your marriage?" Of course, I may have gotten some information about this during the initial two-hour consultation; however, here I want to get more details, especially as they relate to the patient's difficulties. This is an important area of inquiry. Children exposed to ongoing marital animosity are likely to be deprived, and such deprivations may contribute to the development of their sympto- matology. And, if the children become actively embroiled in the parental conflict, there is even a greater likelihood that psychopa- thology will develop. It is reasonable to say that many (but certainly not all) children who develop psychological difficulties do so because of problems in their parents' marriages. If the mother describes difficulties, I will go into detail, especially with regard to those problems that the patient is either aware of or exposed to. Some parents naively believe that children are in no way affected by parental problems that they are not directly exposed to or aware of. I attempt to impress upon such parents that the effects of marital discord tend to filter down to children, even without the awareness of the concerned parties. I try to convince them that, if parents are depressed or otherwise unhappy over difficulties in the marital relationship, this is going to compromise the care of the children.

Some mothers routinely state that their marriages are good ones. This is their automatic response, and they may consider it the socially acceptable thing to say. Along with this, they will often say, "I love my husband." In some cases the marriages are quite poor, but denial mechanisms have resulted in both parents' maintaining a facade that they have a "good marriage." In such cases, I might say,

258 The Intensive Diagnostic Evaluation

"You know, no marriage is perfect. Every marriage, like every human relationship, has strong points and weak points. In every relationship there are things that you like about the other person and things that you don't. There is no marriage in which there aren't occasional fights. What I want you to tell me now are the strong points of your marriage and the weak points. I'd like to hear about the things you agree on, and the things about which you don't agree." When the question is posed this way, it becomes more socially acceptable for the mother to reveal deficiencies in the relationship. When one begins with a discussion of the positive aspects of the marriage, it becomes easier to talk about the negatives. Because mothers are generally more comfortable talking about deficiencies in the marriage than fathers, the information obtained here will be useful to the examiner during the interview with the father.

Some mothers will describe the marital difficulties, but state that their husbands have strictly warned them not to talk about them to me. There are many women who comply with this wish and I never learn about the marital difficulties. This, of course, compromises my evaluation. Other mothers tell me the problems, but request that I not tell their husbands that they revealed the information to me. Sometimes I am successful in my attempts to get such mothers to assert themselves and advise their husbands that they have provided me with this information. Others fear doing so and when I meet with the husband it becomes apparent that their wives have never revealed that they have disclosed the details of the marital problems to me. Sometimes I am successful in "smoking this information out" during the joint interview with the husband and the wife; and other times the mother is so frightened of "rocking the boat" that she continues to hold back. Such mothers are serving as models for passive submission to their husbands and this, of course, is likely to contribute to the child's difficulties. I believe that refusal to discuss marital difficulties is one of the most common reasons why parents do not agree to embark upon the intensive evaluation or, if they do so, it is one of the most common reasons why they interrupt it. Therapists who confine themselves to working exclusively with children, and do not delve deeply into the marital and/or family situation, are likely to attract such parents. However, I believe that the therapy they provide is likely to prove useless.

Sometimes the marital conflict may focus directly on the child.

A mother may say, for example, "The only fights we have are over how to deal with Tom. I believe that if things went well with him, we wouldn't fight about anything." There are two possibilities here. One is that the statement is true, and the marriage is basically a good one with the patient's problems the main source of parental friction. The other possibility is that the youngster is being used as a weapon or tool in the parental conflict and that differences over management are being utilized in the service of less noble goals. It behooves the examiner to inquire further into this issue in order to ascertain which of the two possibilities is closer to the reality. When parents are involved in divorce, the second possibility is generally the more likely. Because divorced parents are living separately, they do not have direct access to one another to vent their rage. The children, who move back and forth freely between the two households, become good candidates to be used as weapons, spies, and tools in the parental conflict (Gardner, 1976, 1977, 1979a).

History of Psychiatric Treatment

I will then ask the mother whether she has ever been in treatment. If so, I want details about the phases of her life when she had therapy, the types of treatment, the reasons for having entered into treatment, and what she recalls of the experience(s). This is a good way of getting into the question of the mother's own psychopathology. Simply to ask the question, "Do you have any psychiatric disturbances?" may produce defensiveness. However, a discussion of previous therapeutic experiences is more likely to provide useful data in this area. I am often amazed at how little people remember of their therapy. I am rarely surprised when an adolescent has little recollection of early childhood therapeutic experiences with me. But it does amaze me how little adults remember of treatment that took place 10 or 15 years previously, treatment that may have occurred while they were adults. They commonly do not even recall the name of the therapist. I am particularly interested in any marital counseling or conjoint therapy that the mother may have involved herself in with the father. This is another way of learning about marital problems. I often try to get information about what the therapist said, especially with regard to each party's contribution to the marital difficulties.

Background Information

Family Background   It may come as a surprise to some readers that my discussion of the acquisition of background information about the mother comes so late in this section. It is important to appreciate that we are not dealing here with the mother's psychoanalysis, but her involvement with her child—especially with regard to maternal capacity. Were we interested in psychoanalyzing the mother we might be much more interested in her early developmental life, her relationships with her parents, and the influences in her development that played an important role in shaping her present personality. Although I am concerned about these subjects (and will discuss them in this section), I consider them to be less important than the areas of inquiry discussed thus far.

I begin with questions about the mother's date of birth, place of birth, and list of places where she has lived during her life. If the mother has moved frequently, especially during the patient's lifetime, then I may have a clue to a factor that may have contributed to the youngster's difficulties. Children who shift around from location to location during their formative years, especially if this involves frequent changes of schooling, may suffer psychologically from the disruptions. I then ask the mother about her own mother, whether she is living or dead, and where she lives at the present time. If dead, I want to find out about the cause of death. If the information hasn't been obtained already, I want to know about the ethnic and religious background of the maternal grandmother. Ethnic factors often play a role in the development of psychopathological processes. I want to know about the maternal grandmother's religion and how religious she was (or is). I am especially interested here in fanaticism or dogmatic religious beliefs that may contribute to the development of psychopathology. I ask the mother to describe the kind of person her mother was and the kind of relationship the mother had with the maternal grandmother during the mother's childhood. I am particularly interested in the kind of maternal care that the maternal grandmother provided the mother.

I also want to know whether the maternal grandmother worked or was a homemaker. If she worked, I want to know about her occupation and whether or not she was mainly out of the home or was actively involved in the mother's child rearing. This may provide information about the mother's own maternal capacity, in that if the model she had as a child was a good one, it is more likely that she is providing good maternal input into the patient. And the opposite is the case if the maternal grandmother was deficient in this regard.

I also want to know about the maternal grandmother's relationship with the mother's husband. If there is dissension between the maternal grandmother and the child's father, it may play a role in the child's difficulties. I am particularly interested in how much grandparental input the maternal grandmother has with her grandchildren, especially my patient. Good grandparenting can play an important positive role in a child's psychological development. The exaggerated high esteem that grandparents often have for their grandchildren can serve as a buffer for the criticism and the undeserved negative feedback that children (like the rest of us) often are subjected to in life. I also ask about the maternal grandmother's psychiatric status, whether she has ever been in psychiatric treatment or has suffered with unusual medical illnesses. I then ask the mother if there is anything else that she can mention about her mother that might be of importance to me.

Next, I ask the mother similar questions about her father. I ask about her father's occupation, especially with regard to how much time he had for input into the mother's own upbringing. Information about the mother's relationship with the father may provide useful data about the mother's relationship with her husband. The female-male relationship patterns laid down in childhood tend to repeat themselves in our subsequent lives. Here too I am particularly interested in the relationship between the maternal grandfather and the patient. This is especially important if there are deficiencies in the relationship between the mother's husband and her child, i.e., the patient and his or her father.

I then ask the mother about the relationship between her parents. That relationship (whether good or bad), which the mother observed during her formative years, is often the model being repeated in the mother's present marital relationship. I am not saying that this is invariably so, only that it is quite a common phenomenon. If a mother, for example, frequently observed her father to be hitting her mother, it is more likely that she will marry a man who will treat her similarly—her vows never to marry such a

man notwithstanding. If the mother's whole extended family operates in this way, it is even more likely that she will repeat the pattern
in her own marriage. One could say that it is the only lifestyle she
knows and that such a mother would be uncomfortable during the
dating period with young men who treated her more benevolently.
She would be like "a fish out of water" in such relationships and
would find them strange and uncomfortable. She might even
provoke men into maltreating her or always anticipate maltreatment—even though there is no evidence that she would be mistreated. And this pattern is likely to transmit itself to a third generation
and exhibit itself in the patient, at a level commensurate with his or
her level of development.

Sometimes, there may have been divorce in the mother's home
during her childhood. In such cases I want to know about the
reasons for the separation and whether or not there were remar-
riages. If stepparents were involved in the mother's upbringing, I
want to know about them and the nature of the relationships
between the mother and stepparents.

I then ask the mother to list each of her siblings and get brief
information about their age, occupation, and marital status. I am
particularly interested in whether or not any of the siblings had
serious psychological difficulties and, if so, the nature of them.
Because genetic factors often play a role in various psychopathological processes, I want to know about the appearance of such
difficulties in the child's aunts and uncles as well as the child's
maternal grandparents.

The First-Memory Question   I sometimes find the first-memory question to be useful. I generally pose it in this way: "Go back
as far as you can and tell me what the first memory of your life is.
I'd like you to go further back than the beginning of school if you
can." Psychoanalysts, especially, are very interested in this question. Although it may not provide useful information, sometimes it
serves as an epitome of many factors that have played a role in the
patient's lifetime. When it does, it can often provide valuable clues
about central psychological themes in the mother's lifetime, themes
that began in childhood and exist to the present time. Sometimes
the actual memory is false and the incident never occurred. However, because the mother believes fully that it did, the response can

still be a useful source of information. At this point I will present a few examples to impress upon the reader the value of this question.

One mother gave this response:

> I was about three years old. I remember my brother and my father urinating. I wanted to do what they did and I tried, but I couldn't.

This mother was an extremely domineering and aggressive individual. She was married to a man who was submissive and passive. This memory clearly reflects the desire to assume the masculine role, and it was certainly the case that she had done so in her marriage.

One mother responded:

> I was three years old and my mother and father and sister were fussing over me because of my dancing.

This woman was an extremely histrionic, hysterical individual. She was markedly exhibitionistic. As a child, she had been an actress and a model. But throughout her life she continued to exhibit her talents, which were probably much less than she professed. She was so self-centered that she gave little attention to her son, who was significantly deprived. It was this deprivation that played a role in the development of his symptomatology.

Another mother responded:

> I was two or three years old. I climbed out of my crib, fell, and broke my arm.

The memory reveals the mother's basic feelings that if she removes herself from a protected environment (a crib) she will be traumatized. The mother was basically an extremely dependent individual who did not view herself as capable of handling many of life's situations and anticipated that if she were unprotected by her husband and her parents, she would indeed meet with disaster. One could argue that the arm fracture incident was a psychological trauma which deserved to be remembered. My response is that this does not negate the aforementioned explanation. There were probably many other falls, accidents, and psychologically traumatic incidents in the mother's life. The fact that she remembered this one—after so many years—is a statement that it lent itself well to epitomizing themes in her life that were central to her personality.

One mother responded:

> After I was two years old, if I misbehaved, I would be tied to a table and spanked and kept there. These are the earliest memories of my childhood.

This mother was an extremely masochistic and martyristic individual. She constantly reminded her children about how much she sacrificed herself for their benefit. She stated that at times she did twenty hours of work a day in order to devote every spare moment to philanthropic work. She constantly reminded those she served (her children and others) how much they were in her debt for her benevolence. The seeds of her masochistic-martyristic tendencies are clearly present in this first memory. This mother worked on the principle that the only way she could get affection from others was to suffer pain. She also used her martyrdom as a mechanism for expressing hostility. She would get people to feel guilty over how ungrateful they were for not appreciating her suffering on their behalf.

Another mother's response:

> I was about three or four years old. We were taking family pictures and I was very shy. I didn't want my picture taken.

The memory reveals the mother's fear of exposing herself and her basic feelings that if she is "seen," the observer will be critical or rejecting of her. And she assumes that others share her own low opinion of herself. These personality qualities were playing a role in her son's difficulties in that he too was shy, submissive, and excessively dependent upon the opinions of others. These were qualities that he acquired by identification with his mother.

Another mother's response:

> I was about three years old. It was in Atlantic City. We had gone there on vacation. I was all sunburned and my mother

made me put on a starched dress. It hurt my arms and I was crying.

This mother grew up in an upper-middle-class home where there was significant emphasis on propriety, attendance at the "proper schools," and appropriate manners and dress. Otherwise, her parents were not particularly interested in her, and her upbringing was given over to various housekeepers and maids. Although the memory suggests that the mother was resentful of this treatment by the maternal grandmother, she was actually reproducing the pattern in the upbringing of her own daughter. The mother worked full-time in order to send her child to the best private schools and gave little meaningful care and attention to them while she was at home.

One more example:

Two memories come to mind. Both when I was about three or four years old. I remember being fed hot peppers by a little boy who lived next door. I thought he was giving me candy. In a second memory I remember being burned on the bottom as I backed into a gas heater.

This mother, although in analysis with another therapist, had never analyzed her earliest memories. I discussed with her their possible psychological significnce and suggested that she try to analyze them. She responded:

I come from a long line of masochists. In both of these memories I'm getting harmed. In the first I was tricked. It really wasn't candy but pepper. I still think men are untrustworthy. When they say they're gonna give you something sweet, it turns out that it isn't. The second one makes me think that I wasn't adequately protected by my parents. I feel they should have protected me.

This mother's analysis agreed with my own guesses as to the psychological significances of these first memories. In both she is harmed. In the first she is harmed by another's duplicity (being fed hot peppers) and in the second she brings about her own misfortune (backs into a gas heater). Both suggest the propensity to being hurt either by gravitating toward those who would maltreat her or by participating in behavior that would result in her being harmed. And these tendencies reflected themselves well in her life in that she married a man who, although superficially loving and benevolent, actually turned out to be an extremely hostile individual who subjected her to vicious litigation at the time of their divorce.

My presentation of these many clinical examples was done in the hope that it would impress upon the reader the great value of this question. Although I am often critical of psychoanalytic theory and technique, it would be a mistake to conclude that my criticism is so vast that I do not appreciate the benefits to be derived from certain aspects of classical psychoanalytic theory. In fact, I believe that much in this book is still very much within the psychoanalytic model, the alterations and modifications notwithstanding.

School Life   I then ask the mother about her elementary school experiences, both in the academic and behavioral realms. I ask about friendships during this period as well as things that might have been going on in her home that might have affected her personality. Similar questions are asked about the junior high school and the high school periods. Just as information about school and neighborhood can provide vital data about the patient, the same questions about the mother can be useful in determining whether or not she has psychopathology. With regard to high school, I am particularly interested in whether the mother dated and, if so, what kinds of experiences she had. I ask about academic and/or emotional problems.

Work History   Next, I ask the mother what she did following graduation from high school. If she went to work, I get details of her work history, particularly with regard to how well she got along with colleagues and superiors. If she had numerous jobs, I want to know the reasons for the various changes, especially if she was repeatedly fired. If she is still working now, I want to know the nature of her job adjustment. I am particularly interested in her work history since the birth of my patient. I want to know how much time she spent out of the home and in it. If she gave the child's care over to housekeepers or other caretakers, I want to know who they were, how long they remained in the home, and the nature of their relationships with the child. This is an extremely important area of inquiry because it tells something about emotional deprivation, a common cause of psychopathology.

The Premarital Relationship with the Father　I then ask the mother about the circumstances under which she met her husband and the qualities within him that attracted him to her. If there were previous marriages, I want to list each one and get information about them. I am particularly interested in any psychopathological trends that may have exhibited themselves in each of the previous marriages. Important questions in this area relate to who initiated the separation, what were the main problems in the marriage, and what criticisms former husbands had of the mother. Here again we see the question of criticisms other persons had of the interviewee. This can often be an important source of information about the interviewee's personality deficiencies, deficiencies that may not readily be revealed by the person him- or herself.

Projective Questions　Projective questions are routinely used in interviews with children. They are not as frequently used in interviews with adults. I too generally use them much more in interviews with children. However, I will occasionally present them to adults as well, when I am having difficulty getting adequate information by direct questions. In this section I will describe some of the projective qustions that I have found most useful.

Five wishes　The traditional question is to ask the person what wishes they would make if three could be granted. However, it is nowhere written that one must limit oneself to three. I generally prefer to ask for five wishes because I am then less likely to get stereotyped responses. The first two or three may very well be routine, everyday answers. When one must "scratch one's brain" and provide one or two more, then one is more likely to tap unconscious sources that may provide more meaningful information.

1. Safety and good health for all of us.
2. Equanimity for myself in daily existence.

3. An ability to see further, to be less narrow, to comprehend more the meaning of the situation *while* it is happening.
4. An ability to make and keep decisions.
5. To be less self-absorbed—to be able to give of myself.

Superficially, the first wish appears to be normal in that most
people will include good health for themselves and their family.
However, the word *safety* does not usually appear. It suggests
unconsious hostility toward her family and then, by a process of
reaction formation, she protects them from trauma. One could,
however, argue that wishing one's family good health also implies
an initial thought of sickness and that response could also be
considered a manifestation of hostility with compensatory reaction
formation. Although this may be true, I can only say that *safety* is a
rare wish whereas *good health* is an extremely common one. This
lends support (but certainly does not prove) my belief that they have
different psychodynamics. In this case this mother did indeed
harbor formidable hostility toward her husband, a domineering and
overbearing individual upon whom she was quite dependent.

The second wish reveals a desire for cessation of her chronic
feelings of anxiety, depression, and inner agitation associated with
her difficult relationship with her husband.

The third wish makes more specific reference to her inability to
think for and assert herself, not only in her relationship with her
husband but with others as well. Her statement, "to comprehend
more the meaning of the situation *while* it is happening" makes
reference to her problem in considering her own thoughts and
feelings when they are contradicted by others. Subsequently, she
sometimes realizes how submissive she has been. Her wish here is
that she be more astute and less inhibited and denying when she is
allowing herself to be suppressed.

The fourth wish also makes reference to her passivity and
dependency on authorities, especially her husband. She cannot
make a decision because she is too beholden to the opinions of
others and to keep them against resistance is extremely difficult for
her.

Last, the fifth wish refers to her self-absorbed state which was
the result of the above-described pathology as well as her deep-
seated inhibition in giving of herself meaningfully in an affectionate

way. This mother significantly deprived her child, the patient, and described how when he was very young she refused to let him come into her bed in the mornings although he stood for hours scratching at the bedroom door. The boy came to treatment at age 16 because of marked antagonism toward his peers, especially girls. Clearly, his hostility stemmed from the deprivations he suffered in his relationship with his parents.

Another mother gave these wishes:

1. Traveling. I'd like to do a lot of traveling. I'd love to go to Europe, to Germany, Denmark, and Spain.
2. I'd like to live very long.
3. I'd like to have a lot of money.
4. I'd like to eat more without gaining weight.
5. I'd like my children to succeed. I'd like them to be as happily married as I am, to enjoy the world, the blue sky and the grass. I don't want them to marry money. I want them to be basic individuals. I don't want them to be impressed by prestige.

These wishes reveal the mother's basic egocentricism. The first four are all concerned with herself, and no mention is made of her husband and children. They all reveal the desire for self-indulgence. The fifth, although possibly a normal response, is not so for this mother. She was an extremely hysterical and histrionic individual. The most mundane subjects were spoken about with extreme enthusiasm and exaggeration. The mechanism of denial was frequently utilized, and no matter how unfortunate or miserable the situation was she tended to see it in the best possible light. Her references to enjoying "the world, the blue sky, and the grass" are all part of the hysterical picture and cannot be considered bona fide desires for her children to enjoy these aspects of living. In addition, her wish that her children not "marry money" and not be concerned with prestige in their choice of a mate was in her case simple reaction formation to her basic desire that they be most concerned with these considerations. This mother was quite involved with social status, but she denied this through frequent utilization of the mechanism of *undoing,* and spoke of her "tolerance" of social and ethnic groups which were usually discriminated against. My patient, her 17-year-old daughter, was exhibitionistic, materialistic, self-indulgent, and exploitive of her father—all qualities that she derived from her mother.

Last, one mother gave these wishes:

1. I wish I could be left alone. I always feel under pressure. I'd relax. I feel under pressure from my husband to be a perfect wife. He wants gourmet cooking. He wants me to be more aggressive and I am not. He wants me to be friendly to people who might be important to him for business purposes. I just can't be that way.

2. I'd like to travel a lot. I've never been to Europe. But we can't go now because my husband would rather spend money on cars. He gets everything he wants. He's very selfish. He always does what he wants and never what I want. I feel helpless because he has control over all the money.

3. To be more self-assured.

4. I wish I was more tolerant of my parents. I don't know what it is, but whenever I'm with them I cringe. I know I'm their whole life. I can't forgive them for not being more affectionate to me when I was younger. They were always working.

5. I'd like to be completely independent so I won't have to rely on my husband for everything. If I wanted to do something I wouldn't have to ask my husband for everything. I'd like to be on my own and have my own money.

These wishes need little psychoanalysis. They describe, quite succinctly, this woman's main psychological and marital difficulties. It was no surprise that near the end of the first interview she stated: "Although I came here for my daughter, I really think I have problems of my own and I guess I want treatment for myself as well."

Verbal Projective Questions   Although I routinely present children with verbal projective questions, I do not usually present them to adults. Again, when direct questions are not adequate to provide me with the information I desire, I may utilize verbal projective questions (Kritzberg, 1966). Whereas with children and young adolescents I generally ask questions about animals and objects, I most often ask older adolescents and adults about people. My usual question to the older adolescent and adult is this: "If you could not be yourself, but could live your life as any other person in history, living or dead, real or fictional, famous or not, whom would you choose?" Following the response, I ask for the reasons for having selected that particular person. I then ask for second and third choices (and reasons) and then the persons who the patient would *not* want to be. Although this question may be immensely valuable for learning about adults, it is often of little value for children because of their limited repertoire of figures from which they can select. In addition, they will often choose superheroes or other age appropriate figures. The stereotyped responses are not as revealing as the atypical. Accordingly, as will be seen below, the verbal projection question for people (as opposed to animals and objects) can be very useful for adults.

One mother gave these responses:

(+)1 Rita Hayworth. I try to copy her to a T. She led a very glamorous life. She was beautiful. She was sexy-looking.

(+)2 Maria Callas, of the Metropolitan Opera—she's not a dying thing. People adore her. People will worship her forever.

(+)3 Happy Rockefeller. She's a dream person. She's not cheap or rowdy. She's elegant. She's wealthy.

(−)1 a) A poor person. I'd never want to be poor.

b) My aunt. She was very promiscuous.

(−)2 My mother. She was very ignorant. She had a low IQ. She wasn't neat.

(−)3 The female murdered in the picture, *I Want to Live.* She kills other women. She was a murderer. She slept with men.

This mother was basically hysterical, exhibitionistic, deeply materialistic, and vain. Her vanity bordered on psychotic grandiosity. She looked upon those who did not profess adoration of her as being hostile. These cravings are well revealed in the verbal projective test. The (+)1, (+)2, and (+3) responses all reveal her desire to be adored by large numbers of people, adored for beauty and wealth. The (−)1b and (−)3 responses reflect her guilt over sexual

272 The Intensive Diagnostic Evaluation

feelings, and (−)3 also reflects her guilt over hostile feelings toward other women.

Another mother gave this response:

(+)1 Jacqueline Kennedy. She has glamor. She's respected and she's elegant. She has many intellectual interests. There is more for her in the future.

(+)2 Picasso. He lives an isolated and contented life. He has inner contentment and satisfaction. He's not dependent on others. He's uninvolved with the rest of the world.

(+)3 Jay. The man I'm now dating. He's serious-minded. He has a flair of enjoying life. He captures both worlds, the real and the unreal.

(−)1 My ex-husband's brother's wife. She has no sense of morals. She has affairs with other men and she shows no reaction, no guilt. Otherwise, she's wonderful.

(−)2 My mother. She's incapable of showing warmth. She always finds the bad side of things. She thrives on misery.

(−)3 Candy, the heroine in a book. It's a sexual satire on a foolish young girl. She has sex with her father, with an uncle, with a resident doctor, with someone in a men's room, and a hunchback in the street.

This mother was an extremely infantile and self-indulgent woman. She was sexually promiscuous and neglected her children in order to go off evenings and weekends with a series of men. She was highly materialistic and extremely exhibitionistic. She was incapable of involving herself in a meaningful way with others. All these qualities are revealed in the verbal projective responses. Her choice of Jacqueline Kennedy for her "glamor" and elegance reveal her exhibitionistic and materialistic qualities. Her inability to involve herself meaningfully is suggested in the reason she gives for wishing to be Picasso, as well as the reasons she gives for not wishing to be her mother. Some guilt over her sexual promiscuity is revealed in (−)1 and (−)3 where she denigrates two other women who themselves were quite promiscuous.

Another mother stated:

(+)1 Margaret Bourke-White. She was formerly a photographer. Now she's sick. She was well-traveled and she led an exciting life. She traveled all over the world. She was married to Erskine Caldwell but they were divorced. She was very creative. She was a very aggressive woman.

(+)2 E. Nesbitt. She wrote children's books. She wrote books on poetry, English, and wild life. She supported her husband and her husband's mistress in her own home. She entertained many interesting people. She was a very strong person. She was lively and full of energy.

(+)3 My Aunt Robb. She was always held up to me as a model. She was beautiful, charming, athletic, and always enjoyed life. She always lived in an academic world, but she was not an intellectual.

(−)1 My mother. She led a hard life. She was always mixed up. I don't like her. She has no common sense. She's done all the wrong things. She favored my brother. She was unfair to me. She gave me no preparation for life. When I had to have my tonsils out, she didn't tell me in advance. I couldn't rely on her. I've never gotten any backing from her and now I can't depend on anyone.

(−)2 My father. He's led a very unrealistic kind of life. He never found meaningful work. Although he graduated from Harvard, he always held menial jobs. I wouldn't want to be him because he married my mother. He was never happy with her.

(−)3 A man at my office. He's a no person. He's a zombie. He has no animation. He's just a dead pan.

This mother was a very intelligent, independent, self-assertive, and a fairly accomplished woman. She was married to a very intellectual man who was quite dependent on her. She was somewhat inhibited in the expression of her maternal feelings. In the (−)1 response, she reveals some of the sources of her exaggerated independence and self-assertion, namely, her own mother's neglect and lack of interest in her. Not being able to depend on her mother she had never felt she could depend on anyone and had thereby become extremely independent and self-assertive. In (+)1 and (+)2 she selects women who have these qualities. The (+)2 choice exhibits this to an extreme degree where she selects a woman who supports not only her husband but her husband's mistress. The (+)3 response is not in itself pathological but tends to support the kind of independent life which this mother considers to be ideal. The (−2)response again gives information about the reasons why this mother could have little respect for men and little belief that she could depend upon them, thereby having to depend only on her own resources. The (−)3 response also makes reference to her emotional inhibition and lack of spontaneity.

Dreams   I will most often ask a mother if she has had any dreams that have repeated themselves throughout the course of her life. I am in agreement with my colleagues in the field of psychoanalysis that this can be an important question. Repetitious dreams most often reflect an ongoing theme in the individual's life. If the mother has not had such experiences, then I ask her if she can recall *any* dream in her life. This, too, may be significant, especially if it is a dream that she had many years previously. The fact that she remembers it so many years later is a statement of its psychological importance. Another kind of dream that should be given serious consideration by the examiner is one that occurs before the first session. Often this may be a rich source of information about the patient's anticipations from treatment or about fundamental life problems. Unfortunately, the dream may be presented at a time when the therapist is less capable of analyzing it because of his or her unfamiliarity with the person. However, to the degree that one can analyze it, to that degree may one learn some useful information. On occasion, one files it away and may find it useful subsequently, when one is more familiar with the person.

One mother related this dream as having taken place just prior to the initial evaluation:

> I was in the waiting room of a dentist's office and there were three dogs there. They got into the garbage cans and the dentist was going to spray the dogs with MACE (that anti-riot stuff that makes you paralyzed).

The patient's father was a physician who spent long hours in his office. The dream reveals the mother's feelings that the father (here depicted as a dentist) sees their three children as unnecessary nuisances who have to be rejected and paralyzed if he is to be freed of the obligations of taking care of them. Their scrounging for food in a garbage can reveals her feeling that he has little to offer them. It is of interest, however, that she is passive to all of this and permits it to occur.

Another mother related this repetitious dream:

> I often dream that there is a fire in the house and I have to get the kids out.

The dream serves as an expression of the mother's hostility toward her children and her desire that she be free of the responsibilities and inconveniences associated with their upbringing. However, another part of her – a part which is genuinely concerned for their well being – salvages them in time. In summary then the dream reflects the mother's ambivalence toward her children.

Between her first and second evaluation sessions, a mother related this dream:

> A service man had to come to service the bidet. He didn't know what he was doing.

I understood this dream to mean that the serviceman was this examiner and it reflected the mother's feelings that I was incompetent. The mother had an hysterical character disorder with much repression of hostility and sexual feelings. I considered the bidet, as a cleanser of her genitalia, to reflect her desires that I might in some way alleviate her feelings that sexuality was dirty, or that I might in some way be involved in cleansing her sexuality. I did not attempt to analyze this dream in this case because I felt that she was not ready to deal with any of my surmised interpretations. Often a dream like this speaks poorly for the parents' commitment to the treatment process because of its implied distrust of the therapist. Fortunately, in this case, this did not turn out to be the case, and the child did well with full cooperation on the part of the parents. My guess is that the mother gradually became more confident in me, in spite of her initial hesitation.

One mother related this repetitious dream:

> I was at AB's house. She was having a birthday party for her daughter C. It really wasn't A's house but she was having a party there. She had an old-fashioned stove there, a potbellied stove. It had a beautiful rare plant growing out of it. The plant had a beautiful odor. I said, "Please tell me where you got this." A said, "Before you leave, I'll either tell you where I bought it or I'll give you a branch to plant yourself." It had pink and white pretty flowers. I kept asking her where she got it. Oh, yes, one other thing. The stove had originally been black, but it was painted white.

The mother had previously been in treatment for a short period, was intelligent, and was interested in analzying this dream. As a result of her associations and my inquiries, we decided that the potbellied stove and plant represented the mother herself. She basically considered herself to be vulgar, inadequate (i.e., "black"), and she attempted to hide these deficiencies by presenting herself with a colorful facade. This was represented by the white paint and the beautiful flowers which everyone admired and which everyone enjoyed smelling. This may have reflected her way of dealing with her inner feeling that she "smells."

This mother was an extremely materialistic and exhibitionistic woman. She was quite wealthy and was obsessed with indulging herself with expensive clothing. She said, "I even dress up to go out for the mail." She was quite shocked after she understood what the dream meant. She subsequently went into therapy with me, and the dream served to catalyze her working on this problem.

Another mother told me she used to have this dream about once a week a few years prior to the evaluation:

> A very short, ugly man came up to me. He was exactly the opposite of the kind that I like. I asked him to make love to me. He was overjoyed at the idea. He couldn't believe his luck. He then made advances to me, and I told him that I changed my mind.

The dream reveals the mother's deep-seated hostility toward men. In the dream she selects an ugly man, that is, one who is most likely to respond with gratitude and enthusiasm to her suggestion of a sexual encounter and then thwarts him in the midst of his excitation. Her hostility toward men here is obvious.

During the evaluation this mother told the following dream:

> I was with a child. I was at Columbia Teacher's College. I went back and forth from making pottery to being in the apartment of a photographer. While I was making pottery, someone said that I should do it in a particular way but I insisted that I could do it better. Which was so.
>
> This photographer was trying to take a picture of a child and he said that he was on the staff at the university. The child didn't want to let his picture be taken. I told the child that he should let the photographer take the picture. The child said that he would be nice to the photographer only until the picture was taken and then he wouldn't be nice any longer.
>
> The child and I then went through many rooms and then we went out the back door and left.

The dream clearly reflects the mother's attitude toward the evaluation. The photographer is a common symbol for the therapist who "sees through," confronts, and accurately portrays the patient. The child is depicted in two ways: first as the pottery which the mother creates, and second in the form of a child. In the dream the mother reveals her feeling that she can do a better job in molding and forming her child's personality than I can and, therefore, insists upon doing it herself. In the dream she also has the child cooperate with me until the picture is taken (that is, until the end of the evaluation) and then has him refuse to cooperate further.

The journey through many rooms signifies the complex inquiry of the evaluation and their leaving through the back door reveals their desire to remove themselves surreptitiously and prematurely, rather than through the front door which would reflect a desire to leave when treatment is completed.

The dream was a perfect statement of what ultimately happened and served as an accurate warning for the examiner. The child did cooperate until the end of the evaluation, and then both he and the parents decided not to pursue treatment. Although the dream was analyzed with the mother and she accepted its implications at the time, I was unable to alter the strong forces which compelled her to follow its dictates.

Another mother described having frequent fearful fantasies and an occasional nightmare that "my husband would lose both of his legs and I'll end up pushing him in a wheelchair."

This mother was extremely masochistic. Although she had a Ph.D. degree, she constantly berated herself intellectually and had always felt that she had to present herself as intellectually average or below average if she were to attract her husband. Her husband was a borderline psychotic who had little involvement with her and devoted himself to his academic pursuits (he was a professor at a university). He had her do most of the "dirty work," that is, boring research and typing, for his own doctoral thesis.

The fantasy reveals not only her unconscious hostility toward her husband, hostility which is expressed through the desire that he lose his legs, but also her feeling that the only way he could really need her was if he were to be helpless. When he was getting his doctorate degree he needed her. Following this he would no longer need her and the fantasy allowed her once again to play a meaningful role in his life. In addition, by burdening herself with a crippled man, she could gratify her masochistic desires.

The mother of an adolescent described this dream on the night before her first individual interview with me. (There had been a previous screening interview when I saw her in association with her son and husband):

> I was on one side of a sliding door. My husband was on the other side. I was trying to shut the sliding door and couldn't.

The dream, coming as it did on the night prior to her first interview with me alone, suggests that she would prefer to place a closed door between herself and her husband so that he would not see certain things which would be unpleasant for her to reveal to me. It suggested that she was not going to tell me freely very much about her real feelings about her husband. In the subsequent part of the interview this prediction turned out to be true. She described her relationship with him as a good one and had absolutely no complaints. Of him she could only say, "He's wonderful. He's good.

Sometimes he talks a little too much, but that's nothing that concerns me. He talks a lot of common sense."

In reality, the husband was a person who was prone to make endless speeches over inanities. He would puff himself up and pontificate over the most simplistic issues as if he was spouting forth great wisdom. Only one of his four children was consciously irritated by these lectures. One of his sons (not my patient) identified with the father and at 21 was already filled with an air of self-importance.

The dream and the mother's subsequent comments revealed her fear of coming to terms directly with this quite alienating trait of her husband's.

I generally spend two interviews with the mothers of adolescents, each one lasting 45 to 60 minutes. I hope the reader can appreciate that the information gained in the individual interviews provides me with a much greater knowledge of what is going on with her than is obtained in the initial two-hour consultation. In every sense of the word, the data collection in the initial interview is indeed superficial. The examiner who does not avail him- or herself of the more extensive interviews is being deprived of vital information—information that is crucial to have if one is to understand thoroughly what is going on with the patient.

Before closing the final interview with the mother, I may ask her how she views herself ten years from now. The answer provided can also be a useful source of information. The same question can be asked about her guesses about the patient a decade from now. I am sure that the reader has a collection of his or her own questions that can also prove useful. In this section I have presented those that I personally have found most valuable.

THE EVALUATION OF THE FATHER

My discussion of the father's evaluation will be significantly shorter than that of the mother. This is primarily because many of the questions are the same and there would be little point in my repeating them in this section. However, another fact relates to my observation that fathers generally are less willing to reveal themselves than mothers and accordingly, their evaluations are often shorter. Whereas the mother's evaluation is generally two (sometimes three) interviews, each of which is 45 to 60 minutes, fathers generally have nothing further to say to me after one (or at most two) interviews of the same duration. They often are much "tighter" when responding to the projective questions, as well.

The Initial Inquiry

As was true with the mother, I begin the interview with an open-end question in which I ask him if there is anything special on his mind that he would like to speak with me about. He may or may not have something to discuss and, of course, I follow his lead. I then ask the father about reactions to the initial two-hour consultation. We then go on to questions in which I ask him his opinion regarding the causes of the youngster's difficulties. I inform him that I recognize that his main reason for consulting with me is that I should provide my opinion regarding the answers to this question. However, I advise him that his guesses and speculations can be an important source of information to me. I then proceed with the questions regarding his and his wife's dealing with the patient, both assets and liabilities. I am particularly interested in whether the father involved himself in sports with the children when they were younger, especially such activities as Little League, soccer, and so on. When investigating this area, however, the examiner should find out whether the father was fanatical about it. If the father was having fist fights with the coaches at the Little League games, he was probably doing his children more harm than good. He was probably using the child for vicarious gratification to a degree beyond the normal. I am also interested in his involvement in school activities, curricular and extracurricular.

Description of the Marriage

We then proceed to a discussion of the marriage. Here, especially, fathers may be particularly unreceptive to revealing difficulties in the marital relationship. A common situation is one in which a mother will claim that her husband had had an affair, and he has told her that he does not wish her to reveal this to me. In the session with me he will studiously avoid discussion of this issue, even though he knows that his wife is aware of the relationship. I ask the father the same questions about the marriage that I ask the mother, especially with regard to its strong points and weak points. If the father initially presents the marriage as "good," with no problems at all, I will state that all marriages have their areas of friction, and I encourage him to discuss those areas in which he and his wife have differences of opinion. Even with this sanction, the father may insist that there are no such difficulties in his marriage. If such a response is given by a father whom the examiner knows is having an affair (by some information provided by the wife), then there is little the examiner can do. It is hoped that she will bring the matter up during the joint session, but often she does not. As mentioned, in such situations, I often let the thing rest. To "rock the boat" may cause a disruption of the marital equilibrium, which may do the child more harm than good.

History of Psychiatric Treatment

I then ask the father whether he has ever been in treatment. Most child therapists will agree that boys are overrepresented in their patient population. In contrast, most adult therapists will agree that women are overrepresented in their patient population. I believe that this phenomenon relates to the fact that boys are generally more rambunctious, assertive, and "fighters." As every teacher and parent knows, boys are "tough customers" when compared to girls. Accordingly, they have greater difficulty complying with social constraints, especially in school. I suspect that there are probably genetic bases for these character traits in that they may have been more adaptive in evolutionary development. Hunters and fighters do better if they are more aggressive, and so men who possessed such qualities survived preferentially over men who did not. However, social and environmental factors have probably played a role as well in engendering these traits. At the adult level, however, men often feel the need to maintain their "macho image" and are less receptive to therapy—a process in which they are encouraged to reveal weaknesses and failings. If the father has been in therapy, I will ask the same questions that I have asked the mother regarding the nature of the problems for which he went into treatment and what benefits, if any, were derived from the therapy. I am especially interested in marital counseling and the marital problems that brought the parents into therapy.

Background Information

The questions to the father regarding background information are essentially the same as those posed to the mother. Specifically, I ask the father about his parents, their relationship with one another, and their relationships with him. I also inquire about his siblings, especially with regard to the presence of psychiatric difficulties. Here, I am particularly interested in the kind of parenting the father received in that his parents probably served as the model for his own parenting. I also want to know about the nature of the relationships between the paternal grandparents and my patient.

Military Service   One difference between the father's and the mother's inquiries relates to military service. If the father served in the military, one does well to find out about how he adjusted there and whether he received an honorable discharge. One should ascertain whether the father had difficulties adjusting in the service and whether he warranted disciplinary action and/or psychiatric treatment. The military generally requires a degree of integration similar to (if not more than) that which is required for adjustment in school. One must be willing to comply to a reasonable degree with authority and to exhibit self-restraint under stressful circumstances. If the father was in combat, one wants to find out whether he suffered with any psychiatric disorders commonly seen under such circumstances.

The First-Memory Question   As was true for the mother, questions about the father's first memory can often provide useful information about underlying psychodynamics. I present here a few examples.

One father gave this memory:

> I was about four years old. I remember leaving my
> mother's and father's store. I climbed over a fence outside of
> the store and ripped my leg open. Then I ran back into the
> store.

This father, although 38 years old, was still working as an
employee in his parents' store. He was extremely dependent on
them and was quite passive in his relationship with them. Although
he spoke on occasion of going out on his own, there was little
evidence that he seriously intended to do this. Although he could
not openly admit it to himself, it was clear that he was waiting for
the day that they would die and then the business would become
his. In his marriage, as well, he was quite dependent on his wife,
who domineered him mercilessly. The memory reveals the father's
basic feeling that were he to leave the domain of his parents he
would be traumatized. The warning serves him well and he returns
to the store where he feels comfortable and safe. The first memory
epitomizes the basic theme of his life and his relationships both with
his parents and with his wife.
Another father had this memory:

> I was about four years old. I was driving a little toy car and
> running over another kid's white shoes. He was a dandy. I was
> a dirty little kid. I liked to get dirty. He went crying to his
> mother. I don't know if after that I was chastised or what.

This father was a bright, somewhat cocky, and basically
arrogant man. He was quick to anger and most of his comments
about people were critical. He was in the plumbing supply business
and psychologically he appeared to be "shitting" on the world. The
memory reflects this life pattern. His greatest pleasure appeared to
be dirtying those who were clean, that is, defecating on others. His
relationship with me was in the same spirit. I felt that he saw me as
a boy with white shoes and his primary mode of relating to me was
hostile. He stated that in grade school his greatest pleasure came
when he was head of the monitors, a position, no doubt that gave
him further opportunity to be sadistic to others. After graduation
from college the father was fired from his first job after six months
of work. He considered his firing the result of his having been

rebellious: "I didn't want to do what they wanted." He finally ended up working for his own father, with whom he described a very competitive and antagonistic relationship.

The father also stated that he feared women, saying: "I see them as aggressive birds who would want to scratch our eyes out." I considered this fantasy to be a reflection of his own hostility projected onto women.

Another father's memory:

> I was in my crib. I must have been about two years old and I was picking the paint off the iron bars and eating it.

This father's parents were quite distant from him and he suffered definite emotional deprivation in his childhood. The recollection is symbolic of the deprivation he suffered in that he had to resort to the ingestion of inedible objects in his attempt to gain symbolic affection. The psychodynamics of this memory are similar to those of children with pica who ingest inedible objects because of neglect and a craving for oral-dependent gratifications.

Another father's first memory:

> I was two or three years old and playing in my backyard. My clothing caught on a fence that I was climbing. A friend of mine came and had to lift me up and take me off.

This father had a schizoid character disorder and was severely dependent on his wife and parents. Although 31 and a law school graduate, he was still unable to function as an adult. He worked for his father, who was also a lawyer, and it was clear that he could not have been able to function independently in another law firm or in his own practice. The memory reveals his basic dependency problem. When he is confronted with an obstruction or some other difficulty in life, he is unable to get himself out of trouble and must depend on others to take care of him.

One father gave this response:

> I was about three years old and I remember trying to eat cement from a wall.

This man's father (that is the paternal grandfather of my patient) was a very intellectualizing man who devoted himself to his scholarly interests instead of spending time with his children. The paternal grandmother had paranoid and depressive episodes for which she received ECT. At times she was suicidal. It is hard to see how this father felt that the love and affection givn to him was as digestible as concrete.

School Life   I ask the father about adjustment at the elementary school level. I am particularly interested in the father's comparison of himself with my patient during this period, especially if the patient is a boy. Many fathers will say that the patient is exhibiting behavior very similar to their own during this phase of their lives. One must consider the possibility that this reflects a genetic component. However, one also wants to ascertain whether the father is sanctioning atypical behavior (antisocial) or criticizing it. Possible genetic contributions notwithstanding, sanctioning may contribute to its perpetuation.

Although things are changing, women still have less necessity to dedicate themselves as assiduously as fathers to school and career planning. I am not claiming that this is a good thing; only that it is a reality of our world, recent changes notwithstanding. Accordingly, if a mother was insufficiently motivated during the high school period, it does not necessarily reflect as much pathology as a father who was similarly unmotivated. The pressures on the father to ultimately be a breadwinner are far greater than those placed on girls during the formative years. Accordingly, a girl's lack of school and work motivation during the high school period does not necessarily reflect as much pathology as in a father who is similarly unmotivated. I am also interested in the father's social relationships throughout his school career. These lay the foundation for adult relationships, including the relationship with his wife.

Work History   It is important to go into the father's work history. A long history of difficulty adjusting in jobs generally reflects psychiatric difficulties. And the father's commitment to work will generally affect the youngster's attitude toward school. If the patient sees the father seriously involved in his work, it is likely that he will thereby serve as a good model for the youngster's involvement in school work. I cannot emphasize this point strongly enough. Many parents present with children who are unmotivated to do their school work. Yet the parents may provide an atmosphere in which work is viewed as odious and there is practically no intellectual curiosity. In such an environment the child is not likely to develop strong school interest unless exposed extensively to other models who demonstrate such commitments.

The Premarital Relationshp with the Mother   I want to find out the circumstances under which the father first met the mother and what his initial attractions were. The examiner does well to appreciate that most people do not provide what a judicious middle-aged person would consider reasonable reasons for marriage. So common are the frivolous criteria for marriage that one has to consider them to be in the normal range. For example, a father may claim that he "fell in love." When one asks what the particular qualities were that he fell in love with, he may be hard put to give other answers other than his wife was physically attractive and that she was "sweet." One should be particularly interested here in any atypical relationships that were established during this period.

Projective Questions   Because fathers are generally more reticent to reveal themselves directly, one would think that projective questions might be useful. However, even in this area my experience has been that they are more reluctant to reveal themselves. This hesitation notwithstanding, one can sometimes still get useful information by the utilization of these questions.

Five Wishes   Some fathers can only go to three wishes. When they reach the fourth and fifth wishes, they become too anxious to continue because they run out of stereotyped responses. I present here some responses of fathers to the five wishes question.
One father gave these responses:

1. That Randy be okay.
2. That I have a happy marriage.
3. That I become independent and self-sufficient.
4. I can't think of anymore.

All three wishes relate to difficulties in the family. The third wish especially epitomized the father's main psychological problem, namely, that he was an extremely dependent individual. Although in his late 30s, he was very much under the thumb of his own father, whom he was working for, who was supporting him, and who controlled almost every aspect of his life.

Another father gave these responses:

1. Wisdom.
2. Patience.
3. Charity.
4. Free access to any library I wanted.
5. The writing style equivalent to George Travelli Macauley.

This father was a highly intellectualized man on the faculty of a major Eastern university. He was most fearful of intimate involvements with others and spent most of his time absorbed in his academic work. For years he had not slept in the same room as his wife and sexual contact was rare. Three of his five responses make direct reference to his intellectual and academic ambitions (#1, #4, and #5). In addition, this man flaunted his intellectual accomplishments in an attempt to bolster a very low self-esteem. This is well shown in wish #5 where he mentions the name of a person who was unknown to this examiner. When I asked him who Macauley was, he responded with condescending incredulity that I didn't know that Macauley was a famous historian. The implication of his facial expression was one of: "How stupid can you be, not ever to have heard of Macauley?"

Conspicuous by their absence are responses that refer to any human beings other than himself.

Another father gave these answers:

1. Good health and long life.
2. To be a contented, respected millionaire. To have enough material comfort to free me from worry.
3. To have stature and power. To be a better lawyer than anyone else and to be recognized as such. To be a member of the establishment.

4. For my children to have the same luck with their wives as I have with mine and to have as much money as I have.

5. The question I wonder about is whether it would be better for my wife or for me to die first? It would be better for her if I went first, but you won't get me to say that I want her to die first. No, the best thing would be if there was an accident and we both died together.

This father was an extremely grandiose, self-centered, manipulative, and hostile individual. He actually considered himself to be uniformly admired, respected, and envied by all around him. In actual fact he had no real friends. His cruelty to his daughter (more verbal than physical) resulted in her being a very withdrawn and timid child.

Response #1 is within the normal range. Wishes #2, #3, and #4 reflect the already described grandiosity, materialism, and power fantasies. Wish #5 reveals his hostility toward his wife, which he then denied. Actually, the man's wife (my patient's mother) had significant personality problems, and the marriage was fraught with difficulties. However, he had to deny this in order to maintain the image of having a "perfect marriage." Under these circumstances there was formidable hostility toward his wife, reflected in his death wishes, but he could not allow these feelings entrance into conscious awareness.

Verbal Projective Questions   Presented below are some verbal projective questions that provided important information in the fathers' evaluation.

One father gave these responses:

(+)1 Caruso or Lawrence Melchoir. I can't sing very well, and I'd love to be a great singer, to be able to entertain people that way.

(+)2 Jacques Cousteau. He leads an active, interesting life. He's adventurous; he's in the outdoors; he does a lot of skin diving.

(+)3 Dr. H. He's a very good surgeon. He does a lot of good for the people. His hours probably aren't too bad.

(−)1 Frank Sinatra or the Beatles, or others in the public eye. They have no private life. They're mobbed wherever they go.

(−)2 A politician. Most of them are phony phonies. They lie all the time. I couldn't keep track of all the lies.

(−)3 Just plain Joe. I want to get some recognition in life.

My full clinical evaluation of this man revealed him to be relatively stable and free from significant psychopathology. Although one might find evidences of psychopathology in the above responses, I considered them to be within the normal range. The (+)1 and (+)3 responses suggest that this father might have inordinate desires to be famous. However, his life situation was one in which he appeared to be very secure and adjusted in a fairly respectable but certainly not famous position. He was an engineer who was owner of a small manufacturing company. The (−)2 reply suggests the possibility that the father himself engages in duplicity or would like to do so. However, this was not substantiated by the rest of my clinical evaluation. It is important for the reader to appreciate that repression of unacceptable material exists in all people, and projective tests reveal what is being repressed. In our culture there is probably a tendency in most people to lie at times and to crave fame. Lying and inordinate ambition are not acceptable traits and may very well be repressed. This does not mean that the person harboring such desires is suffering with psychopathology. It is only when there is acting out, obsessive preoccupation, or when these trends interfere significantly with one's life pattern that the term psychopathology can justifiably be applied.

Another father gave these responses:

(+)1 Elvis Presley. He's rich and famous. He's honest; he doesn't gamble. He's a good family man. I've always been a great fan of his.

(+)2 Mickey Mantle. I like to play ball. He's my idol. I adore his strength and skill as a ball player. He's also an upright family man. He doesn't have much of an education, just like me.

(+)3 John Kennedy. He had a close relationship with the common man, in spite of all his money. But he wasn't a big shot. He had compassion for the common man.

(−)1 Fidel Castro. He deceived people. He manhandled people. He causes a lot of pain and heartache.

(−)2 Hitler. He mistreated the Jewish people terribly. He rose to power by stepping over everybody.

(−)3 Jimmy Hoffa. He engaged in many underground activities. He's a vicious leader who robbed the union membership.

This 28-year-old father worked at the dairy counter at a supermarket. He graduated high school with mediocre grades and married at the age of 20. The paternal grandfather showed the father little warmth, and abandoned the home when the father was 18 years old.

The persons that this patient selected in both positive and negative categories could very well be within the normal range. However, the reasons he gives for choosing these people reflect certain manifestations of his personal psychopathology. In the (+)1 and (+)2 responses he introduces the "family man" theme, which are clearly personal associations to these figures, and certainly not typical. They suggest preoccupation with and cravings for a close-knit family in compensation for the deprivations he suffered as a child. In the (+)3 response he chooses John Kennedy, in part because of his "compassion for the common man." His (−)1, (−)2, and (−)3 responses are all people who in one way or another have taken advantage of, deceived, and even killed the common man. These responses reveal his father's basic feelings of impotency in a world which he sees as malevolent and overpowering. He craves the protection of a benevolent authority symbolized by John Kennedy.

Another father gave this response:

(+)1 Paul Getty, for his business shrewdness. He got the oil reserve depreciation bill passed by Congress. He had no family life, so I wouldn't want to be like him for that.

(+)2 My old hometown doctor, Dr. O. He's someone who has done a lot of good for many people. He could talk to you about anything. He was a good family man.

(+)3 Supreme Court Justice White. He's an athlete. He's smart. He leads a well-rounded life.

(−)1 Adolph Hitler. He was a killer. His super-race idea was all wrong.

(−)2 Walter Reuther. He's a legalized crook. He warps our economy with the strength of his union.

(−)3 Malcolm X. He was trying to get a job done and wasn't doing it the right way. He was using violence rather than discussion.

This father had little interest in the patient, his adopted stepson, and spent 16 to 20 hours a day, six to seven days a week at work. He had strong psychopathic tendencies as well.

The (+)1 response reveals both his psychopathic tendencies as well as denial of his disinterest in family life. In the (+)2 reply we again see the denial of his lack of interest in his family via his admiration for Dr. O, the "good family man." I considered the (+)3 and (−)1 responses to be within the normal range. The (−)2 response again relates to the father's psychopathy because I considered the father himself to be a "legalized crook." The (−)3 response as it stands cannot provide too much information. Had time been available to discuss the Malcolm X associations further, more revealing information might have been obtained.

One father gave these responses:

(+)1 Nathaniel Bowdich. He was a 19th century New Englander. He was a self-taught navigator and ship owner. He established many of the principles of navigation for whaling ships. Mariners still use Bowdich's book on navigation. He was very sharp and skilled. He taught mathematics at Harvard as well.

(+)2 Thomas Jefferson. He was a happy man. He had many interests. He enjoyed life.

(+)3 Jerry G., a colleague of mine. He's articulate, outgoing, and gets a bang out of life.

(−)1 Nat Turner. Although he was free, he was really still a slave. He had obsessions that he could not let go of. He was a double-dealing shackled madman.

(−)2 Nixon. He doesn't know what he wants. He doesn't know where he's going. He's not up to the responsibility. He has no convictions of his own.

(−)3 A psychiatrist. There's too much intimacy. They're bowed down with the inner world, which is a horrible one.

This father, athough a successful professional man, was a borderline psychotic whose main symptoms were withdrawal and obsessive ruminations. He had little genuine interest in his family and only out of a sense of duty did he make attempts to involve himself with them. Consistent with this lack of involvement is the fact that in none of these responses is any mention made of family involvement. The (+)1 person, although admirable in many ways, appears to epitomize 19th century new England independence and self-assertion. He is the kind of a person who rises above hostile forces in nature and the hardships of life in a determined and single-minded manner. The choice of the navigator probably relates to the father's feelings that he himself needs some navigation and direction if he is to weather the storms of his life, especially those associated with the welling up of feelings (as represented by the ocean waves) which are so threatening to him. In the (+)2 and (+)3 responses the father reveals his desire to get some pleasure out of life, something he was not getting because of his psychiatric disturbances.

The (−)1 response reveals the father's basic feelings about himself. He, like Nat Turner, is enslaved by his obsessions and his duplicity (which was associated with his contrived and artificial involvement in his family) and cause him to think of himself as "a double-dealing shackled madman." In the (−)2 response reference is made to the father's indecisiveness related to his obsessive doubting and massive ambivalence. The (−)3 response again makes reference to the father's psychic conflicts and fears of relevation of his primitive eruptions from the unconscious.

One father was asked the animal questions in addition to the person questions. These are the responses he gave:

(+)1 A poodle dog. It gets good treatment.

(+)2 A black panther. It's shrewed and it's cunning. It's fast.

(+)3 A turtle. It goes on slowly but looks back to see if it's right or wrong.

(−)1 A cat. It's too self-reliant. It doesn't give. It just takes.

(−)2 A pig. It's only here to be eaten.

(−)3 A reptile or snake. It's misunderstood. People kill them and don't realize that they're just doing their own thing.

This father was an extremely psychopathic person. He had little interest in the patient, his adopted stepson, and spent most of his time away from the home at his job. He was a very conniving and materialistic individual who used people ruthlessly in order to obtain his own ends. His primary attraction to his wife, who was 10 years his senior, was that she was a good cook.

The (+)1 response reveals his strong impulses to passively lead a life of luxury. The (+)2 response reflects his admiration for psychopathic qualities. The (−)3 response suggests unconscious respect for the psychopathic personality type who is most circumspect, calculating, and reflective of his behavior.

In the (−)1 response the father's criticism of the cat who "doesn't give, just takes" is a clear statement of his denial of these qualities within himself, because he was a most taking person. The (−)2 response relates to the same attitude in that the father, seeing the world as a place where one is "eaten," chooses to be the "eater." The (−)3 response is a clear-cut rationalization for psychopathic behavior. The reptile and the snake are highly symbolic of the devious, the unacceptable, the cunning, and the surreptitious. The father cannot provide a logical justification for accepting such behavior but merely requests that these animals be accepted because they are "doing their own thing," and that in itself should be enough for people to accept them.

The verbal projective questions can also be used with adults to describe other family members. Just as the child is asked to select animals and objects that will suit his or her mother and father, the parent can be asked to present people, animals, and objects that will suit other family members, especially spouse and children. This father gave the following responses when asked to select animals that suited hs wife's personality:

> (+)1 A mynah bird. It's like a parrot. It's always jabbering.
> (+)2 A rhinoceros. It goes where it wants. It doesn't have much of a brain. It tromps over everything in order to get what it wants.
> (+)3 A Pekingese house dog. It has no worries. It's fed, then taken out to shit, and then put to bed.
> (−)1 A mallard. It's graceful; she's not.
> (−)2 A leopard. It's quiet and stealthy. She's loud. She has no tact. She's noisy.
> (−)3 An alligator. He lives in the water and she's afraid of the water.

This father had very little respect for or involvement with his wife and the verbal projective associations clearly reflect this. The responses illustrate the massive feelings of disdain and disgust he had for her, and each response reveals a different type of deprecation. Here we see how all of these derogatory attitudes are on the conscious level.

Another father gave these responses when asked to select animals that suited his wife's personality:

> (+)1 A lion. It's majestic. It's a leader. It's quiet and unassuming. It has perseverance. It likes to get things done in a quiet way. She's respected like the lion by the rest of the animal kingdom.
> (+)2 A Mastiff dog. It protects the house. It's a strong animal yet it's gentle. It's respected by everyone.
> (+)3 A deer because of its beauty and gracefulness. It's shy except when protecting its young and then it becomes very forceful. It's clear. It leads a quiet life. It's a choice food of carnivorous animals.
> (−)1 A cat. They're nice until you go against them. Then they will turn against you. She won't do that.
> (−)2 A snake. She's not repulsive. She doesn't instill fear in anyone.

(−)3 A bat because it's a spreader of disease. It's repulsive. It's a scavenger. It hides away from view.

This father was extremely passive and submissive in his relationship to a remarkably domineering masochistic-martyristic wife. She was extremely controlling and coercive to all members of the family, but her manipulations were rarely overt. She played on their guilt through her martyristic self-sacrificing tendencies. Both the father and the children were very much in fear of her.

These qualities are reflected throughout the verbal projective responses. She, like the lion, is the "leader" and gets things done in a "quiet" and "unassuming" way. The "respect" that the lion enjoys from the "rest of the animal kingdom" is clearly the fearful subservience she has extracted from the members of her family.

The Mastiff dog, of course, exhibits qualities similar to the lion. The mother, like the Mastiff, is the "protector of the house" and is "respected" (= feared) by everyone. In the (+)3 response the statement that the deer is "the choice food for carnivorous animals" reflects the father's primitive and repressed hostility toward the mother. By identifying himself with a carnivorous animal for whom the deer is "choice food," he can vent the rage he feels toward her. In addition, the fantasy probably represents a desire to acquire her strength through primitive incorporative, cannibalistic maneuvers.

The (−)1 response is denial pure and simple. The mother is a person who will turn against the father if he turns against her, and he lives in fear of her retribution. The (−)2 response reveals his true feelings towards the mother, namely, that she is repulsive and he lives in fear of her. The (−)3 response is again a clear statement of the real feelings the father feels about the mother. He sees her as "repulsive" and "a scavenger." The subtle and somewhat surreptitious coercive maneuvers that the mother utilizes are reflected in the comment that the bat "hides away from view."

Another father gave these responses:

(+)1 A tiger. She's ferocious at times. She yells and screams a lot.

(+)2 A horse. She likes horse races. She watches many on TV. She loves all sorts of gambling, but not to excess. She's a $2.00 better.

(+)3 Dogs, any kind of dog. She loves them and I despise them. She'd want to be a dog. (What kind?) A brown Scotch Terrier. I can just associate her with dogs. I don't know why.

(−)1 A cow. It's fat, cumbersome, and odd. She's not like that.

(−)2 A giraffe. It has a high neck and long strides. She doesn't have a high neck and she takes short strides.

(−)3 A snake. It's slimy. She's not.

The 12-year-old daughter of this man was constantly bickering with her mother, whereas he tended to indulge his wife. The mother was not a very strongly maternal person, and the patient turned to her father where she felt she could get greater affection. An hereditary loss of hair was a source of serious concern to the mother, although the father denied that it in any way lessened his attraction for her. When first seen, the family was going through what I would consider an "oedipal crisis," with the father and daughter strongly attracted to one another and denying their attraction with intermittent bickering. The mother was quite jealous over the relationship between the father and daughter and directed much of her jealous rage toward the daughter.

The (+)1 response refers not only to the father's awareness of the mother's overt hostility expressed toward the daughter but, in addition, probably reveals his sensitivity to some of the mother's additional hostilities as well. The (+)3 response reveals the father's inability to overtly express his anger and his lack of physical attraction to his wife. He could only go as far as saying that he "despises" dogs and he somehow associates his wife with a dog. Denial and reaction formation were strong defense mechanisms in this man. In the (+)1 response he reveals his basic feelings about her lack of attractiveness, and there is also suggested his awareness that she is not a very maternal person in that the cow lends itself well to being viewed as a powerful maternal symbol. Although the (−)2 and (−)3 responses could also reveal his lack of attraction to her, they also could be considered to be within the normal range of responses.

Dreams One father reported the following repetitious dream:

> I dream that I am submerged under water. I think that I can't breathe and that I'm trying to get to the surface. I then discover that I can breathe under water and I feel much better.

The father was completely dependent upon his own father who owned a large business. As he grew up he always knew that no matter how poorly he did in school he would ultimately end up owning the business. He never applied himself and each time he failed out of prep school or college, his father managed to buy him into another. He had many psychopathic qualities and felt no obligation to spend time with his children, be faithful to his wife, or commit himself in any way to anyone.

The dream reveals his basic life pattern—that he will be magically saved from catastrophe. Actually others would have suffered the consequences of such a life of self-indulgence, but he seems to feel that he has come away unscathed. Others get drowned; he can breathe under water. The dream epitomized his life pattern, especially his relationship to his overprotective father.

This father described the following repetitious dream:

> I was taking a test and I never had time to finish it. I felt pressured and pushed. I kept feeling that I wasn't going to finish.

This is a common repetitious dream of people from homes where the academic pressures have been great. In analyzing this dream with both parents and patients, I have most often found it to reflect a feeling that the people will not be able to live up to the standards of their parents, both in the academic as well as in the nonacademic areas of life. Because so much emotional investment has been directed to the academic realms, it serves as a general symbol for success in life. I have also found the dream to reflect ambivalence on the person's part toward successful achievements in life. Failing the test is not simply the academic test, but the test of life's success as well. Often the parents of such a patient have been ambivalent themselves with regard to their children's successful performance.

This father was a borderline psychotic who was a highly educated and moderately successful professional man. However, his extreme psychopathology prevented him from getting anything but the slightest gratification from his professional and nonprofessional life.

Another father related this dream:

> I was reading one of my competitor's private reports. He walked in and I was ashamed. I put the papers down.

Although this father did not exhibit specific psychopathic trends in the clinical interview, he was a fiercely competitive, materialistic, grandiose, and coercive individual. Although he was ostensibly ethical in his business dealings, the dream reflects an aspect of his personality that was not apparent in the clinical evaluation, but would certainly be consistent with his character structure. This dream demonstrates how a parent's dream may provide the examiner with added information about character structure—information that may be useful in understanding the child's psychopathology. In this case, some of the child's antisocial behavior could be considered the result of identification with his father's psychopathic traits and the desire to fulfill the unconscious wishes of the parent.

Throughout his life, one father had this repetitious dream:

> I had a gym all to myself. I spent a lot of time there with kids, teaching them to play basketball. I have no problems there when I am in the gym.

The father, although 38 years old, was still very much a child. He was still employed by his parents in their small store, and he was very much under the domination of his wife. He spent much time out of the house coaching young boys in various sports. This activity not only served as a way of removing himself from the domination of his wife, but also provided him with a feeling of authority and competence—which he lacked in his relationship with both his parents and his spouse. Furthermore, sports enabled him to express vicariously much of his pent-up hostility. Last, the dream enables him to engage in childish activities beyond the extent to which he involved himself in reality. It is a dream of an adolescent dreamed by a man who psychologically was still an adolescent.

Concluding Comments

My goal here is to show that the individual, whether mother or father, who is reluctant to give information directly may provide meaningful data with projective tests. However, analyzing such material can be risky. I am certain that many examiners may have come to different conclusions regarding the interpretations I have given to the material presented. In my defense, I might say my interpretations are made on the basis of my direct clinical experiences with the families. Analyzing the material in isolation from such clinical data is extremely risky and is generally a poor idea. But even when one does have clinical information, there is no question that there is still a certain amount of speculation. These drawbacks notwithstanding, I find such projective material useful, especially for the parent who is not comfortable revealing him- or herself in the direct clinical interview.

THE EVALUATION OF THE PATIENT

INTRODUCTION

I generally devote three 45- or 60-minute sessions to the intensive evaluation of the adolescent. With regard to this phase of the evaluation, one can generally divide adolescents into two groups. The younger adolescents are usually unreceptive to direct discussion of their problems. They are similar, therefore, to pre-adolescent children in this regard. However, they differ from such younger children in their receptivity to storytelling and other projective games. They generally appreciate that such instruments are vehicles for the revelation of their innermost thoughts and feelings—revelations that they are not willing to provide. We find ourselves in the position, then, with such youngsters of having a patient that is too old to utilize the old standby, storytelling and other projective material, and too young to reveal him- or herself directly. Such youngsters, accordingly, are not comfortable sitting in a session for 45 to 60 minutes with the therapist's "beady eyes" staring at him or her asking for intimate revelations. With these youngsters I will often spend more of the evaluation sessions utilizing verbal projective questions, dream discussion, the Draw-a-Person test, the Draw-a-Family test, and other instruments described in this section. With older adolescents, generally those over the age of 15, I am usually more successful in engaging them in direct discussion which, in itself, provides useful data. However, this does not preclude my utilization, to a lesser degree, of the other instruments described in this section.

When purely psychogenic problems are present, I generally devote three sessions to the intensive evaluation of the youngster. And this is the kind of evaluation I will be describing here. If, on the basis of the information I obtained in the initial two-hour evaluation, I concluded that neurologically based difficulties are present, then a longer, extended evaluation is often warranted. I not only have to assess for the presence of the neurologically based problems, but for psychogenic problems as well. And the latter may fall into two categories. The first are those psychogenic problems that are secondary to the neurological impairment. They are derivatives of such impairment and would presumably not be present if the patient did not have a basic organic disorder. The second are those that are independent of the neurological disturbance and often result from family problems and/or improper child-rearing practices. Of course, the two categories may overlap and each contribute to the intensification of the other. Obviously, the evaluation for these difficulties is much more complex and generally takes five to six meetings with the patient.

It is important for the examiner to appreciate that the purpose of the extended evaluation is more than simply data collection. An equally, if not more, important goal is to lay the foundation for a good therapeutic relationship. This is not likely to be accomplished in one or two pressured interviews. The more relaxed the circumstances, the greater the likelihood the therapist will be able to engage the child meaningfully.

Direct Verbal Inquiry

When engaging adolescents in direct verbal discussion, it is important for the examiner to appreciate that most adolescents, especially the younger ones, do not have insight into the fact that they have "problems" and the examiner is well advised not to attempt to get such patients to develop what we call "insights." Although younger adolescents are cognitively capable of creating linkages between their symptomatology and the unconscious (and even conscious) psychological processes that are producing their symptoms, their denial mechanisms are often so formidable that they will be unreceptive to inquiries designed to bring to conscious awareness these associations and linkages. Accordingly, the examiner should not be looking for any kind of testimonials from these patients. Furthermore, what we call "problems" are not generally viewed as such by adolescents, especially the younger ones. To them the problem is often the people who are "on their backs" trying to get them to do things they don't want to. But even those youngsters who have differentiated clearly the behavioral patterns which their parents consider pathological from those which their parents deem acceptable and desirable are not likely to be motivated to direct themselves to alleviating the "unhealthy traits."

Therapists working with adolescents do well to appreciate that if the parents and they have been successful in getting "the body in the room" they are very much "ahead of the game." It is important for examiners to appreciate that if the adolescent *really* doesn't want to go for treatment, there is nothing that either he or she or the parents can do about it. Therapists also should refrain from trying to analyze defensive rationalizations that give the youngster a face-saving excuse for attending the meetings. For example, when a 16-year-old fullback on his high school's football team (six feet 2 inches tall and 200 pounds of solid muscle) tells you that the only reason he comes is that his "mother (four feet eleven inches, 98 pounds) makes me come here," the therapist does well to respond with such comments as: "Yeah, many mothers are kind of pushy," or "I know how you feel, my mother used to coerce me into things when I was your age." The worst possible response is to say some-something along these lines: "Now look, you know and I know that your mother cannot make you come here if you really don't want to. You could pick her up off the floor by her collar, look her squarely in the eyes, and say something like 'Look, Ma, if you don't get off my back about seeing that doctor, I'm going to carry you over to the window and drop you out.' Once you start accepting the fact that you're here because you really want to be here and that, at some level, you recognize that you have problems, then you'll be making the first step toward doing something about them." Therapists who talk this way are going to lose their patients and, if in private practice, are not going to have many child and adolescent patients. Such a response loses sight completely of the fact that the adolescent needs the rationalization to protect him- or herself from the ego-debasing realization and appreciation that they have weaknesses, deficiencies, and areas of imperfection. Accordingly, the therapist does well to accept, gloss over, or sidestep the rationalization and proceed with the discussion with comments such as: "Well, as long as you're here, what would you like to tell me?" or "Well, as long as the money's being spent and the session paid for, we might as well use up the time. What would you like to talk about?" With such reassurances, the youngster is more likely to reveal him- or herself.

A good example of this phenomenon occurred a number of years ago during the course of a custody evaluation. A 13-year-old girl entered the interview and stated firmly: "Let's get something straight right now. I know why you want me here. You want me to tell you who I want to live with. You want me to say things about which parent I prefer over the other. Well, you're not going to get a word out of me on that subject. My best friend's parents are also splitting and they're seeing a shrink and their shrink wants to see her also and ask her who she wants to live with. We're very good friends and we made a vow. We promised each other that we'd never tell you shrinks who we want to live with. We're blood sisters. We cut our fingertips and mixed the blood. We made a vow that we'll never break that promise. I'll talk about other things, but I won't talk about that subject."

I recognized that the girl's comments revealed an attempt to protect herself from the feelings of disloyalty she would have if she were to make a direct statement about which parent she preferred. She recognized that such a revelation might compromise her relationship with the non-preferred parent. However, I also suspected that a part of her probably did wish to divulge her preference in order to protect herself from being assigned by me and the court to the non-preferred parent. Her statement that she would be willing to talk about other subjects lent support to this suspicion. In addition, from previous experiences in such cases, I knew well that such youngsters often need to have the feeling that the decision was imposed upon them by a "crazy judge" and they can thereby protect themselves from the feared alienation of a non-preferred parent. Following the decision, they can complain to the non-preferred parent how they repeatedly expressed preference for that parent and it was only the insanity of the legal process that resulted in the youngsters' being assigned to the other parent.

With this understanding I responded to the girl: "I want you to know that I fully respect your thoughts and feelings on this issue and I would not consider it proper of me to use any kind of coercive techniques to get you to talk about that subject. Accordingly, I promise you that I will not ask you that question, so you can breathe freely and rest assured that we will consider that issue "off limits." I then said to her: "Accordingly, in line with this respect for your wishes, I will be willing to talk with you about anything else that you wish to discuss. We have almost the full session so you'll have ample opportunity to tell me about anything *else* that you wish to talk about."

With such reassurance the girl began to speak: "Well, I don't know what to speak about. Nothing much has really been happening with me . . . my mother and I went shopping today. There's nothing really to say about that. You know, doctor, I can't go shopping with my father. He doesn't know anything about lipstick, cosmetics, things like that. Also, girls my age really can't confide in their fathers. I can talk to my mother about my periods and my feelings about boys. I could *never* talk to my father about things like that. He just wouldn't understand. . . ." The girl continued to "roll" and tell me about the other manifestations of the close relationship she had with her mother, continually contrasting it with the more distant relationship she had with her father. There was no question that she was telling me her parental preference without consciously realizing that she was doing so. She constructed the interview, however, in such a way that she did not have to feel disloyal and yet could provide me with this vital information. Her statements played an important role in my decision to recommend that she remain living with her mother. Following the court's decision that she remain with her mother she vociferously denigrated me to her father with such statements as: "That Dr. Gardner is an idiot. I told him that I wanted to live with you. I told him about all the terrible things that my mother did with me. But he didn't listen. And then he told the judge to have me live with *her*, the bitch." Of course, with her mother, she plays me for my judiciousness, sensitivity, and appreciation of the importance of her remaining living with her mother.

These reservations about insights notwithstanding, I will usually start the interview with the traditional open-ended question: "So what's doing with you?" or "So what would you like to talk about?" If this question proves unsuccessful in getting the youngster to open up (the usual case), I may then ask a more specific question such as: "I'd like to know what your reactions were to our last interview" (referring here to the initial two-hour evaluation).

As I will elaborate in Vol. II (1999a), abstractions and conceptualizations are of far less therapeutic value than concrete examples. Accordingly, questions beginning with "Why?" and far less valuable than questions beginning with "When, Where, What, or How?" Of course, as therapists we are interested in knowing *why*, but we are less likely to learn the reasons *why* from *Why* questions than we are from questions utilizing other interrogatory words. For example, to ask a youngster why he or she misbehaves in school is generally not productive. To ask the same patient a series of questions about when, where, with whom, and under what circumstances there is trouble in school is more likely to provide useful data. Even here, due to the youngster's defensiveness, one may not get reasonable answers because the questions are related to the patient's "problems"—a touchy subject if there ever was one. Under such circumstances one might lead into revelations about academic problems, for example, by asking specific concrete questions such as: "What grade are you in?" and "How many boys and girls are at that grade level?" Then one might go on to ask such questions as: "Who's the smartest kid in the class?" "What do you like about him (her)?" "What don't you like about him (her)?" "Who is the poorest student?" and "Do you like him (her)?" Such questions may ultimately result in the youngster's talking about his or her own attitude toward academics. Other questions that might lead into a discussion of the patient's academic problems are: "What subject do you like the most in school?" "What subject do you like the least?" "What subjects are you best at?" and "What subjects are you worst at?"

In order to discuss behavioral problems one might lead into the issue with questions such as: "Who are the kids in your class who get into trouble?" "What kinds of things do they do?" "What does the teacher do when they get into trouble?" The reader will note that I am talking here about *other* parties, not the patient. "Does the teacher yell at them?" "What does the teacher say to them when they get into trouble?" "What do the other kids feel about those troublemakers?" "What kinds of punishment do they get?" "Who's the best person in the class in conduct?" "Do you like him (her)?" From this point one might say, "*All* kids get into trouble once in a while in class, what kinds of things do *you* do that get *you* into trouble?" By stating first that "all" youngsters get into trouble, at times, it becomes easier for the patient to describe the situations when he or she has behavioral difficulties. The reader will note also that I rarely ask yes-no questions. These are most often of little value because, after one has received an answer, one does not know if it is really valid. Questions requiring specific answers are much more likely to be useful.

In order to learn more about peer difficulties, one might start off with specific, nonthreatening questions, for example: "Tell me the names of some of the kids who live in your neighborhood?" "Who are the ones you spend the most time with?" "Who is your best friend?" "What is it about that person that makes you like him (her) so much?" "What kinds of things do you like doing most with him (her)?" "Of all the kids in the neighborhood which one do you dislike or hate the most?" "What is there about that person that makes you dislike or hate him (her) so much?" "What do you think are the things that a person can do that will turn off other kids?" For the patient who is teased and/or scapegoated, one might ask what are the specific things other youngsters say to him or her when taunting is occurring. These patients might also be asked what things their parents and siblings tell them they do that get them into trouble. One might also talk here about the various activities the youngster involves him- or herself in and, if there are difficulties, the details regarding why.

With regard to pathological behavior in the home, again, the examiner does well to follow the aforementioned principles. Some good lead-in questions: "What do you like doing most with your mother (father)?" "Of all things you like doing in the house, what things are the most fun?" "What are the things you don't like doing with your mother (father), the things that are no fun at all?" "All kids get scolded sometimes. What kinds of things do your parents scold you over?" "All kids get punished sometimes. What kinds of things are you punished for?" "Who punishes you?" "What kinds of punishments does your mother (father) give you?" "How long do they last?" "Are these fair punishments?" "I want you to tell me the best things you can about your mother?" "Now tell me the worst things about your mother?" "Now I want you to tell me the best things you can about your father?" "Now tell me the worst things about your father?" "What's the best thing that ever happened to you in your whole life?" "What's the worst thing that ever happened to you in your whole life?"

One can question the patient, as well, to get information about parental capacity. This can be done by going through the events of the day, from the time the youngster gets up in the morning until the time he or she goes to sleep at night. In association with each event, one tries to find about which parent is involved and the nature of the involvement. For example, one might ask which parent gets the patient up in the morning and whether there are difficulties, and continue with such questioning about the whole course of the day. Particular emphasis should be given to those times when both parents are available. Most often, this is during the evening. In the discussion one could ask about homework—who helps with the homework, who has the most patience, and whether there is any conflict and fighting over it.

The examiner must appreciate that most adolescents generally have weak egos and will utilize a variety of maneuvers to avoid direct confrontation with their deficits. They commonly utilize such phrases as "I don't know." Accordingly, the examiner should pose questions that circumvent embarrassing confrontations. To say to an adolescent, "Tell me about the things you're scared of?" or "What are the things that frighten you?" is an injudicious way of finding out about fears. A preferable way of getting information in this area is to say: "Most people have some things that scare them once in a while. What things scare you?" By presenting fears as a normal response, the patient is more likely to divulge what his (hers) are. Also, by starting off with the positive, easily admitted aspects of an issue, it is often easier to get into the embarrassing opposite. For example, one might ask, "What are the things about yourself that you are most proud of?" I will then go into a detailed inquiry of the sources of the child's pride. With ego enhancement as a buffer, one is in a better position to ask the question: "All people have times when they do, say, or think things they're ashamed of. I'd like to hear one thing that you're ashamed of." Again, the question is so posed that shame is presented as a normal phenomenon and all I'm asking of the patient is to mention one thing that has caused him or her shame.

Some patients are particularly fearful of expressing their feelings. On occasion, feelings are relegated to the unconscious, and questions about them prove futile. However, there are some youngsters who can verbalize their feelings but are uncomfortable doing so. The worst way to elicit the expression of feelings from a repressed child is to ask the question: "How do you feel about that?" or "How does that make you feel?" One could ask the question, but should not be surprised if the repressed child does not answer. In such cases, the examiner might say, "You must have felt really sad when your parents told you they were going to split up." "You must have *really* felt lonely when the other kids didn't want to be with you." Even then one might get the answer: "It doesn't bother me!" One might respond then with, "Well, I find that hard to believe. I believe that you *do* have feelings about it but that you're not comfortable talking about it now. I hope the time will come soon when you'll feel more comfortable talking about these things."

There are occasions, however, when the aforementioned kinds of catalytic questions do serve well to precipitate an emotional response. They serve to fan and enlarge sparks of feelings that were only dimly appreciated by the patient. Another way of facilitating the expression of such feelings is to precede them with comments that make them socially acceptable: "Most kids get very upset when they learn that their parents are going to get a divorce. What were the kinds of feelings *you* had?"

A discussion of the youngster's interests and hobbies can be very useful. Sometimes, the examiner does best to start the interview with this topic, because it is the least threatening. At other times, it may be useful as a way of decompressing a situation and diverting a patient from a particularly difficult area of inquiry. One might ask very simply: "What are your hobbies?" or "What are your favorite games?" or "What do you like doing after school?" "What's your favorite sport?" These can serve as a point of departure for a discussion in which the therapist discusses his or her own knowledge of this area. Such discussion can serve to entrench the therapist-patient relationship. Sometimes the discussion may reveal pathological trends. One boy may say that his hobby is computers. However, the discussion of computers reveals that he has such a massive preoccupation with the subject that he spends little time on anything else. When asked about his favorite TV program, one child responded, "Divorce Court." A very common "hobby" of many youngsters at this time is the game "Dungeons and Dragons." This game facilitates group discussion of a wide variety of often morbid and hostile fantasies. It is particularly attractive to children who have rich fantasy lives, some of whom are borderline and others even psychotic. Recently, there have been reports in the newspapers about youngsters who have acted out these fantasies, even to the point of attempted murder and I know of at least one homicide reported in association wth the game. Examiners do well to investigate the depth of involvement with this game and discourage it for those who are excessively involved.

Three Wishes

Whereas I generally ask adults for five wishes, I usually ask children for only three. My main reason for this is that I have found this question to be less useful for children. Most often children provide so much stereotyped responses that are age appropriate and not particularly valuable sources of information, e.g., "a million dollars," "all the money in the world," or "all the toys in the world." Adolescents are somewhere in between. Some will give five meaningful, idiosynchratic responses that can be a useful source of information. This is especially true of older adolescents. Younger adolescents, in contrast, may often provide the stereotyped wishes and for them, I will generally quit after three.

A very mature ten-year-old girl (she could easily pass for 13) presented with symptoms of depression, stuttering, poor relationships with peers, and generalized tension. Her mother was extremely punitive and her father passively permitted the mother's sadistic behavior. Her first wish: "To have magical powers to make someone exactly like me. We'd then go and live in a big mansion in

Florida." I considered the first wish to reveal her desire to have a "clone," someone just like herself. She would then have a playmate to compensate for the deprivation she suffered in her household. The playmate, of course, would be kind to her, unlike her mother. She would also remove herself from the home and go to Florida, which represented, I believe, a climate of emotional warmth, ease, and relaxation. Her second wish: "I'd have a farm of horses." Although this might be a normal response, in this girl's situation I suspected that it related to her desire to be in the company of animals because her experiences with human beings had been so difficult. In addition, the horses probably had some sexual connotation for her. Her third wish: "To grow up fast and get married to a man who would love me a lot and take good care of me." Considering this child's background, the meaning of the wish is obvious. It is another reflection of the patient's general unhappiness in her home situation. Although ten, she was preoccupied with sexual fantasies involving teenage dating, seductivity, and kissing. This was partially derived from her mother who, in addition to her hostility, was a seductive woman, preoccupied with sex, but was basically a sexually inhibited person.

First Memory

An adolescent's first memory is generally a less valuable source of information than that of adults. One might argue that the adolescent's first memory is more likely to be a useful source of information because the time gap between the event and the time the question is posed is much shorter than the time lag for adults. When adults are asked this question, however, they are reaching back into the distant past and are selecting the event from a much larger storehouse of recollections, and thus it usually has a much greater psychological significance. One cannot label an adolescent immature or regressed if he or she remembers being in a crib, being fed a meal, or being taken care of in bed when sick. As is true in all projective information, one must take care to differentiate the age-appropriate from the idiosyncratic and atypical.

A very bright 11-year-old boy had great difficulties in his relationships with his parents. His mother was an extremely cold, critical, coercive, and controlling individual. His father did not protect the boy adequately from his mother's maltreatment of him. When asked for his first memory, the patient responded: "I was being put into a crib a few minutes after I was born." I believe that the patient was being honest with me; however, I also believe that the fantasy had a reality for him because it was so deeply entrenched in his psychic structure and so well lent itself to symbolizing his life situation with his mother. It reflected well his feelings of having been separated from his mother a few minutes after he was born and placed where he could not enjoy any contact with her.

This 12-year-old boy's parents both had minimal involvement with him. His father was a hard-driving businessman, a workaholic, who was often absent from the home because of long business trips. His mother was a frustrated, angry, embittered woman who ranged from tolerance of the patient to utilization of him as a scapegoat. This was the first memory he provided: "I was in kindergarten. The school nun was there. The milk she gave me was frozen and I was scared to tell her that the milk was no good. The other kids told her for me. I was afraid that if I bothered her, she would yell at me." The fantasy needs little analysis. The frozen milk is a clear statement of the patient's view of his mother as unmaternal. In addition, he fears complaining about her lack of affection because he might then be traumatized in retaliation and thereby add to the difficulties he was already suffering in association with his emotional deprivation.

A 14-year-old girl was referred because of severe outbursts of rage. She described this event occurring when she was five:

> My mother went down a one-way street in a car. She went the wrong way. A policeman stopped her. I didn't like police at that time. I thought they were mean. I was scared of them. I cried a lot and said, "Don't hurt my mother." I was screaming and crying and yelling. It got him so frustrated that he said, "The heck with it," and he got rid of us. And he didn't give us a ticket.

The patient's mother was a woman who felt overwhelmed by the world and was often confused about where she was heading and what her future would be. One manifestation of this was her poor sense of direction, which prevented her from adequately driving distances more than a few miles from her home. The patient's recalling mother's going down a one-way street is a statement of her view of her mother as a woman who doesn't know which way she is going in life. The patient's recollection of avoiding the consequences of her behavior by having a violent outburst of rage epitomizes her life pattern. The patient's temper outbursts did indeed enable her to avoid the consequences of her unacceptable behavior. Early in life she had learned that if she were to rant and rave long enough, she would get her way. In this case the policeman, the symbol of the punitive authority, is dissuaded by her tantrums from administering appropriate punishment.

Draw-a-Person and Draw-a-Family

I generally confine the Draw-a-Person and Draw-a-Family tests to the initial two-hour evaluation. On occasion, I will administer the instruments again during the course of the extended evaluation. The examples presented here were derived from that phase.

An 11-and-a-half-year-old girl came to treatment because of antisocial behavior both at home and at school. She was very resistant to the idea of coming for treatment, told this to her family, but not to the therapist. This is the story that she told about the family she drew:

> This family was very happy. They had one dog, but he didn't get his picture taken. He wanted to be in he picture, but the family wouldn't let him be in it.
>
> The next-door neighbors, they were snooping around trying to find out why the family wouldn't let the dog have his picture taken. They found out that the dog kept jumping on the cameraman all the time. They had to shut the dog up in a closet so that he couldn't get on the cameraman.
>
> The reason the dog was always jumping on the cameraman is because the dog thinks that every time the cameraman would take a picture, a gun would come out of the camera and kill the family. Finally, one day the neighbors told the family why the dog was doing that—because he thought the cameraman had a gun. The family laughed and said, "There's nothing. There is no gun."

But then the cameraman did shoot the family. He was a robber and he wanted jewelry. Then the neighbors called the police and the police put him in jail and gave the dog a medal for capturing the cameraman.

The dog, of course, represents the patient. In the beginning of the story the dog's failure to get his picture taken reflects early treatment anxieties in which the patient does not want to be seen by the eye of the camera, that is, by the therapist. Depicting herself as a dog also reflects her feelings of low self-esteem. She sees herself as being rejected by the family and "locked in a closet." The cameraman's murder of the family represents her own hostility toward her family members and the cameraman is used as the perpetrator of the crime, thereby assuaging her own guilt over the act. The dog has little remorse over their demise. By having the cameraman jailed she further assuages the guilt she feels over her hostility. Providing the dog with a prize serves further to reinforce suppression of hostility.

Verbal Projective Questions

The verbal projective questions of N.I. Kritzberg (1966) can provide useful information about the adolescent's underlying psychodynamics. As mentioned, questions about the people whom the patient would like to be transformed into are not generally useful for pre-adolescent children in that their repertoire of individuals from whom they can choose is somewhat limited and they tend to select ego-appropriate stereotyped people. Younger children, however, do better with the animal and object question. In the adolescent period youngsters begin to expand significantly their repertoire of individuals from whom they can choose and the question thereby becomes more meaningful. And, the older the adolescent, the more likely the question is going to prove valuable. This does not preclude, however, utilizing animal and object questions for the adolescent, nor does it preclude asking the adolescent questions about which animals and objects would most suit the parents if they had to be so transformed.

This 11-year-old boy came to treatment because of severe conflicts with his father, a shrewd businessman who prided himself on his business acumen. However, he was insensitive to others, to the point of being psychopathic. The mother was passively submissive in her relationship with her husband, thereby abandoning the boy to her husband's maltreatment of him. These are the responses he gave to the question regarding which persons he would choose to be changed into had he to be so transformed:

(+)1 The actor who played "Oliver." He was an orphan boy. He lived in an orphanage. He had very little food. He unknowingly meets his grandfather, and then he lives happily ever after with his grandfather.

(+)2 Mr. Robinson. He's the father in the TV program *Lost in Space*. It's a space family and they go around exploring space. In one program the father was drifting from the ship into space, and they catch him just in time. They catch him just in time to get away from monsters. He's the pilot. He's the leader of the family.

(+)3 President Johnson. He signs civil rights bills, making sure that all races have equal rights.

(−)1 Mary Martin. I saw her in that play, *The Sound of Music*. She makes this mean father into a nice man. He was very strict to his kids and she changes him so he isn't strict. I would not want to be there in the beginning of the picture when she was married to the mean father.

(−)2 My sister Ruth (age 14). She's a real kook. She thinks of love all the time. If the house was on fire and she was talking to her boyfriends, she wouldn't make an attempt to get out.

(−)3 My sister Jane (age 16). She's a big shot. She thinks she's real great. She bosses everybody around all the time. She snitches on me to my parents.

Response (+)1 reveals the patient's feelings of having been abandoned and rejected by his father and his desire to be protected by him. The (+)2 response reflects the patient's ambivalence toward his father. On the one hand, he would want him separated and removed (drifting into space) and exposed to the dangers of monsters. On the other hand, he would want him retrieved. In the (+)3 response, his desire to be President Johnson stems here from the wish to be assured equal rights, that is, to be given humane treatment from his parents.

The (−)1 response reflects the patient's desire that someone come into his home and transform his father into a benevolent and loving person. The (−)2 and (−)3 responses are, in part, normal responses for a 12-year-old boy and reflect usual sibling rivalry problems. However, in (−)2 the introduction of the house burning down theme reflects the patient's hostility toward his family. There is possibly a sexual element here as well: the fire repressing his sexual desires which he harbors toward his sister and the devastating results should he express such.

Both of this 14-year-old girl's parents were extremely rejecting and angry people. The patient herself harbored deep-seated retaliative hostility toward her parents which she was unable to express. I considered such feelings to be playing a role in the anxiety attacks which she presented for treatment.

> (+)1 A bird, a small one, a bluejay. It's sweet. It can sing and fly. They care for their children even though they are animals.
>
> (+)2 A deer. It's gentle, sweet and pretty. Deers care for their children.
>
> (+)3 An otter. It's playful. Their main objective is not to kill.
>
> (−)1 A lion. All animals are scared of you. Lions kill, and I wouldn't want to do that.
>
> (−)2 A snake. They're mean and ugly and horrible.
>
> (−)3 A bug or spider. They're horrible. They're so horrible and creepy, but I couldn't kill it. I can't kill any insect.

In (+)1 and (+)2, the patient admires birds and deer because they "care for their children," a quality which she does not enjoy from her parents. The (+)3 choice, the otter, whose main objective is "not to kill," reveals the patient's desire to repress her own murderous rage.

The same holds true regarding her desire not be a lion (−)1 because a lion kills, that is, she wishes to disown her own hostility. The (−)3 response clearly reveals her basic feelings that she is like a bug or spider, prone to be obliterated by overwhelming forces. In addition, her inability to kill small insects reveals her great conflict about the expression of hostility.

This 11-year-old boy came to treatment because of severe passive-aggressivity in the home and at school. His obstructionism was a constant source of irritation to his teachers and school personnel. The patient's father was an extremely insecure and inadequate man who compensated with a pathetic pseudo-intellectuality. He fancied himself an arm-chair philosopher and as a man who was exquisitely sensitive to the deeper processes and workings of the human mind. His seemingly erudite pontifications were most often fatuous. When frustrated, he exhibited severe rage outbursts. These are the responses the patient provided to the question regarding which animals would most suit his father if his father had to be so transformed:

> (+)1 Half-gorilla and half-lamb, because sometimes he yells and sometimes he's nice.
> (+)2 Half-cat and half-lion, because sometimes he yells and sometimes he's nice.
> (+)3 Half-tiger and half-playful dog, for the same reason. Sometimes he screams a lot and other times he's nice.
> (−)1 A gorilla. He doesn't always yell.
> (−)2 A tiger, because he doesn't always yell.
> (−)3 A lion, because he doesn't always yell.

When providing answers to these questions, it was clear that the patient was not going to exert himself or in any way inconvenience himself to think of elaborate answers. The easiest thing for him to do was to perseverate the same reasons for his choices. However, his resistance notwithstanding, he provided meaningful material. The perfunctory way in which he gave his responses, as well as their repetitious similarity, revealed his basic passive-aggressivity. His (+)1, (+)2, and (+)3 responses all indicate that the patient appreciated his father's dual personality. On the one hand, the father is "half-gorilla," a reflection of the patient's appreciation of his father's rage outburst problem. On the other hand, his father is "half-lamb," a reflection of the patient's appreciation that his father is basically a weak person. The gorilla is also a facade and serves to compensate for the basic feelings that his father is a lamb. The $(-)1$, $(-)2$, and $(-)3$ answers are basically repetitions of the gorilla, tiger, and lion themes, given without much thought and deliberation. Nevertheless, they reveal his appreciation of the compensatory personality traits of his father.

At this point, I present in detail (with many verbatim vignettes) an adolescent's responses to the verbal projective questions. I will demonstrate here not only the use of the child's responses as a source of information about underlying psychodynamics, but as a point of departure for the acquisition of additional information and therapeutic interchange. Charles was brought to treatment at age 13 because of destructive behavior in the classroom, poor academic performance in spite of high intelligence, defiance of his parents at home (especially his mother), and alienating behavior toward peers. He was fiercely rivalrous with his nine-year-old brother who was more successful in the classroom, in the neighborhood, and in his relationship with their parents.

During the initial consultative sesson I was not able to determine the sources of Charles' difficulty in the family. Charles' mother was a housewife and, to the best of my knowledge, was dedicated to his upbringing and showed no manifestations of significant psychopathology. His father, however, was a somewhat "uptight" individual who was inhibited in expressing his feelings. In spite of this he did devote significant time to the boys, especially on weekends, and involved himself extensively in their recreational activities which he served as a coach for a variety of sports.

Charles' problems are said to have started when he was three-and-a-half years old, following the birth of his younger brother. By the end of my two-hour consultation I concluded that fierce sibliing rivalry was probably playing an important role in Charles' difficulties, and I could not ascertain any other significant family problems that might have contributed to his antisocial behavior. In addition, Charles had a weight problem from excessive eating—a problem for which he was frequently criticized by his parents (especially his father).

In the second session, the first of my extended evaluation, I asked Charles the first animal question. His response: "A tiger because I would be able to defend myself from other animals. Also, they're very fast."

Charles' second choice: "A bird." Consistent with the principle that one does well to ask for species in that there are a wide variety of birds that can symbolize many different things, I asked Charles what bird he woud like to be. He responded, "A robin because they can fly wherever they want." I then asked Charles where he would fly to if he were a robin. He responded, "To Florida. I've never been there. I want to go there with my family."

Charles' third choice: "A seal because everyone likes them. They can swim wherever they want."

Before we had the opportunity to go on to the animals Charles would *not* want to be, he asked me if it was all right to change his first choice from a tiger to a chimpanzee. I told him there would be no problem there, but asked him why he wanted to be a chimpanzee. He responded, "Because they're smart and intelligent. They're active and people love them because they're cute." He then told me he would like to leave the tiger answer as his fourth choice. Again, I told him there would be no problem with that.

We then went on to the animals he would not want to be. His first choice: "A rhinoceros because everyone hates them because they're strong and they kill other animals. People are afraid of them because of the way they look with their big horns."

His second choice: "A hippopotamus because they're big and ugly. People are scared of them because of their looks."

His third choice: "A shark because everyone is scared of them. No one wants to be near them. They're killers."

I believe that Charles' request to substitute the chimpanzee for the tiger was a reflection of his strong desire for the chimpanzee response to take priority over the other three. His reasons for selecting the chimpanzee related to the problems for which he entered treatment. He described the chimpanzee as smart, intelligent, active, and "people love them because they're cute." Doing poorly in school, Charles did not consider himself smart or intelligent. Both he and the chimpanzee are "active." Charles' "activity" was associated with antisocial behavior and resulted in his being alienated from others. The chimpanzee's activity, however, does not result in such alienation; rather, "people love them because they're cute." The response reveals Charles' desire to be loved in spite of his alienating behavior. The robin and the seal responses share in common the desire to be free from constraints. At times this is a normal response, given by many children who view school and home restrictions to be constraints from which they wish to free themselves. Last, Charles' original first choice, the tiger, was chosen because of its capacity to defend itself from other animals. The response suggests that Charles sees himself as vulnerable to attacks by outsiders and would like to be strong enough to defend himself.

The three animals that Charles chose not to be share in common the hostility element. The rhinoceros "kills animals." People are "scared of" the hippopotamus. And sharks are "killers." In addition to the hostility there is the appearance element described in the rhinoceros and hippopotamus responses. Of the rhinoceros Charles stated: "People are afraid of them because of the way they look with their big horns." And with regard to the hippopotamus: "People are scared of them because of their looks." The hostile elements in the undesired animals may very well be in the normal range. However, they may also reflect inordinate hostility which Charles wished to disown. One cannot justifiably come to this conclusion from these three responses taken in isolation from other data, especially because they were given in response to the question regarding what animals he would *not* want to be. Not wanting to be an animal that is ferocious is within the normal range. Bringing in the element of appearance, however, is definitely idiosyncratic and suggests that Charles has special feelings about how he looks. This may have related to his mild obesity problem in that Charles was frequently criticized by both of his parents (especially his father) for being overweight.

Charles was then asked what objects he would want to be changed into, if he had to be so transformed. His first response: "I'd want to be a computer. It knows a lot of stuff. It knows more than a man. It's smart and intelligent. People like to use them." We begin to see here a theme emerging on the issue of intelligence. The responses suggest that Charles has feelings of intellectual inadequacy associated with his academic underachievement. His revised first choice on the animal question was the "smart and intelligent" chimpanzee and now his first choice on the object question again relates to intelligence.

Charles' second choice of object: "A pen because people would use me a lot and I'd have a lot of people around me." Charles was then asked what was the paritcular value of that and he replied,

"People *need* them. People need them to write and writing is important." The responses here not only reflect Charles' need for others to respect him for his abilities, but the particular quality for which he wants respect: writing. And writing, of course, is best done by those who are "smart and intelligent."

Charles' third object: "A stereo. People love to listen to music. I'd be used a lot." The response reflects Charles' desire that he be liked and be needed by other people, probably a reaction to the alienation he suffered from parents and peers because of his psychological problems.

The first object Charles would not want to be: "A box for corn flakes because once people are through with it they throw you away." Again we see the theme of being needed and the fear of being viewed as useless.

His second choice: "A baseball bat. You're always getting hit with a ball and someone can break you. People don't treat you well. You're just a piece of wood to them. They just throw you around." The response again reveals Charles' feelings of being rejected by others and being viewed as subhuman, as someone whose feelings are not considered. In addition, there is the element here of maltreatment from others, and this response is similar to one of the reasons why he did not wish to be a tiger, namely, because it is unable to defend itself from other animals.

The last object he would not want to be: "A gun because I wouldn't want to be used to hurt anyone else." Although one might ascribe hostility here, it is also possible that the response reflects a humane attitude toward others. Of course, both needs would be gratified by this response.

Charles was then asked what animals would suit his mother if she had to be so transformed. His first response: "A chimpanzee. They're nice, but when you get on their bad side they won't be nice to you." I then asked Charles how he gets on his mother's bad side. He replied, "If I don't listen to her she gets mad." I asked him what he could do about this and he responded, "By stopping myself from being on her bad side." I next asked him why he was still continuing to be on her bad side and why he couldn't stop doing so. His reply: "I know I shouldn't. If I get into my moods I just think 'Who does she think she is bossing me around like that?' " I finally tried to elicit from Charles information about what factors contributed to his getting into one of his "moods." He was unable to provide me with any meaningful response and so we proceeded.

Charles' second choice of animal that would suit his mother: "A bird." Again, I generally do not accept readily such a response and asked him what specific *kind* of bird would most suit his mother's personality. He replied, "A bluejay because she is a nice person. Bluejays keep on coming back if you are nice to them and give them food. If you are nice to them, they'll be nice to you, and it's like that with my mother. I've got to stop being on her bad side." I asked Charles if he thought he could do so and he replied, "Yeah, I've got to try harder. If I put my mind to it. The problem is, I've got to put my mind to it." When asked why he had not done so in the past, he replied, "I don't know. I just get into one of my moods." Again, Charles was asked what situations get him into one of his moods. He replied that when he has trouble with other children, he gets moody. Although I was able to get him to see that his difficulties with peers related to provocative behavior on his own part, I did not feel at that point that my message was sinking in. And so we proceeded.

The third animal that Charles considered to suit his mother's personality: "An owl because they're smart. She's smart. She knows a lot of things I don't know. She knows a lot of math and she can help me with my math." Again, the issue of intelligence emerges and Charles is stating here that he views his mother to be a smart woman, as someone who could help him with his studies. Children generally view their parents as smarter because that is the reality of the situation. Parents do help children with homework and generally have a much vaster fund of knowledge. I suspect, however, that Charles' response here is not simply related to this reality. Rather, it probably relates to feelings of intellectual inadequacy resulting from his academic underachievement.

Charles was then asked what animals would not suit his mother's personality. His first response: "A shark because she isn't a mean person. A shark is." His second animal: "A pig, she's a neat person and she's smart. A pig isn't." His third animal: "A gorilla, because she's not like a savage." The first and third responses could very well be considered to be within the normal range. The pig, however, again reveals the theme of intelligence, lending weight to the conclusion that this issue is very much on Charles' mind.

I then proceeded to ask Charles what animal would suit his father if he had to be so transformed. His first response: "An owl, just like my mother. I have the same answers for my father as I do for my mother." At this point I urged Charles to come up with different responses for his father in that his father and mother were two different people and I was sure that he could think of animals that indicated these differences. Giving the same answers is a common avoidance maneuver, and the examiner should encourage children to ponder the question a little longer before taking the easy route of giving identical responses for both parents. In response Charles replied, "Okay then, a cheetah. He's fast and he can defend himself."

At that point, Charles interrupted and asked me if he could give me another animal that would suit his mother because one had just come to mind. Of course, I agreed and he responded: "A dog and a cat." I suggested that we start with the dog and that he name a specific kind of dog. I cannot emphasize this point strongly enough to the reader. There are a wide variety of dogs, each breed of which lends itself well to symbolizing a different personality characteristic. And, as the reader will see in just a few seconds, my asking Charles to select a specific kind of dog provided useful information. His response: "A Saint Bernard, because you can depend on them. If you have a problem, you can tell them and they'll help you. They're famous for rescuing people in the snow." The response reveals Charles' view of his mother as nurturing and protective. However, it also suggests that he feels himself in a situation of emotional deprivation (lost in the snow). Perhaps this relates to his father's problems in expressing feelings and his mother's capacity to provide him with the affection that his father cannot.

Because Charles had stated that his mother resembles a "dog and a cat," I asked him then why he had chosen a cat. He responded: "You can also depend upon them. If you need a friend it's always there, and they're always by your side." The response again is a statement of Charles' view of his mother as warm, nurturing, and reliable. It is important to appreciate that this response, coming as it did as an interruption, must be given extra attention and credibility when assessing a child's responses. Just as the chimpanzee interruption provided useful information earlier in the inquiry, this interruption did so as well. The examiner does well to view these interruptions as reflecting significant pressure by unconscious processes to express important issues. The comments about Charles' mother's warmth, protectiveness, and affection came in the midst of descriptions of his father. They suggest that his descriptions of his father's coldness was anxiety provoking and that he needed his mother's warmth and protection as an antidote.

We then continued and Charles gave as the second choice of animal that would suit his father: "A dog, a Saint Bernard." Again, I asked Charles if he could give me a different animal because I considered the Saint Bernard response to be a manifestation of resistance in that he had just given that animal as one that would suit his mother. Without much delay he stated, "A Dalmation, because you can depend on them for help." It is difficult to assess his answer, coming as it did immediately after one that described Charles' mother as being someone on whom he could depend. I believe that Charles' father *was* dependable in certain areas such as involvement with Charles in sports. What he could *not* depend upon from his father were open displays of emotion, intimacy, and warm tender feelings. His father could, however, *do* those things that were necessary for adequate child rearing.

The third animal that would suit Charles' father: "A beaver because it works hard." Charles' father's work occupied him for long hours during weekdays; however, he was available to a significant degree on weekends to devote himself to his sons. From the ensuing discussion I could not be certain whether or not Charles felt any deprivation in association with his father's midweek work obligations. He denied such feelings. I suspect that the reality was that Charles did not consciously experience his father as depriving because he was there to a significant degree on weekends. The deprivation that he was not consciously aware of was emotional, which is more subtle—but deprivation nevertheless.

In answer to the question as to which animals are not similar to his father, Charles replied: "A lion because he is not mean or savage." The second animal unlike his father: "A fox because he is not a con artist." And the third: "A snake because he is not a slippery snake that goes around biting people." I considered the first and third responses (the lion and the snake) to be within the normal range, not only with regard to the animals chosen but the reasons why. However, the second response is, in my experience, atypical. And atypicality is one of the criteria for ascertaining psychopathology. It certainly is an unusual response and suggests that the patient, at some level, may consider his father to be duplicitous. It may be of interest to the reader to learn that on the day following this interview I did have an individual interview with the father. There was no question that he was not candid with me. He described the marriage as always having been a good one and denied that there were any problems. Charles' mother, however, during the interview prior to the one with Charles in which the verbal projective test was administered, described a number of serious marital problems, among which were infidelty on her husband's part. Although Charles' response here created only a mild suspicion that his father was duplicitous, and although such a view was not supported by subsequent responses on the test, there was indeed "fire beneath the smoke," and the initial suspicions engendered in me by this response proved to be verified in the next interview with his father.

Charles was then asked questions regarding the objects that would suit his mother's personality. His first response: "A bandaid because she helps me heal." His second response: "A chair because she is comfortable." And his third response: "A computer because she is smart and so intelligent." The first two responses, of course, make direct reference to his mother's nurturing and protecting roles. The third again is another example of the theme related to intellectual functioning which, as we know, was an area of difficulty for Charles.

When asked what objects would not suit his mother's personality, his response was, "A knife because she's not a dangerous person." His second response: "A machine gun because she doesn't go around hurting people." And his third: "A camera because she doesn't spy on people." As is usually the case, it is more difficult to make firm statements about the meaning of the negative responses than the positive. Negative responses do not necessarily indicate unconscious material that the patient is guilty and/or anxious about and must thereby relegate impulses to unconscious awareness.

They can also be explained simply as age-appropriate negative attitudes that the child has derived from the environment. Here again, one looks for atypicality for leads to psychopathology. The knife and machine gun are, in my experience, normal responses, although the machine gun may be a little strong in that a simple gun is more often chosen. The camera serving as a vehicle for spying, however, is a more atypical response and suggests feelings that the patient has that his mother spies on him. However, most children have these feelings, and so I cannot consider this response to be significantly representative of psychopathology, especially because there was no repetition or pattern of such imagery throughout the assessment.

Charles was then asked what objects would suit his father's personality. His first response: "A computer because they're smart." Once again, we see the concern with intellectual capacity.

His second response: "A thermostat because it keeps you warm and cool." This was an unusual and somewhat confusing response and so I questioned Charles for further details. Accordingly, Charles was then asked to elaborate on the point that his father, like the thermostat, keeps one "warm." In response he stated, "If I have a problem, he'll say don't worry about it and that makes me feel better." When asked to elaborate on the association between his father and the thermostat helping someone become "cool," he replied, "He's comforting and he helps you." When I tried to understand better what Charles was referring to here, the best I could determine was that he was using the word *cool* in the sense that many adolescents use it, that is, to refer to one's being unemotional and not taking upsetting experiences seriously. To the degree that this response implies improper suppression and repression of feelings, to that degree it is pathological. In my subsequent interview with Charles' father, I found him to be quite inhibited in expressing his feelings and suspected that Charles' response here related to this aspect of the father's personality.

Charles' third response: "A car." Again, just as I asked Charles to tell me the specific *kind* of dog and bird he had selected, I asked him to tell me the specific *kind* of car that would suit his father's personality. There are many different kinds of cars and they lend themselves to different kinds of symbolization. In response, he stated, "A Ferrari, because he has one and he's interested in cars."

The response suggests that Charles' father may be swept up in the common materialism of our society. This is not to say that every person who buys a Ferrari is necessarily exhibitionistic; only that there are many purchasers of this car who certainly are so, and the response should alert the therapist to look into this issue.

Charles was then asked to name those objects that would not suit his father's personality. His first response: "A hand grenade because he doesn't kill people." His second response: "A knife because he doesn't stab people." His third response: "A match because he doesn't burn people." Although the level at which normality ends and pathology begins may be difficult to ascertain with the negative questions of the verbal projective test, I believe that the responses here go beyond the normal frequency of dangerous implements that one gets in response to these questions. They suggest Charles' view of his father as inordinately hostile—hostility that Charles is trying to suppress and repress. Considering that Charles had an acting-out problem, the responses here suggest that a contributing factor to this symptom related to Charles' relationship with his father, especially with regard to hostile elements that often contribute to such difficulties.

As mentioned, the interchanges derived from my administration of the verbal projective test with Charles are presented in detail in order to familiarize the reader with the administration of the test and its utilization not only for learning about psychodynamics but for providing material that may serve as a point of departure for further inquiry, both diagnostic and therapeutic.

Dreams

Children are less capable of analyzing their dreams than are adults. The dream may nevertheless be a rich source of information about a youngster's underlying psychodynamics. The ability to utilize the dream metaphor probably exists at about the age of two or three in most children. However, the ability to appreciate the process, that is to separate cognitively the symbol from the entity that it denotes, is a later phenomenon and for the average child does not take place until the age of ten or eleven, the age at which the child reaches what Piaget refers to as the stage of formal operations. Accordingly, I do not generally spend much time attempting to help children below the age of ten or eleven gain insight into the dream's meaning. Adolescents, however, are often capable of analyzing their dreams and this is especially the case for older adolescents. I generally ask the youngster to tell me any dreams he or she can remember and inform the patient that I am particularly interested in repetitious dreams. These often provide valuable information about basic themes that pervade the patient's personality structure. Here I describe and analyze some dreams that adolescents presented me during the intensive evaluation. I will offer my understanding of the dream, but I will not go into detail about any discussions I may have had about the its meaning. My primary purpose here is to demonstrate how a youngster's dream can often be a rich source of information about underlying psychodynamics. Even when the youngster is not interested in or capable of analyzing the dream, the examiner's hunches and speculations can often be useful in the patient's treatment. Elsewhere (Gardner, 1986a, 1996) I discuss in detail my views on dream analysis and their utilization in treatment.

An 11-year-old girl presented with psychosomatic complaints, especially headaches, nausea, vomiting, and occasional diarrhea. She had a variety of allergies as well. Her mother, who was an extremely tense and angry woman, had little meaningful capacity for child rearing. The mother openly stated that she should have never become a parent. Her relationship with her husband was a difficult one because he too felt frustrated over his wife's tension and rejection of him. When either he or the children (the patient had a 14-year-old sister) would express any anger toward the mother, she would have violent rages which were extremely frightening to both the children and their father. The patient related this dream during the extended evaluation:

> I was at the beach with my friend at Atlantic City. I was in the water. A giant wave came. I had to duck under. Another big wave came and it drowned me.

This is a common dream. I consider the most likely explanation for a dream in which a patient is being drowned or submerged by waves to reflect the feeling that suppressed or repressed emotions are going to break out of the unconscious into conscious awareness. The emotions, however, are viewed as dangerous and even lethal.

Often patients will wake up from the dream relieved that they have not been drowned. And I believe that this explanation was applicable to this girl. The feelings here represent the massive hostility she felt toward her mother – hostility that could not be expressed overtly lest she suffer even further rejection and retaliation. Her feelings overwhelm her and she will drown in them. I considered many of her symptoms to be manifestations of the tension she felt in association with her attempts, both conscious and unconscious, to suppress and repress her anger toward her mother. Her dream confirmed my clinical speculations.

This 14-year-old boy asked his parents to bring him to therapy because of strong homosexual fantasies. His father was an extremely domineering, controlling individual who always presented with a facade of reasonableness. However, in any discussion in which differences of opinion were expressed, he maintained a rock-like rigidity. The patient's mother was passive and submissive in her relationship with the father. Neither parent had much capacity to involve themselves emotionally with the patient and his older sister, then 17. During the extended evaluation, he described this repetitious dream:

> My family and I were in a car going up to the driveway to my school. It was a school day. There was a little shack next to the school. I went into the shack. There was a hand there in a white glove. It was a mechanical hand. I had to be very quiet. It was very dangerous, so I couldn't make any noise. Once I sneezed and the hand went over my mouth.

I considered the little shack, next to the school, to symbolize the patient's view of himself as isolated from the mainstream of his peers and possibly his family as well. I considered the mechanical hand, covered by a white glove, to represent his father who did not allow the patient to express his genuine thoughts and feelings. Even the sneeze, which the patient could not control, is suppressed by the white-gloved hand. It is a statement of his great pressure for expression of the patient's repressed thoughts and feelings. Viewing his father as a mechanical hand in a white glove is a statement of his belief that his father is machine-like rather than human. The white glove implies sterility and cover-up of "blackness" and other undesirable personality qualities. It also symbolizes the father's veneer of reasonableness to disguise inhumane (mechanical) qualities.

Concluding Comments

The kinds of inquiries and assessment instruments described above are the primary ones that I utilize in the extended evaluation of the adolescent. They generally provide me with a wealth of information. However, on occasion, I may utilize *The Talking, Feeling, and Doing Game* (Gardner, 1973b), especially with the younger adolescents. My main purpose here is not simply to gain some data. Rather, I am interested in ascertaining how successful I will be in engaging the younster. By the mid- and late adolescent period, youngsters will generally be more comfortable talking directly and do not need this vehicle for helping them express themselves.

JOINT INTERVIEW
WITH THE PARENTS

Following the individual interviews with each of the parents alone, I will conduct a joint interview with both parents together. It is extremely important that the examiner conduct this interview as part of the extended evaluation. At times, parents may object because they will claim that each has already provided information. Sometimes, they will even claim that the information has already been given twice, in that the mother has related it during her individual interview and the father during his. When I explain to them that I often get different renditions of what is happening in the home, they will become more receptive to the joint interview because they recognize that it is important that any distortions which have been introduced into the evaluation should be corrected. Besides utilizing this interview to gain the most accurate data, the examiner is able to observe interactions between the parents. This is truly a situation in which the whole is greater than the sum of the parts. It is a rare situation in which I do not learn new things from the joint interview. This relates to both the acquisition of new information as well as the things I learn from the interactions. During the initial two-hour consultation, only a limited time is spent in the joint interviews so that the opportunity for observation of interactions is small.

The Correction of Distortions and
Other Kinds of False Data

It is extremely important for the reader to appreciate that all human beings distort their perceptions in situations of stress. At the Columbia University School of Law, it is not uncommon for a professor to stage a totally unanticipated interruption in the class. Specifically, a group of young men and women may suddenly charge into the classroom. There is screaming, a scuffle, shouts, shrieks, and angry words. Feigned gun shots, knife stabbings, and other forms of violence are likely to ensue. Then, as quickly as it began, the group suddenly leaves the room. The professor then asks each member of the class to write exactly what he or she observed. He advises them that they have been witness to a crime and that they will be asked to testify under oath regarding what they have seen and heard. The class is generally around 300 young people, just about all of whom have been extremely high in their college classes and have performed extraordinarily well on the Law School Aptitude Test. Presumably we are dealing here with a very bright group of young men and women. The professor generally receives 300 different renditions of what occurred. And each of these young people is being honest. Such is the nature of the human mind. So great is the capacity to distort under situations of stress.

Another example of this phenomenon. As the reader may know, I lecture extensively throughout the United States and occasionally abroad. Most often, I give a full-day of presentations, generally three or four lectures. The most common format is four one-and-a-half hour presentations, two in the morning and two in the afternoon. Frequently, a person will ask me a question in which there is a misquotation and/or a misunderstanding of what I had previously said. When I inform the person that I have been completely misunderstood and that I said exactly the opposite of what he or she is attributing to me, the individual often responds with incredulity. I have often had the thought that a wonderful experiment would be to make a videotape of the first presentation. Then, I would hand out an objective test (such as one with multiple-choice questions) that would be based *entirely* on the material just presented during the previous hour and a half. I am convinced that most people in the audience would give some incorrect answers and would, in addition, swear that their recollection of what I said was accurate. Then, we would get the videotape's opinion regarding what I said. These individuals would react with amazement that they could have so misunderstood me.

Our memories play tricks on us, especially if the topic is emotionally charged. And when one lectures in the field of psychiatry, one is likely to touch on emotionally charged situations. If I am lecturing on the subject of divorce, there are likely to be many individuals in the audience who have been or are going through the process of divorce, making this a charged subject for them. Under such circumstances, distortion is almost inevitable. I am not being critical of these individuals who distort or misinterpret what I say. I myself would be likely to make such errors occasionally were I in their situation. And when one is interviewing parents about their marriage and the ways in which they deal with their children, especially in a psychiatric interview, it is inevitable that distortions will arise. The joint interview can serve to correct these for both the parents and the examiner.

It is extremely important for the examiner to appreciate that one's interpretation of any situation is determined by two factors. One is the actual facts, the actual reality, and the other is what one brings to it, what one interprets it to mean, what one *wants* to understand about the significance of the events. I often say that life is like a Rorschach test. In fact, one could view this as a fundamental dictum of human experience. All phenomena can be divided into two factors: the reality and what the human being brings to the reality. The viewer's hopes, anticipations, denial mechanisms, et cetera, are all going to play a role in determining what the individual sees and how he or she reacts. Both the external entity and the viewer's thoughts and feelings about it are realities in their own right, and both play an important part in determining how one will react in a particular situation. There is a glass with water in it. One person sees it as half full, another sees it as half empty. And when parents are talking about their marriage and their children, the likelihood of these superimposed attitudes playing an important role in their discussions is very high. In fact, it is so great that I consider it to be universal. Accordingly, distortions, misrepresentations, and exaggerations are inevitably going to be present, and it is in the joint interview, especially, that the examiner is in the best position to determine what these are.

Accordingly, the examiner must recognize that the information gathering process in this interview occurs at two levels. An attempt must be made to ascertain, to the degree possible, exactly what is happening. Sometimes this can happen if the two individuals come to some kind of a compromise or when one's credibility is clearly greater than the other's. At other times it may not be possible and the examiner does well to go on to the next issue. In such cases, I might say, "Well, you say one thing and your husband (wife) says just the opposite. We've gone back and forth a few times and you each stick to your own position. I suggest we go on to another issue. Perhaps in the future, I'll learn what's really going on."

The other level, and possibly the more important, is the attitudinal. It relates to the thoughts and feelings of the individual about the particular event. Shakespeare's Hamlet said it well: "There's nothing either good or bad, but thinking makes it so." A father, for example, may put his three-year-old son on his lap while driving the car, and while both of their hands are on the steering wheel, the father gives the child the impression that he is helping drive the car. Early in the marriage, when there was a loving relationship between the parents, the mother may have considered the father's act to be a benevolent one, one designed to help the child feel like "a big man." In contrast, at a time when the marriage has deteriorated, she may complain vehemently to the examiner about the kinds of dangerous things her husband used to do with the boy, and she may give this as an example.

In the individual interviews, one may get diametrically opposed stories resulting in a complete inability to find out what has really gone on. In the joint interview, one can sometimes "smoke out the truth." For example, in the individual interviews, each parent might describe attendance at all school functions to which parents are invited, both curricular and extracurricular. However,

332   *The Intensive Diagnostic Evaluation*

during the joint interview the mother may say, with regard to the father, "Yeah, he came, but I always had to pull him. It was a big struggle. And when he finally got there, he used to fall asleep during the plays and recitals." The father may then sheepishly admit that he "sometimes" did fall asleep for short periods, but that his wife is exaggerating the frequency and the duration of the time spent sleeping. In the subsequent discussion, the father may admit reluctance and occasional sleeping. Although the two may differ regarding the degree of reluctance and the frequency and duration of sleeping episodes, the examiner has still learned about the father's lack of enthusiasm for these events. And this I would consider to be a parental deficiency.

"The Whole May Be Greater Than the Sum of Its Parts"

The joint interview with the parents is one of those situations in which the whole may be greater than the sum of its parts. In fact, in most of the interviews, I find this to be true because information is derived which was not or could not have been obtained in the individual interviews. This phenomenon is the result of the inter-action between the parents. Because of the shortness of the joint interview during the initial two-hour evaluative session, time often does not allow for the emergence of this additional information. It is only under more relaxed circumstances, during the extended evaluation, that there is a greater likelihood that this additional data will become available.

Let us take the example of a passive and somewhat quiet man who is married to an assertive and more talkative woman. In the short joint interview, during the two-hour screening evaluation, one may sense that this is the nature of the relationship, but questions are still being directed toward both parties. In the individual interview(s) with the father, the examiner is spending most of the time posing questions (as described in detail in the above section on the interview with the father). More than 95 percent of the time is spent with the father's talking. He is a "captive audience." The individual interview should not be conducted like a classical psychoanalytic session in which the examiner sits back silently and waits for the patient to talk. (This does not preclude, however, an occasional open-ended question.) Rather, the examiner is generally concerned with obtaining answers to a whole series of questions. In the joint interview, however, one may observe directly how the mother may actually consume 99 percent of the time, while the father sits silently, allowing her to "roll." Now that he is no longer a captive audience, now that the examiner is not posing one question after another, now that he is being permitted to either talk or remain silent as he chooses, his severe problem in verbal inhibition becomes apparent. In addition, his passivity problem also manifests itself, especially when he remains silent on issues of disagreement with his wife. The father may say, "I was never one who had much to say in social situations. I never had the 'gift of gab.' I guess one of the reasons why I was attracted to my wife was because she always had something to say at all times." And, with this lead, the examiner may also learn about the father's passivity in his relationshp with the mother and his fears of asserting himself. A derivative of this would be a discussion of the patient's identifications in these areas, with the father and/or the mother.

A father may claim in the individual interview(s) that the marriage is a good one, that there were never any difficulties, and that there was never any talk of separation. In her individual interview(s), however, the mother may claim that on two occasions during the course of the marriage, she found love letters from other women. She suspects that there were probably more infidelities that she cannot be certain of. She claims also that when her husband was confronted with these letters he admitted to her that he had been unfaithful and that he would discontinue the affairs. In some circumstances I will recommend that the mother bring up the issue of infidelity in the joint meetings with her husband, and on other occasions I will not. On the one hand, I may consider it important for the child's treatment to do so, especially if the mother has good reason to believe there is an ongoing affair taking place during the time of the evaluation. On the other hand, I may consider it antitherapeutic to do so in that it might cause additional marital discord which I suspect both parents would rather avoid. One just doesn't go after the truth, no matter what the consequences. One goes after the truth in the service of doing what is best for the child's treatment. In order to determine whether or not this issue should be brought up, I will ask the mother her opinion on the subject, and her input here will be very important. Of course, I too will have input into the decision. All marriages involve a certain amount of acceptance and resignation of qualities in the other party that one would prefer did not exist. The examiner must respect such equilibria and not attempt to change every single source of marital difficulty. If one is going to "rock the boat," then one should be sure that one is in a position to deal completely with the repercussions of such a disruption of the marital equilibrium.

Let us say that both the mother and I decide that it would serve the best interests of the marriage and the patient for her to bring up the affair in the joint session. In the joint meeting, the mother confronts the father with her supsicions about ongoing infidelity. She expresses incredulity that his "business meetings" so frequently go on until two in the morning. She also expresses her disbelief that they always take place where he cannot be reached and cannot call her to tell her that he has been detained. She expresses her belief that he is with other women, either at their homes or in hotels. In response the father somewhat sheepishly and unconvincingly gives various explanations. At this point the mother may say, "Doctor, I've been living with this man for 15 years. I know him inside out. Right now he's lying. Look at that shit-eating grin on his face. That's how he looks when he's lying." The father might still hold to his original story and claim that his wife has a vivid imagination and that she has "delusions of jealousy." On occasion, under such circumstances, the mother may turn to me and ask my opinion on the subject. My response, under these circumstances, has been along these lines: "Well, I can't be 100% certain. Your wife, however, is certainly giving some very convincing reasons why she suspects infidelity, and your responses don't seem to have much credibility to me. Although I'm not sure at this point—pending more convincing information from you—I'm inclined to believe that your wife has good reasons to be *very* suspicious."

However, I do not stop there. I will then say something along these lines: "Regardless of whose version is valid here, there is no question that you and your wife have some serious marital difficulties. However, you are not candidates for marital counseling at this point, at least on this issue. Either she is delusional and believes her delusions or you are lying. In either case, people like yourselves, with this kind of a conflict, are not candidates for marital counseling." I then proceed with other issues. My point here is that the joint interview enables the examiner to learn better about a parent's personality characteristics. In the example cited above, I learned about the father's probable duplicity. On other occasions, under the same circumstances, I have learned something about the mother's delusional system. In both situations, the confrontation by the spouse provided important input in my determining what was most likely the situation.

Many other forms of interaction can be observed in the joint interview. For example, sado-masochistic tendencies that may not have been apparent in the initial screening interview may manifest themselves. As the joint interview progresses, a father may become increasingly hostile toward the mother, speak in a condescending way to her, and denigrate her. Rather than asserting herself and expressing her resentment that her husband is treating her so shabbily, she may passively sit and accept his deprecations. These personality traits of the parents are likely to be playing a role in the child's difficulties. Or, a mother may continually interrupt her husband with nitpicking and hairsplitting corrections. Rather than tell her how offended he is by her behavior, he passively explains himself repeatedly, continually trying to justify himself. Again, these patterns are not likely to have manifested themselves in the individual interviews.

The Marriage

It is in the joint interview, with both parents together, that one is likely to learn much more about the marriage than in the individual interviews. Confrontations between the parents not only enable the examiner to correct distortions but to make observations in which the interactions often provide more information than actual statements. Because marital difficulties are such an important factor in bringing about psychogenic pathology in children and adolescents, I will often devote a significant portion of the joint interview to the details of the marital relationship. Although some parents who bring children to treatment will not have any difficulties in this area, my experience has been that this is uncommon. Accordingly, I most often have little trouble getting parents to discuss the marital problems; often each has discussed them at some length during the individual interviews.

On occasion, a parent who has discussed the marital problems in individual interview will show hesitancy in discussing them in the joint interview. Most often, I consider such discussion warranted. Therefore, in order to catalyze the discussion I may make a comment such as: "Each of you has told me at length what you consider to be both the assets and the liabilities, the strengths and weaknesses, of your marriage. I would now like to discuss them here with the two of you together. Why don't we start off with the strong points." At this point, I do not specify which parent I would like to start; rather, I leave it open because I would like to ascertain which parent is going to be the more assertive and forthright with regard to the marriage, both its assets and liabilities. Suggesting that they talk about the assets first generally "breaks the ice" and makes it easier to discuss the liabilities thereafter.

On occasion, one or both parents will be reluctant to discuss the marriage and say that they don't understand how their marital difficulties have anything to do with their youngster's problems. Others will go further and state that my delving into the marriage is improper and that if they wanted marital counseling, they would have asked for it. I try to explain to such parents that their view of child therapy as a process which is focused on the child primarily, if not exclusively, is improper and injudicious. I explain to them that I cannot separate their child's difficulties from their own, that there are therapists who would be willing to treat their child without any contact with them, but I am not that kind of therapist. I try to explain to them that children exposed to and/or embroiled in marital problems are likely to develop psychological difficulties themselves. The parents may respond that they have been completely successful in protecting their children from any knowledge of their marital difficulties. In such cases I try to explain to the parents that this is practically impossible. I try to get across the point that if the parents are unhappy this is going to compromise their parenting, even if the children don't know exactly what the parents are unhappy about.

I also advise them that my view of therapy involves my counseling parents on how to take care of the children and deal with their problems, and I hope that they will be receptive to this part of the therapeutic program. It is the rare parent who is unreceptive to this; in fact, I cannot recall a parent saying that he or she did not want my advice regarding how to handle the children's problems. I also advise them that treatment for their own problems is an overlapping but separate issue. If they *wanted* treatment for their problems, I would be happy to discuss with them the question of whether I should do such counseling or someone else should. In such discussions I point out the advantages of my doing it, but try to avoid giving the impression that "I am looking for extra business." Rather, I impress upon them the fact that by having one therapist treat the whole family, I will be more in touch with those issues that are affecting the child than I would be if another therapist were to do the marital counseling.

On occasion, it will become apparent that the youngster's problems are a small and incidental spinoff of the parents' difficulties and that the main thrust of the therapeutic approach will have to be with the parents if there is to be any hope of alleviation of the patient's problems. (I will discuss this issue in the section devoted to the final presentation of my findings.) On occasion, it has become apparent that one of the parents is basically using the youngster's symptoms as an "admission ticket" for marital treatment. At some level the parent recognizes that the major problems lie within the marriage, and the hope was that by bringing the child, the parental difficulties would surface and perhaps a reluctant parent would be more motivated for therapy. My experience has been that this is a common situation and that the mother, much more than the father, is likely to have been the initiator in such a process.

On a number of occasions, it has become more apparent during this joint interview that the marital problem must be considered a fixed constant in the youngster's treatment. Sometimes one of the parents is adamantly against any kind of counseling. My experience has been that the person who is most often resistant to the counseling is the father. On other occasions, a parent may recognize that there are serious problems in the marriage but may be afraid to "rock the boat." My experience here has been that it is the mother, more than the father, who is often in this position. One has to respect defenses in a marriage. One has to respect the equilibria and the benefits of maintaining the status quo, the drawbacks of such silence notwithstanding. All marriages involve a delicate balance between healthy and pathological forces, and the examiner must respect these balances and not bulldoze the parent into "putting everything out on the table." The likelihood of people gaining anything for such tactics is small, and the therapist, under such circumstances, may do the family much more harm than good.

Dealing with the Children

The second important area that I generally focus on in the joint interviews is the parental dealings with the children. Generally, I have asked each of the parents in the individual interviews to describe him- or herself and the other parent with regard to this area. Here I want to get feedback from each parent regarding the other's comments. I generally encounter far less reluctance and resistance in the discussion of child-rearing practices than I do in the discussion of the marriage. I usually start with a broad question such as: "Now let's talk about the children and how each of you has handled the various problems that have arisen." This is generally enough to get things moving. Sometimes I will have to be more specific with questions such as: "Although we've covered child-rearing practices to some degree in the individual sessions, I'd like to go into further detail here, especially with regard to how you see each other in this area. So why don't we talk first about what you see as your own strong points and the other party's strong points in dealing with the children." Again, I do not ask a particular parent to start speaking. Rather, I want to see who initiates the discussion.

Following a discussion of the strong points and assets, I then shift to the more difficult subject of liabilities. Again, I want a statement by each person regarding how he or she sees his or her own weaknesses and how the other party sees them. Sometimes I will divide the liabilities issue into specific areas of inquiry. For example, I may ask a mother what she suspects her husband's criticisms of her have been with regard to disciplinary techniques and/or what she recalls him to have said in this area. Then, I will turn to the husband and ask him directly what his criticisms are. I will then repeat the procedure with the father's stating first what his recollections are of the mother's criticisms of his disciplinary techniques and then ask the mother directly to state them.

In the course of the discussion on child-rearing practices, I may give advice. Although my primary goal in the extended evaluation is to collect as much data as possible, this does not preclude my spending time providing recommendations. I am not referring here to the kinds of recommendations that can only emerge from extended experience; rather, I am referring to those that are simple, short, and do not detract significantly from the time spent in the data-collection process. But such *en passant* recommendations can also serve the purpose of data collection in that parents' reactions to my suggestions often provide additional information that may be useful. I am particularly interested in the parents' degree of receptivity to my advice. And there is a whole range here from the parents who passively and gullibly accept every bit of advice to those who are completely resistant and antagonistic to it. The ideal is that they be at some point close to the receptive end of the continuum, but not to the point of blind acceptance of everything I say. I would like them to have conviction for my recommendations because when they do, it is far more likely that they will implement them effectively. In addition, parents who are too passive in their relationship with me serve as poor models for their children. The children should not view me as their parents' "boss"; rather, they should view their parents as receptive to my advice but retaining the final decision-making power.

Concluding Comments

The joint interview with the parents not only serves the goal of data collection but, if successful, can help entrench the parents' relationship with the therapist. The establishment of a good relationship with parents is one of the cornerstones of effective therapy with the youngster. It is here, more than in the other interviews, that one may learn about criticisms each has about the therapist, criticisms that may not have been revealed in the individual interviews. Here, one parent may bring these criticisms up in the presence of the other. And it is crucial that they be discussed. Otherwise, the parents may harbor their resentments silently, and this can compromise the treatment and even bring about its cessation – without the therapist's knowing exactly what has gone on to compromise the treatment.

Before closing the joint interview with the parents, I discuss the family interview. Generally, I want teenagers present and those younger children who can be relied upon to contribute significantly. My experience has been that a good cutoff age is five or six. Although one may learn from the observations of interactions between the parents and the preschool nonpatient sibling, the disruptions of their presence throughout the course of the interview may outweigh the advantages of such observations. Furthermore, even children of five to eight may not be valuable contributors and may just sit there quite bored during the course of the family interview. After eight or nine, the older the youngster, the greater the likelihood of meaningful input. (The reader should not view these ages as fixed guidelines; rather, they are approximate.)

Once the decision has been made regarding which children shall participate, we discuss the issue of what to tell the siblings regarding the purpose of the family meeting. I generally advise the parents to say to them that it will be helpful to me in my work with their brother or sister to get information from them about what is happening in the family. I advise the parents to reassure the siblings that they want them to be open and honest and that there will be no repercussioins for their divulgences. On occasion, parents are reluctant to tell the siblings about the patient's treatment because they fear that the siblings might taunt the patient, tell others, or involve themselves in other inappropriate reactions to the disclosure. Most often, I advise the parents to tell the siblings about the treatment and to deal with any inappropriate reactions if and when they arise. I impress upon them that keeping the patient's treatment a secret is likely to contribute to and even intensify the patient's feelings of low self-worth, because such withholding implies that the patient is suffering with a disorder that he or she should be ashamed about. There are occasions when a sibling is so sadistic and disturbed that the divulgence might indeed work against the patient, but this has been a rare situation in my experience.

THE FAMILY INTERVIEW

Elsewhere (Gardner, 1986a) and in Vol. II (1999a) I discuss in detail the family interview techniques that I utilize. Here I discuss only some basic principles of the family interview in the extended evaluation. It is important for the examiner to appreciate that both the patient and the siblings may be quite tense at the beginning of the family interview. The patient is likely to be uncomfortable over the fact that his or her siblings are now going to discuss embarrassing issues. And the siblings may be fearful of criticizing their parents or may appreciate that what they say may be upsetting to the patient. Accordingly, I generally do not sit silently at the outset of this session and wait for someone to open up. Rather, I myself begin with some reassuring statement to the various parties. I will turn to the siblings and say something along these lines: "I appreciate your coming here today. I want you to know that my experience has been that brothers and sisters can often provide me with very valuable information that helps me in the treatment of their brother or sister. I know that this is probably uncomfortable for you. But I know that I speak for your parents when I say to you that they want you to be open and honest with me and that you shouldn't be afraid that there'll be any terrible consequences afterwards if you say critical things about them." At this point, I may actually ask the parents to make some statements along these lines. I will also say to the siblings: "I want you to know, also, that I understand that I am placing you in a difficult position with regard to the things that you're going to say about your brother or sister. However, I hope you'll appreciate that it's important for me to have this information and that you, probably more than anybody else, can provide it to me."

I will then turn to the patient: "I know that this is difficult for you, as well. I know that I'm asking your brother and/or sister (or whatever the number and sexes are) to say things about you that may be upsetting and embarrassing. I hope, however, that you're big and strong enough to appreciate that it's important for me to get this information if I'm to help you." When I make this statement, I generally do not expect the child to agree with me that such divulgences are likely to be in his or her best interests; I make the statement, however, in the hope that some of it does get through, and the child does appreciate my sensitivity to his or her situation.

I will then ask the siblings why they think their brother (sister) is coming to see me. This is an important base from which to operate. The derivative questions make more sense if this issue is brought out first. On occasion, the siblings do not know of the basic problems, but most often they do. In addition, their opinions regarding the problems may be at variance with the parents and this can also be useful as clarifying data. Furthermore, their confrontations may help the patient gain some insight into the fact that he or she has problems although, as mentioned so many times previously, I don't push for this.

At this point I may ask the siblings to talk about the parents. I may ask them to say good things about their parents and things about their parents that they do not like. I start with the parents here because I want to take the focus off the patient and discuss criticisms of the parties who have "thicker skins." Often, the information about the parents that the children provide me proves quite useful. They frequently come up with parental characteristics that were not previously brought to my attention. I may then go on to the subject of exactly how they see their parents' personality problems and difficulties to have contributed to the patient's. Sometimes siblings will give me very insightful information about this relationship. For example, a teenage sister might say, "I think Billy's main problem is my mother. She spoils him sick. He's the big baby of the family. She doesn't know how to say no to him like she used to say to me and my brother." Although I may recognize jealousy as an element in such criticism, there also may be significant truth to the allegations. I will then use this as a point of departure for family discussion. For such a criticism, I may turn my attention to the mother and ask for her response. I may ask Billy himself what he thinks about this criticism. The likelihood is that Billy (age 14) does not consider himself to be too indulged; in fact, he may believe that his mother is too withholding from him and indulging of his sister.

The general principle I follow when conducting family interviews is that I use each issue as a point of departure for further back and forth confrontations and discussion. Usually I ask each party what he or she thinks about what the other party has just said. Sometimes I will ask an individual what he or she thinks about what has been said previously by a few members on a particular point. I try not to let things become chaotic; rather I try to come to some tentative conclusions on each issue raised. Getting input from the other family members serves to clarify as well as generate family discussion, interaction, and information about their various relationships. Last, the family interview may have direct therapeutic benefits in that it may open up, sometimes for the first time, the kinds of discussions that have taken place previously—and this cannot but be therapeutic for the patient. I cannot emphasize this point strongly enough. The data collection interviews are often stressful to the patient and other family members. To the degree that one can help the family derive therapeutic benefits during the course of these interviews, to that degree will the therapist be compensating the family for these negative elements in the extended evaluation.

I generally do not set aside a standard 45-minute interview for the family. Rather, I will take an hour to an hour-and-a-half, depending upon how much information I suspect will be emerging. It is not my intention during this time to follow up every issue to its limit. Rather, I want to focus on major problems and collect some information about each of them. I am not conducting family therapy here; rather, I am collecting data about the family, my patient, and the various interactions of the family members. On occasion, a second family interview may be warranted. Also, on occasion, the initial family interview may have served as a breakthrough for them, and ongoing family therapy may be agreed upon. What was originated, then, as a diagnostic data-gathering procedure, ends up being an important therapeutic experience.

PREPARATION OF THE PRESENTATION

I recognize that the extended evaluation I conduct is probably more time-consuming and involved than that employed by most examiners. In fact, I myself do not *routinely* conduct such extended evaluations. On occasion, on the basis of the two-hour initial consultation, I sense that all the aforementioned interviews may not be necessary. For the purposes of this book, however, I have described in detail the full evaluation and recognize that the reader (like myself) will find situations in which it is not warranted. Similarly, the preparation of the final presentation may not necessarily be as intensive as that which I describe here. Again, for the sake of this book, I present the full preparation procedure.

The ideal way of organizing the formidable data that the examiner may have accumulated is with the use of a word processor. The examiner who has one available will save much time. Those who do not have one must utilize the more primitive procedure that I used prior to my acquisition of this valuable instrument. Accordingly, I will first describe the method I use with the word processor and then describe the more painstaking method that I utilized previously. In addition, if the examiner enjoys the indulgence of a secretary, this can obviously save time. If not, then the examiner must perform these procedures him- or herself. Fortunately, I have both a word processor and a secretary and can indulge myself in these shorter and more efficient procedures.

I begin the dictation by instructing my secretary to set up on the word processor a series of basic topics. Then, I will go through my material—from beginning to end—and dictate comments and quotations within each of these categories. The secretary scrolls up and down the screen inserting the material within each of the topics. The topics are: Basic Data, Presenting Problems, Mother's Assets, Mother's Liabilities, Father's Assets, Father's Liabilities, Patient's Psychodynamics Derived from Patient Interviews, Patient's Psychodynamics Derived from Parents and Family Interviews, Conclusions and Recommendations. When dictating the material, I do not concern myself with organization of the material *within* each of the categories. Rather, it serves the purpose of the final presentation to the parents to have just the aforementioned degree of organization. If I want to use this material in the preparation of a written report, then I will reorganize (again by word processor) the material *within* each category, but utilize the aforementioned outline as my starting point. On occasion, when the question of the child's having a neurologically based learning disability has also been raised, I will include a section in which the results of special tests in this area are also presented. I place this immediately after the section on the child's presenting complaints. I generally entitle it: Evaluation for the Presence of the *Group of Minimal Brain Dysfunction Syndromes* (GMBDS) (Gardner, 1979b, 1987b).

The basic data material is often taken directly from the face sheet of the parents' questionnaire (Appendix II). It generally includes the patient's name, age, date of birth, grade, and whether in a regular or special class. It also includes the names and ages of the parents and their occupations. In addition, I include the names and ages of the siblings and what grades they are in. Stepparents also are included.

With regard to the chief complaints, I most often start with those that have been presented by the parents (and sometimes the patient) at the beginning of the two-hour consultation. I select here only those problems I consider to be psychological difficulties and not those mentioned by the parents which I have decided are not. I include here, as well, those problems described on page 2 of the questionnaire where I request the parents provide me with a three-line summary of the main difficulties. I will then scan pages 9 through 12 of the questionnaire and select those symptoms that I consider worthy of therapeutic focus. I do not generally include here every single item checked off by the parents because some parents will list as a symptom atypical behavior of normal frequency, my warning to this effect in the introduction on page 9 notwithstanding.

In the section on parental assets and liabilities, one does well to include quotations. These enhance the accuracy of the presentation and may also prevent inappropriate antagonism toward the therapist. If one takes care to quote criticisms from the opposite parent, one is likely to prevent such occurrences. Such quotations are especially important if a written report is to be prepared. In these days of burgeoning malpractice, one wants to be certain that the written report is not used to one's disadvantage in any possible subsequent litigation. And accurate recording of quotations can serve this end in that it is not the therapist who is making the critical allegation but one of the family members. (It is a sad commentary on our times that this must be mentioned here, but not to do so would be a disservice to the reader.)

When dictating the section on the patient's psychodynamics, I not only describe each observation, but the meaning that I ascribe to it. This might include a behavioral manifestation and then an interpretation, or it might refer to some verbal projection and my interpretation. For example, I might quote certain key statements from the story that the patient told in association with a human figure that was drawn, and then I will dictate my understanding of the meaning of the story. The same is done with the verbal projective questions. With regard to the verbal projective questions about those people, animals, and objects that would suit the parents, I make sure to state that this is my interpretation of how *the child* sees the parents and emphasize to the parents that this may not necessarily be the way they are, but the way the child sees them. This is not only a more accurate way of stating things, but also can assuage the pains and discomforts of more defensive and/or insecure parents.

In the conclusions and recommendations section I will summarize the major themes in the family that are contributing to the child's difficulties. This generally ranges from two or three to about ten or twelve elements. It may include genetic predisposing factors and psychodynamic issues, both interpersonal and intrapsychic. This summary statement can also be useful in the course of therapy in that I may refer to it from time to time to refresh my memory about the variety of problems for which the patient has presented as well as to assess progress. I then state the recommended treatment program with regard to the number of sessions per week (generally one or two) as well as who shall be involved in the treatment. If the reader does not have a secretary and word processor, then the aforementioned must be done by hand. One generally writes the titles on separate sheets of paper and then skips back and forth from page to page inserting the proper information under each category.

PRESENTATION OF THE FINDINGS
TO THE PARENTS

I generally set aside an open-ended session for this presentation. It takes about two hours, sometimes longer. I make it open-ended in order to insure that we are not rushed. The adolescent and both parents are seen together during the interview, which I usually begin by explaining to them how I prepared the presentation. I directly show them the computer printouts and enumerate the various categories within which I have placed the information as it has been dictated. I then go step by step, from one section to the next, reading and commenting on what has been written therein. I advise the parents to interrupt me at any point if they have questions or wish further discussion. I prefer that the issues raised serve as points of departure for limited discussion, but not the kind of extended discussion that might be more appropriate during therapeutic interviews. Sometimes, I may have been in error with regard to a particular point or quotation and I invite the parents' correction. I inform them that my goal here is not to be "right" but to be "accurate." Unless there are a formidable number of such errors, the parents will generally appreciate my receptivity to corrections. I invite the patient's participation as well.

On occasion, I will have ordered psychological tests. I make a photostatic copy of the psychological report, give the parents one copy, and we read them over together in detail. This report is their property and they take it with them at the end of the meeting (regardless of whether or not they have chosen to have a full written report prepared by me). Examiners who do not give the parents a copy of this psychological report are asking for trouble. The parents are entitled to it and not to give it to them exposes one to justifiable criticism. They are also entitled to discuss the report in detail with the examiner, especially because such reports are often confusing and anxiety provoking to parents. Obviously, when such a report is discussed in the final presentation, it is going to add to the meeting's length.

The discussion of the final treatment program is quite important. Because it comes last, I want to be sure that we have the time to discuss this in depth. And this is one of the main reasons why my final presentation is open-ended. Parents will often ask how long the treatment will take. I generally advise them that I cannot know in advance and that the most important determinants relate to how successful I will be in engaging their youngster and how receptive they themselves will be to involvement in the therapy. Of course, by this time I have definite information in this area and will make comments on it. It is a serious error for the therapist to even proffer a guess with regard to the number of weeks, months, or years treatment will take. No matter how many qualifications he or she may give, the parents are still likely to put a circle on their mental calendar (if not their real calendar). Only the number becomes branded in the parents' brains; the qualifications never seem to have reached their ears. Even if accused of being vague, obstructionistic, or hostile, the therapist should not speculate about how long the treatment will take. It would be a rare situation in which he or she would not regret having made such a speculation.

I also discuss the nature and degree of the parental participation in the youngster's treatment. The exact degree of parental participation in an adolescent's treatment presents certain technical difficulties. When working with younger children I generally utilize the parents to a significant degree during the child's sessions. I refer to my treatment of these younger children as *individual child psychotherapy with parental observation and intermittent participation.* The parents serve very much as my *assistant therapists.* In the treatment of adults, I obviously do not have parents actively involved although this does not preclude my seeing the parents of my adult patients once or twice (generally along with the patient) if the situation warrants it. Parental involvement in the adolescent's treatment is somewhere in between these two extremes. As mentioned previously, I will not accept into treatment an adolescent who refuses to have me involve the parents. Nor is it warranted that the parents actively participate in every session. The adolescent requires a certain amount of autonomy during this transition phase from childhood dependence to adult independence. The adolescent must have a sense of separateness and keeping the parents in the room too frequently may compromise this healthy process.

I generally advise the parents that I will be expecting them to remain in the waiting room throughout the course of the youngster's session. Often, I have the parents join me at the outset with the quieter and more reticent patients, because they are similar to pre-adolescent youngsters in this regard. When the youngster is more talkative, I will generally not begin with the parent but reserve the right to bring the parent in as warranted throughout the course of the session. This is especially useful when the youngster runs out of things to say. Generally, the parent who then joins us can be relied upon to bring up issues that can serve as points of departure for discussion. Because mothers are the ones most often available to bring the youngster, I advise the fathers that they should make attempts to bring the adolescent from time to time and to join us (no advance notice required) when available. I also inform the parents that I will be recommending sessions where both the parents and the youngster will be present and that if situations arise which warrant their requesting such a session, I am most receptive to scheduling it. One wants to maintain ongoing relationships with both parents; otherwise, the youngster's treatment is going to be compromised. One wants to create a setting in which the various family "Pandora's boxes are open" and family skeletons are taken out of the closet. Joint interviews are often the most efficacious way of doing this.

I will also talk about the difference between counseling the parents on dealing with the patient vs. treating the parents for marital difficulties which they may have. It is important that the examiner not coerce the parents into treatment regardless of how formidable the marital problems are. Rather, the examiner does well to ask questions like: "Do you consider yourself to have marital problems?" "Have you ever given thought to having therapy for such problems?" and "What do you think about obtaining therapy for these problems?" It is crucial that the examiner take a passive attitude here and merely sound the parents out on their receptivity. To use coercive or guilt-evoking tactics is contraindicated, for example: "If you want to salvage your marriage, you're going to have to go into treatment. I can't imagine the marriage surviving without it" or "For the sake of your child, it's important that you people have treatment for your marriage. If you don't, it's going to be extremely difficult, if not impossible, for me to help your youngster."

People who enter treatment in response to such threats are not likely to be helped. If the parents decide that they want therapy for the marital problems, then the therapist does well to make a statement along these lines: "Well, as I see it, you have two choices here. One is to work with me and the other to work with someone else. As you know, I do treat parents of my child and adolescent patients and have often found the combination useful, but recognize that some parents feel more comfortable working with someone else on their marital problems, while being counseled by me regarding how to deal with their child. I am interested in your thoughts and feelings on this; however, it's important that you be direct and honest with me and not hold back your true feelings from fear that I might be offended. Many parents have chosen to see others and I respect that choice." This approach, I believe, protects the therapist from the parental reaction that "he (she) is looking for business." It does, however, provide the parents with an option that they may not have appreciated they had and helps them clarify both the pros and cons of each alternative—information they are entitled to have.

If medication is warranted, I will discuss this with the parents at this point. Here again, one must leave ample time for such discussion in order to assuage unnecessary or irrational fears that the parents may have. It is likely that they have some unrealistic ideas about what medication can do and cannot do, and the therapist must give them the opportunity to express their ideas if he or she is to correct distortions. For parents who are very reluctant to have their child on medication, I will emphasize that I am only suggesting a *trial* on medication and that they not commit themselves to a full course of treatment before knowing about the drug and ascertaining empirically whether or not it will prove helpful. Often, by reassuring them that a few pills are not likely to produce lifelong damage to the youngster's body, they will be more receptive to the trial.

Before closing this meeting, the therapist should invite the parents to ask any further questions. Often they may have heard of quicky-type treatments that promise results in a shorter perioid. I will generally ask them about the particular form of treatment and present them my views on it. When contrasting psychotherapy with these other forms of therapy, the examiner should be cautious with regard to making any claims about the efficacy of psychotherapy. The examiner does well to emphasize to the parents that there is no "proof" that psychotherapy works but that the examiner has definite convictions that it can be useful for certain children and their families, especially those who involve themselves with commitment to the process.

Finally, before closing the session, I ask the parents if they would like a full written report prepared. Examiners who charge for the extra work involved in the preparation of such a report should have told the parents about this much earlier. I make mention of it in the face sheet to my questionnaire so that the parents know about it even prior to the first meeting. Examiners who do not use such a document do well to mention this charge during the initial consultation. Otherwise, I believe parents have a justifiable complaint when they are advised of this new extra expense at such a late point. Even here many parents have "forgotten" about this charge and will express surprise (and even resentment) that it will cost them more money for me to prepare this report. If the parents choose to have a written report, I prepare a copy for them, give it to them directly, and let *them* decide whom they wish to give it to. This is an important point; in fact, it may be the most important point I make in this book. In these days of burgeoning malpractice litigation, the safest course is to give the parents the report themselves and let them decide whom they wish to give copies to, whether it is the school, the child's pediatrician, or anyone else. In this way, the examiner cannot be accused of having sent out critical and/or personal information to parties to whom the parents did not wish to have this information available.

Sometimes parents will ask me to prepare a modified report for certain parties, such as a school. I generally refuse to do this. I say to them, however, that if they wish to delete certain parts of the report before turning it over to the school, that is their privilege. However, I strongly urge them to make a copy of the report, cut out the deleted paragraphs, and advise the school of such deletions. Some may do this, some may not. I tell them about the injudiciousness of not telling the school that the report has been altered. But, if they do not follow my advice, I cannot be considered to have been at fault. The therapist does well to appreciate that we are living in a time when there is approximately one lawyer for every 850 individuals in the population. With such a ratio, there are many hungry lawyers who view malpractice litigation to be a very promising livelihood. (Remember the bumper sticker: *Become a Doctor, Support a Lawyer.*) Giving parents the report and letting them make copies for distribution to others is an excellent way of protecting oneself in this unfortunate atmosphere.

RICHARD A. GARDNER, M.D.
P.O. BOX R
155 COUNTY ROAD
CRESSKILL, N.J. 07626-0317

Dear

Attached please find the questionnaire I would like you to fill out about your child. Please bring it with you at the time of your first appointment. In addition, I would appreciate your bringing copies of any other material that you suspect might be useful to me, e.g. reports from psychologists, psychiatrists, child study teams, learning disability consultants, teachers, etc. I am also interested in recent report cards and scores on standardized tests of academic achievement such as the Iowa, CAT, and SAT. Please make copies of these reports so that I can have them for my files.

Unless there are special reasons to do otherwise, my usual procedure is to see the child and both parents in the initial two-hour consultation. The three parties are seen individually and in various combinations, as warranted.

My fee for consultations is $150/60-minute session. Unlike reports from other medical specialists, child psychiatric reports are generally quite lengthy and time consuming to prepare. Accordingly, if a written report is desired, there is an additional charge for its preparation, dictation, and review--which is prorated at the aforementioned rate.

My fee for 45-minute treatment sessions ranges from $110 down to $80. My fee for full-hour sessions ranges from $140 down to $100. The exact fee is determined at the time treatment is instituted. When deciding on the fee it is most helpful to know exactly what insurance coverage (if any) you have. Accordingly, please try to have this information available at the time of the initial consultation. I will discuss with you my policy for payment for missed sessions at the time of the initial consultation. Payment is due at the time services are rendered.

    hours have been reserved for the initial consultation with your child. I would appreciate your paying my secretary the $ fee at the time of the consultation. My secretary will be pleased to provide receipts and assist you in the preparation of forms for subsequent reimbursement to you by insurance companies and other third-party payers.

Please know that I will do everything possible to be helpful to your child. If you have any questions regarding the above, please do not hesitate to call my office.

Sincerely,

APPENDIX II

RICHARD A. GARDNER, M. D.
155 COUNTY ROAD
CRESSKILL, N. J. 07626
—
TELEPHONE 201 - 567-8989

PLEASE BRING THIS COMPLETED FORM WITH YOU AT THE TIME OF YOUR FIRST APPOINT-

MENT ON_____AT____ _____

IT IS PREFERABLE THAT BOTH PARENTS ACCOMPANY THE CHILD TO THE CONSULTATION.

Child's name_____Birth date_____Age___Sex_____
            last   **first**   **middle**

Home address_____
            street   city   state   zip

Home telephone number_____
                 area code   number

Child's school_____
           name   address   **grade**

Present placement of child (place check in appropriate bracket):

	Column A Adults with whom child is living	Column B Non-residential adults involved with child
Natural mother	( )___	( )___
Natural father	( )___	( )___
Stepmother	( )___	( )___
Stepfather	( )___	( )___
Adoptive mother	( )___	( )___
Adoptive father	( )___	( )___
Foster mother	( )___	( )___
Foster father	( )___	( )___
Other (specify)	_____ ___	_____ ___

Place the number 1 or 2 next to each check in Column A and provide the
following information about each person:

1. Name_____Occupation_____
         last   first
   Business name_____Business address_____

_____Business tel. No. ( )_____

2. Name_____Occupation_____
         last   first
   Business name_____Business address_____

_____Business tel. No. ( )_____

Place the number 3 next to the person checked in Column B who is most involved
with the child and provide the following information:

3. Name_____Home address_____
                             street

_____Home tel. No. ( )_____
  city   state   zip
  Occupation_____Business name_____

Business address_____Bus. Tel. No. ( )_____

Source of referral: Name_____Address_____

_____Tel. No. ( )_____

Purpose of consultation (brief summary of the main problems):_____

_____ ___

_____ _____

_____ _____ _____ __

_____ _____ _____

PREGNANCY
  Complications:
    Excessive vomiting_____hospitalization required_____

    Excessive staining or blood loss_____

    Threatened miscarriage_____

    Infection(s) (specify)_____

    Toxemia_____

    Operation(s) (specify)_____

    Other illness(es) (specify)_____

  Smoking during pregnancy_____average number of cigarettes per day_____

  Alcoholic consumption during pregnancy_____describe, if beyond an occa-
    sional drink_____

  Medications taken during pregnancy_____

  X-ray studies during pregnancy_____

  Duration_____weeks

DELIVERY
  Type of labor: Spontaneous_____Induced_____
  Forceps: high_____mid_____low_____
  Duration of labor_____hours

  Type of delivery: Vertex (normal)_____breech_____Caesarean_____

  Complications:
    cord around neck_____

    cord presented first_____

    hemorrhage_____

355

infant injured during delivery_____

other (specify)_____

Birth Weight_____
Appropriate for gestational age (AGA)_____
Small for gestational age (SGA)_____

POST-DELIVERY PERIOD (while in the hospital)
Respiration: immediate_____delayed (if so, how long)_____

Cry: immediate_____delayed (if so, how long)_____

Mucus accumulation_____

Apgar score (if known)_____

Jaundice_____

Rh factor_____transfusion_____

Cyanosis (turned blue)_____

Incubator care_____number of days_____

Suck: strong_____weak_____

Infection (specify)_____

Vomiting_____diarrhea_____

Birth defects (specify)_____

Total number of days baby was in the hospital after the delivery_____

INFANCY-TODDLER PERIOD
Were any of the following present--to a significant degree--during the
first few years of life? If so, describe.

Did not enjoy cuddling _____

Was not calmed by being held and/or stroked _____

Colic_____

Excessive restlessness_____

Diminished sleep because of restlessness and easy arousal _____

Frequent headbanging_____

Constantly into everything_____

Excessive number of accidents compared to other children_____

DEVELOPMENTAL MILESTONES
 If you can recall, record the age at which your child reached the following developmental milestones. If you cannot recall, check item at right.

	age	I cannot recall exactly, but to the best of my recollection it occurred		
		early	at the normal time	late
Smiled				
Sat without support				
Crawled				
Stood without support				
Walked without assistance				
Spoke first words besides "ma-ma" and "da-da"				
Said phrases				
Said sentences				
Bowel trained, day				
Bowel trained, night				
Bladder trained, day				
Bladder trained, night				
Rode tricycle				
Rode bicycle (without training wheels)				
Buttoned clothing				
Tied shoelaces				
Named colors				
Named coins				
Said alphabet in order				
Began to read				

COORDINATION
 Rate your child on the following skills:

	Good	Average	Poor
Walking			
Running			
Throwing			
Catching			
Shoelace tying			
Buttoning			
Writing			
Athletic abilities			

COMPREHENSION AND UNDERSTANDING

Do you consider your child to understand directions and situations as well as other children his or her age?_____If not, why not?_____

_____

How would you rate your child's overall level of intelligence compared to other children? Below average_____Average_____Above average_____

SCHOOL

Rate your child's school experiences related to academic learning:

	Good	Average	Poor
Nursery school			
Kindergarten			
Current grade			

To the best of your knowledge, at what grade level is your child functioning: reading_____spelling_____arithmetic_____

Has your child ever had to repeat a grade? If so, when_____

Present class placement: regular class_____special class (if so, specify)

_____

Kinds of special therapy or remedial work your child is currently receiving

_____

Describe briefly any academic school problems_____

_____

_____

Rate your child's school experience related to behavior:

	Good	Average	Poor
Nursery school			
Kindergarten			
Current grade			

Does your child's teacher describe any of the following as significant classroom problems?

Doesn't sit still in his or her seat_____

Frequently gets up and walks around the classroom_____

Shouts out. Doesn't wait to be called upon _____

Won't wait his or her turn_____

Does not cooperate well in group activities_____

Typically does better in a one-to-one relationship_____

Doesn't respect the rights of others_____

Doesn't pay attention during storytelling_____

Describe briefly any other classroom behavioral problems_____

_____

_____

PEER RELATIONSHIPS

Does your child seek friendships with peers?__ _____

Is your child sought by peers for friendship?_____

Does your child play primarily with children his or her own age?_____

younger_____older_____

Describe briefly any problems your child may have with peers_____

_____

_____

HOME BEHAVIOR

All children exhibit, to some degree, the kinds of behavior listed below.
Check those that you believe your child exhibits to an excessive or exaggerated degree when compared to other children his or her age.

Hyperactivity (high activity level)_____

Poor attention span_____

Impulsivity (poor self control)_____

Low frustration threshold_____

Temper outbursts_____

Sloppy table manners_____

Interrupts frequently_____

Doesn't listen when being spoken to_____

Sudden outbursts of physical abuse of other children_____

Acts like he or she is driven by a motor_____

Wears out shoes more frequently than siblings_____

Heedless to danger_____

Excessive number of accidents_____

Doesn't learn from experience_____

Poor memory_____

More active than siblings_____

INTERESTS AND ACCOMPLISHMENTS
  What are your child's main hobbies and interests?_____

_____

  What are your child's areas of greatest accomplishment?_____

_____

  What does your child enjoy doing most?_____

_____

  What does your child dislike doing most?_____

_____

MEDICAL HISTORY
  If your child's medical history includes any of the following, please note
  the age when the incident or illness occurred and any other pertinent information.
  Childhood diseases (describe any complications)_____

_____

  Operations_____

_____

  Hospitalizations for illness(es) other than operations_____

_____

  Head injuries_____

  _____with unconsciousness_____without unconsciousness_____

  Convulsions_____

  _____with fever_____without fever_____

  Coma_____

  Meningitis or encephalitis_____

  Immunization reactions_____

  Persistent high fevers_____highest temperature ever recorded_____

  eye problems_____

  ear problems_____

  poisoning_____

PRESENT MEDICAL STATUS

Present height_____Present weight_____

Present illness(es) for which child is being treated_____

_____

Medications child is taking on an ongoing basis_____

_____

FAMILY HISTORY - MOTHER

Age_____ Age at time of pregnancy with patient_____

Number of previous pregnancies_____Number of spontaneous abortions

(miscarriages)_____Number of induced abortions_____

Sterility problems (specify)_____

School: Highest grade completed_____

　Learning problems (specify)_____grade repeat_____

　Behavior problems (specify)_____

Medical problems (specify)_____

Have any of your blood relatives (not including patient and siblings) ever

had problems similar to those your child has? If so, describe_____

_____

_____

FAMILY HISTORY - FATHER

Age_____Age at the time of the patient's conception _____

Sterility problems (specify)_____

School: Highest grade completed_____

　Learning problems (specify)_____grade repeat_____

　Behavior problems (specify)_____

Medical problems (specify)_____

Have any of your blood relatives (not including patient and siblings) ever

had problems similar to those your child has? If so, describe_____

_____

Most children exhibit, at one time or another, one or more of the symptoms listed below. Place a P next to those that your child has exhibited in the PAST and an N next to those that your child exhibits NOW. Only mark those symptoms that have been or are present to a significant degree over a period of time. Only check as problems behavior that you suspect is unusual or atypical when compared to what you consider to be the normal for your child's age. Then, on page 12, list the symptoms checked off on pages 9-12 and write a brief description including age of onset, duration, and any other pertinent information.

Thumb-sucking ___

Baby talk ___

Overly dependent for age ___

Frequent temper tantrums ___

Excessive silliness and clowning ___

Excessive demands for attention ___

Cries easily and frequently ___

Generally immature ___

Eats non-edible substances ___

Overeating with overweight ___

Eating binges with overweight ___

Undereating with underweight ___

Long periods of dieting and food abstinence with underweight ___

Preoccupied with food--what to eat and what not to eat ___

Preoccupation with bowel movements ___

Constipation ___

Encopresis (soiling) ___

Insomnia (difficulty sleeping) ___

Enuresis (bed wetting) ___

Frequent nightmares ___

Night terrors (terrifying night-time outbursts) ___

Sleepwalking ___

Excessive sexual interest and pre-occupation ___

Frequent sex play with other children ___

Excessive masturbation ___

Frequently likes to wear clothing of the opposite sex ___

Exhibits gestures and intonations of the opposite sex ___

Frequent headaches ___

Frequent stomach cramps ___

Frequent nausea and vomiting ___

Often complains of bodily aches and pains ___

Worries over bodily illness ___

Poor motivation ___

Apathy ___

Takes path of least resistance ___

Ever trying to avoid responsibility ___

362

Poor follow-
through ___

Low Curiosity ___

Open defiance of
authority ___

Blatently un-
cooperative ___

Persistant
lying ___

Frequent use of
profanity to
parents, teachers,
and other author-
ities ___

Truancy from
school ___

Runs away from
home ___

Violent outbursts
of rage ___

Stealing ___

Cruelty to animals,
children, and
others ___

Destruction of
property ___

Criminal and/or
dangerous acts ___

Trouble with the
police ___

Violent assault ___

Fire setting ___

Little, if any,
guilt over behavior
that causes others
pain and dis-
comfort ___

Little, if any,
response to pun-
ishment for anti-
social behavior ___

Few, if any,
friends ___

Doesn't seek
friendships ___

Rarely sought by
peers ___

Not accepted by
peer group ___

Selfish ___

Doesn't respect
the rights of
others ___

Wants things own
way with exag-
gerated reaction
if thwarted ___

Trouble putting
self in other
person's position ___

Egocentric
(self-centered) ___

Frequently hits
other children ___

Argumentative ___

Excessively cri-
tical of others ___

Excessively
taunts other
children ___

Ever complaining ___

Is often picked
on and easily
bullied by
other children ___

Suspicious,
distrustful ___

Aloof ___

"Wise-guy" or
smart aleck
attitude ___

Brags or boasts ___

Bribes other
children ___

Excessively
competitive ___

Often cheats when
playing games ___

"Sore loser" ___

"Doesn't know
when to stop" ___

Poor common
sense in social
situations ___

Often feels
cheated or
gypped ___

Feels others
are persecuting
him when there
is no evidence
for such ___

Typically wants
his or her
own way ___

Very stubborn ___

Obstruction-
istic ___

Negativistic
(does just the
opposite of what
is requested) ___

Quietly, or often silently, defiant of authority ____

Feigns or verbalizes compliance or cooperation but doesn't comply with requests ____

Drug abuse ____

Alcohol abuse ____

Very tense ____

Nail biting ____

Chews on clothes, blankets, etc. ____

Head banging ____

Hair pulling ____

Picks on skin ____

Speaks rapidly and under pressure ____

Irritability, easily "flies off the handle" ____

Fears
dark ____
new situations ____
strangers ____
being alone ____
death ____
separation from parent ____
school ____
visiting other children's homes ____
going away to camp ____
animals ____
other fears (name)

_____ ____
_____ ____

Anxiety attacks with palpatations (heart pounding), shortness of breath, sweating, etc. ____

Disorganized ____

Tics such as eye-blinking, grimacing, or other spasmodic repetitious movements ____

Involuntary grunts, vocalizations (understandable or not) ____

Stuttering ____

Depression ____

Frequent crying spells ____

Excessive worrying over minor things ____

Suicidal preoccupation, gestures, or attempts ____

Excessive desire to please authority ____

"Too good" ____

Often appears insincere and/or artificial ____

Too mature, frequently acts older than actual age ____

Excessive guilt over minor indiscretions ____

Asks to be punished ____

Low self-esteem ____

Excessive self-criticism ____

Very poor toleration of criticism ____

Feelings easily hurt ____

Dissatisfaction with appearance or body part(s) ____

Excessive modesty over bodily exposure ____

Perfectionistic, rarely satisfied with performance ____

Frequently blames others as a cover-up for own shortcomings ____

Little concern for personal appearance or hygiene ____

Little concern for or pride in personal property ____

"Gets hooked" on certain ideas and remains preoccupied ____

Compulsive repetition of seemingly meaningless physical acts ____

Shy ____

Inhibited self-expression in dancing, singing, laughing, etc. ____

Recoils from affectionate physical contact ____

Withdrawn ___	Mute (refuses to speak) but can ___	Flat emotional tone ___
Fears asserting self ___	Gullible and/or naive ___	Speech non-communicative or poorly communica-tive ___
Inhibits open expression of anger ___	Passive and easily led ___	Hears voices ___
Allows self to be easily taken advantage of ___	Excessive fan-tasizing, "lives in his (her) own world" ___	Sees visions ___
Frequently pouts and/or sulks ___		

As requested above, please first list below symptoms marked with the letter P and next to each symptom give descriptive information such as age of onset, age of termination, and other important data. Then list symptoms marked with an N and provide similar information.

P or N	Symptom	Brief Description
___	___	___
___	___	___
___	___	___
___	___	___
___	___	___
___	___	___
___	___	___
___	___	___
___	___	___
___	___	___
___	___	___
___	___	___
___	___	___
___	___	___
___	___	___
___	___	___

365

SIBLINGS

	Name	Age	Medical, social, or academic problems
1.			
2.			
3.			
4.			
5.			

LIST NAMES AND ADDRESSES OF ANY OTHER PROFESSIONALS CONSULTED

1. _____
2. _____
3. _____
4. _____

ADDITIONAL REMARKS

Please use the remainder of this page to write any additional comments you wish to make regarding your child's difficulties.

RICHARD A. GARDNER, M.D.
P.O. BOX R
155 COUNTY RD.
CRESSKILL, N.J. 07626-0317
201-567-8989

Policy for Missed Sessions

Unlike physicians in other medical specialties, I do not have other patients in my waiting room when an appointment is missed. Accordingly, please inform me or my office as soon as you know about anticipated missed appointments. The more advance notice I have, the greater the likelihood I will be able to fill the appointment with another patient. In contrast, the shorter the advance notice, the less the likelihood of my filling the appointment. If I am able to fill the appointment, there will be no charge; if not, then I charge for the time set aside for the appointment. I do not have a cut-off point for determining whether or not there will be a charge; rather, the earlier the advance notice of cancellation, the greater the chance the appointment will be filled.

This policy holds regardless of the reason for the cancellation--whether it be car breakdown, conflicting obligatios, weather conditions, illness, or any other reason for missing the appointment. Of course, if I am not in the office, for any reason whatsoever (including weather conditions), you will be informed in advance and there will be no charge. In situations in which the primary patient is a child who cannot attend, I can usually use the session with a parent. In marital counseling the time can often be used productively by the available spouse. In order to increase the chances of my filling missed sessions calls will be accepted during evenings, weekends, and holidays.

I recognize that some may consider this policy stringent. I hope that those who do so will try to place themselves in my position regarding cancellations. I think the best way for patients to view my policy is to consider themselves to have made a commitment for a time slot in my schedule and that on rare occasions a session will be paid for that was not attended.

I recognize that patients who come to me for treatment have committed themselves to pay me for my services and to comply with my payment policy. I in return promise to commit myself to do whatever I reasonably can to be of help to them and their families.

REFERENCES

Alexander, F. (1950). Analysis of the therapeutic factors in psychoanalytic treatment. *Psychoanalytic Quarterly* 19:482–500.

Alexander, F., and French, T. (1946). The principle of corrective emotional experience. In *Psychoanalytic Therapy: Principles and Application,* pp. 66–70. New York: Ronald Press.

Bandura, A., and Walters, R, H. (1958). Dependency conflicts in aggressive delinquents. *Journal of Social Sciences* 14:52–65.

Bandura, A., Ross, D., and Ross, S. A. (1963). Imitation of film-mediated aggressive models. *Journal of Abnormal Social Psychology* 66:3–8.

Becker, E. (1973). *The Denial of Death.* New York: Free Press.

Berkowitz, L., and Rawlings, E. (1963). Effects of film violence on inhibitions against subsequent aggression. *Journal of Abnormal Social Psychology* 66:405–415.

Bieber, I., et al. (1962). *Homosexuality: A Psychoanalytic Study of Homosexuals.* New York: Basic Books.

Bowlby, J. (1944). Forty-four juvenile thieves: their characters and homelife. *International Journal of Psychoanalysis* 25:19–53.

——— (1952). *Maternal Care and Mental Health.* Geneva: World Health Organization.

Comstock, G., Chaffee, S., and Katzman, N. (1978). *Television and Human Behavior*. New York: Columbia University Press.

—— (1983). Media influences on aggression. In *Prevention and Control of Aggression*, ed. A. Goldstein. New York: Pergamon.

—— (1986). Sexual effects of movie and TV violence. *Medical Aspects of Human Sexuality* 20(7):50ff.

Coolidge, J. C., Tessman, E., Waldfogel, S., and Miller, M. L. (1962). Patterns of aggression in school phobia. *Psychoanalytic Study of the Child* 17:319–333. New York: International Universities Press.

Eisenberg, L. (1958). School phobia: a study of communication and anxiety. *American Journal of Psychiatry* 114:712–718.

Erikson, E. H. (1950). *Childhood and Society*. New York: Norton.

—— (1968). *Identity: Youth and Crisis*. New York: Norton.

Freud, S. (1909). A phobia in a five-year-old boy. In *Collected Papers*, vol. 3, pp. 149–209. New York: Basic Books, 1959.

——(1924). The passing of the Oedipus complex. In *Collected Papers*, vol. 2, pp. 269–276. New York: Basic Books, 1959.

Gardner, R. A. (1968). The mutual storytelling technique: use in alleviating childhood oedipal problems. *Contemporary Psychoanalysis* 4:161–177.

—— (1969). The guilt reaction of parents of children with severe physical disease. *American Journal of Psychiatry* 126:636–644.

—— (1970). The use of guilt as a defense against anxiety. *Psychoanalytic Review* 57:124–136.

—— (1971). *Therapeutic Communication with Children: The Mutual Storytelling Technique*. Northvale, NJ: Jason Aronson.

—— (1972). Little Hans—the most famous boy in the child psychotherapy literature. *International Journal of Child Psychotherapy* 1(4):24–50.

—— (1973). *Understanding Children: A Parents' Guide to Child Rearing*. Cresskill, NJ: Creative Therapeutics.

—— (1975). *Psychotherapeutic Approaches to the Resistant Child*. Northvale, NJ: Jason Aronson.

—— (1976). *Psychotherapy with Children of Divorce*. Northvale, NJ: Jason Aronson.

—— (1977). *The Parents Book About Divorce*. New York: Doubleday.

—— (1979a). *The Parents Book About Divorce*. New York: Bantam.

—— (1979b). *The Objective Diagnosis of Minimal Brain Dysfunction*. Cresskill, NJ: Creative Therapeutics.

—— (1982). *Family Evaluation in Child Custody Litigation*. Cresskill, NJ: Creative Therapeutics.

—— (1984). *Separation Anxiety Disorder: Psychodynamics and Psychotherapy*. Cresskill, NJ: Creative Therapeutics.

——— (1986a). *The Psychotherapeutic Techniques of Richard A. Gardner.* Cresskill, NJ: Creative Therapeutics.

——— (1986b). *Child Custody Litigation: A Guide for Parents and Mental Health Professionals.* Cresskill, NJ: Creative Therapeutics.

——— (1987a). *Differentiating Between Fabricated and Bona Fide Sex-Abuse Allegations of Children.* Audiocassette and videotape. Cresskill, NJ: Creative Therapeutics.

——— (1987b). *Hyperactivity, the So-Called Attention Deficit Disorder, and the Group of MBD Syndromes.* Cresskill, NJ: Creative Therapeutics.

——— (1987c). *The Parental Alienation Syndrome and the Differentiation Between Fabricated and Genuine Child Sex Abuse.* Cresskill, NJ: Creative Therapeutics.

——— (1987d). *Sex Abuse Legitimacy Scale (SAL Scale).* Cresskill, NJ: Creative Therapeutics.

——— (1999a). *Individual and Group Therapy and Work with Parents in Adolescent Psychotherapy.* Northvale, NJ: Jason Aronson.

——— (1999b). *Psychotherapy of Antisocial Behavior and Depression in Adolescence.* Northvale, NJ: Jason Aronson.

Hatterer, L. J. (1970). *Changing Homosexuality in the Male.* New York: McGraw-Hill.

Hess, E. H. (1966). Imprinting. In *Readings for an Introduction to Psychology,* ed. R. A. King, pp. 39–46. New York: McGraw-Hill.

Holmes, D. J. (1964). *The Adolescent in Psychotherapy.* Boston: Little, Brown.

Kardiner, A., and Ovesey, L. (1951). *The Mark of Oppression.* Cleveland, OH: World Publishing.

Kolb, L. C., and Brodie, H. K. H. (1982). *Modern Clinical Psychiatry.* Philadelphia: W. B. Saunders.

Kritzberg, N. I. (1966). A new verbal projective test for the expansion of the projective aspects of the clinical interview. *Acta Paedopsychiatrica* 33(2):48–62.

Kubie, L. (1956). Psychoanalysis and marriage: practical and theoretical issues. In *Neurotic Interaction in Marriage,* ed. V. W. Eisenstein, pp. 10–43. New York: Basic Books.

Leventhal, T., and Sills, M. (1964). Self-image in school phobia. *American Journal of Orthopsychiatry* 34:685–695.

Levy, D. M. (1937). Primary affect hunger. *American Journal of Psychiatry* 94:644–652.

Lorenz, K. (1937). The nature of instinct. In *Instinctive Behavior: The Development of a Modern Concept,* ed. C. H. Schiller. London: Methuen.

——— (1950). The comparative method in studying innate behavior patterns. *Symposium of the Society of Experimental Biology* 4:221–268.

Machover, K. (1949). *Personality Projection in the Drawing of the Human Figure.* Springfield, IL: Charles C Thomas.

———— (1951). Drawing of the human figure: a method of personality investigation. In *An Introduction to Projective Techniques,* ed. H. H. Anderson aand G. L. Anderson, pp. 341–370. Englewood Cliffs, NJ: Prentice-Hall.

———— (1960). Sex differences in the development pattern of children as seen in human figure drawings. In *Projective Techniques in Children,* ed. A. I. Rabin and M. R. Haworth, pp. 230–257. New York: Grune & Stratton.

Malamuth, N. M., and Donnerstein, E. (1982). The effects of aggressive-pornographic mass media stimuli. In *Advances in Experimental Social Psychology,* ed. L. Berkowitz, vol. 15, pp. 103–136. New York: Academic Press.

Marshall, R. J. (1983). A psychoanalytic perspective on the diagnosis and development of juvenile delinquents. In *Personality Theory, Moral Development and Criminal Behavior,* ed. W. S. Laufer and J. M. Day, pp. 119–144. Lexington, MA: D. C. Heath.

Piers, G., and Singer, M. B. (1953). *Shame and Guilt.* Springfield, IL: Charles C Thomas.

Ravitch, D., and Finn, C. E. (1987). *What Do Our 17-Year-Olds Know?* New York: Harper & Row.

AUTHOR INDEX

SUBJECT INDEX